Time Out

2012

things to do in London

timeout.com

Time Out Guides Ltd
Universal House
251 Tottenham Court Road
London W1T 7AB
United Kingdom
Tel: +44 (0)20 7813 3000
Fax: +44 (0)20 7813 6001
Email: guides@timeout.com
www.timeout.com

Published by Time Out Guides Ltd, a wholly owned subsidiary of Time Out Group Ltd.
Time Out and the Time Out logo are trademarks of Time Out Group Ltd.

© **Time Out Group Ltd 2011**

10 9 8 7 6 5 4 3 2 1

This edition first published in Great Britain in 2011 by Ebury Publishing.
A Random House Group Company
20 Vauxhall Bridge Road, London SW1V 2SA

Random House Australia Pty Ltd 20 Alfred Street, Milsons Point, Sydney, New South Wales 2061, Australia
Random House New Zealand Ltd 18 Poland Road, Glenfield, Auckland 10, New Zealand
Random House South Africa (Pty) Ltd Isle of Houghton, Corner Boundary Road & Carse O'Gowrie,
Houghton 2198, South Africa

Random House UK Limited Reg. No. 954009

Distributed in USA by Publishers Group West
1700 Fourth Street, Berkeley, California 94710

For further distribution details, see www.timeout.com.

ISBN: 978-1-84670-231-0

A CIP catalogue record for this book is available from the British Library.

Printed and bound by Firmengruppe APPL, aprinta druck, Wemding, Germany.

The Random House Group Limited supports The Forest Stewardship Council (FSC®), the leading international
forest certification organisation. Our books carrying the FSC label are printed on FSC® certified paper. FSC is the
only forest certification scheme endorsed by the leading environmental organisations, including Greenpeace. Our
paper procurement policy can be found at www.randomhouse.co.uk/environment.

Time Out carbon-offsets its flights with Trees for Cities (www.treesforcities.org).

MIX
Paper from
responsible sources
FSC® C004592

Published by

Time Out Guides Limited
Universal House
251 Tottenham Court Road
London W1T 7AB
Tel +44 (0)20 7813 3000
Fax +44 (0)20 7813 6001
email guides@timeout.com
www.timeout.com

Contributors Simon Coppock and Ruth Jarvis, plus Elena Andreou, Ismay Atkins, Helen Babbs, Charles Betts, Sarah Cobbold, William Crow, Katie Dailey, Euan Ferguson, Sarah Guy, Derek Hammond, Mina Holland, Zoe Kamen, Jenny Landreth, Florentyna Leow, Leo Miranda, Anna Norman, Cath Phillips, Candice Pires, Cyrus Shahrad, Hui Shan Khoo, Sarah Thorowgood, Jamie Warburton.

The Editor would like to thank Simon Coppock, Dan Craig, Dominic Earle, Patrick Field, Sarah Guy, Kei Ishimaru, Ruth Jarvis, Anna Norman, Dan Jones, Scott Moore, Katie Mulhern, Hillary Peachey, Chris Pierre, Daniela Prinz, Johnny Pym, Ben Rowe, Lara Thornton, Jamie Warburton, Stephanie Wolffe.

Street Shop Illustrations Ben Rowe.

Cover photography Heloïse Bergman, Ian Cumming/ZSL, Elisabeth Blanchet, Ben Rowe, Rob Greig, Jonathan Perugia, Ant Clausen/Shutterstock, Lisa Payne, Mauro Bighin/Shutterstock, Ming Tang-Evans.

Photography page 3 Getty Images/ODA; 5 (top left), 9 (top and middle), 69 LOCOG; 5 (top right), 301 Slinkachu/Andipa Gallery; 5 (bottom left), 278/279 S.Borisov/Shutterstock; 5 (bottom right), 35 Angelos Giotopoulos; 7 (left), 46, 48, 100, 124, 171, 219, 242, 251, 253, 266, 274 Jonathan Perugia; 7 (top right), 92 Tyson Benson; 7 (bottom), 36, 77, 155, 222, 235, 248, 249 Elisabeth Blanchet; 10/11, 56, 79, 98, 112, 138, 139, 191, 211, 243, 259, 273, 282 (top), 303 Britta Jaschinski; 14 (top left) Eamonn McCabe; 14, 15, 207 National Portrait Gallery London; 17 Avella; 18, 33, 57, 58, 82, 90, 103, 107, 136, 152, 158/159, 164, 170, 175, 182/183, 190, 195, 202, 229, 244, 257, 267, 297 Rob Greig; 19 Anika Mottershaw; 20 Museum of London; 23, 68, 143, 187, 221, 298 Andrew Brackenbury; 25 Sarah Cuttle/Vertical Veg 2010; 26 Helen Babbs; 27, 115 Jitka Hynkova; 28, 65, 232, 236 Celia Topping; 30 Oleg Skrinda/ www.skindra.com; 31, 81, 153 Marzena Zoladz; 9 (bottom), 38/39, 133 Olivia Rutherford; 43 Matt Clayton; 44, 126, 129, 151, 206 Tricia de Courcy Ling; 45, 47, 49, 64, 198, 220, 282 (bottom), 287, 292 Michelle Grant; 50, 51 Tom Nelson; 52, 134/135, 271, 277 Scott Wishart; 53, 62/63, 75, 179, 180, 196, 203, 204, 285 Ben Rowe; 61 Dan Burn-Forti; 71 (top) Walt Disney Pictures/Photofest; 71 (bottom) Warner Bros./Photofest; 72 Universal Studios/ Photofest; 73 Fox Searchlight Pictures/Photofest; 78 Andy Lane; 3 (bottom right) Richard Gibson; 84 Linus Lim; 85, 166, 225 (bottom right), 286, 299 Heloïse Bergman; 87 (top) Alistair Hall; 87 (bottom) Yemesi Blake; 88 Miriam Douglas; 89 Alamy; 93 Gordon Rainsford; 94 Paula Glassman; 96, 122 Lisa Payne; 99, 226 Rogan MacDonald; 102 Rod Currie; 105 Elena Schweitzer/Shutterstock; 106 James Thurston/Shutterstock; 109 Haris Artemis; 110/111 Arcelor Mittal Orbit, designed by Anish Kapoor & Cecil Balmond; 118, 132 Nick Ballon; 121 Dan Craig; 127 DALiM; 128 Susannah Stone; 131, 167, 188, 262, 268, 269, 291 Ming Tang-Evans; 137 Alex Yeung; 140 Lauren O'Farrell; 141 Laurence Davis; 142, 160, 172, 173, 174 Stephanie Wolffe; 144, 145, 193, 208, 217, 245, 265 Alys Tomlinson; 149 Adrienne Katz; 154 Carl Court; 156, 161, 176, 250, 256 Ed Marshall; 165 iStockphoto; 169 Jo Duck; 178 Duncan McKenzie; 185 Kelly Hill; 197, 200 Padmayogini/Shutterstock; 199 Shutterstock; 201 (right) Christina Trampenau; 212, 213 Trustees of the British Museum; 214, 215 Michel Franke; 218 (top) Stephen Emms; 223 Magnus Andersson; 225 Christina Theisen; 230/231 Allison Moore; 239 Nigel Tradewell; 247 Sir John Soane's Museum; 255 Karl Blanchet; 260 National Gallery London; 270 Abigail Lelliott; 274 (left) Chris Harvey/Shutterstock; 275, 280 Jael Marschner; 283 Chris Tubbs; 284 Anthony Shaw Photography/Shutterstock; 288 Getty Images for LOCOG; 289 Will Robson Scott; 293 (top) Print of the Terrific Combat between the Lion, Tiger and Tigress in the Tower of London on Friday, December 3rd, 1830. © Board of Trustees of the Armouries; 293 (bottom) Historic Royal Palaces; 294 Oliver Knight; 295 Belinda Lawley; 296 David Jensen/ZSL; 300 Jonty Wilde; 302 Peter Kindersley.

The following images were provided by the featured establishments/artists: pages 7 (top left) 16, 41, 55, 68, 69, 83, 88, 95, 97, 113, 114, 116, 117, 123, 147, 162, 163, 201 (left), 218 (bottom), 241, 254.

Contents

LONDON 2012 WILL BE THE BIGGEST SPORTING EVENT IN HISTORY AND THE NATIONAL LOTTERY HAS HELPED MAKE IT POSSIBLE.

- Every week, National Lottery players raise £28million for good causes.

- The National Lottery funds art, sport, heritage and voluntary projects, creating a better life for people across the UK.

- The National Lottery funds a wide range of projects ranging from large national institutions to small-scale community organisations.

Getty Images

Up to £1.8 billion of Lottery money has helped create world-class facilities for the London 2012 Olympic and Paralympic Games. It has also helped fund the preparation of UK athletes, turning the Olympic and Paralympic dreams of many into reality.

London 2012 is not just about sport. It is also helping to fund the Cultural Olympiad. Spread over four years, it will get more people involved in dance, music, theatre and other activities, creating a lasting legacy across the UK.

While making the most of our wonderful capital city, you will discover several museums, parks and theatres that are Lottery-funded. Iconic landmarks have been preserved and visitor attractions improved, making London a spectacular host city for the London 2012 Olympic and Paralympic Games.

National Maritime Museum, London

LONDON VISITOR ATTRACTIONS TO HAVE RECEIVED NATIONAL LOTTERY FUNDING:

- Tate Modern
- Victoria and Albert Museum
- Royal Opera House
- Shakespeare's Globe Theatre
- Wembley Stadium
- Battersea Park
- National Maritime Museum
- British Museum
- Millennium Bridge
- Kew Gardens

The National Lottery®
Funding a better future

About the guide

Telephone numbers

All phone numbers listed in this guide assume that you are calling from within London. From elsewhere within the UK, prefix each number with 020. From abroad, dial your international access code, then 44 for the UK, and then 20 for London.

Disclaimer

While every effort has been made to ensure the accuracy of information within this guide, the publishers cannot accept responsibility for any errors it may contain. Businesses can change their arrangements at any time so, before you go out of your way, we strongly advise you to phone ahead to check opening times, prices and other particulars.

Advertisers

The recommendations in *2012 things to do in London* are based on the experiences of Time Out journalists. No payment or PR invitation of any kind has secured inclusion or influenced content. The editors select which venues and activities are listed in this guide, and the list of 2,012 was compiled before any advertising space was sold. Advertising has no effect on editorial content.

Let us know what you think

Did we miss anything? We welcome tips for 'things' you consider we should include in future editions and take note of your criticism of our choices. You can email us at guides@timeout.com.

LINKS
LONDON

Official Jewellery Collection of Team GB

linksoflondon.com

Introduction

Thanks to the London 2012 Olympic and Paralympic Games, 2012 is set to be a terrific year for the capital. With a packed programme of cultural and sporting events, the buzz extends far beyond the bounds of the state-of-the-art Olympic Park. You'll be able to watch Marathon runners pound past on the streets, stroll a floating walkway on the Thames or take in world-class theatre, art, music and dance. Even the most distinguished London landmarks are joining in the fun: stately Somerset House will become Casa Brasil, a vibrant showcase for Brazilian culture, while thousands of tonnes of sand will transform Horseguards Parade into a Beach Volleyball venue to remember.

To mark this landmark year, we've come up with 2012 don't-miss things to do and places to go, for visitors and locals alike. However well you know this great city, there's always something new to discover: a secret garden squeezed between the office blocks; a speakeasy serving heady cocktails; a Victorian velodrome; or a flying trapeze class held in a park. To really get to the heart of London, it's no good being too methodical. This city has a way of subverting even the best-laid intentions and itineraries, luring you in myriad different directions. Taking a lead from this glorious serendipity, the 2012 things that made the final cut aren't set out in order of merit, or neatly categorised. Instead, rather like a wander through the city streets, this book offers fresh surprises at every turn.

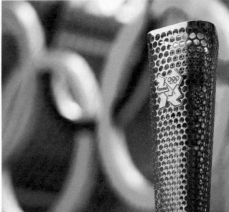

Suggestions of what to include came in thick and fast, from all kinds of sources: photographers, poets, cabbies, cyclists, athletes, authors, gardeners, bloggers and London obsessives of every stripe. Curators from the city's most celebrated museums and galleries chose their favourite exhibits and recounted the tales that lay behind them, while a stellar assortment of chefs revealed their favourite places to eat. The result? A list of 2012 inspirational ideas, running from a print-your-own newspaper service to mudlarking down by the river. London is full of adventures, if you know where to look.

Elizabeth Winding, Editor

1

Eat gelati at Gelupo...

Blood orange, burnt almond, chestnut, espresso: the flavours of the gelati, sorbets and granitas at this Soho ice-cream parlour (7 Archer Street, W1D 7AU, 7287 5555, www.gelupo.com) will transport you to straight to Italy. For an alternative ice-cream fix, bite into a 'burger' – a gelato-filled doughnut, batches of which arrive fresh from Brixton's Wild Caper bakery each morning.

Get Set...

Official Publisher of Travel and Tourism Guides to the London 2012 Olympic Games and Paralympic Games

... Then sample the best of the rest

Bull & Last
Own-made flavours such as prune and armagnac and millionaire shortbread are sold at this smart gastropub – and are available to take away.
168 Highgate Road, NW5 1QS (7267 3641, www.thebullandlast.co.uk).

Chin Chin Laboratorists
At London's first 'nitro ice-cream parlour', styled to look like a mad scientist's lab, be-goggled staff make ice-cream to order with liquid nitrogen.
49-50 Camden Lock Place, NW1 8AF (07885 604284, www.chinchinlabs.com).

Fortnum and Mason's Parlour
Treat yourself to a three-scoop ice-cream 'flight', with a jug of Amedei chocolate sauce, in this opulent, David Collins-designed parlour.
181 Piccadilly, W1A 1ER (7734 8040, www.fortnumandmason.com).

Freggo
This luxury Argentinian ice-cream chain has arrived in London: if the signature dulce de leche is too sweet, try a scoop of malbec and berry.
27-29 Swallow Street, W1B 4QR (7287 9506, www.freggo.co.uk).

Gelato Mio
This rapidly expanding mini-chain does it the proper Italian way. Appealing seasonal specials might include Pimm's in summer.
138 Holland Park Avenue, W11 4UE (7727 4117, www.gelatomio.co.uk).

Gelateria Valerie
All Valerie's gelato is handmade on site daily. Enjoy a cone, waffle or wafer as you people-watch on Duke of York Square.
Duke of York Square, SW3 4LY (7730 7978, www.patisserie-valerie.co.uk).

La Grotta Ices
Kitty Travers pops up at Maltby Street market on most summer Saturday mornings, selling her wares from a Piaggio three-wheeler. Her imaginative concoctions might include fennel and citrus sorbet or a Perigord cherry refresher.
Maltby Street, SE1 3PA (no phone, http://lagrottaices.tumblr.com).

The Icecreamists
The enfant terrible of the ice-cream world, this Covent Garden parlour hit the headlines with its controversy-courting breast milk ice-cream. Such gimmicks aside, the ices are pretty good.
23-47 The Market Building, WC2E 8RF (8616 0721, www.theicecreamists.com).

Marine Ices
Family-run, retro, and utterly charming, Marine Ices is a much-loved north London institution. The kaleidoscopic array of gelati, sorbetti and sundaes are own-made and delicious – albeit no longer uniquely so.
8 Haverstock Hill, NW3 2BL (7482 9003, marineices.co.uk).

Morelli's Gelato
The inspired array of gourmet ices features surprises such as honey and rosemary and mango mojito, though chocolate remains a firm favourite.
Harrods, 87-135 Brompton Road, SW3 1NE (7893 8959, www.harrods.com).

Oddono's
With a minimalist interior and retro seating, this place is all about quality. Its focus is on premium ingredients and classic flavours; the pistachio is among the best you'll ever taste.
14 Bute Street, SW7 3EX (7052 0732, www.oddonos.co.uk).

Paul A Young
The cachet and craft of this chocolatier extends to a range of ice-creams and sorbets, made fresh every morning with all-natural ingredients. Decadent and delicious.
33 Camden Passage, N1 8EA (7424 5750, www.paulayoung.co.uk).

Scoop
Matteo Pantani's enthusiasm for his product is contagious – and justified. Many of the ingredients are imported from suppliers in Italy, from mascarpone to Marsala wine. There's now a second branch in Brewer Street, too.
40 Short's Gardens, WC2H 9AB (7240 7086, www.scoopgelato.com).

William Curley
Like Curley's truffle creations, the ice-creams at this Belgravia chocolatier are often infused with classic Japanese flavours, such as toasted sesame, kinako and green tea.
198 Ebury Street, SW1W 8UN (7730 5522, www.williamcurley.co.uk).

Curator's top ten

16-25

*Sandy Nairne, Director of the
National Portrait Gallery*

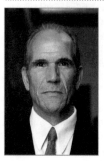

Holbein *Cartoon of
Henry VIII* (c1536-1537)
This large preparatory
drawing is for the
left-hand section of a
mural commissioned by
Henry VIII for Whitehall
Palace. The mural
was destroyed with
the palace in a fire in
1698, but this drawing
remains the record of
Holbein's encounter
with Henry, sketching his face from life.
Room 1: The Early Tudors

Marcus Gheeraerts the Younger *Queen
Elizabeth I, 'The Ditchley Portrait'* (c1592)
A portrait of power, this painting shows
Elizabeth standing on a map of England, with
her feet on Ditchley in Oxfordshire, for which
it was commissioned. The stormy sky, with
clouds parting to reveal sunshine, and the
inscriptions on the painting make it clear that
the portrait's symbolic theme is forgiveness.
Room 2: Elizabethan England

John Donne (c1595)
This remarkable image is one of the earliest
surviving examples of an Elizabethan author
portrait. The poet is depicted with his
head set back in the shadows,
topped by a wide-brimmed hat
and his collar left untied at the
neck – a fashionable literary
affectation of melancholy. The
Latin inscriptions suggest that
the picture may have been
intended as a plea to a lover.
*Room 2: Elizabethan England
(due to return from restoration
in November 2011)*

William Shakespeare (c1610)
This is the Gallery's number one:
the first portrait to be acquired by
the Gallery in 1856, and also the
only portrait of
Shakespeare that
has any claim to have
been painted from life.
We believe it to be by
a painter called John
Taylor, who was an
important member of
the Painter-Stainers'
Company.
*Room 4: The
Jacobean Court*

Rubens *Thomas
Howard, Earl of
Arundel* (1629)
This wonderful portrait
of the Earl of Arundel
is by Rubens, and not
many visitors are aware that we have
works by Rubens on display. As a sketch,
it has an exceptional liveliness in its
characterisation of a man with a somewhat
knowing view of the world.
Room 5: Charles I & Civil War

Sir Godfrey Kneller *Sir Christopher Wren*
(1711)
I have a personal reason for admiring this
painting: I am privileged to be a member
of the Fabric Advisory Committee of St Paul's
Cathedral, and a small but very engaging part
of my life is taken up with Wren's magnificent
creation. But I also love this picture as an
example of what portraits do best – speak
to us across time.
Room 10: The Arts in the Early 18th Century

Patrick Branwell Brontë *The Brontë Sisters*
(c1834)
This is the only surviving group
portrait of the three famous
novelist sisters, and it was
thought to have been lost until
discovered folded-up on top of
a cupboard. In the centre of the
group a male figure, previously
concealed by a painted pillar,
is almost certainly a self-
portrait of the artist, their
brother Branwell Brontë.
Room 24: Early Victorian Arts

Albert Charles Challen
Mary Seacole (1869)
This is the only known painting of

Mary Seacole, the black Victorian nurse regarded as one of the most significant figures to emerge from the Crimean War. As well as being a nurse, Seacole was an adventurer and writer whose bravery, compassion and determination mark her out as an exceptional figure in Victorian society.
Room 23: Expansion & Empire

Marc Quinn *Self* (2006)
An unusual self-portrait of the artist Marc Quinn, cast from many pints of his blood and kept in a special refrigerated display. The artist makes a new version of *Self* every five years, and it's the ultimate reminder of our own mortality.
Room 38: Science & Technology

Michael Craig-Martin *Zaha Hadid* (2008)
Taking him into the realm of portraiture, this commission marked a new departure for Michael Craig-Martin, a key figure in the first generation of British conceptual artists. Although the structure of the portrait is fixed, the colours are controlled by computer software that makes constantly randomised choices, in infinite combinations, ensuring that it never looks the same twice.
Ground floor – not currently displayed; check online for details.

National Portrait Gallery *St Martin's Place, WC2H 0HE (7306 0055, www.npg.org.uk).*

26 Go to Oktoberfest without leaving town

If you fancy some beery Bavarian carousing without the expense of flying to Germany, buy a ticket to the Bavarian Beerhouse's version of the event, now in its ninth year. Swig steins of beer, snack on würst, listen to oompah bands and obey the organisers' exhortation to 'eat, drink, sing and dance on the benches'. It's held at two locales: Old Street (190 City Road, EC1V 2QH) and Tower Hill (The Arches, 9 Crutched Friars, EC3N 2AU, 0844 330 2005, www.bavarian-beerhouse.co.uk).

27 Spend Apple Day at Fenton House

You'll be hard-pushed to find a better place to celebrate the British apple than Fenton House in Hampstead. Within its walled kitchen gardens, the 17th-century brick mansion has a 300-year-old orchard, where around 30 types of apple flourish. Apple Day, held in late September every year, is the perfect opportunity to savour some of its rare and delicious apples, along with goodies such as apple-blossom honey.
Fenton House *Windmill Hill, NW3 6RT (01494 755563, 7435 3471, www.nationaltrust.org.uk).*

28

Take a dip in the Ladies' Pond

Apologies to the gents, but our choice for pond-dipping is strictly for the fairer sex: Kenwood Ladies' Pond trumps the men-only and mixed versions by a country mile. But you'll have to take our word for it: uniquely among Hampstead Heath's bathing lakes, the Ladies' Pond is fenced off and screened by woodland. This seclusion is part of its charm: whether you're taking a dip or lounging in the idyllic meadow, you feel 400 miles from central London, rather than four. Fleet river currents tickle your toes as you swim, and you might spot a kingfisher. Go now: flood-control plans under consideration might affect the lovely natural landscaping.
Kenwood Ladies' Pond *Millfield Lane, NW6 3ED (7485 3873, www.cityoflondon.gov.uk).*

29 *Develop a taste for tea*

Tea Smith's sleek, minimalist premises are a world away from traditional teashops – and so is the tea, with a changing menu that takes in white, green, oolong, red, black, aged and puer teas. There's a once-monthly Masterclass (£35), with accompanying cakes and chocolates courtesy of pâtissier William Curley, but you can experience an impromptu tasting session for much less. The super-knowledgeable staff are happy to talk customers through the various teas, and help them choose a brew; what's more, you're given three or more precision-timed infusions from each pot, so you can taste how the flavours develop.
Tea Smith *6 Lamb Street, E1 6EA (7247 1333, www.teasmith.co.uk).*

30 *Go carbon-neutral karting*

Powered by lithium ion batteries and lighter (thus faster) than many conventional karts, Team Sport's sleek electric eco karts can reach speeds of up to 40mph. Set in a converted biscuit factory, the two-level track's a beauty, too, with its flyovers, hairpins and banked corner. Take part in a race session or hire the whole place for your own Grand Prix-style showdown; note that you have to book ahead.
Team Sport Tower Bridge *Tower Bridge Business Park, 100 Clements Road, SE16 4DG (0844 998 0000, www.team-sport.co.uk).*

31 *Explore Islington's treehouses*

Treehouses for children, built by children, is the brilliant new project set up by Islington Play Association (www.islingtonplay.org.uk). The treehouses, shelters and dens are in 24 adventure playgrounds across the borough, including Toffee Park (Ironmonger Row, EC1V 3QN) and Lumpy Hill (Market Road, N7 9PL).

32 *Visit a 'national house'*

Representatives of pretty much every nation will be arriving in London this summer, thanks to the 2012 Games – and it has become something of a Games tradition for delegations to host events promoting their home country at temporary 'national houses' in the host cities. For the London 2012 Games, Somerset House is to become Casa Brazil (Rio hosts the 2016 Games), Alexandra Palace will turn Dutch orange and resonate to brass bands, while the Russians hope to promote the Sochi 2012 Winter Games with an unseasonal 1,000-capacity ice-rink by Hyde Park. Other locales include the Museum of London Docklands (Germany) and Old Billingsgate Market (France).

33 *Prop up the barre at Frame*

Frame is a dynamic dance workout studio in Shoreditch, that aims to take the misery, if not the hard work, out of exercise. Each season they reinvent the workout with quirky new dance tutorials – with anything from Prince routines to sequences straight out of *Footloose*, all suitable for enthusiasts with two left feet. Following the release of *Black Swan*, and the ensuing revival in a taste for the barre, Frame swiftly introduced a series of ballet based workouts with a twist, from Cardio Barre (syncing ballet moves with heart racing gym workouts) to the more classic Ballet Barre and beginners' Basic Barre.
Frame *29 New Inn Yard, EC2A 3EY (7033 1855, www.moveyourframe.com).*

34-42 *Count the hours*

Is there any sound so soothing as that of a perfectly regulated clock? The Clockmakers' Museum (Guildhall, Aldermanbury, EC2V 7HH, 7332 1868, www.clockmakers.org) is an enchanting single-room exhibition, and a sanctuary of whirring, ticking and chiming amid the City's hurly-burly – linger, and you'll start to believe the Clockmakers' Company motto: *tempus rerum imperator* ('time is the commander of [all] things').

Not far away, at the start of noisy Fleet Street, St Dunstan-in-the-West (186a Fleet Street, EC4A 2HR, 7405 1929, www.st dunstaninthewest.org) has one of the capital's silliest – and oldest – clocks. Completed in 1671, this was London's first public clock with a minute hand. Its most appealing feature, though, are the two (rather small) giants, clad in leaves and destined to strike the hours and quarter-hours with their clubs for all eternity.

More modern time-related automata include the 1964 clock found above the entrance to Fortnum & Mason (181 Piccadilly, W1A 1ER, 7734 8040, www. fortnumandmason.co.uk), from which the frock-coated founders appear each hour, with tea tray and candelabra, to nod respectfully at one another.

The water clock on the Neal's Yard Holland & Barrett (21-23 Shorts Gardens, WC2H 9AS, 7836 5151) was constructed in 1982. A tube is filled with water to indicate the minutes; on the hour, a row of gardeners pour their watering cans into a trough, causing plastic flowers to grow. Its inventor, Tim Hunkin (www.timhunkin.com), only gives the Neal's Yard clock a single star on his website ('beware of disappointment'), but his 2008 clock outside the Tropical Aviary at London Zoo (Regent's Park, NW1 4RY, 7722 3333, www.zsl.org) gets a full five-star endorsement ('worth an expedition to see'). This Victorian eccentric's version of a cuckoo clock has toucans pecking at the pendulum and a top-hatted gent revealing a shiny green bird under a cloche; other birds appear, disappear and escape from a cage to wheel squawking overhead.

No London clock tour would be complete without acknowledging the Clock Tower of Parliament – known as Big Ben, after the nickname of its largest bell. Few people are aware that you can arrange tours of Big Ben: if you're a British citizen, simply contact your local MP three to six months before your visit.

Wander west along Victoria Street and you can also say hello to Little Ben. This late Victorian folly, found outside the Victoria Palace Theatre, is made of cast iron and stands about nine metres tall.

Looking at clocks is fun, but doesn't tell you much about their inner workings. Combine education and entertainment at the marvellous exhibitions on the history of timekeeping in Rooms 38-39 of the British Museum (Great Russell Street, WC1B 3DG, 7323 8299, www.britishmuseum.org) and the Time Galleries at the Royal Observatory Greenwich (Greenwich Park, SE10 8XJ, 8312 6565, www.rog.nmm.ac.uk).

In the former, seeing Sir William Congreve's rolling ball mechanism in action is mesmerising, while the latter displays fully functioning examples of John Harrison's H1, H2 and H3 marine chronometers, successive designs of the clock that enabled the problem of longitude to be solved nearly three centuries ago.

Interestingly, the clocks at the Royal Observatory all remain on Greenwich Mean Time throughout the year – there's no British Summer Time here.

Fortnum & Mason

43-47

Spend less on a night at the flicks...

If you're a member (£10 a year), seats at the Prince Charles (7 Leicester Place, WC2H 7BY, 7494 3654, www.princecharlescinema.com) go for as little as £1.50; even at peak times they're never more than £6. A lesser-known gem is the Roxy Bar & Screen (128-132 Borough High Street, SE1 1LB, 7407 4057, www.roxybarandscreen. com), set at the rear of a pub. It charges £3 a screening; arrive early to order a pint and a pie, and nab a cosy, sagging sofa.

For the name alone, we've got a soft spot for the Duke Mitchell Film Club – a free, once-monthly film night, held in King's Cross. Past installments have celebrated spaghetti westerns, Vincent Price and 1980s action movies; get the latest on upcoming themes by following the club on Facebook or Twitter.

In Loughborough Junction, the 60-seater Whirled Cinema (259-260 Hardess Street, SE24 0HN, 7737 6153, www.whirledart.co.uk/cinema) is an independent members' cinema; fork out £30 a year, and all screenings are free. Another south London champion of affordable cinema is Deptford Film Club (www.deptfordfilmclub.org), hosting screenings at the Amersham Arms. For £3, you can enjoy some stellar classic and arthouse films, among Deptford's cinematic cognoscenti.

48-49

... Or splash out in style

For an altogether more luxurious viewing experience, head east to the 45-seater Aubin Cinema (64-66 Redchurch Street, E2 7DP, 0845 604 8486, www.aubincinema.com), where there are two-seater sofas and a bar serving cocktails, or west to the Electric Cinema (191 Portobello Road, W11 2ED, 7908 9696, www.electriccinema. co.uk), which has all of the above, plus leather seats and posh snacks.

50

Sign up to Bandstand Busking

This enterprising initiative is using bandstands for what the Victorians designed them for – our entertainment. Join the mailing list at www. bandstandbusking.com to find out about the free gigs, which attract up to 200 like-minded music-lovers. Past performers include Wild Beasts, Ed Harcourt and folk heart-throb Johnny Flynn.

51
Take refuge in the V&A Reading Rooms

Just around the corner from the V&A Museum, the elegant, airy V&A Reading Rooms is a perfect retreat on rainy afternoons: a bookshop with its very own wine bar. Sip a glass of chablis as you peruse the shop's well-curated selection, ranging from the V&A's own glossy fashion and design titles to children's books and biography.
V&A Reading Rooms 8 Exhibition Road, SW7 2HF (7225 0594, www.vandareadingrooms.co.uk).

52
Follow your nose

Set up by scent obsessive Lizzie Ostrom – aka Odette Toilette – Scratch+Sniff (www.scratch andsniffevents.com) runs monthly 'adventures in olfaction' at the Book Club in Shoreditch (100-106 Leonard Street, EC2A 4RH, 7684 8618, www.wearetbc.com). Featuring expert guest speakers, its events explore themes such as Scent and Childhood, with a cloud of evocative smells.

53-55
Cross the Thames by ferry

Various Transport for London River Bus routes flit from bank to bank, but there are only three proper there-and-back services. Hammerton's ferry is an appealingly (or worryingly, depending on your river-legs) small craft that shuttles passengers and cycles between the banks near Marble Hill House, Twickenham, and Ham House, Ham. The service is summer-only and costs £1 each way; see http://hammertonsferry.co.uk.

Less romantic, but convenient in a bridge-less stretch, TfL's River Buses ply the crossing between Hilton Docklands and Canary Wharf pier for £3.30 (www.tfl.gov.uk). In the east, meanwhile, the free Woolwich Ferry (8853 9400) is one of London's most enjoyable experiences. Two craft chuff across the Thames between north and south Woolwich, loaded with cars, cyclists and foot passengers, there to enjoy the wide-horizon views and an ice-cream while they wait.

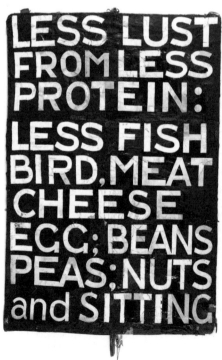

56
Choose a champion conker...

One of our favourite hunting grounds for conkers is Bushy Park (Hampton Court Road, Middx TW12 2EJ, 8979 1586, www.royalparks. gov.uk). Keep your eyes to the ground as you walk along the venerable Chestnut Avenue, looking for glossy, firm-fleshed nuts – then prepare for a knuckle-bruising battle.

57
... Or celebrate Chestnut Sunday

Late spring, meanwhile, is the prettiest time to stroll Bushy Park's magnificent avenue of horse chestnut trees, established during William and Mary's reign. The trees 'candles' are in full bloom, providing a good excuse for an annual shindig on the second Sunday in May. Along with a parade along the avenue, 'Chestnut Sunday' involves musket-brandishing historical re-enactments, pony rides, hawk displays and more; see www.royalparks.org.uk for details.

58
See the Protein Man's placard

For 25 years Stanley Green, known as the 'Protein Man', cycled to central London to warn the public that eating protein was to blame for sexual and anarchic impulses in the world. To spread the message, he would distribute a self-published leaflet, 'Eight Passion Proteins. With Care', brandishing a placard that read: 'LESS LUST FROM LESS PROTEIN: LESS FISH BIRD, MEAT CHEESE EGG; BEANS PEAS; NUTS and SITTING'. ('Sitting' refers to Green's peculiar belief that a sedentary lifestyle could cause a build-up of protein energies that manifest themselves in oubursts of passion and rage). The placard can now be admired in the '1950s – Today: World City' exhibition at the Museum of London.

Museum of London *150 London Wall, EC2Y 5HN (7001 9844, www.museumoflondon.org.uk).*

59

Ski across Hyde Park

London being somewhat short on snowy and suitable terrain, cross-country skiing isn't the easiest of hobbies to pursue. Help is at hand, though, thanks to the enterprising folk at Rollerski (8348 2540, www.rollerski.co.uk). On Saturday mornings, they don ski boots and rollerskis (shorter than skis, and with wheels at the ends) to power across Hyde Park, leading groups of learners. You may get a few funny looks, but it's great preparation for the real thing; Ben Fogle and James Cracknell used rollerskis to train for their race to the South Pole.

60-66

Watch Euro 2012 amid a home crowd

The UEFA Euro 2012 footie tournament will run from 8 to 24 June, in Poland and Ukraine. Should your home team falter, alleviate the misery by becoming an honorary fan of another side, and watching a match among a throng of passionate – and partisan – footie fans. Here are a few ideas (assuming, of course, that their teams make it through). For fixtures, see www.uefa.com.

Czech Republic

This West Hampstead establishment shows all international and domestic Czech matches. Sparta Prague scarves mounted on the wall leave little doubt as to the favoured home team, and Czech beer and grub – beef goulash, potato pancakes – ensure an authentic matchday experience.

Czechoslovak Bar & Restaurant *74 West End Lane, NW6 2LX (7732 1193, www.czechoslovak-restaurant.co.uk).*

France

Le Bar des Magis is French through and through, with a dedicated football following. Home support is generally for Olympique Lyonnais, but also has a soft spot for Le Arsenal. The neighbouring restaurant, Le Bouchon Bordelais, sponsors local Gallic-tinged Sunday league side the Mavericks.

Le Bar des Magis *7-9 Battersea Rise, SW11 1HG (7738 0307, www.lebouchon.co.uk).*

Germany

The Bavarian Beerhouse claims to be London's only authentic Bavarian pub, and shows regular Bundesliga action as well as Germany's national games. There's an excellent choice of beer, as you'd expect, and lots of dumplings to soak it up.

Bavarian Beerhouse *190 City Road, EC1V 2AH (0844 330 2005, www.bavarian-beerhouse.co.uk).*

Netherlands

De Hems has long been a refuge for the Dutch in London: first as a retreat for homesick sailors, later, as a base for the Dutch Resistance during World War II. A shirt signed by national hero Dennis Bergkamp is in pride of place behind the bar, and success is toasted with Benelux brews.

De Hems *11 Macclesfield Street, W1D 5BW (7437 2494).*

Portugal

Considered by many to be the best drinking option in Stockwell's Little Portugal, Bar Estrela is the ideal spot to join the locals in supporting their home team, with matches beamed in on Portuguese TV. Cold Super Bocks, custard tarts and portions of stew and sundry pork dishes served to your table add to the Iberian charm.

Bar Estrela *111-115 South Lambeth Road, SW8 1UZ (7793 1051).*

Spain

To see if hotly tipped Spain will reign, head to King's Cross tapas bar Camino; the atmosphere's electric whenever the current European and World champions play. Get in the mood with a glass of Sagres and sizeable sharing platter.

Camino *3 Varnishers Yard, Regents Quarter, N1 9FD (7841 7331, www.camino.uk.com).*

Sweden

All Swedish football fixtures are shown at the Harcourt, which also screens ice-hockey matches. Kopparberg pear and apple ciders are dispensed at the bar, while the menu runs from meatballs and mash to herring and apple salad.

Harcourt Arms *32 Harcourt Street, W1 4HX (7723 6634, www.theharcourt.com)*

Take home a memory of your 2012 adventures in London

Choose from a great selection of gifts available at the London 2012 Shops, conveniently located at St Pancras International and Paddington stations, Heathrow Terminals 3 and 5, Stansted Airport, John Lewis Stratford City and John Lewis Oxford Street.

london2012.com/shop

67-73

Take a brews cruise

There was a moment in 2006, when the Young's brewery in Wandsworth closed, when it looked as if Fuller's (of London Pride fame) might be the only beer-maker left in town. Five years on, and there's been a most welcome resurgence – and many of the new breweries are open to visitors.

Brodie's Beers

From their one-room Leyton brewery, brother and sister James and Lizzie Brodie concoct a terrific variety of beers. Set up in 2008, the brewery has just received organic certification. We love the seven-hop IPA – and the fact that the tour is free.
816A High Road, E10 6AE (07976 122853, www.brodiesbeers.co.uk).

Fuller's Brewery

The current brewery was officially established in 1845, though the Chiswick site of Fuller's Griffin Brewery has seen 350 years of continuous brewing. On an average day, 640 barrels of beer are produced; regular tours guide visitors through the industrial process, and the beautiful building.
The Griffin Brewery, Chiswick Lane South, W4 2QB (8996 2063, www.fullers.co.uk).

Ha'penny Brewing Company

On a farm near the eastern end of the Central Line, this cask brewery began as a weekend project for two friends. The beers are named after characters of London lore: the Guildhall giants Gog and Magog, and, from *Sweeney Todd*, Mrs Lovett's Most Efficacious. Tours are available on request.
Unit 8, Aldborough Hall Farm, Aldborough Road North, Aldborough Hatch, Ilford, IG2 7TD (07961 161 869, www.hapenny-brewing.co.uk).

Kernel Brewery

Evin O'Riordain began brewing commercially under the Bermondsey railway arches in 2009, and has already scooped up awards for his fine ales. On Saturdays you can sample the current range of bottled beers in situ, and Evin is happy to show interested parties around.
98 Druid Street, SE1 2HQ (07757 552636, www.thekernelbrewery.com).

Meantime Brewing Company

This Greenwich-based brewery, whose award-winning output ranges from raspberry beer to

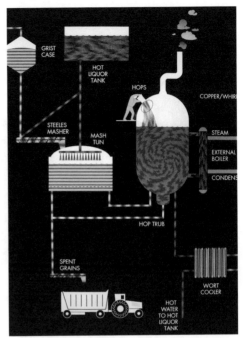

porter, runs Tuesday evening tours for £15. The £40 tour includes dinner at Meantime's sister restaurant in the Old Royal Naval College.
Blackwall Lane, SE10 0AR (8293 1111, www.meantimebeers.com).

Redemption Brewing Company

Andy Moffat began brewing Redemption cask ales in 2010 at this small north London site. He uses only British hops and malt, powers with renewable energy and composts spent grain at a local allotment. Five ales are currently brewed, including a pale ale (3.8 per cent) and the Urban Dusk bitter (4.6 per cent), with a rich, burnt sugar sweetness.
Unit 2 Compass West Industrial Estate, West Road, N17 0XL (8885 5227, www.redemption brewing.co.uk).

Sambrooks Brewery

Founded in 2008, this Battersea brewery sources its ingredients from within 100 miles. The deep amber Junction ale and lighter Wandle ale were recently joined by a new porter. Groups of ten or more can book a brewery tour (£10 per person); individuals can attend the open evenings (third Wednesday of the month at 6.30pm, £10).
Unit 1 & 2 Yelverton Road, SW11 3QG (7228 0598, www.sambrooksbrewery.co.uk).

Grow
your own

Even the smallest nooks and crannies can support a wealth of greenery, as Helen Babbs *discovers.*

For someone lacking green fingers, the idea that a blank balcony could ever become an urban jungle takes quite an imaginative leap. But it is possible. In a matter of months, despite having no real gardening knowledge and very little spare cash, I managed to turn a small flat roof in Holloway into an aerial, edible garden. And I'm by no means unique. Undeterred by spatial limitations, plenty of Londoners are growing their own – despite not having their own gardens.

In north London, garden-less Mark Ridsill-Smith is practically self-sufficient in fruit and veg. Every window ledge and balcony of his Camden home supports some kind of edible plant life. Methodical in his approach, Mark has calculated that he grew over 80kg of food last summer, worth £590.

Reassuringly, he admits his first attempt at balcony growing resulted in one solitary serving of rocket. Since then, he's got more serious, and says detailed planning is the key to a year-round supply of fresh produce purely from pots.

March to June is his busiest time – he spends about half an hour a day watering, plus half a day a week sowing, staking and planting out. After that, the workload lessens. Mark estimates that he spends one day in total over a month from July to October, and half a day each month from November to February. He's not obsessed, but he is focused – and keen to teach other people about food growing.

Full of newfound urban farming knowledge, Mark has set up www.verticalveg.org.uk in a bid to get more landless people growing. He recommends starting with leafy herb or salad crops. The most delicious of all are pea and broad bean shoots, which grow to edible size in just three weeks, from May until October. Climbing crops are great for limited spaces, too – think vine tomatoes, winter squash, French beans and mange-tout.

Mark is taking his balcony allotment growing to something of an extreme, but this doesn't have to be your approach. A few herbs on a kitchen

window ledge will transform your meals, and there's a lot of joy to be had in a single hanging basket of tumbling tomatoes or strawberries.

For me, it all began when I escaped the house-share from hell and moved to a tiny first-floor flat in Holloway that just happened to have an accessible rooftop. It was, admittedly, a rather bleak grey space – but one that was ripe to become something special. The roof was fenced and able to bear weight, and my bedroom door opened straight on to it. It was framed by views of chimney tops and townhouses, and buffeted by birdsong and traffic noise.

It took me a while to get started in earnest. The roof was appealing, but I wasn't a gardener; there was much thought, but little action for a long time. I would stare at it through condensation-curtained windows during that first winter, and think I'd like to get to know my balcony better.

Come summer, it was a space for dozing rather than vegetable growing, but things changed. I became increasingly interested in urban nature, fascinated by the number of creatures that call London home, and I was starting to understand the environmental importance of city gardens. While London is celebrated as one of the world's most verdant cities, green space is still endangered here. Private garden land covers a significant swath of the capital and is a precious resource, but it is continually under threat from hard surfacing and development. Lots of land is lost to decking and extensions, so creating a brand new garden felt like a small but valuable contribution.

I decided to transform myself into an aerial edible gardener, and try to create a true living room – an outside space that would become an extension of my small home. The rooftop area was three metres square and, despite being sandwiched between the Camden and Holloway Roads, it managed to feel calm. The plan was to weave green walls around the rooftop and turn it into a fragrant tangle of vegetables, fruit and flowers.

I didn't know what I was doing. I read a few books and drew strange diagrams, but really I just experimented. Some stuff worked well, other things didn't. All my crops had to bear an entirely container-bound life, and I discovered that things like runner bean, tomato, courgette, potato, garlic, radish, strawberry, salads and herbs all cope well. I also planted flowers, especially night blooming ones. Spring was painted with the yellows and purples of daffodils, violas and alium star bursts, while summer evenings were perfumed by tobacco plant, evening primrose and jasmine.

Of course there have been problems in my rooftop paradise. I've been terrorised by obese and angry squirrels that eat my strawberries and tomatoes, and behead my flowers out of nothing but spite. Slugs and snails, meanwhile, have devoured my hard-grown lettuces. Watering in the hot months can be time consuming, and I've been guilty of neglect. Overall, though, making myself a little roof garden has been pure pleasure. However humble your attempt, I heartily recommend you give it a go.

Helen Babbs is the author of My Garden, the City and Me: Rooftop Adventures in the Wilds of London, *published by Timber Press. For more, see www.aerialediblegardening.co.uk.*

A beginner's guide

Growing your own could get expensive, but the thrifty gardener can survive on a shoestring budget. Next time you buy a chilli, keep the seeds and plant them; plant a garlic clove and it'll transform into a bulb (after a few months). Seek out seed swaps and farmers' markets for cheap seeds and plants, and treat yourself to a Sunday afternoon at Columbia Road Market; to get the best deals, head there when the traders are packing up.

Decent compost and plant food are key, and anyone interested in being environmentally friendly should seek out soil that's organic and peat-free. Local councils sometimes offer great deals on compost. Islington has been known to sell 60 litre bags (made from north Londoners' food waste) for a mere £3.

Be creative when it comes to containers. The city's streets are littered with wooden veg boxes that stall and shop owners will happily let you have, possibly after a bit of banter. People are constantly throwing away things that make great plant pots; old baskets, paint pots, colanders and even wooden CD racks.

Numerous plants will survive and thrive in containers, whether it be a basket of tomatoes hanging beside a shared front door; a kitchen window ledge box planted with culinary herbs; or larger troughs and pots sitting on a balcony, hosting anything from courgettes to potatoes

and everything in between. Here are a few pot-happy suggestions to get you started.

Fruit
Strawberries, tomatoes

Vegetables
Beans, carrots, courgettes, squashes, potatoes, radishes, garlic, peppers, chillies, salad leaves

Herbs
Bay, rosemary, chives, chervil, parsley, basil, sage, oregano, thyme, mint, lemon balm

Flowers
Lavender, jasmine, evening primrose, night flowering tobacco, rose, viola, daffodils, alium

75
Lunch at Sweetings' convenience

Heavens above, no – there'll be no fish suppers served at Sweetings. The City institution is only open at lunchtime, Monday to Friday, 11.30am to 3pm. And what's that? You'd like to make a booking? Don't be ridiculous, out of the question. What you *are* permitted is excellent, plain fishy dishes – cod and chips, potted shrimps, smoked eel and market-fresh fish (grilled, steamed or fried, on or off the bone) – and spotted dick for pud. No time for coffee though, sir: it isn't served, so as to speed up the considerable customer turnover. **Sweetings** *39 Queen Victoria Street, EC4N 4SA (7248 3062).*

76
Shake up Shakespeare

Fresh from celebrating its 50th anniversary in 2011, the Royal Shakespeare Company (0844 800 1110, www.rsc.org.uk) will be producing a World Shakespeare Festival (23 Apr-9 Sept 2012). Part of the London 2012 Festival, it will provide all sorts of fresh takes on the Bard. The RSC itself is to stage a series of plays on Shakespearean shipwrecks called 'What Country, Friends, is This?', directed by (among others) the company's Artistic Director Michael Boyd and the excellent Rupert Goold, but they're also importing such exotic fare as a circus-theatre take on *Richard III* from Rio de Janeiro and an Iraqi *Romeo and Juliet*, in which the feud between the Capulets and Montagues is reimagined between Sunnis and Shias. London venues are likely to include Camden's Roundhouse, the Barbican in the City and, on the South Bank, the National Theatre.

77
Tweak your tyres at a communal bike pump

The City of London has two sleek municipal bike pumps, at London Wall (Moorgate) and Banyard House Car Park on Queen Victoria Street. The tubular, stainless steel design looks like a space-age street bollard: look a little closer, and you'll discover it's a fully functioning bicycle pump.

78-80
Be at one with bats

From late spring – when bats emerge from hibernation – until September, twilight bat walks run in various London locales. Armed with an ultrasonic bat detector, an expert will lead you through wood and wetland in search of the elusive (and endangered) mammals. Evening Bat Watch events among the oaks and hornbeams of Highgate Woods are free, but hugely popular; be sure to book ahead (Muswell Hill Road, N10 3JN, 8444 6129). The London Wetland Centre (Queen Elizabeth's Walk, SW13 9WT, 8409 4400, www.wwt.org.uk) is another bat-watching hotspot, with seven species in residence; its bat walks (£10) also take in a talk, and a visit to the sculptural-looking Berkeley Bat House. The London Wildlife Trust (7261 0447, www. wildlondon.org.uk), meanwhile, runs free bat- and moth-spotting evenings in various nature reserves, including Byng Road in Barnet. For a list of other walks, see www.londonbats.org.uk.

CHEESE BURGER £
BACON BURGER £
CHILLI BURGER £
DOUBLE BUBBLE BUR
DEAD HIPPY BURGER
PHILLY CHEESE STEA

Meatwagon

81-85

Bag a burger...

Tired of the big burger chains? Order up a burger at one of London's smaller specialists, and taste the difference. With outposts across the city, Byron (97-99 Wardour Street, W1F 0UD, 7297 9390, www.byronhamburgers.com) is generally agreed to serve up some of the best in town, featuring Scottish beef, perfectly proportioned buns and juicy pickles on the side. Haché (24 Inverness Street, NW1 7HJ, 7485 9100, www.hacheburgers.com) offers more variants (tuna, Moroccan lamb), but still gets the classics right.

Dollar Grill & Martinis (2 Exmouth Market, EC1R 4PX, 7278 0077, www.dollargrillsandmartinis.com) makes its flavoursome burgers from minced American steak; alternatively, upgrade to a Wagyu beef burger. For a taste of New York's Lower East side, join the Soho set at the speakeasy-style Spuntino (61 Rupert Street, W1D 7PW, no phone, http://spuntino.co.uk). Its 'sliders' are tiny, starter-sized burgers in toasted brioche buns: the beefburgers contain bone marrow to keep them moist. If you can resist its trademark steaks, the Hawksmoor (11 Langly Street, WC2H 9JG, 7856 2154, www.thehawksmoor.co.uk) also has burger-making down to a fine art: juicy patties of Longhorn beef, anointed with melted Ogleshield and served with triple cooked chips.

86

... Or follow the Meatwagon

Revered by London's gourmets and gluttons, the burgers made by Yianni Papoutsis are oozing, sprawling monsters, made from 28-day dry-aged steak and paired with onion rings and own-made 'slaw. Punters flocked to his van, the Meatwagon, until it was nicked; downcast but not deterred, Yianni now runs a pop-up joint, the Meateasy. Check www.themeatwagon.co.uk for his latest location, or join his legion of Twitter followers.

87

Appreciate art from the top deck

Part of the Cultural Olympiad, the Bus Tops project (http://bus-tops.com) will be positioning 33 digital art installations – one for each of the 32 London boroughs, plus the City of London – on the roofs of bus shelters across the city by January 2012. They'll continue to brighten commutes until the end of the Paralympic Games, on 9 September.

88

Seek enlightenment in NW1

The Camden School of Enlightenment (www.csofe.co.uk) isn't your usual night school. Held on the second Tuesday of every odd numbered month at the Camden Head (100 High Street, NW1 0LU, 7485 4019, www.camdenhead.com), this 'cabaret for the inquiring modern mind' takes in mini-lectures, poems, stories, music and comedy from regulars, guest speakers and members of the audience. Past events have included talks on fetishes, snooker legends and a puppet re-enactment of the life of Sylvia Plath.

89-91

Fashion your own footwear

Design your own footwear – from sandals to boots – at the Dalston workshops run by I Can Make Shoes (54 Cazenove Road, N16 6BJ, 07954 252287, http://icanmakeshoes.com), or enrol on a two-day course at the Prescott & Mackay School of Fashion & Accessory Design (7388 4547, www.prescottandmackay.co.uk), held at Black Truffle's shoe shop on Warren Street. Part of London College of Fashion, meanwhile, Cordwainer's (Golden Lane, EC1Y 0UU, 7514 7552, www.fashion.arts.ac.uk) is a shoemaking specialist, whose alumni include Olivia Morris, Emma Hope and Jimmy Choo. Alongside full-time study, it also offers evening classes: perfect for dipping a toe into the business.

92
Learn tango for free

From May to September, Tango Fever (07530 493826, www.tango-fever.com) runs free 'monthly milonga' evenings in Bishops Square in Spitalfields. Tango is the sexiest and subtlest of partner dances, but don't worry too much about picking up the finer points – just try an absolute beginners' class at 6.30pm and give it a whirl, with DJs and dancing until 9.45pm. It's free to attend; simply turn up and join in.

93
Pedal in plus fours

Dapper dress is de rigueur on the Tweed Run (http://tweedrun.com), a ten-mile ride through London that will celebrate its fourth installment in April 2012. Flat cap, tweeds and plus fours are the order of the day, along with well-groomed whiskers for the gents; extra kudos for riding a tandem or suitably old-fashioned steed. Entry costs a fiver, but you'll have to be quick off the mark: tickets generally sell out within the hour.

94
Celebrate Private Eye's 50th

Scourge of the British establishment, the scurrilous, scandal-mongering *Private Eye* has survived untold libel lawsuits, and will celebrate its 50th anniversary in October 2011. This momentous occasion will be marked by an exhibition at the V&A (19 October 2011-8 January 2012), promising a choice array of covers, original artwork and memorable content, plus a recreation of the editor's desk in the Soho office. **V&A** *Cromwell Road, SW7 2RL (7942 2000, www.vam.ac.uk).*

95
Borrow a desk

A rather lovely desk, that is, at the Mill Co Project (Lime Wharf, Vyner Street, E2 9DJ, 07866 549216, www.themillcoproject.co.uk), on the Regent's Canal in Hackney. It provides a shared working space, where you can bring your laptop, hook up to the Wi-Fi and rent a space for a day (£15) or a month (from £180). There's a communal kitchen and reception, community arts classes and events, and 1960s-style decor.

Shop this street

96-105

Tin Pan Alley:
Denmark Street, W1

Running between Charing Cross Road and St Giles High Street, Denmark Street's every door seems to lead to a room packed with new or vintage guitars, pedals and amps. Whether you're seeking a '30s Gibson acoustic, a £20 ukulele or a neon-green lightning bolt DIME-series Dean electric, no other street offers such variety.

From a 17th-century estate turned 18th-century slum, Denmark Street grew into a row of theatres, instrument shops, music printers and cheap domiciles for musicians, earning it the nickname 'Tin Pan Alley'. In the 1960s it became a launch pad for the UK rock scene: the Beatles and Jimi Hendrix recorded their first tracks in makeshift basement studios here, while the Rolling Stones recorded their debut album at Regent Sound Studio. The late Malcolm McLaren had one of the divier basements, while David Bowie – who couldn't afford a flat at the time – lived out of a van. Today, most of the recording studios have gone, but the remaining guitar shops are still a magnet for rock stars and music fans.

Starting at the St Giles High Street end, at no.4, Regent Sound Studio (7379 6111) is Europe's largest Fender dealer. It also stocks Gretsch, Music Man, Squier, Tokai, Hofner, Vox and Danelectro guitars, basses, amps and accessories. Next door, Rockers (no.5, 7240 2610) offers everything from beginner-level to professional thrash-ready guitars by Fender, Gibson, ESP, Ibanez and Dean. Staff will let you demo your chosen axe with a HIWATT amp, and you'll be melting faces in no time.

Moving on, Vintage & Rare Guitars (no.6, 7240 7500, www.vintageandrareguitars.com) is a treasure trove of 1950s and '60s pre-CBS Fender and Gibson electrics, vintage Martin and Guild acoustics and collectable instruments. Also on sale are rare handmade 'boutique' fuzz and effect pedals from LovePedal and Death by Audio. The Sex Pistols lived in the building behind the shop.

A newer arrival, at the Charing Cross Road end, is the Early Music Shop (no.11, 7632 3960, www.earlymusicshop.com), where you can pay a tenner for a plastic Yamaha soprano recorder and up to £3,500 for a Paetzold sub bass model, moving through handmade wooden recorders by the likes of Blezinger and Mollenhauer. It also stocks harps, baroque cellos, zithers and more. On the opposite side of the street, at no.20, Wunjo (7379 0737, www.wunjoguitars.com) houses three rooms of wall-to-wall new and used guitars of all types.

Heading back towards St Giles High Street, you'll find Bass Cellar (no.22, 7240 3483), selling standard, fretless, five-, six-, seven-string and lefty models by Fender, Warwick, Rickenbacker and others, as well as a host of bass rigs. Acoustic and classical guitarists, meanwhile, shouldn't miss London's largest Martin dealer, Hank's, at no.27 (7379 1139, www.hanksguitarshop.com). After establishing its original Tin Pan Alley shop in 1958, the family-owned Macari's (no.25, 3301 5481, www.macaris.co.uk) moved to Charing Cross Road, but recently opened a Denmark Street branch. The shop is the UK's official Gibson and Marshall dealer. The owner's father co-founded Colorsound effects pedals, producing the first English-made 'fuzzbox', used by Jimmy Page on *Led Zeppelin I*.

Finally, Music Ground Inc (no.27, 7836 5354) is packed with vintage electric guitars, from Gibson, Fender, VOX and National to 'oddball' European brands.

If all that has whet your appetite for some guitar-driven sounds, duck into the 12 Bar Club (no.26, 7240 2120, www.12barclub.com). This cherished hole in the wall is a gathering place for London's musically minded types, with live music every night. The size (capacity of 100, a stage that barely accommodates a trio) dictates a predominance of singer-songwriters, tiny tables crowd around the stage, and the graffiti-covered walls just add to the effect.

106-129 *Breakfast like a champion*

Best For... *Swish surrounds*

Dean Street Townhouse
The full English in more ways than one, this hotel restaurant features starched linen and uniformed service – though its streetside seating soaks up the Soho buzz.
69-71 Dean Street, W1D 4QJ (7434 1775, www.deanstreettownhouse.com).

202 Café
The café in Nicole Farhi's boutique is as elegant as its clients, and the menu juggles flavours with flair: sausages with fennel, say, or sweet potato with pancetta.
202-204 Westbourne Grove, W11 2RH (7727 2722).

The Wolseley
One of the grandest places in town to dip into a boiled egg and soldiers, the Wolseley offers silver tea pots, crisp linen and a selection of newspapers to peruse.
160 Piccadilly, W1J 9EB (7499 6996, www.thewolseley.com).

Best For... *Superior fry-ups*

Pavilion Café
Scoring a seat at this lakeside café isn't easy in fair weather, but Aussie chef Brett Redman's high-end fry-ups are worth the wait.
Victoria Park, E9 5DU (8980 0030, www.the-pavilion-cafe.com).

Roast
As you'd expect, Roast's menu is big on meats of pedigree, from Ayrshire streaky bacon to black pudding from Ramsay of Carluke.
Borough Market, Stoney Street, SE1 1TL (0845 034 7300, www.roast-restaurant.com).

St John Hotel
In a plain, white-tiled dining room, St John Hotel sets you up for the day with good, hearty fare – including a plate of Old Spot bacon with eggs and fried bread.
1 Leicester Street, off Leicester Square, WC2H 7BL (3301 8020, www.stjohnhotellondon.com).

Tom's Kitchen
The tiled walls of Tom Aitkens' brasserie ring to the sound of satisfied brunchers every weekend. English breakfasts sit alongside American pancakes and exceptional waffles.
27 Cale Street, SW3 3QP (7349 0202, www.tomskitchen.co.uk).

Best For... *Better baking*

Boulangerie Bon Matin
Breakfast standouts at this light-filled French bakery and café include fruit-filled crêpes and cinnamon-spiked French toast.
178 Tollington Park, N4 3AJ (7263 8633).

Breads Etcetera
The tables at this artisan bakery are set with toasters; breakfasting options range from smoked salmon and scrambled eggs on rye to 'DIY' combinations of toast and toppings.
127 Clapham High Street, SW4 7SS (07717 642812).

Gail's
Breakfast at this upmarket bakery might bring buttermilk pancakes or mushrooms on toast with spinach, taleggio and fried egg.
48 The Broadway, N8 9TP (8348 6323, www.gailsbread.co.uk).

Lowry & Baker
A domestic oven sits at the heart of this café, whose menu mixes pastries and cinnamon toast with colourful cooked breakfasts – rosemary and potato pancake, perhaps, topped with bacon, a poached egg and fresh thyme.
339 Portobello Road, W10 5SA (8960 8534, www.lowryandbaker.com).

Best For... *Global inspiration*

Dishoom
Dishoom skillfully blends western and Indian influences to offer Bombay breakfast bakes (eggs baked on a lentil bhaji mash), fruit-filled roti and the signature bacon naan roll.
12 Upper St Martin's Lane, WC2H 9FB (7420 9320, www.dishoom.com).

Kipferl

Breakfasts at this Austrian café include a rich bergkäse (mountain cheese) omelette, with mushrooms, pickles and caraway bread.
20 Camden Passage, N1 8ED (7704 1555, www.kipferl.co.uk).

Kopapa

A Kiwi-style café fusing international influences to deliver some inventive fare: ricotta pancakes with avocado and roasted grapes, or 'Turkish eggs' with whipped yoghurt and chilli butter.
32-34 Monmouth Street, WC2H 9HA (7240 6076, www.kopapa.co.uk).

Nopi

Ottolenghi's Soho offshoot does breakfasts with a difference – such as black rice with coconut milk, banana and mango.
21-22 Warwick Street, W1B 5NE (7494 9584, www.nopi-restaurant.com).

No.67

The South London Gallery café has got the breakfast spectrum covered, from Greek yoghurt, fruit and granola to the 'full Spanglish': fried eggs, grilled mushrooms, grilled chorizo, morcilla and spicy own-made beans.
South London Gallery, 67 Peckham Road, SE5 8UH (7252 7649).

Best For... *A leisurely brunch*

Breakfast Club

The inviting all-day brunch menu at this four-strong chain runs from porridge and pancakes to breakfast wraps and eggs any style.
12-16 Artillery Lane, E1 7LS (7078 9633, www.thebreakfastclubcafes.com).

Modern Pantry

A chic black and white interior belies a brunch menu bursting with colour: French toast is spiced with vattalapam (a Sri Lankan coconut custard) and accompanied by tamarind, maple syrup and bacon.
47-48 St John's Square, EC1V 4JJ (7553 9210, www.themodernpantry.co.uk).

Penk's

The well-judged weekend brunch menu at this local favourite mixes the usual suspects with artful alternatives, like cardamom and clove-infused kedgeree with bacon and boiled egg.
79 Salusbury Road, NW6 6NH (7604 4484).

Raoul's Café

Brunch is a served until 6pm daily at this brasserie and deli. Enjoy juices and eggs any which way in the banquette-lined interior or claim one of the streetside tables.
113-115 Hammersmith Grove, W6 0NQ (8741 3692, www.raoulsgourmet.com).

The Table

At weekend brunches, tackle this sleek café's signature 'stack' of own-made beans, chorizo, poached eggs, hollandaise and red pepper pesto.
83 Southwark Street, SE1 0HX (7401 2760, www.thetablecafe.com).

Village East

This haven for the hungover takes its weekend brunches very seriously, with three variations on the Bloody Mary to go with a free range full English.
171-173 Bermondsey Street, SE1 3UW (7357 6082, www.villageeast.co.uk).

Best For... *Breakfast alfresco*

See also **Pavilion Café**.

Lido Café

The poolside café at this restored art deco is the perfect place to unwind over a terrific free range breakfast.
Brockwell Lido, Dulwich Road, SE24 0PA (7737 8183, www.thelidocafe.co.uk).

Towpath

This cash-only café sits right on Regent's Canal: ignore the ringing of bicycle bells and it's an oasis of calm. The porridge with stewed fruit and cooked offerings are both top-notch.
Regent's Canal Towpath, between Whitmore Bridge & Kingsland Road Bridge, N1 5SB (no phone).

Discover the best of Britain...

130

Pay homage to Pina Bausch

With a posthumous 3-D documentary about her from Wim Wenders winning rave reviews last year, German choreographer Pina Bausch's profile has never been higher – notwithstanding her sudden death, just before her 70th birthday. For the London 2012 Festival, the troupe she led for four decades – Tanztheater Wuppertal Pina Bausch – will dance the new commission 'World Cities 2012' (6 June-9 July 2012) at Sadler's Wells and the Barbican. Made up of pieces individually premiered across the globe over the last two decades, 'World Cities 2012' uses the company's characteristic combination of everyday gestures and the abstractions of contemporary dance to explore Hong Kong, Los Angeles, Santiago in Chile, Rome, Saitama, São Paulo, Kolkata, Istanbul, Palermo and Budapest.

131 *Listen out for the Fleet*

The Fleet is one of London's lost rivers, chanelled underground as the city developed. It rises in Hampstead Heath and runs to the Thames via Camden, King's Cross and Clerkenwell (beneath Farringdon Road). It was once a major landmark, known at various points in its history for its healing waters, tidal mills, busy wharves and foul pollution – Alexander Pope described the Fleet ditch as disgorging 'its large tribute of dead dogs to Thames'. Gradually covered over in the 18th and 19th centuries, the river is remembered in the city's nomenclature (Turnmill Street, Seacoal Lane, Clerkenwell, Fleet Street) and its waters emasculated into little more than a trickle. You can hear them gurgling through a nondescript grating outside the Coach and Horses pub on Ray Street, EC2, and watch their unsung outfall into the Thames, just west of Blackfriars Bridge.

132-138

Be perfectly coiffed

Party like it's 1949 with London's retro hair salons and services, which specialise in teasing the tresses of pin-ups and hepcats.

It's Something Hells

This red velvet and leopard upholstered salon is big on rockabilly, with a measure of goth thrown in. Miss Betty styles the girls, Mr Ducktail the teddy boys.

2.16 Kingly Court, W1B 5PW (07896 153491).

Lipstick & Curls

These mobile beauticians give lessons in vintage hair styling and make-up, specialising in 1920s to '60s looks.

07879 076449, www.lipstickandcurls.co.uk.

Nina's Hair Parlour

One of the first salons to offer retro hair styling, and also one of the best – no one primps a marcel wave or pin curl quite like Nina and her team.

Alfie's Antiques Market,1st floor, 13 Church Street, NW8 8DT (7723 1911, www.ninasvintageand retrohair.com).

The Painted Lady

Staff at this lovely little East End beauty parlour will soon transform you into a sleek, modern take on *Mad Men*'s Betty (or Don) Draper.

65 Redchurch Street, E2 7DJ (7729 2154, www.thepaintedladylondon.com).

Pimps & Pin-ups

The decor is retro gone turbo at this lively rockabilly salon, specialised in making its clientele look like the cast of *Grease*.

14 Lamb Street, E1 6EA (7426 2121, www.pimpsandpinups.com).

The Powder Room

Pink-clad beauticians dispense Dita Von Teese-style screen siren make up and up-dos.

136 Columbia Road, E2 7RG (7729 1365, www.thepowderpuffgirls.com).

Vintage Secret

This little collective organises sporadic fashion and beauty 'Secret Salons', that are so heavily vintage themed, you'll feel as if you've walked into an episode of *Goodnight Sweetheart*.

www.vintagesecret.com.

139

Join the throng for the Opening Ceremony...

The London 2012 Olympic Games will open on 27 July, with an elaborate Opening Ceremony, overseen by Oscar-winning film director Danny Boyle and Tony Award winner Stephen Daldry. The details are top secret, but Boyle is said to be keen to start at sunset, using the darkness to create spectacular lighting effects. The Opening Ceremony was one of the hottest tickets in the ballot, but there's no need to watch it alone on TV if you weren't lucky enough to get a ticket. Instead, join the spectators whooping at the action on big screens at Live Sites around town. Potters Field Park on the South Bank, Hyde Park and Victoria Park in east London are likely locations, plus Trafalgar Square for the Paralympics only.

Pimps & Pin-ups

140-154

... And have a picnic ready for the key 2012 showdowns

Making predictions about sport is a treacherous business, but there are some mouthwatering prospects for the London 2012 Olympic and Paralympic Games. The key date for non-ticket-holders to grab their picnic blanket and head to a Live Site to soak up the sporting atmosphere is 5 August 2012. This is the day of the final of the Men's 100m, when the mighty Usain Bolt is likely to be taking on Asafa Powell and Tyson Gay to find out who is the fastest man in the world, in what could be the most exciting 100m Final since Atlanta 1996, when the defending gold medallist, the reigning world champion and the man with fastest 100m time of the year all raced head-to-head. The 100m (T44) Final in the Paralympic Games will also be a titanic clash: Oscar Pistorius (the South African double amputee, famous as 'the Blade Runner') has been trading victories with his lesser-known US rival Jerome Singleton.

Another hotly anticipated possible showdown is between American Michael Phelps, eight-times gold medallist of Beijing 2008, and Australian Ian Thorpe, a five-times Olympic gold medallist who is returning from retirement expressly to compete at the London 2012 Games. They should meet in the 100m Freestyle and 200m Freestyle.

There are a number of potential red letter days for British sports fans. Jessica Ennis's bid to add Olympic gold to her World Championship gold in the Heptathlon will come to a climax on 4 August, when Mo Farah also should be running in the 10,000m Men's Final (he is also aiming for the 5000m Men's Final on 11 August). On 5 August, the same day as the Men's 100m Final, Paula Radcliffe will attempt to make one of the comebacks of all time and beat her Olympic hex to take gold in the Marathon; Christine Ohuruogu will also be running in the 400m. The Triple Jump contest between Frenchman Teddy Tamgho and flamboyant local boy Phillips Idowu is a heady prospect for 9 August. In the pool, names to watch will probably include Rebecca Adlington, who contests the 800m Freestyle Swimming (2-3 August), and Tom Daley in the Diving (7, 11 August). There might also be a rare opportunity to see siblings contest the same event – Alistair and Jonathan Brownlee share medal aspirations in the Triathlon (7 August) – and an even rarer opportunity to see some British tennis success, should Andy Murray make it to the Singles Tennis Final – again on 5 August.

Given how fashionable bicycles now are in London – and the British team's successes at Beijing 2008 – events in the Velodrome might yet generate the keenest Live Sites audiences. In the Track Cycling, watch out for Victoria Pendleton, Chris Hoy and Bradley Wiggins (2-7 Aug). There are high hopes too that Manx sprinter Mark Cavendish will overcome his Beijing disappointments to win gold in the Cycling Road race (28 July).

155 Engage your mental muscle at chessboxing

The ultimate in sweat-soaked intellectual thrills, this hybrid sport alternates rounds of boxing with speed chess: imagine a Grandmaster Muhammed Ali. Competitors must possess both brain and brawn, as a match can be won either way. You can challenge your mind and muscles every Saturday at Boxing London (20 Hazelville Road, N19 3LP, 07956 196780, www.londonchessboxing. com) where training for serious boxers, would-be grandmasters and everyone in between is available for £12 per session.

156 Find peace in the London Library

On the corner of St James's Square, mere minutes from the throng of Piccadilly Circus, the London Library is the world's largest independent lending library. Founded in 1841, it has long been a haunt of eminent literati – Dickens, Kipling and TS Eliot among them. Join up, and you might find yourself browsing the 15-mile maze of book-crammed shelves alongside Sir Tom Stoppard, Simon Schama or Simon Callow, all of whom are members. If the hefty annual fees (£435; £220 concessions) are beyond your means, free, 45-minute tours afford a peek inside this venerable literary haven, every Monday at 7pm.
The London Library *14 St James's Square, SW1Y 4LG (7930 7705, www.londonlibrary.co.uk).*

157

Admire a great survivor
Built in the 1920s, Battersea
Power Station has become
an iconic feature of the city's
skyline. Like St Paul's Cathedral,
it miraculously survived the Blitz,
despite suffering major damage
in September 1940. Since ceasing
operations in 1983, though, the
Grade II-listed building has had a troubled history. After plans to
open a theme park on the site in 1990 foundered, it was left without
a roof and exposed to the elements: over the decades, it has sunk
deeper and deeper into disrepair. Now, with planning permission
granted on a new scheme (www.battersea-powerstation.com), there
are hopes Sir Giles Gilbert Scott's masterpiece will finally be saved.

158 Brew a batch of elderflower cordial

Elder is one of the UK's most common shrubs, and you'll find it along the edge of canals, in wastelands, and woven through hedgerows and woodland across London. In spring, clusters of tiny white elderflowers appear, boasting a sweet, delicate flavour. With a little savoir faire, you can turn them into cordial that will taste wonderful diluted with Prosecco.

Having found your elder, pick 20 fully open flower heads. Zest four lemons, chop them into quarters and put both the zest and fruit into a bowl. Inspect the flowers for bugs, but don't wash them, then add them to the bowl. Dissolve 1kg of white granulated sugar into 1.5 litres of water to make a syrup. Pour the hot syrup over the lemons and flowers, and stir it in. Add 55g of citric acid (found behind the counter at your local chemist), and cover the concoction with a tea towel. Leave it to steep overnight, then strain the mixture through muslin into bottles. Seal the bottles well, then freeze them or drink within a month.

159 Cycle to the seaside

The 120-mile overnight Dunwich Dynamo (www.southwarkcyclists.org.uk/content/dunwich-dynamo) ride from London to the Suffolk coast is not for the faint-hearted, but it's perfectly possible for even not very sporty cyclists; there aren't many hills and you've got all night to do it. Plus there's usually a cake-and-tea stop at a village hall somewhere midway. It's usually held on a short midsummer night with a full moon, so for the most part you're riding in spectrally beautiful natural light, along narrow, empty lanes. Starting in Hackney, on the Saturday evening, it arrives at the Suffolk coastal town of Dunwich early the following morning – just in time for a revitalising swim and breakfast, which is laid on for a small fee. The ride itself is free, except for a £1 donation for a route sheet. You can also book a place on a coach back, but there's otherwise no support other than of the mutual variety, from the 1,500 or so other riders all making for the dawn.

160 Eat sweets in Chinatown

There may be an abundance of eateries in Chinatown, but only one specialises in Asian desserts. As a result, the pocket-sized, first-storey Candy Café is always chock-full of in-the-know Chinese, Thai and Singaporean students. The gorgeous pomelo mango dessert comes with fresh fruit and little sago pearls; for something less sweet, try the glutinous, generously filled black sesame rice balls in soymilk.

Candy Café *3 Macclesfield Street, W1D 6AU (7434 4581).*

161 Enjoy a right royal knees-up

On 2 June 1953, the coronation of 27-year-old Queen Elizabeth II took place in Westminster Abbey. Sixty years on, you can celebrate her continuing reign over a four-day Diamond Jubilee. Celebrations will centre on Sunday 3 June 2012, when the Queen will lead a flotilla of hundreds of boats along the Thames, aboard the Royal Barge. The following evening, 2,012 beacons will be lit across the UK, and a concert will be held at Buckingham Palace. If you drink our sovereign's health a little too enthusiastically (Her Majesty's preferred tipple is said to be gin and Dubonnet), don't worry: there are bank holidays on Monday and Tuesday on which to recover.

162 Make the city your gym

After the daily grind of nine to five, pushing weights and pounding the treadmill in the confines of the gym isn't everyone's idea of fun. Rat Race Urban Gym (01904 409401, www.ratrace.com) offers a fast-paced alfresco alternative, running circuit training sessions around Broadgate and St Paul's. Do pull-ups on railings, dips on benches and bound up flights of steps, astonishing passing commuters.

A few of my favourite things

163-173

Giles Deacon,
fashion designer

Dover Street Market (17-18 Dover Street, W1S 4LT, 7518 0680) is incredibly specialist and well-thought out. It has a really diverse series of collections, from Japanese street fashion through to high-end design. They sell great Undercover pieces, which are hard to get hold of outside Japan, and I really like Bleu de Paname for their French denim. And the Comme des Garçons collection is super, of course, as label head Rei Kawakubo created the store. I also love Angela Hill's IDEA Books concession: she has a selection of really interesting magazines and rare editions of fashion and design books.
Artwords Bookshop in Shoreditch (69 Rivington Street, EC2A 3AY, 7729 2000, www.artwords.co.uk) also has a terrific selection of fashion, art and architecture magazines, and contemporary titles and rare editions from small publishers. They're a small, independent shop, and have been there for a long time. They put a lot of effort in to it, and are great at ordering things in very quickly.
Fortnum & Mason (181 Piccadilly, W1A 1ER, 7734 8040) is a bit of a guilty pleasure for me. I remember people talking about it when I was a kid, and never knowing what it was. Since my first visit, I've had a real obsession. The hampers make really lovely gifts. It's got a unique British quality: something peculiarly old school that I find very attractive.
I cycle everywhere in central London, but like to take the overland train with my bike from near my house in Dalston to Richmond Park (TW10 5HS, 8948 3209). My favourite bit is by the deer house, but I also enjoy just cycling with no destination and disappearing

into the park. You can feel as if you're in the middle of nowhere in no time at all.
I'm not very good at sitting still, so I like to relax by taking a walk from Lincoln's Inn Fields to Camden. You see an amazing cross section of London, and its urbanisation and modernisation. I walk around the back of the Royal Courts of Justice, through Bloomsbury to Regent's Park and back over to Camden. Sometimes I'll then follow the Regent's Canal to London Fields. It's on a bit of a leyline, and quite hidden away. Even though I walk past things that I've seen a thousand times before, I always notice something new. And I have to do it with a good soundtrack on my headphones.
My favourite place to eat in London is Bistrotheque (23-27 Wadeson Street, E2 9DR, 8983 7900, www.bistrotheque.com). I love the mix of cabaret and food, and the design and layout of the restaurant upstairs. With the bar downstairs too, it's a great one-stop shop for a whole evening's fun.
I love the raclette at St John Bread & Wine (94 Commercial Street, E1 6LZ, 3301 8069, www.stjohnbreadandwine.com), which is near our studio. I like the nose to tail ethic of Fergus and Margot Henderson's cooking, but it's not just for meat eaters; they make a delicious beetroot salad. It's not a generic food hall, and they source all kinds of interesting ingredients. It's very particular and precise; that draws me to places.
I'm not a big one for overly glam places. I enjoy going to the Drapers Arms (44 Barnsbury Street, N1 1ER, 7619 0348, www.thedrapersarms.com) in Islington. It's very relaxed, and there are always interesting people in there. It's terrific on a Saturday afternoon. I find pretty much anywhere in London is welcoming for a drink though, really.
Also in Islington is 69 Colebrooke Row (69 Colebrook Row, N1 8AA, 07540 528593, www.69colebrookerow.com). It's small and intimate, but has an awful lot of character. The cocktails are absolutely incredible, especially the mint julep. They're also behind the cocktail bar at the Zetter Townhouse (49-50 St John's Square, EC1V 4JJ, 7324 4545, www.thezettertownhouse.com).
A bit more central and very special is the cigar bar in Claridge's, which is called the Fumoir (Brook Street, W1K 4HR, 7629 8860). It's all dark with dim mirroring – just beautiful. It's all terribly quiet and discreet, and you can chat away for hours.

174 See zoological curiosities at the Grant Museum

Recently re-opened in a former Edwardian library in the UCL complex, the Grant Museum retains the air of an avid Victorian collector's house. Its 67,000 specimens include the remains of many rare and extinct creatures, including skeletons of the dodo and the zebra-like quagga, which was hunted out of existence in the 1880s. Visitors are engaged in dialogue about the distant evolutionary past via the most modern means available, including iPads and smartphones.

Grant Museum *Rockefeller Building, University College London, University Street, WC1E 6DE (3108 2052, www.ucl.ac.uk/museums/zoology).*

175 Pay your respects to Jeremy Bentham

In his will, philosopher Jeremy Bentham asked that his body should be preserved at University College London (Gower Street, WC1E 6BT, 7679 2000, www.ucl.ac.uk/Bentham-Project). Sure enough, it's still there for all to see, in a cabinet at the end of the South Cloisters. While the clothes and skeleton are Bentham's own, the head is wax; his real head used to repose between his feet, but after being stolen and held to ransom by waggish students, is now in secure storage. Visitors are welcome on weekdays, between 7.30am and 6pm.

176

Make a pilgrimage to the Whovian shop

Program your Tardis to E6, present day, and you'll find just what the Doctor ordered – a shop specialising in all things Whovian, from a Weeping Regenerating Angel figurine to a film print signed by Nick Briggs, the owner of the original Dalek voice. Stacked with paraphernalia and memorabilia, the shop is often host to visiting cast members, from the mighty David Tennant to Gilly Brown – who you'll know played Ohica in 'Brain of Morbius'.

The Who Shop *39-41 Barking Road, E6 1PY (8471 2356, www.thewhoshop.com).*

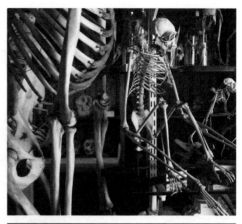

177 Meet the people behind the London 2012 Games

The final part of the 'Road to 2012' trilogy of photographic exhibitions (http://roadto2012. npg.org.uk) will run from late July through to September 2012 at the National Portrait Gallery (St Martin's Place, WC2H 0HE, 7306 0055, www.npg.org.uk). Commissions for the series have included intimate portraits of Olympic and Paralympic stars, as well as the people who secured the bid and are working to make the London 2012 Games happen. The final exhibition will also include the best of the preceding shows.

178 Kip on a cultural beacon

If you've ever enjoyed a night at the Southbank Centre so much you didn't want to go home, A Room for London will be your idea of heaven. Part of the London 2012 Festival, this unique artistic and architectural collaboration will place a boat-shaped, timber-built room on the roof of the Southbank Centre's Queen Elizabeth Hall, offering guests and invited artists a place of refuge and reflection, high above the riverfront throng. The designers hope occupants will keep a 'logbook' of their experiences; during each stay, a flag will be raised to indicate the boat has been boarded. Members of the public will be able to spend a single night in A Room for London between January and December 2012; booking opens in September 2011 (www.living-architecture.co.uk).

179 *Lunch at LASSCo*

A rootle around the LASSCo salvage yard is always a delight. From old sets of traffic lights and London Underground signs to Vicorian trunks, its stock is endlessly inspiring. You can browse more curiosities in its excellent café, in the Georgian Brunswick House. The menu is seasonal and delicious (roast fennel and Berkswell tart, say, or smoked mackerel with beetroot). Generally a daytime affair, it's open in the evenings from Thursday to Saturday, and mixes a mean cocktail.
Brunswick House Café *30 Wandsworth Road, SW8 2LG (7720 2926, www.brunswickhousecafe.co.uk).*

180 *See London anew*

Visit 'Another London' at Tate Britain (Millbank, SW1P 4RG, 7887 8888, www.tate.org.uk/britain) to see how some of the world's most renowned photographers captured the city. Comprising 150 classic 20th-century photographs, the exhibition runs from 31 July to 16 September 2012.

181-182 *See a bisected boat and a Quantum Cloud*

Standing on the foreshore of the Greenwich Peninsula, sculptor Richard Wilson's *Slice of Reality* (2000) is delightfully peculiar. A towering vertical section of a sand dredger, it was commissioned as a temporary installation in honour of the Millennium: afterwards, Wilson exploited a loophole of maritime law to get a mooring permit, and now occasionally uses its habitable sections as a studio. Even more brilliantly, it's sometimes open to visitors on Open House weekends; visit www.londonopen house.org to see if it's on this year's programme. It's just off the Thames Path, round the back of the North Greenwich Arena.

Afterward, follow the path to the Thames Clipper pier to see Antony Gormley's vast *Quantum Cloud* (1999). Taller even than his celebrated *Angel of the North*, it consists of a seemingly random cloud of steel sections: look at it straight on, and you'll see the artist's body outlined at the centre.

183-186
Shop like a celebrity

In need of sartorial assistance? Then call on a personal shopping service. That scene in *Pretty Woman* that sees Julia Roberts presented with a procession of clothes whisked from the shop floor for her wearing pleasure can be re-enacted for you, too – just don't expect Richard Gere to pick up the tab.

At the top end of the spectrum is Harrods by Appointment (87-135 Brompton Road, SW1X 7XL, 7893 8000, www.harrodsbyappointment. com) – a lifestyle concierge service, whereby you can request anything from new-season Prada to a private jet. It's free, but an immaculate eyebrow is likely to be raised if you leave with nothing.

Selfridges (400 Oxford Street, W1A 1AB, 0800 123 400, www.selfridges.com) and Harvey Nichols (109-125 Knightsbridge, SW1X 7RJ, 7259 6638, www.harveynichols.com) also excel at personal shopping. The in-house stylists have a comprehensive handle on the stock, and knowledge of key season trends – plus you get access to the plush private changing rooms.

For the more modest of budget, Topshop's personal shopping service, tucked away in the bowels of the store (36-38 Great Castle Street, Oxford Circus, W1W 8LG, 0844 243 5544, www.topshop.com) is free, good fun and now available for men at the Oxford Circus flagship. All services are by appointment.

187
See the priciest painting ever sold

Picasso's *Nude, Green Leaves and Bust* broke records in May 2010 when it became the most expensive painting ever sold at auction, selling for $106.5m (£66m) to an unknown bidder. The 1932 work is one of a series of portraits of Picasso's then muse and mistress, Marie-Thérèse Walter, and can now be appreciated by the British public at Tate Modern, lent by its anonymous owner. You'll find it in the Pablo Picasso: Convulsive Beauty room, on the gallery's third floor.
Tate Modern *Bankside, SE1 9TG (7887 8888, www.tate.org.uk).*

188
Catch next year's West End hit today

South Bank fringe theatre the Menier Chocolate Factory (51-53 Southwark Street, SE1 1RU, 7378 1713, www.menierchocolatefactory.com) has a golden touch with West End transfers. Revivals of musicals such as *Little Shop of Horrors* and *La Cage aux Folles* are among the productions to have moved on to successful Theatreland runs, and there's a surprisingly good bar-restaurant too.

189
Pay less for your espresso

With its cheery red awning, the Algerian Coffee Stores is a beacon for impecunious coffee-lovers, right in the heart of Soho. It has traded from its old Compton site for over 120 years, still with the original wooden counter and shelving – chock-a-block with house blends, single origin beans and rarities. Its takeaways must be the best coffee deal in London: a pound for an espresso or double espresso, £1.20 for a latte or cappucino.
Algerian Coffee Stores *52 Old Compton Street, W1V 6PB (7437 2480, www.algcoffee.co.uk).*

Want to see the London sights without taking all day over it? If you've got a bit over half an hour to spare and an Oyster card with £1.30 of credit, you're ready to receive the quintessence of tourist London. (Even without an Oyster, a single bus ticket is only £2.20.) You can do this tour any day and at any time – just avoid rush hour on weekdays (8-9.30am and 4.30-7pm).

Climb aboard the first no.11 to arrive at Stop B of Liverpool Street bus station. Head upstairs and do your utmost to secure one of the front window seats; the views just aren't as good from anywhere else. Tower 42 will suddenly appear straight ahead. Yes, it's boringly straitlaced in black and grey, but it rears its head impressively over the six-floor banks that cluster at its knees like attendant pages.

Just before the bus turns right on to Threadneedle Street, look high above the corner sandwich shop to spot a grasshopper motif. It is the symbol of Sir Thomas Gresham, pioneering Tudor financier and sometime arms smuggler. He established the Royal Exchange, the third version of which will shortly be on your left. On your right, the Bank of England is squat and grey at ground level, but white and rather impressive at top-deck height. We like the burly chaps in bas-relief, especially the last, who has had the foresight to preserve his modesty behind a huge bunch of keys.

The Duke of Wellington stares across the junction at Mansion House, official residence of the Lord Mayor of London (elected by Aldermen to rule the City of London, and not to be confused with the plain old Mayor of London, elected by all of us). As the bus crosses the junction, glance back over your left shoulder to see Sir Richard Rogers' inside-out Lloyd's of London building, whose lifts and cooling pipes are visible on the exterior rather than hidden away within. Don't gaze too long: at a right-angle left you can also see Nicholas Hawksmoor's St Mary Woolnoth. A student of Sir Christopher Wren, Hawksmoor created six London churches, each a budget-busting combination of dark Gothic and elegant neo-classical styles. St Mary's had a key role in TS Eliot's *The Waste Land*, calling his fellow bank clerks into work with 'a dead sound on the final stroke of nine.'

Next you make an infuriatingly pointless (for commuters) and wonderfully accommodating (for sightseers) loop... that brings you right up by St Paul's Cathedral. As you draw alongside, look left across the Millennium Bridge to Tate Modern – you'll see why the bridge was dubbed a 'blade of light'. Just after St Paul's is a statue of Queen Anne in the plaza. Beyond her is Temple Bar, also attributed to Wren. This gate used to mark the point where the City becomes Westminster, as well as displaying the heads of executed traitors on spikes. Back in 1878, it was removed to ease traffic, and languished in the garden of a stately home for a century, before being returned to its new City location.

You now plunge down the hill to Ludgate Circus. At the crossroads, look diagonally left. The white layers of St Bride's 'wedding cake' spire can be seen over the grey buildings. This is another Wren creation and, as the official church to journalists, pretty much the last vestige of old Fleet Street. In 2005, Reuters (on the left at no.85) was the last news organisation to leave, but the jet-black art deco Daily Express (on the right at nos.121-128) is still impressive. Having topped the hill, look right. See those elaborate chimes, struck by a pair of camp giants, and the massive clockfaces? These belong to St Dunstan-in-the-West, whose rector was the poet John Donne. Next, on the same side, you can't miss the Royal Courts of Justice, seeming oddly frivolous when the sun shines. Shortly before the Courts, you'll have passed a griffin, in the middle of the street, that marks the original location of Temple Bar.

You're now on the Strand – location of Burlington Bertie's morning consitutional in the music hall song. To your left, enjoy flashes of the Thames. You are, though it doesn't look like it, on the riverbank. 'Strand' has the (now rather poetic) sense of 'shore of a sea, lake or river'. That's exactly what this street was

until 1874, when Sir Joseph Bazalgette, saviour of London from noxious sewage, completed the grand Embankment that pushed the river southwards to its current location.

St Mary-le-Strand, on your right, is as grubby as a proper city church should be, its sombre colour a perfect contrast for the lush tree in its courtyard. Left, note the blue railings and lamps of Somerset House before the buildings briefly open into the flat greyness of Waterloo Bridge. Here, lovers Terry and Julie watch a 'Waterloo Sunset' in the Kinks' song. Next are boarding-school trad carvery Simpson's-in-the-Strand, then the strange vision of a golden knight atop a shiny art deco canopy. It's the entrance to the Savoy, and you're looking down the only bit of Britain where you must drive on the right.

Here you'll probably run into traffic by McDonald's, behind black cabs queuing to pick up fares from Charing Cross station. In front of the station is a roughly conical structure that contrives to look frothy. In 1290, after the death of his wife Eleanor, the uxorious Edward I ordered crosses to be erected to mark the 12 points at which her funeral train halted. In 1863, long after the original cross was crunched into paving, this replica was erected.

Up ahead, Nelson's Column marks Trafalgar Square. The bus makes to the left, passing (on your right) an equestrian statue of Charles I, set on a woozily skewed roundabout. Behind him, a small plaque marks the official centre of London. Poking over trees is your next big-money sight: Big Ben... or rather the clocktower that holds a vast bell called Big Ben. You're on Whitehall. Keep looking right for Horse Guards, where you might spot a mounted sentry in his dazzling cuirass. Just after the Women of World War II memorial, glance left across the river for the London Eye, then right for Downing Street, home of the prime minister. You now pass Sir Edwin Lutyens' Cenotaph, memorial to the dead of both world wars, and – still looking right – the exquisite triple arch that marks the beginning of King Charles Street.

If your neck doesn't already have a crick, you're about to get one. Half an hour gone, and you're in Parliament Square. White Westminster Abbey, with its square towers, will probably strike you first; in front of it, the much older St Margaret's Church is dwarfed. The tobacco-yellow Houses of Parliament are unmissable on your left.

The next section is a bit dull, but keep alert for a leftwards glimpse of the domed, red-brick Westminster Cathedral, its spire like a square minaret. Next on the left there's a glimpse of Victoria station. At the next junction, just as the bus starts into a tree-laden square, look hard right on Buckingham Palace Road: that yellowy-brown building in the distant park is Buckingham Palace.

You could stay on for Sloane Street and the neo-classical squares of the King's Road, before alighting at the terminus, Fulham Town Hall. But ding the bell now and you can get the tube from Victoria – having ticked off London's major sights in double-quick time.

225-235

Test the water at London's lidos

For full details of London's lidos (and to join the campaign to reopen those that have closed), visit www.lidos.org.uk.

Brockwell Lido

Transformed by a Heritage Lottery Fund grant, this 1930s lido now sports a poolside café, a gym, and yoga and Pilates studios.

Brockwell Park, Dulwich Road, SE24 0PA (7274 3088, www.brockwell-lido.co.uk).

Finchley Lido

There are two indoor pools here, but it's the outdoor pool and sun terrace that make it such a draw for locals in summer.

Great North Leisure Park, Chaplin Square, High Road, N12 0GL (8343 9830, www.gll.org).

Hampton Pool

The water is heated to 28°C at Hampton Pool, and there's a learner pool for babies and toddlers.

High Street, Hampton, Middx TW12 2ST (8255 1116, www.hamptonpool.co.uk).

London Fields Lido

This east London lido measures an Olympian 50m – which is why the US Paralympic team plans to train here. It's heated to around 25°C, and has two cafés at which to refuel. There are lanes for slow, medium and fast swimmers and usually for general swimming too (but check first).

London Fields Westside, E8 3EU (7254 9038, www.gll.org).

Oasis Sports Centre

This heated 28m outdoor pool is open year round, and is particularly appealing in winter, when steam rises from the surface (it's a chilly dash from the changing rooms, mind). There's a 25m indoor pool, too.

32 Endell Street, WC2H 9AG (7831 1804, www.gll.org).

Park Road Pools

Crouch End's 50m lido dates from 1929. The centre includes diving areas, a children's pool, exercise studios, a steam and sauna room, and strips of lawn that lend themselves to lounging when the sun's out.

Park Road, N8 8JN (8341 3567, www.haringey. gov.uk/leisure).

Parliament Hill Lido

Built in 1938, Parliament Hill Lido measures a generous 60m by 28m. It's unheated, but wetsuits are permitted at the lifeguard's discretion. There's a paddling pool for under-fives, and a café.

Gordon House Road, NW5 1NB (7485 3873, www.cityoflondon.gov.uk/hampstead).

London Fields Lido

Pools on the Park

This sports complex inside the picturesque Old Deer Park features a 33m heated outdoor pool, and one the same size inside.

Old Deer Park, Twickenham Road, Richmond, Surrey TW9 2SF (8940 0561, www.springhealth.net).

Serpentine Lido

This picturesque freshwater pool is a London institution, beloved by swimmers and ducks. During the London 2012 Games, the Serpentine will host the Swimming 10k Marathon as well as the swimming element of the Triathalon.

Hyde Park, W2 2UH (7706 3422, www.serpentine lido.com).

Tooting Bec Lido

At 94m by 25m, Tooting Bec's art deco beauty is the second largest open-air pool in Europe. There's a paddling pool for splash-happy toddlers.

Tooting Bec Road, SW16 1RU (8871 7198, www.wandsworth.gov.uk).

Uxbridge Lido

Originally opened in 1935, Uxbridge's Grade II-listed art deco lido was rescued from dereliction and reopened in 2010. Additions include heated shallow pools for kids (the main pool is unheated) and decorative fountains.

Gatting Way, Park Road, Uxbridge, Middx UB8 1NR (0845 130 7324, www.fusion-lifestyle.com).

236 *Have a cuppa at Rasa Sayang*

Teh tarik, which literally means 'pulled tea' in Malay, is frothy, incredibly milky and extremely satisfying whatever the weather (it can be served hot or cold). Popular across South East Asia, it has its origins in Indian chai, and is prepared by successively pouring a mixture of black tea and sweetened condensed milk from one mug to another, at an impressive height. This 'pulling' process creates a cappuccino-like foam on top, as well as mixing the two ingredients and cooling the tea down to optimum drinking temperature. A good place to sample it is Malaysian/Singaporean eaterie Rasa Sayang; while you're there, don't miss the standout *chye tow kuay* (Chinese-style fried carrot cake) and fried fish noodles in soup.

Rasa Sayang *5 Macclesfield Street, W1D 6AY (7734 1382).*

237 *Discover London's last music hall*

Opened in 1853, Wilton's (Graces Alley, E1 8JB, 7702 2789, www.wiltons.org.uk) used to entertain the masses with acts ranging from Chinese performing monkeys to acrobats, contortionists to opera singers – and, more than 150 years later, still does much the same. Even better, the management decided not to renovate the severely dilapidated interior: above the wonderfully distinctive twisting columns, for example, you can still see charring on the roof timbers from the huge 'sun-burner' chandelier, which was powered by 300 gas jets. If you can't get tickets for a show, drop in to the Mahogany Bar, built around 1725. It now opens 5-11pm on weekdays, with free retro music or cabaret performances every Monday.

238 *See some right royal stationery*

At the back of British heritage brand Smythson's New Bond Street store (no.40, W1S 2DE, 7629 8558, www.smythson.co.uk) is a small but perfectly formed museum devoted to its wares. The firm's pedigree is evident in official stationery from the Royal Palaces, from Queen Victoria's time onwards – including the die used to print the Duke of Windsor's letterheads, and Princess Diana's writing paper, topped with a crowned 'D'.

Practice makes perfect

Elizabeth Winding **watches the Royal Ballet practising their pliés.**

Standing by the barre in the Clore Studio, Marianela Nuñez is warming up. Seemingly effortlessly, she swings her leg in ever-increasing, impossible arcs, as Merrill Ashley, who is leading tonight's working rehearsal, explains why it is so crucial. Her male lead, the precociously talented Sergei Polunin – at 20, one of the Royal Ballet's youngest-ever principals – has been comandeered to step into another production this week. That, in turn, has squeezed the already tight schedule for the *Ballo della regina* – which, as Ashley explains, is a hugely challenging piece, performed at breakneck speed.

Held around once a month, generally on Monday evenings, Royal Ballet in Rehearsal sessions offer a rare – and thrillingly close-up – glimpse behind the scenes at this most venerable of companies. The 90-minute sessions are held in the Linbury Studio Theatre or the Clore Studio Upstairs, with capacities of 400 and 170 respectively. This is ballet at its most stripped down: no sets, no exquisite costumes and no grand stage. Instead, there's just the piano, the squeak of shoes on the scuffed grey floor, and the intent concentration of the dancers. The sessions are, invariably, a sell-out.

The casting is generally only revealed on the night, and before we go in, the old hands eagerly scan the programme to find out who will be rehearsing. It could be the leads practising an elaborate pas de deux, or new recruits from the corps de ballet learning the steps to *Swan Lake* or *Nutcracker* for the first time. 'We wait until the night to reveal the programme as things often

change due to dancer injury, and we don't want to raise false expectations,' says Insight Programme Manager Tom Nelson, who co-ordinates the sessions. 'It's also a nice surprise to turn up and find out you've got two principals.'

Tonight, we're in luck: a pair of the Royal Ballet's highest-profile principals, plus Ashley herself. A star of the New York City Ballet for 30 years, she danced the lead in the first production of *Ballo della regina* in the 1970s. In fact, legendary choreographer George Balanchine created the role for her, lending her instructions to the dancers a particular authority. Now, she's here to teach the steps to the Royal Ballet's dancers.

The pianist begins, and Polunin launches himself into a spectacular entrance: a series of whirling leaps that are over in the blink of an eye. ('It's a shock to come out and do that,' the mic'ed-up Ashley drily observes.) The rehearsal is good natured but intense; after a relentless series of pas de chat and en pointe pirouettes, Nuñez leans over to rest, elbows on knees, panting with exertion. At times, it is inexpressibly lovely; a moment later, Ashley's pithy instructions bring proceedings back down to earth. ('Over-cross like that and you'll hit Sergei in the nose!'). Watching a work in progress like this, rather than a polished final performance, brings home the sheer physicality and meticulous timing demanded by each sequence, jump and entrance – and it's hard graft.

Faced with the endless repetitions and stop-starts, the dancers' resilience is astonishing. Asked to try a particularly punishing, drawn-out sequence yet again, Nuñez rises gracefully en pointe. As she turns, for what must be the sixth excruciating time, and 'sees' her partner, her whole face lights up with joy, just as it did the first time she rehearsed the steps.

Sometimes things do go awry. Nelson cites one rehearsal in which Valentino Zucchetti was being rehearsed by ballet master Christopher Carr in *The Tales of Beatrix Potter*. It was the first time Zucchetti had ever rehearsed the role of Squirrel Nutkin, and donned the costume head. 'The heads are notorious for impairing dancers' vision and throwing them off balance,' says Nelson. 'The audience actually gasped as Zucchetti nearly lost his footing during a grand jeté – a scary but thrilling moment to see in rehearsal.'

Despite having watched countless rehearsal sessions, Nelson says that he still finds it spellbinding. 'What you are witnessing is such a personal, physical, often very raw process. Every event is utterly unique, and I can't think of another art form where the process of creation is laid bare for audiences to see at such an early stage. You'd never be allowed into a painter's studio as they paint, or a composer's study as they compose…'.

Royal Opera House *Covent Garden, WC2E 9DD (7304 4000, www.roh.org.uk).*

South Bank

240-249

Frolic in a fountain

When Somerset House (The Strand, WC2R 1LA, 7845 4600, www.somersethouse.org.uk) opened to the public a decade ago, the choreographed water jets in its courtyard made almost as much of a splash as its art collection. They've since inspired a clutch of other play-friendly fountains at cultural spaces, including the low-level jets in Duke of York Square, outside the Saatchi Gallery (King's Road, SW3 4SQ), and the five banks of fountains at More London Riverside, near Tower Bridge. Over in Piccadilly, 12 fountains bubble up in the dignified Palladian courtyard of the Royal Academy (Burlington House, W1J 0BD, 7300 8000, www.royalacademy.org.uk); at the V&A (Cromwell Road, SW7 2RL, 7942 2000, www.vam.ac.uk), you can paddle in the spring-like fountains of the John Madejski garden courtyard. We're also hoping Jeppe Hein's 'Appearing Rooms' jets will be back on the Southbank Centre's terrace (Belvedere Road, SE1 8XX, 7960 4200, www.southbankcentre.co.uk) for summer; to find them, follow the shrieks of laughter.

Elsewhere, the fountains in Russell Square (WC1B 5BE) delight intrepid children, gradually getting higher and higher; if that's too alarming, there's a gentle teapot spouter at Cannizaro Park (SW19 4UE, www.cannizaropark.com). Another option on hot days is the lovely fountain within

a huge, shallow pool at Swiss Cottage, outside the leisure centre/town hall complex. Another good place to make a splash is the Thames Barrier Park (North Woolwich Road, E16 2HP), whose fountain plaza features no less than 32 jets.

250-252

Party in a public convenience

Toilets in clubs get a bad rap; clubs in toilets are another matter altogether. Over the years, a clutch of enterprising developers have converted Victorian public toilets into fully functioning bars and nightclubs – and they're less seedy than they sound.

Public Life (82A Commercial Street, E1 6LY, 7375 1631, www.publiclife.org.uk) is the raviest of the bunch – a concrete corridor that regularly heaves with tough techno sounds. The centrally located Cellar Door (Aldwych, WC2E 7DN, 7240 8848, www.cellardoor.biz) is a more glamorous affair, running burlesque, cabaret and jazz nights for intimate audiences (the maximum capacity is 56 people), while Ginglik (1 Shepherds Bush Green, W12 8PH, 7348 8968, www.ginglik.co.uk) is the largest of the three. Set in toilets built for the 1908 Olympic Games in White City, it has the most varied programme – from club nights and comedy to gigs, album launches and martial arts classes.

The beauty of cycle cafés is that riders can often get small repairs attended to while they avail themselves of coffee, flapjack, cycle chat and free Wi-Fi. Cycle cafés tend to be engaging, small-scale operations – appealing to non-cyclists too.

Container Cafe
On the perimeter of the Olympic Park, this place serves great food: it's on the Greenway, and cycle hire is available by arrangement from BikeWorks (8983 1221, www.bikeworks.org.uk) – at least until spring 2012.
The View Tube, The Greenway, Marshgate Lane, E15 2PJ (07530 274160, www.theviewtube.co.uk).

Cyclelab
Near enough to the City to draw in cycle couriers, Cyclelab combines knowledgeable service for all types of riders, a few bikes, a workshop and a healthy little café. Freshly squeezed juices and smoothies are the speciality, but there's also coffee, tea and cakes. Seating is limited to a few stools inside, and a bench next to the cycle path.
18a Pitfield Street, N1 6EY (3222 0016, www.cyclelab.co.uk).

Full City Cycles
Open weekdays only, this place is courier central – which speaks volumes for the coffee, vibe and servicing skills.
72 Leather Lane, EC1N 7TR (7831 7081).

Lock 7
With a plum location on the towpath of Regent's Canal, beside Broadway Market and a short ride from Victoria and Haggerston Parks, Lock 7 combines an all-day café with repairs, second-hand sales and bike hire.
129 Pritchard's Road, E2 9AP (7739 3042, www.lock-7.com).

Look Mum No Hands!
This friendly repair shop and café, strong on cakes, salads and pies (and with Square Mile coffee) has become a bit of a cycle community clubhouse, hosting events and screening live races. It's licensed (good beers), so an enjoyable evening hangout for all.
49 Old Street, EC1V 9HX (7253 1025, www.lookmumnohands.com).

Micycle
A few cycles (Bianchi and Kona, mostly), a small café and a workshop that, unusually but laudably, allows members to use the shop's tools to carry out their own repairs for free. A lovely garden too.
47 Barnsbury Street, N1 1PT (7684 0671, www.micycle.org.uk).

Towpath
Kick back with some Italian-influenced snacks and a coffee while you get your bike fixed at Route Canale next door. Strung along the towpath, this seasonal café (April to October) is great for people- and bicycle-watching, especially with a glass of wine on a summer evening.
Regent's Canal towpath, between Whitmore Bridge & Kingsland Road Bridge, N1 5SB (no phone).

Berry Bros & Rudd

With 300-plus years of expertise as a wine importer, BBR offers one-day classes as well as four- to six-week evening courses and examination courses for wine geeks. Classes are held in the cellar of the venerable St James's Street premises.

3 St James's Street, SW1A 1EG (0800 280 2440, www.bbr.com/wine-knowledge/school).

Borough Wines

Borough Wines has a new Hackney outpost, full of neighbourhood charm. It specialises in the output of small (mainly French) producers, some of whom visit to talk customers through their wares. On Friday to Sunday evenings, a tenner buys you three samples of wines chosen by staff, who circulate to tell the story behind them.

67 Wilton Way, E8 1BG (7923 2258).

Bottle Apostle

Self-service Enomatic wine dispensers allow you to sample individual tasters of your choice of wines, armed with a Bottle Apostle smart card. If you'd prefer a little more guidance, book a place on one of the regular wine and cheese evenings, seafood soirées or themed tasting events (an introduction to rioja, say).

95 Lauriston Road, E9 7HJ (8985 1549, www.bottleapostle.com).

Cellar Gascon

One of London's best-kept secrets is the wine-matched dinner held here every month: five small plates and five complementary wines, to a theme, for an eminently reasonable £35. An expert is on hand to talk you through the glasses, and the food is always impeccable.

59 West Smithfield, EC1A 9DS (7600 7561, www.cellargascon.com).

Decanter Education

Not content with sharing its expertise in print, *Decanter* magazine also hosts wine tastings in the South Bank's very cool Blue Fin Building. The tutors are as distinguished as you'd expect, and there's the occasional special guest, such as Andrew Jefford. Mainly regional themes.

Blue Fin Building, 110 Southwark Street, SE1 0SU (3148 5000, www.decanter.com).

Institut Français

Here, French wine is imbibed in the august surroundings it deserves: the Institut's panelled library, with its large wooden tables. Six wines are accompanied by commentary and sometimes fromage, in regional or specialist selections.

17 Queensberry Place, SW7 2DT (7073 1350, www.institut-francais.org.uk).

Leiths School of Food and Wine

The tutors at Leiths' evening wine tastings (subjects might include champagne, food and wine matching, or dessert wines) are often Masters of Wine, the ultimate viniferous accolade. Look out for Nancy Gilchrist, who is an inspiring host.

16-20 Wendell Road, W12 9RT (8749 6400, www.leiths.com).

Noble Green Wines

This capacious shop has a huge range of wines, including a monthly-changing selection on an Enomatic tasting system. Unusually, 25ml tasters are free, and there are also casks of the resident Twickenham and Dark Star ales for sampling. Walk-in tastings feature prominently on its events calendar, along with ticketed events.

153-155 High Street, Hampton Hill, TW12 1NL (8979 1113, www.noblegreenwines.co.uk).

Planet of the Grapes

This unpretentious, welcoming wine shop showcases its wares in a pleasant basement tasting room. Prices for events such as 'Australian Icons' will set you back around £50, but you'll taste the quality in the glass. Private tastings for up to 20 people can be arranged on request.

9 New Oxford Street, WC1A 1BA (7405 4912, www.planetofthegrapes.co.uk).

Roberson Wine

Acclaimed wine supplier Roberson runs a wine school from its Kensington shop. There's an imaginative programme of evening tastings, with some interesting speakers and guests. Look out for the free introductions to wine tasting (or sign up to the mailing list): if you'd prefer to take the DIY approach, order its Wine School in a Box.

348 Kensington High Street, W14 8NS (7371 2121, www.robersonwine.com).

RSJ

A long relationship with the wines and winemakers of the Loire means that the events at this unstuffy French restaurant provide plenty of personal insight. Vignerons sometimes visit to talk about their output in person, while the tasting dinners offering up to nine food-matched wines are not to be missed.

33 Coin Street, SE1 9NR (7928 4554, www.rsj.uk.com).

The Sampler

This award-winning establishment was one of the first places in town to invest in wine sampling machines, which dispense tasters of some 80 wines, from 30p a tot. Like its sister establishment in South Kensington, it runs regular tastings and meet-the-producer events, as well as an inexpensive 'Sunday School'.

266 Upper Street, N1 2UQ (7226 9500, www.thesampler.co.uk).

28°-50° Wine Workshop & Kitchen

Wine to sip, not glug, is served to complement the French menu at this shrine to the grape. There are regular wine dinners – food matching is a speciality – and workshops, where suppliers and makers explain what your palate is experiencing.

140 Fetter Lane, EC4A 1BT (7242 8877, www.2850.co.uk).

Vagabond Wines

Thanks to its high-tech wine preservation system, Vagabond is able to offer try-before-you-buy tasters of 100 bottles, with 35ml samples for 50p. Conduct a DIY tasting, or attend one of the informal weekly tutored events; themes might run from an introduction to sherry to a look at small, independent champagne producers.

18-22 Vanston Place, SW6 1AX (7381 1717, www.vagabondwines.co.uk).

Vinopolis

After an introduction to wine-tasting, you're furnished with a wine glass and an audioguide for a self-guided tour exploring the history of winemaking, covering cultures, grape varieties and vineyards. Exhibits are set out by country, with six or more (depending on your ticket) opportunities to taste wine or champagne from different regions. 'Mini masterclasses' cost £5 extra, and there are monthly evening tastings.

Bankside, next to Shakespeare's Globe, SE1 9BU (7940 8322, www.vinopolis.co.uk)

West London Wine School

This independent wine school offers a wide range of courses based on regions, countries and levels of knowledge. It also runs a packed programme of one-off tastings (from £20) – looking at the English wine industry, perhaps, or setting Loire wines against rival New World offerings.

The Wine Cellars, Big Yellow Storage, 71 Townmead Road, SW6 2ST (8144 2444, www.westlondonwineschool.com).

Wine & Spirit Education Trust

WSET trains the industry, and it's serious classroom-type stuff. Alongside its professional courses, though, it offers tutored evening tastings for all – generally on more specialised topics. Chablis masterclass, anyone?

39-45 Bermondsey Street, SE1 3XF (7089 3800, www.wsetglobal.com).

The Winery

You follow a printed tasting tour at the Winery's monthly events, designed to showcase its wines: somewhat unusually, these are sourced direct from small producers. Staff are on hand to elaborate, and it's free and enjoyably social. Get yourself on the mailing list to score an invite.

4 Clifton Road, W9 1SS (7286 6475, www.thewineryuk.com).

278-283

Walk among the bluebells...

Intrepid bluebell-hunters, take note: peak season is from late April until May, although a harsh winter can mean they bloom a few weeks later.

The Isabella Plantation

Set behind high ornamental gates, this 40-acre plantation may be part of Richmond Park (0300 061 2200, www.royalparks.org.uk), but feels like a secret garden. A stream runs through the centre, bordered by ferns and forded by a series of little bridges, while regal-looking black swans glide across the pond. Spring brings a sea of bluebells, along with camelias, daffodils and magnolias.

Osterley Park

Just eight miles from Piccadilly Circus, Osterley (8232 5050, www.nationaltrust.org.uk) is one of London's last surviving country estates – and a stronghold for native British bluebells, which grow in glorious swathes here. There's a guided bluebell walk every year; for this year's date, call or check online in early April.

Oxleas Wood

On the south side of Shooter's Hill, the tract of ancient woodland at Oxleas Wood (8921 6885, www.greenwich.gov.uk) is famed for its profusion of bluebells. Explore on your own, or join the annual bluebell walk. While you're down there, call by the café (8856 4276), perched at the top of the hill, for a restorative cup of tea and a fry-up.

Claybury Woods

The mossy, 70-hectare patch of oak and hornbeam at Claybury Woods (8921 6885, www.redbridge.gov.uk) provides the perfect conditions for bluebells, which grow alongside white-flowering clusters of ramson (wild garlic). The conservation team runs a free walk in bluebell season; call for details.

Downe Bank

For 40 years, Charles Darwin lived at Downe (01622 662012, www.kentwildlifetrust.org.uk), on the southern fringes of Greater London, and it was here that he penned *On the Origin of Species*. In 1843, he noted 'large areas were brilliantly blue with bluebells' – and a sea of flowers nod here in spring. It's easiest to drive: park at Downe village, then it's a half-mile walk.

Linder's Field

All that remains of a larger ancient woodland, destroyed in the 1920s, the four-hectare nature reserve at Linder's Field (www.eppingforestdc.gov.uk) is sprinkled with bluebells, and a lovely spot for a picnic. Access is from Roebuck Lane, and through an intricate steel gate, entwined with birds, butterflies, plants and animals.

284

... And help monitor the Spanish invasion

With Britain's bluebells under increasing threat from non-native species and hybrids, the National History Museum has set up a survey to help monitor flowering patterns and prevalence. Print off an observation form at www.nhm.ac.uk/nature-online, find a patch of bluebells, then send your findings to the team. The way to tell a native bluebell from its pernicious Spanish cousin is to look at the pollen colour: creamy white for natives, pale green or blue for Spanish bluebells and hybrids. The native species also has narrower blooms, with distinctive curled-up tips, and a graceful, drooping stem.

285-286

Test your mettle

Competitive yet courteous, fencing is a throwback to the days of duelling dandies and swashbuckling heroics. Channel the spirit of D'Artagnan and Errol Flynn by signing up for a fencing class; try the London Fencing Club (www.londonfencing club.co.uk) or Blades Club (07779 123715, www.bladesclub.com), both of which offer tuition for all ages and abilities.

287 Peruse the Olympic Park

In the run-up to the London 2012 Games, you won't be able to get into the Olympic Park, but you can spot the key venues – the Olympic Stadium, the Aquatics Centre and, in the distance, the Velodrome – in the course of a pleasant walk on the Greenway and the banks of the Lea Navigation. Every morning at 11am (and at 6pm on Wednesday evening, and 1.45pm on Saturday), a Blue Badge guide leads a two-hour walk from Bromley-by-Bow tube station, around the perimeter of the Olympic Park, showing you how things are shaping up. For more information, call 7936 2568 or visit www.toursof2012sites.com.

288-289

Hold a street party...

In 2011, the Royal Wedding whetted the national appetite for bunting, trestle tables and tea urns. Happily, 2012 offers two golden opportunities to take to the streets and celebrate: the Queen's Diamond Jubilee, in early June, and the London 2012 Olympic and Paralympic Games. You'll need to contact your local council three months in advance, but unless you plan on charging or want live music, odds are the bureacracy will be simple and you may not need insurance (though don't forget to apply to your highways department to close the road). For more information, consult www.streetparty.org.uk.

290

... Or a Big Lunch

If, like many Londoners, you'd struggle to recognise the people who live on your street, the Big Lunch (www.thebiglunch.com) offers a chance to put things right. Dreamt up by the people behind the Eden Project, the idea is that on Sunday June 5, neighbours across the country get together for lunch, rediscovering a bit of good, old-fashioned community spirit. In 2011, a million people did exactly that; in 2012, the date falls on the Queen's Diamond Jubilee weekend, offering even more reason to celebrate.

291 Wrestle yourself fit

A spectacle and a sport in one, Lucha libre ('free fighting') is Mexico's wrestling phenomenon, involving colourful costumes, larger-than-life characters, and violence so cartoonish is makes the WWF look restrained. Fancy yourself as a luchadore (wrestler)? Then attend a beginners' class at the London School of Lucha. First, decide whether you're going to be a *técnico* (good guy) or *rudo* (bad guy). Next, select a mask. Once you don a mask, it stays on; for an opponent to succeed in tearing it off is the most humiliating thing any luchadore can suffer.

London School of Lucha *Resistance Gallery, 265 Poyser Street, London, E2 9RF (www.lucha britannia.blogspot.com).*

292-294 Rack your brains

Forget your average – generally guessable – general-knowledge pub quiz and try, if you dare, the fiendishly difficult specialist version. Attended by genre nerds and journalists, who are intensely competitive beneath their casual veneer, this lot will really test your mettle.

As well as pitching unanswerable questions on cooking history and techniques, the monthly food quiz at the Coach & Horses (26-28 Ray Street, EC1R 3DJ, 7278 8990, www.thecoachandhorses. com) includes a hand-on tasting round. If you're lagging on the leaderboard, find consolation in one of the pub's justly famed scotch eggs.

Around the corner, the Three Kings (7 Clerkenwell Close, EC1R 0DY, 7253 0483) is known for its killer Monday night music quiz. Prizes are given on the night and for the season, and competition is fierce. Finally, the IMAX Film Café at the British Film Institute (1 Charlie Chaplin Walk, SE1 8XR, 7199 6000, www.bfi. org.uk) hosts a monthly event, grilling punters on obscure cinematic trivia and the latest BFI screenings. Sample questions on the website tackle such subjects as Russian film pioneers and Sidney Lumet's back catalogue: be afraid.

295 Take a tour of the 20th century

Set in the arches between the Royal Festival Hall and Waterloo station, Topolski Century (150-152 Hungerford Arches, SE1 8XU, 7928 5433, www. topolskicentury.org.uk) used to be the studios of Polish-born satirical painter Feliks Topolski. Topolski travelled the world between 1933 and his death in 1989, showing an uncanny knack of popping up at key events in world history – the liberation of Bergen-Belsen, the coronation of Queen Elizabeth II – all of which he worked into this cluttered, stylistically varied and thoroughly extraordinary mural. You can see all the great figures of the 20th century, from Churchill and Mao to Bob Dylan and Malcolm X. At present, you can only see it via a pre-booked private tour, though plans which would see the addition of a café and artist's studio are in place for 2012.

296 *Stargaze in Hampstead*

An undistinguished-looking dome at the edge of Hampstead (Lower Terrace, near Whitestone Pond, NW3, 8346 1056, www.hampsteadscience.ac.uk/astro) conceals a 100-year-old telescope that offers stunning views of the night sky. From September to April (when the nights are dark enough), all-comers are welcome to turn up from 8pm to 10pm on Friday and Saturday and look into the heavens. A helpful stargazing guide on the website allows you to time your visit for maximum celestial activity.

297 *Meet a merman*

In Victorian times, enterprising characters in the Far East would approach wealthy travellers with tales of rare, exotic creatures, offering to obtain specimens in return for princely sums. One such oddity, described as a 'Japanese monkey-fish', was donated to the Wellcome Collection in 1919. In 1982, it moved to the Horniman, where it became known as the 'merman'. Initially, it was thought to comprise the head of a monkey, a fish tail and a carved wooden body, but recent research revealed the grotesque model to be pieced from bird claws and the tail and jaws of a fish, embellished with wood, wire, papier mâché and clay.

Horniman Museum & Gardens *100 London Road, SE23 3PQ (8699 1872, www.horniman.ac.uk).*

298
Seek out the secret room at the National Gallery

For just one afternoon a week, the enigmatic Room A opens to the public, in the depths of the National Gallery (Trafalgar Square, WC2N 5DN, 7747 2885, www.nationalgallery.org.uk). Open every Wednesday from 2pm to 5.30pm, it contains almost 800 paintings, hung in old-fashioned density on the walls and dividing boards. Among the apparent jumble of pictures, spotting a Titian, Rembrandt, Frans Hals, Sisley or Corot feels like making your own thrilling discovery.

299-305
Fill up on pie and mash...

Long favoured by impecunious Londoners, thanks to its filling properties and bargain price, pie and mash remains a hearty, handy standby. Aficionados can argue the merits of various pie and mash purveyors until the cows come home: one safe bet, though, is F Cooke (9 Broadway Market, E8 4PH, 7254 6458), with its tiled interior, old-fashioned signage and flavoursome, home-made parsley liquor. Other East End favourites include G Kelly (414 Bethnal Green Road, E2 0DJ, 7739 3603) – which also does a soya veggie variant, and a good line in fruit pies – and Maureen's (6 Market Way, Chrisp Street Market, E14 6AH, 07956 381216), now run by the son of its eponymous owner. Down south, Harringtons (3 Selkirk Road, SW17 0ER, 8672 1877) is a classic, sporting a beautiful art deco sign and green-tiled frontage, while the pies at Manze's (204 Deptford High Street, SE8 3PR, 8692 2375) are proudly monogrammed with the letter M. Flying the flag in West London, meanwhile, is Cookes (48 Goldhawk Road, W12 8DH, 8743 7630), where a plate of pie, double mash and liquor will set you back a mere £4. In the centre of town, M Manze (87 Tower Bridge Road, SE1 4TW, 7407 2985, www.manze.co.uk) is the city's oldest pie and mash shop. Founded in 1902, it still serves the same grub: squeeze on to one of the narrow wooden benches and partake of pie (with liquor or gravy) or a portion of eels (stewed or jellied).

306-308
... or feed your guests for less

If catered canapés are out of your reach, or you don't fancy cooking for a dinner party, you can order in a couple of dozen ready-to-heat pies with mash and liquor for around £100 from http://eelhouse.co.uk. M Manze (www.manze.co.uk) also offers courier-delivered party packs of pies, while the esteemable Goddard's (0800 862 0400, www.pieshop.co.uk) will deliver to your door – good news for those who mourned the passing of its excellent shop in Greenwich. Serve with Fuller's London Pride.

309 Walk on water at Blackfriars

The London 2012 Games will bring a host of daring temporary initiatives to the city – not least the London River Park. This 12m-wide, half-mile-long river pontoon will sit below Blackfriars Bridge, providing a continuous walkway north of the river to rival the South Bank promenade. Along it will be eight pavilions devoted to culture, sport and other aspects of city life.

Even before the River Park is floated into position, Blackfriars Bridge is worth a look. It not only has splendid red-and-white painted Victorian ironwork, but is the perfect vantage point on London's first cross-river train station. Using empty pillars left over from an 1864 rail bridge, the platforms of the renewed Blackfriars station will run right across the Thames.

310

Spot hawks patrolling St Pancras

Gaze skywards at St Pancras, and you'll get an eyeful of the train shed's magnificent Victorian iron-and-glass roof. The sharp of eye might also spot something more unusual: Harris hawks, swooping in flight, or perched atop the statue of Sir John Betjeman. Comet and Elektra, the hawks, handled by bird specialist Mark Bigwood, are responsible for ensuring the station remains pigeon-free – much to the astonishment of unsuspecting commuters. The birds are flown here two to three times a week, but times and days vary: if the hawk turns up at regular intervals, the canny pigeons get wind of the ruse.

311

Attend the Rare Plant Fair

The Rare Plant Fair's collective of specialist nurseries (0845 468 1368, www.rareplantfair.co.uk) holds annual events in the lovely surrounds of Syon Park and the Inner Temple Gardens. Sellers' specialities run from unusual edibles and Alpine shrubs to ferns, native wildflowers and some glorious traditional rose varieties.

312 See a lost London on celluloid...

BFI Southbank screens a wonderful array of blockbuster and obscure art-house films from across the world, but our favourite programming strand couldn't be more local. Capital Tales has shown everything from rare footage of the London docks saved from an early colour-process experiment to the charming tale of a street urchin secretly living in Tower Bridge with his pet seagull. Check the 'Events' section of the BFI website for the programme and book ahead; these screenings often sell out.
BFI Southbank *South Bank, SE1 8XT (7928 3232, www.bfi.org.uk).*

313

... Or investigate the archives

At the Mediatheque (details as above), you can access the BFI's collection of over 2,000 archived films and television programmes. Chose what you fancy, and watch it in a private booth: it's absolutely free, with no booking required. An Audrey Hepburn screen test (1952), an 'election special' episode of *The Clangers* (1974) and a social history of the jellied eel, 'Noted Eel and Pie Houses' (1975), are among the delights.

314

Watch the Globe go global

Over six weeks from 23 April 2012 (the Bard's traditional birthday), Shakespeare's Globe will undertake an ambitious season for the London 2012 Festival. They will stage all 37 Shakespeare plays, each performed in a different language. Alongside the plays in such rarely heard tongues as Lithuanian, Aborginal, Maori and Shona, we're especially looking forward to the Deafinitely Theatre production of *Love's Labour's Lost*, in British Sign Language. All in all, a fine way for the reborn Globe to celebrate its 15th birthday.
Shakespeare's Globe *21 New Globe Walk, Bankside, SE1 9DT (7902 1400, www.shakespearesglobe.com).*

Shoreditch Sisters

315-316 *Join the sisterhood*

If you associated the Women's Institute with staid basketweaving sessions in the sticks, you'd be wrong on two counts. First, even in the sticks, the WI is about much more than that, with activities ranging from literary discussion and campaigning to a range of crafts and skills. And two of the latest branches to form are deep in urban London: the Shoreditch Sisters (http:// shoreditchsisters.blogspot.com) and the Dalston Darlings (www.dalstondarlings.com). The Shoreditch interpretation of home crafts is to launch an embroidery campaign at louche lingerie boutique Coco de Mer and serve delicious teas from their festival marquee, at, for example, Paradise Gardens, while the Darlings' busy programme ranges from Martini-making evenings to talks from a sex therapist, Kylie's stylist and the founder of Home Jane handywomen. Both organisations charge the regular £30 annual WI stipend, but you can usually drop in to a taster meeting first. Check the websites to find out more, and for times of meetings.

317

See all the city in a single room As well as hosting thought-provoking temporary exhibitions, the New London Architecture HQ (Building Centre, 26 Store Street, WC1E 7BT, 7636 4044, *www.new londonarchitecture.org*) is home to a highly unusual permanent exhibit: the Pipers Central London Model. Covering an area east from Paddington to a little beyond the Royal Docks and south from King's Cross all the way to Battersea, this 12 metre long, 1:1,500 scale model highlights in white every significant London building for which planning permission has been granted, giving you a giant's-eye view of the future of the city.

318-337

Have lunch in a park

Central

Garden Café at Russell Square

An Italian family-run café, perfect for people watching in this leafy Bloomsbury square.
Russell Square Gardens, WC1B 5EH (7637 5093).

Inn the Park

Part Modern British restaurant, part stylish café, Inn the Park is ideal for breakfast (eggy bread with streaky bacon, anyone?), lunch or even a romantic supper.
St James's Park, SW1A 2BJ (7451 9999, www.innthepark.com).

Lido Café Bar

On the southern bank of the Serpentine, this place has lakeside tables and crowd-pleasing grub: eggs florentine for breakfast, hot smoked salmon salad or fish and chips come lunchtime, and mid-afternoon ice-cream sundaes.
Hyde Park, W2 2UH (7706 7098, www.companyofcooks.com).

Serpentine Bar & Kitchen

At this Benugo-run eaterie on the edge of Hyde Park's boating lake, a wood-fired oven turns out crisp-based pizzas, as well as more upmarket offerings.
Serpentine Road, Hyde Park, W2 2UH (7706 8114, www.serpentinebarandkitchen.com).

North

Brew House

Enjoy homely (and often organic) grub and own-made cakes in neoclassical splendour – but be prepared to queue at peak times.
Kenwood House, Hampstead Lane, NW3 7JR (8341 5384, www.companyofcooks.com).

Finsbury Park Café

A pleasant park café serving decent snacks, with easy access to Finsbury Park's boating lake, children's play area, splash fountain and sandpit.
Hornsey Gate, Endymion Road, N4 2NQ (8880 2681, www.finsburyparkcafe.co.uk).

Garden Café Regent's Park

Enjoy seasonal dishes – Sussex Slipcote salad, perhaps, or goat's cheese and courgette tart – in a chic 1960s building, surrounded by glorious rose beds.
Inner Circle, Regent's Park, NW1 4NU (7935 5729, www.companyofcooks.com).

Karmarama

Gladstone Park is a rolling, 97-acre expanse of green, with a sweeping panorama of London, At the northern end, this tiny, family-run café is generally open Friday to Sunday.
The Stables Courtyard, Dollis Hill Lane, NW2 6HT (no number or website).

Pavilion Café at Highgate Woods

With its picket fence and sheltered seating area, this charming café is always packed. It serves Mediterranean-influenced dishes, from feta and sweet potato fritters to chorizo and rocket salad.
Highgate Woods, Muswell Hill Road, N10 3JN (8444 4777).

Serpentine Bar & Kitchen

Pavilion Café at Highgate Woods

South

Café on the Rye
Sandwiched between Peckham Rye Park and the Common, this café goes the extra mile, using fair trade, locally sourced ingredients to create wholesome daily specials (own-made chickpea madras, tortilla), sarnies and cakes.
Strakers Road, Peckham Rye Common, SE15 3UA (8693 9431, www.cafeontherye.co.uk).

Common Ground
The cosy back-room of this child-friendly café, which overlooks the cricket ground, is a welcoming retreat on a winter's day.
Wandsworth Common, off Dorlcote Road, SW18 3RT (8874 9386).

Fulham Palace Café
This café is set in the graceful drawing room of the former residence of the Anglican Bishops of London – so taking tea here feels a bit like attending an aristocratic garden party.
Bishop's Avenue, SW6 6EA (7610 7160, www.fulhampalace.org).

Lido Café at Brockwell Lido
This poolside café serves stellar breakfasts; later in the day, a seasonal, bistro-style menu is served. Look out for pop-up supper events too.
Brockwell Lido, Dulwich Road, SE24 0PA (7737 8183, www.thelidocafe.co.uk).

Old Brewery
Slake your thirst with Meantime Brewery ales in the expansive walled garden of this award-winning eaterie. If you'd prefer to picnic in Greenwich Park, food can be taken away.
The Pepys Building, The Old Royal Naval College, SE10 9LW (3327 1280, www.oldbrewery greenwich.com).

Pavilion Café at Dulwich Park
On sunny afternoons, children run amok as adults sustain themselves on Monmouth coffees and delicious doorstep sandwiches.
Dulwich Park, SE21 7BQ (8299 1383).

Pavilion Tea House
Tuck into hearty soups and other snacks at this hexagonal café, while the kids eat ice-cream in the garden (it's hedged off from the park's central thoroughfare).
Greenwich Park, Charlton Way, SE10 8QY (8858 9695, www.companyofcooks.com).

East

Pavilion Café at Victoria Park
This café is still probably London's best place to enjoy a perfectly brewed coffee alfresco. The fry-ups and cakes are justly famed too.
Victoria Park, corner of Old Ford Road & Grove Road, E9 7DE (8980 0030, www. the-pavilion-cafe.com).

West

Chiswick House Café
Everything from eggs benedict to sourdough sandwiches, scones and pots of tea are served in this architectural box of a café, designed by Caruso St John.
Chiswick House & Gardens, Burlington Lane, W4 2RP (8995 6356, www.chiswickhousecafe.com).

Fait Maison in the Park
Run by catering company Fait Maison, this place offers daily mix and match salads, children's meals and terrific custard tarts.
The Tea House, Ravenscourt Park, Paddenswick Road, W6 0UL (8563 9291).

Holland Park Café
One of the nicest – and possibly the cheapest – places to eat in Kensington, set in an historic Dutch garden. It serves toasties, salad boxes and other no-nonsense grub.
Holland Park, Ilchester Place, W8 6LU (7602 6156).

Curator's top ten

338-347

Rebekah Higgit, Curator of the History of Science and Technology, the National Maritime Museum

Chocolate from Scott's Antarctic expedition

Part of Scott's food supplies for his first Antarctic expedition in 1901, these two squares are all that remain of the 3,500lbs of chocolate and cocoa he was provided with by Cadbury's. Chocolate was among the supplies left behind by Scott's team when they left camp for the last time. Several years later, Shackleton's *Nimrod* expedition (1907-09), attempting to reach the South Pole for the first time, used Scott's old hut. The chocolate was then recovered, and eventually brought back to England.
Oceans of Discovery Gallery

Toy pig from RMS Titanic

This small musical pig belonged to fashion journalist and first-class passenger Edith Russell. Despite going on to become one of the first female war journalists (she spent time in the trenches during World War I), Russell was too frightened to jump into a lifeboat, until her toy pig was thrown into Lifeboat 11 and she felt compelled to follow. Both the pig and Edith survived.
Voyagers Gallery

18th-century guillotine

There is nothing more evocative of the French Revolution than a guillotine. This one found its way to the Caribbean island of Guadeloupe. By the time the Royal Navy captured the island in 1794, it had been used to remove the heads of more than 50 French royalists.
Atlantic Worlds Gallery

Nelson's Trafalgar Coat

Two hours into the Battle of Trafalgar, at about 1.15pm, Hardy realised Nelson was no longer by his side. The admiral collapsed on the spot where John Scott, his secretary, had been killed an hour earlier – it is Scott's blood that can be seen on the tails and the left sleeve of the coat. Nelson was one of many casualties caused by marksmen in the rigging of the French *Redoutable*. The hole left by the fatal musket ball can be seen on the left shoulder.
The above items are displayed in the Maritime London Gallery, National Maritime Museum, Romney Road, SE10 9NF.

Harrison sea clocks

John Harrison's four sea clocks, now known as H1, H2, H3 and H4, were built over the course of 30 years. He hoped to provide a means of finding longitude at sea, and to receive a substantial reward from the Board of Longitude. The Board not only encouraged Harrison's efforts – to the tune of several thousand pounds – but tested H1 and H4 at sea. Harrison's work was of extraordinary quality and included a remarkable number of technical innovations, including caged ball-bearings and bimetallic strips.
Time & Longitude Gallery

Bradley zenith sector

Once one of the most famous instruments in the world, this telescope looks like a rusty drainpipe. It was made by George Graham in 1727 for James Bradley, later Astronomer Royal, and helped to make the reputation of both men. A zenith sector, designed to observe only stars straight overhead, provides accurate observations by cutting out atmospheric distortion. Hoping to observe stellar parallax, Bradley

instead discovered and measured 'nutation' (the 'wobbling' of the Earth's axis) and 'aberration of light' (the first observational proof that the Earth orbits the Sun).
Meridian Building

Airy transit circle

Most visitors to the Observatory stand astride the Prime Meridian, but many walk straight past this huge, confusing instrument, which actually defines longitude 000° 0' 0'. It was used to make observations of the Sun, Moon, planets and stars as they crossed its meridian, in order to determine time and provide vital data for navigators and astronomers. These observations mean that this meridian became the reference point for the nation's maps, and Greenwich Mean Time became British standard time – and ultimately an international standard. *The above items are displayed in the Meridian Building, Royal Observatory Greenwich, Greenwich Park, SE10 9NF.*

Harrison's sea clock

JMW Turner *The Battle of Trafalgar*

Turner's *Trafalgar* is his largest work, and his only royal commission. It was painted for George IV as a dramatic pair with Philip de Loutherbourg's *Lord Howe's Victory* of 1795. When hung in St James's Palace in 1824, the Turner caused such controversy (his painting shows key sequential events as if they happened simultaneously) that in 1829 the King gave both pictures to the Naval Gallery in the Painted Hall at Greenwich.

Sir Joshua Reynolds Commodore *The Honourable Augustus Keppel*

In 1749, Augustus Keppel, captain of the *Centurion*, took Joshua Reynolds – a talented young artist from Plymouth – to Minorca so he could go on to study in Rome. On his return in 1752, he painted this full-length portrait of Keppel to 'show what he could do'. It made his name: he rose to be artistic leader of his age, was knighted and became first president of the Royal Academy. Reynolds never sold the picture.

William Hogarth *Captain Lord George Graham in His Cabin*

Hogarth's group portrait from about 1742 shows Captain Lord George Graham about to dine in his cabin with his former tutor – to musical accompaniment that includes a howling spaniel. Neither the spaniel's significance, nor the reason Hogarth's pug is shown wearing the captain's wig have been explained. Graham was the youngest son of the Duke of Montrose. Though 'a brave and able commander', he died aged only 31, and this cheerful but puzzling picture is the main reason he is now remembered at all.
The above items are displayed in Queen's House, Romney Road, SE10 9NF.

The National Maritime Museum (8312 6565, www.nmm.ac.uk) is made up of three sites: the Maritime Galleries, the Royal Observatory and the Queen's House.

348-352

Roll with it

If you want to join London's legion of roller and inline skaters, there are plenty of options. The Friday Night Skate (www.thefns.com) sets off from Wellington Arch, Hyde Park Corner, every Friday at 8pm; more laid-back (and therefore recommended for less confident skaters) is the Sunday Roller Stroll, which meets at 2pm on Serpentine Road, Hyde Park, and is run by the same people. There's also the London Skate (www.londonskate.com), gathering at the same spot on Wednesday nights in summer at 8pm. The routes for each change every time, but are usually around ten miles long and last two hours or so. The Easy Peasy Skate (www.easypeasy skate.com) is a more family-oriented affair, meeting by the Peace Pagoda in Battersea Park at 10.30am on dry Saturdays. There are no roads to negotiate as you take in laps of the park. For further information, sign up to the *Week on Wheels* newsletter at www.lfns.co.uk.

If you'd like to have lessons before heading off (recommended if you're planning to skate on roads), Citiskate London (7193 5866, www.citiskate. co.uk) offers private and group tuition.

353-354

Engage your brain at a 21st-century salon

Located near the heart of academic Bloomsbury, the School of Life (70 Marchmont Street, WC1N 1AB, 7833 1010, www.theschooloflife.com) operates under the slogan 'Ideas to live by'. Part bookshop, part classroom, it runs courses and talks led by such bright sparks as Rosie Boycott, Alain de Botton, Ilse Crawford and Martin Parr. It was founded by former Tate curator Sophie Howarth, who says it's about 'the practical application of philosophy on life core subjects – love, politics, work, family and play'.

In the west of town, the Idler Academy (81 Westbourne Park Road, W2 5QH, 0845 250 1281, http://idler.co.uk/academy) takes a similar approach, but is centred on a café rather than a shop. Born out of *The Idler* magazine, it hosts how-to classes on topics as wide ranging as Latin grammar, ukelele-strumming and life-drawing, talks from the likes of Will Self, Oliver James and Molly Parkin, and opportunities to philosophise (Sunday Free School, 11.30am Sun) or get busy with a needle and thread (Mending Morning, 11am Wed) over coffee.

355
Peruse Joe Orton's library books

In 1959, playwright Joe Orton moved into a bedsit on Noel Road in Islington with his lover, Kenneth Halliwell. Bored with the books on display at the local library, the pair smuggled out various volumes and set about writing lurid blurbs in the jackets and adorning the covers with collages. John Betjeman's poems were pasted with an image of a tattoo-covered middle-aged man, while the faces of *The Great Tudors* morphed into skeletons, monkeys and other unsuitable personages. After sneaking the books back on to the shelves, Orton and Halliwell would linger at a discreet distance to enjoy readers' reactions. In 1962 they were finally caught, and sent to prison for six months.

Their own story had an even darker end: consumed with jealously over Orton's promiscuity, Halliwell bludgeoned him to death with a hammer in 1967, then took an overdose. The offending tomes, meanwhile, are now the pride and joy of Islington Local History Centre, where four of the surviving 44 covers are on display.
Islington Local History Centre *Finsbury Library, 245 St John Street, EC1V 4NB (7527 7988, www.islington.gov.uk).*

356
Send the kids to Fairy School

Most of the merchandise in Mystical Fairies is pink and sparkly, pertaining to princesses, ballerinas, pixies and elves, as well as its namesake sprites. Down in the shop's fairy light-decked basement, meanwhile, the Fairy School promises to imbue its students in the mysteries of fairy folk, with crafts, games and role plays; there are sessions for toddlers and four to eights, and week-long holiday workshops.
Mystical Fairies *12 Flask Walk, NW3 1HE (7431 1888, www.mysticalfairies.co.uk).*

357-358
Cheer on the Torch Relays

The key symbolic precursor to the London 2012 Games will be the arrival of the Olympic Torch at Land's End, in the far west of the country, on 19 May. The Torch doesn't arrive in London until 21 July, where it completes a 70-day, 8,000-mile journey that encompasses the whole country. The last of the long chain of Torchbearers – athletes and ordinary members of the sport-loving British public, half of whom will be under 25 – will enter the Olympic Stadium at the climax of the Opening Ceremony. The Paralympics has its own Torch Relay, with the Flame arriving in the Olympic Stadium on 29 August.

359
Smoke a stogie...

Smoking ban, schmoking ban: at the lavish Boisdale restaurant and jazz venue in Canary Wharf you can sample cigars before you buy at the shop, keep them on the premises in a personal locker and smoke them on a covered, heated terrace with a tartan rug to keep your knees warm.
Boisdale *Cabot Place, E14 4QT (7715 5818, www.boisdale-cw.co.uk).*

360
...with a whisky in hand

Another luxurious vice in which the Boisdale is expert. The bottles number in the hundreds; as well as a fine selection from Ireland, the US, Japan and Wales, every Scottish region is comprehensively represented. Highlights include rare bottlings from the likes of Glen Albyn, Glenallachie and Mortlach. The list reaches Munro-like heights at the Macallan 1953 49-year-old (over £2,000 for 50ml), but there's plenty to choose from at more realistic prices.

361-426 *See London on film*

All human life is here, along with a multitude of memorable backdrops: little wonder film-makers are irresistibly drawn to the capital. Each of these movies offers a different glimpse of life in the city: comic, romantic, violent and beautiful in turn.

1920s

Blackmail *Alfred Hitchcock*, 1929
Britain's first talkie, culminating in a classic showdown at the British Museum.

The Lodger: A Story of the London Fog *Alfred Hitchcock*, 1926
Opaque silent movie from the master of suspense.

Piccadilly *EA Dupont*, 1929
An incongruously familiar West End sets the scene for this 1920s silent film noir, based around a Piccadilly nightclub.

Underground *Anthony Asquith*, 1928
The denouement of this working-class love story takes place atop Battersea Power Station, while the story revolves around the tube.

1930s

Sabotage *Alfred Hitchcock*, 1936
London landmarks are under threat of terrorist attack in this classic '30s thriller.

The 39 Steps *Alfred Hitchcock*, 1935
Spies and suspense on the streets of Whitehall, in what is perhaps the best of Hitchcock's London films.

1940s

Fires Were Started
Humphrey Jennings, 1943
Drama-doc war propaganda about the London Fire Brigade.

Hangover Square *John Brahm*, 1945
London *noir*, and a stylish evocation of the Edwardian city.

It Always Rains on Sunday
Robert Hamer, 1947
Fascinatingly downbeat post-war drama, set in Bethnal Green.

Passport to Pimlico
Henry Cornelius, 1949
Pimlico declares independence in this genial Ealing comedy. Outdoor scenes were filmed on a Lambeth bombsite.

1950s

Genevieve *Henry Cornelius*, 1953
Delightful antics on the London to Brighton Veteran Car Run, with a final scene playing out on Westminster Bridge.

The Ladykillers
Alexander Mackendrick, 1951
Classic Ealing (black) comedy, set around King's Cross and St Pancras.

The Lavender Hill Mob
Charles Crichton, 1951
Another cockney-spiv spoof heist tale from Ealing Studios.

Night and the City *Jules Dassin*, 1950
London by night is a wonderful sight.

1960s

Alfie *Lewis Gilbert*, 1966
What's it all about, Michael?

Bedazzled *Stanley Donen*, 1967
Heaven, hell and London-set remake of the Faust legend, starring Peter Cook and Dudley Moore.

Blowup *Michelangelo Antonioni*, 1966
Swinging London caught in unintentionally hysterical fashion.

A Hard Day's Night *Richard Lester*, 1964
Good evening London! The Fab Four's introduction to the Big Smoke.

Mary Poppins

The London Nobody Knows
Norman Cohen, 1967
Extraordinary, James Mason-narrated walking tour of obscure backstreets of the captial.

Mary Poppins *Robert Stevenson*, 1964
Our perception of Edwardian London's skyline has never been the same since.

Oliver! *Carol Reed*, 1968
Colourful – and musical – take on high- and low-life in Dickensian adaptation.

My Fair Lady *George Cukor*, 1964
Running the gamut of London accents, from Covent Garden to Kensington.

Peeping Tom *Michael Powell*, 1960
Voyeuristic, Soho-set murder flick.

Up the Junction *Peter Collinson*, 1968
The gritty film of Nell Dunn's novel depicts life in the slums of 1960s Battersea.

Victim *Basil Dearden*, 1961
Ground-breaking thriller, attacking the laws surrounding homosexuality.

1970s
Death Line *Gary Sherman*, 1972
Sole survivor of subterranean race of cannibals abducts travellers from Russell Square tube.

Performance *Donald Cammell & Nicolas Roeg*, 1970
East End crim camps out in Mick Jagger's flat in W11: Notting Hill before *Notting Hill*.

Quadrophenia *Franc Roddam*, 1979
Hell on Wheels! Or 1960s London, anacronistically recalled in the late '70s.

10 Rillington Place *Richard Fleischer*, 1970
Story of British serial killer John Christie, who committed most of his crimes at 10 Rillington Place, Notting Hill.

1980s
An American Werewolf in London
John Landis, 1981
Terror reigns in Tottenham Court Road tube station in this gore-splattered romp.

84 Charing Cross Road
David Hugh Jones, 1987
Post-war London's dusty second-hand book street gets a shot in the arm from the Big Apple.

The Elephant Man *David Lynch*, 1980
Freakshows, corruption and cruelty in seamy Victorian London.

Hope & Glory *John Boorman*, 1987
South London suburbia gets shaken up by Adolf's Luftwaffe, much to the delight of the local kids.

▶

My Fair Lady

The Long Good Friday
John Mackenzie, 1980
Quintessential Docklands gangland thriller.

Mona Lisa *Neil Jordan*, 1986
Seedy King's Cross is the setting for this
low-budget thriller starring Bob Hoskins.

My Beautiful Laundrette
Stephen Frears, 1985
Saeed Jaffrey and Daniel Day-Lewis wash
dirty linen in public in Thatcherite London.

Prick Up Your Ears *Stephen Frears*, 1987
The rise and fall – via a few of London's
public libraries and lavatories – of the
playwright Joe Orton.

Withnail & I *Bruce Robinson*, 1987
Cultish low-life comedy, set in Camden and
the countryside.

1990s

The Krays *Peter Medak*, 1990
Biopic of the East End's most notorious duo.

Lock, Stock & Two Smoking Barrels
Guy Ritchie, 1998
Here come the Mockneys!

Life is Sweet *Mike Leigh*, 1990
Hopes and dashed dreams in Enfield.

London *Patrick Keiller*, 1994
Arthouse trilogy (with *Robinson in Space*,
1997, and *Robinson in Ruins*, 2010) of
documentary fiction tracing London's byways.

Love is the Devil *John Maybury*, 1998
Francis Bacon's masochistic Soho life,
darkly remembered.

Nil by Mouth *Gary Oldman*, 1997
First-hand account of violence, alcoholism,
drug addiction and petty criminality in
south-east London.

Bourne Ultimatum

Notting Hill *Roger Michell*, 1999
Slick Hugh Grant/Julia Roberts rom-com
that changed the face of the eponymous
west London neighbourhood forever.

Shakespeare in Love *John Madden*, 1998
The Bard's London, lavishly brought to the
big screen.

Truly Madly Deeply *Anthony Minghella*,
1990
Comedy weepie with Juliet Stevenson and
Alan Rickman that makes great use of the
South Bank.

Wonderland *Michael Winterbottom*, 1999
Intimate, suburban panorama of life between
south London and Soho.

2000s

Bourne Ultimatum *Paul Greengrass*, 2007
Pacy thriller with a brilliantly staged CCTV
scene in Waterloo Station.

Bridget Jones's Diary
Sharon Maguire, 2001
London's perennially single, big knicker-
wearing heroine lived in Borough long
before the market became famous.

Closer *Mike Nichols*, 2004
Jude Law, Natalie Portman, Julia Roberts
and Clive Owen conduct their affairs across
the capital. Among the locations, look out for
the restaurant of the National Portrait Gallery.

Harry Potter & the Order of the Phoenix *David Yates*, 2007
Stunning aerial shots of London's skyline.

Kidulthood *Menhaj Huda*, 2006
The trials and tribulations of teenage life in west London in the noughties.

Layer Cake *Matthew Vaughn*, 2004
Daniel Craig gets embroiled in drugs crime amid the looming towers of Canary Wharf.

London River *Rachid Bouchareb*, 2009
Two parents search for their children in the aftermath of the 7 July bomb attacks on London.

Love Actually *Richard Curtis*, 2003
Eight couples and their interwined lives, set all over London.

Shaun of the Dead *Edgar Wright*, 2004
Shuffling zombies invade Crouch End.

Somers Town *Shane Meadows* 2008
Thoughtful study of the friendship between two teens, set in the nether regions of King's Cross.

Sweeney Todd: the Demon Barber of Fleet Street *Tim Burton*, 2008
A blood-soaked, musical take on the tale of Sweeney Todd, scourge of Victorian London.

Tube Tales *Amy Jenkins*, 1999
Nine short films inspired by Underground-related stories provided by *Time Out* readers.

28 Days Later/28 Weeks Later *Danny Boyle, 2002/Juan Carlos Fresnadillo*, 2007
Post-apocalyptic horror on the deserted streets of the city.

Vera Drake *Mike Leigh*, 2004
The enthralling story of a backstreet abortionist, set in drab, postwar London.

V for Vendetta *James McTeigue*, 2006
Guy Fawkes-themed dystopia.

2010s

Another Year *Mike Leigh*, 2010
Ruminative study of domestic contentment and allotment-tending in the suburbs, with a quietly tragic flipside.

The King's Speech *Tom Hooper*, 2010
Colin Firth's Bertie (later George VI) stutters to glory and the throne in 1930s London.

You Will Meet a Tall Dark Stranger *Woody Allen*, 2010
The capital looks good in Allen's latest London foray, but the film itself met mixed reviews.

28 Days Later

Help out at a festival

Go through Oxfam (www.oxfam.org.uk) or the Workers' Beer Company (www.workersbeer.co.uk) to volunteer at a festival and everyone wins: you get free entry and camping, the festival gets motivated volunteers, and charities receive donations. Proms in the Park and Get Loaded in the Park (Hyde Park being the park in question) are on the WBC's books, while Oxfam serves major festivals nationwide. London's cultural festivals often need volunteers, too. We know that the London Film Festival (www.bfi.org.uk/lff), East End Film Festival (www.eastendfilmfestival.com), Pride (www.pridelondon.org) and London Open House (www.londonopenhouse.org) have all signed them up in the past. Follow any events you're interested in on Twitter.

433

Taste timewarp treats from the Iron Curtain era

Proudly boasting an interior 'unchanged today to the original style and decor', the Czechoslovak Restaurant (74 West End Lane, NW6 2LX, 7732 1193, www.czechoslovak-restaurant.co.uk) may look and feel like a chilly Eastbourne guest house from the 1950s, but nothing recalls the grey postwar era as surely as its delicacies of dumplings, schnitzels and pork knuckles. There's a real timewarp vibe here – along with a warm welcome and cold Czech beers on draught.

434

Get closer to Don McCullin

Learn more about Don McCullin's work and modern conflict in 'Shaped by War: Photographs by Don McCullin' at the Imperial War Museum. The exhibition runs from 7 October 2011 to 15 April 2012, and includes over 200 photographs.
Imperial War Museum *Lambeth Road, SE1 6HZ (7416 5320, www.iwm.org.uk).*

Canoe through Camden

Strolling along the Regent's Canal, you may have spotted a strange, turreted brick building on the bank near Camden, jutting out over the water. Turns out it's swarming with pirates – namely the volunteers who run Pirate Castle, an independent watersports centre. Set up in the 1960s, when it operated from its founder's back garden, it's now a fully-fledged charity. Along with its community work, the centre offers drop-in canoe and kayak sessions for young people and adults, plus longer courses and school holiday schemes. With prices starting at £1 a session for eight to 17s, and £5 for adults, it's an affordable way to get on the water.
Pirate Castle *Oval Road, NW1 7EA (7267 6605, www.thepiratecastle.org).*

436

Have a storming Bastille Day

Tricolores flutter in the breeze, apéros are quaffed and precision pétanque is played: to sample a vibrant slice of French culture, attend the free July Bastille Day Festival in Battersea Park (www.bastilledaylondon.com). This celebration of all things Gallic also incorporates a market proffering cheese, oysters and wine, music from French DJs, bands and wandering accordion players, and cabaret and costumery aplenty.

437-439

Watch the wheels of justice turn

Justice may be blind, but that's no reason to miss seeing it in action – any member of the public can watch proceedings at Britain's three highest courts, so long as they follow a few rules.

At the Old Bailey and Royal Courts of Justice there's no admission for under-14s (if you're young, you may be asked to show proof of age), you mustn't bring in cameras, video cameras or other recording devices, and you shouldn't carry phones, bags, food or drink. To find out which trials are taking place, check the daily listings on www.hmcourts-service.gov.uk. Things are a little different at the Supreme Court, which positively encourages people to visit – notwithstanding the stringent, airport-style security checks.

None of the courts has space to store your belongings, so leave behind banned items and anything you're not happy to carry with you.

Central Criminal Court (Old Bailey)

The figure of Justice atop the Central Criminal Court's dome – sword in one hand, scales in the other – is a familiar symbol of British justice, and the Old Bailey (as the court is universally known) is probably the world's most famous criminal court. It has hosted any number of high-profile trials, including those of Oscar Wilde, Crippen and the Krays. The public galleries are open to anyone who wishes to see a trial in session.
Old Bailey, EC4M 7EH (7248 3277, www.cityoflondon.gov.uk).

Royal Courts of Justice

Unless there's a notice on the door marking a trial as 'In Camera' or 'In Private', these 88 courtrooms are open for public visits. The complex houses two of the country's highest appeal courts: the Court of Appeal and the High Court, which is further divided into the Queen's Bench, Chancery and Family Division. Peckish? You can get snacks and drinks on the premises at Café 26 (9am-3pm Mon-Fri). To learn more about the court's role, take a guided tour – call 7947 7684 and leave a message or email rcjtours@talktalk.net.
The Strand, WC2A 2LL (7947 6000, www.justice.gov.uk).

Supreme Court of the United Kingdom

The Supreme Court opened opposite the Houses of Parliament on 1 October 2009 with very little fanfare, but represents a major constitutional shift. This is now the country's absolute final court of appeal, established in part to remove those powers from the House of Lords (which held them for six centuries), but also to open up the legal process to the public. To that end, there are guided tours, a quiz sheet for children and – in the converted cells downstairs – a café and exhibition about the court's work. The neo-Gothic building is reasonably interesting (look out for a balustrade engraved with a quote from Ovid: 'Laws were made to prevent the strong from always having their way'), but the real thrill is to sit in the back of one of the three courts, listening to the Justices make and rebut arguments that will ultimately establish the laws of the land.
Parliament Square, SW1P 3BD (7960 1900/ 7960 1500, www.supremecourt.gov.uk).

Ride the rapids

Whitewater rapids in east London? Kathryn Miller *holds on tight.*

Think of a challenging whitewater rafting or kayaking course and a gutsy river such as Zambia's Zambezi or the Whataroa in New Zealand might spring to mind. But London's Lee Valley Park? When I heard that the London 2012 Games Canoe Slalom would take place in north-east London, I was intrigued. And when I was invited to try whitewater rafting at the Lee Valley White Water Centre, how could I refuse?

I arrived for my half-day adventure on a sunny April morning. I was sharing a raft with three other novice rafters – Tom, Vicki and Becky – and instructor Paskell Blackwell. Although the centre officially opened in December 2010, until now it's only been used by professionals; in April 2011, it opened to the public for whitewater rafting and 'have-a-go' kayak sessions. I'm among the lucky few who'll get to try out the course before it closes in preparation for London 2012 in September; once they're over, and the world's elite's athletes have slalomed down the course, it will re-open for general use once again.

The day before my visit, I spoke to GB slalom kayaker and 2012 hopeful Huw Swetnam. He helped to develop the Lee Valley course, and

trains there every day. 'The centre's the best [artificial] whitewater facility in Britain and one of the best in the world,' he told me. 'It imitates some of the best natural whitewater rivers, such as the Etive in Scotland, the Grandtully course on the Tay, and the Tryweryn in Wales.' Swetnam explained that the course is particularly special because it's possible to change the features to make it harder or easier to negotiate.

The centre, which cost £35 million to build, is highly impressive. The roomy, wood-decked viewing terrace traps sunlight all day, while the offices, changing rooms and reception lobby, housed in a sleek cedar-clad building, remain cool. There are two water courses: the 300m Standard Competition Course we'd be using, and the 160m Legacy Loop course.

Having been kitted out with wetsuits and given a safety briefing, we climbed on the raft. Our first run was a straightforward top-to-bottom to make us feel at ease and get us used to the water. But for the second run, Paskell, who captains the GB rafting team and has competed around the world, thought we needed to up the adrenalin and took us 'surfing' – we paddled

towards the rapids, the boat span 360 degrees, and we all got drenched and shrieked a lot.

'There are manoeuvres that make a run more or less tricky,' explained Paskell. 'For conservative groups we keep it simple, but we can easily test the nerves of more plucky people!'

The course for the Games is 300m from start to finish, and has a 5.5m drop. Five powerful machines pump up to 15,000 litres of water per second, so there's plenty of white froth. The rapids are equivalent to a grade three or four river, but because the course isn't as long as a river, rafting sessions involve four or five runs that take about an hour and a half. And there's no hauling the boat up a steep bank – one of the best bits is the giant conveyer that takes you and your canoe or raft to the starting pool (it's rather like being cranked to the top of a big dipper).

During the moments of calm, Paskell explained future aims to promote and develop watersports for Londoners. 'Legacy is important to us. It's not just about building a venue for five days of competition in 2012. The centre enables novices to have flatwater sessions in kayaks and open canoes and progress through to the 2012 course. Slalom paddlers are traditionally from places like Scotland and Wales, where the best courses are. Now we've got this fantastic centre, it opens up the possibility of a watercourse champion from inner-city London.'

The site is already attracting overseas competitors; on the day of my visit, Australian kayaker Jessica Fox was training and the Slovakian 2012 team had just arrived for a week of practice sessions. Inspired by watching the Aussie pro, we opted for a more daring descent. At one point the boat was vertical on its side. Vicki, momentarily losing her balance, executed a dramatic flip and fell head first into the water. 'It's terrifying and disorienting and you don't know what direction you're going in, but it's strangely exciting at the same time,' she grinned when safely back on board.

For the last run I sat in the 'party seat' on the floor at the front of the boat, facing my fellow rafters so I was travelling backwards. I had nothing to hold on to, and as we zipped through the rapids I thought I'd be catapulted in. I managed to stay safely in the boat, but did get thoroughly soaked. Though Lee Valley Park can't compete with the dramatic natural vistas of the Zambezi, I'd ridden a challenging competitive course, surfed rapids and been more playful on a raft than would be possible on a natural river. It had been great fun – and though I was secretly disappointed that I, too, hadn't had a spectacular fall to boast about, there's always next time!

Lee Valley White Water Centre *Station Road Waltham Cross, Herts EN9 1AB (0845 677 0606, www.leevalleypark.org.uk).*

441

Visit the other Diana Fountain

Mention the Diana Fountain, and most Londoners immediately think of the Princess Diana Memorial in Hyde Park (www.royal parks.gov.uk) – a modern cascade, built from Cornish granite. Less well known is the superb classical fountain on Chestnut Avenue in Bushy Park. Commissioned by Charles I, the fountain first reposed at Somerset House, until Oliver Cromwell had it moved to the privy garden at Hampton Court Palace. It was finally placed at the centre of the pool it now presides over in 1713 as part of Sir Christopher Wren's redesign and expansion of the Palace grounds. Although popularly known as the Diana Fountain after the Roman goddess of hunting, the gilded figure in fact represents Diana's nymph, Arethusa.

Bushy Park *Hampton Court Road, Middx TW12 2EJ (8979 1586, www.royalparks.org.uk).*

442-454

Dispense with the bother of booking

Securing a table at London's destination dining spots can take days (or even weeks) – bad news if you've forgotten to book an anniversary dinner, or just want to be spontaneous. Save face by taking your beloved to one of these sought-after eateries, none of which accepts advance bookings.

Albion at the Boundary Project

Reservations are only taken for groups of seven or more at this laid-back all-day eaterie. Food is of the stoutly British, old-school variety: think chops, pies and fruit crumbles. After dinner, take the lift up to the Boundary's rooftop bar for a nightcap under the stars.
2-4 Boundary Street, E2 7DD (7729 1051, www.albioncaff.co.uk).

Anchor & Hope

Join the good-natured throng in the bar, sipping tumblers of wine as they wait for a table in the dining room. The short, meaty, menu rarely disappoints; the only reservations taken are for the 2pm sitting on Sunday.
36 The Cut, SE1 8LP (7928 9898).

Barrafina

The set-up is spartan (customers perch on a row of high stools, ringing the cramped counter and open kitchen); the tapas, sliced, grilled and assembled before your eyes, is utterly superb.
54 Frith Street, W1D 4SL (7813 8016, www.barrafina.co.uk).

Bibendum Oyster Bar

Fulham Road's eccentric, white-tiled Michelin Building celebrated its centenary last year. The ground-floor oyster bar takes no reservations, and is a beautiful setting to indulge a taste for champagne and crustacea.
Michelin House, 81 Fulham Road, SW3 6RD (7589 1480, www.bibendum.co.uk).

Polpo

Corner Room

This informal but elegant little dining room delivers wonderfully inventive food, and hits way above its price bracket. Word is well and truly out about this place, so turn up early to avoid a lengthy wait.

Town Hall Hotel, Patriot Square, E2 9NF (no phone, www.viajante.co.uk).

Morito

If you've failed to get a table at Moro, head for its little sibling next door – an intimate, pared-back operation, dispensing little plates of Moorish tapas, cerveza and sherries. No bookings are taken in the evening. If it's full when you arrive, leave your number and repair to a nearby bar; you'll get a call when a perch comes up.

32 Exmouth Market, EC1R 4QE (7278 7007).

Polpo

A noisy, lively Venetian-style wine bar, bang in the centre of Soho. Sample small dishes and *cicheti* (snacks), with rustic jugs of wine. You can book at lunchtime, but it's every diner for himself at supper time.

41 Beak Street, W1F 9SB (7734 4479, www.polpo.co.uk). ˙

The Princess of Shoreditch

Although the more formal first-floor dining room takes bookings, it's first come first served down in the bar, where the same menu is offered; high-quality gastropub dishes, cooked with considerable flair.

76 Paul Street, EC2A 4NE (7729 9270, www.theprincessofshoreditch.com).

Le Relais de Venise L'Entrecôte

Perfect for indecisive carnivores, this place only serves steak-frites and salad. Orders are scribbled on paper tablecloths, mains arrive with alacrity, and the house red goes down a treat.

120 Marylebone Lane, W1U 2QG (7486 0878, www.relaisdevenise.com/marylebone).

Spuntino

You definitely can't pre-book at this stylish Soho eaterie: it doesn't even have a phone. If you want to sample its terrific truffled cheese on toast and playful 'small plates', you'll have to take your chances on the night; be prepared to queue.

61 Rupert Street, W1D 7PW (no phone, www.spuntino.co.uk).

Tapa Room

Reservations are recommended at the Providores; below it is the more laid-back Tapa Room, which doesn't take bookings. Always surprising and hugely imaginative, this is fusion food at its best.

109 Marylebone High Street, W1U 4RX (7935 6175, www.theprovidores.co.uk).

Tapas Brindisa

Although this Spanish stalwart is an old-timer, it remains enduringly popular: get your name on the clipboard as soon as you walk in, then squeeze into the bar for wine and olives while you wait.

18-20 Southwark Street, SE1 1TJ (7357 8880, www.brindisa.com/restaurants/tapas-brindisa).

Vinoteca

The 25 wines by the glass change weekly, while the food is punchy and accomplished: Devon crab risotto with peas and dill, perhaps, or rabbit and pork rillettes. No bookings are taken for supper.

7 St John Street, EC1M 4AA (7253 8786, www.vinoteca.co.uk).

455

Eat food from the sky

Perched atop Thornton's Budgens in Crouch End, Food from the Sky (http://foodfromthesky.org.uk) is an unlikely apparition: a thriving community garden, where radishes and rainbow chard flourish alongside edible flowers, fig trees and tomatoes of every hue. The organic fruit and veg are sold in the supermarket below, while the garden doubles up as an educational resource for the local community. 'Tiny kids learn how to plant, grow and harvest the produce,' says project founder Azul-Valerie Thome. 'Then they tell their parents to come and buy it, which is great!' Visits are by appointment (check online for details), and new volunteers warmly welcomed. And if you're passing on a Friday (harvest day), pop in for some fresh produce with zero food-mile guilt.

456 Remember the Winchester Geese

Behind the iron gates of an unprepossessing Transport for London storage lot on Redcross Way in Southwark lies an almost-forgotten relic of this once famously bawdy parish of London. Finally closed in 1853, when it was 'completely overcharged with dead', Crossbones (www. crossbones.org.uk) was an unconsecrated burial ground dating back to medieval times. It was used for the disposal of people not considered fit for Christian burial – namely the working girls known as the 'Winchester Geese' who were given licence (by the Bishop of Winchester no less) to ply their trade in the district's seedy streets.

As well as monthly get-togethers at the site to remember the 'outcast dead', each Halloween sees performances of local playwright John Constable's *Southwark Mysteries*, a cycle of mystery plays inspired, he says, by the spirit of a Winchester Goose who first visited him on 23 November 1996 on Redcross Way. Candles are lit, flowers and memorial tokens tied to the gates and poems recited; gin is also poured on the ground, in tribute to the fallen ladies' favourite tipple.

457 Encounter an army of alfresco dancers

The biennial celebration of leaps and pirouettes returns – and it's bigger than ever for the London 2012 Festival. Big Dance 2012 (7-15 July, www. bigdance2012.com) will have five Big Dance Hubs in London to encourage participation right across the city, led and co-ordinated by East London Dance, the English National Ballet, Greenwich Dance, Sadler's Wells and Siobhan Davies Dance. The focal event will be choreographed by Wayne McGregor, the Artistic Director of Wayne McGregor | Random Dance and Resident Choreographer at the Royal Ballet. He plans to gather 2,000 dancers to perform an entirely new piece, under the lions' noses in Trafalgar Square.

458 Learn to love a Lomo

The Lomography phenomenon began in the 1990s, when a group of Austrian art students rediscovered the Lomo LC-A 35mm Soviet-era compact. So began a seemingly boundless nostalgia for the good old pre-digital days. The Lomography shop stocks a collection of reissued 'toy' cameras such as the Diana (Hong Kong), the Chinese Holga and the Russian Lomo, as well as fisheyes, pinholes and accessories. Check out the Lomo wall, which displays thousands of 'Lomographs'. Would-be Lomographers can attend workshops and neighbourhood walkabouts to test-drive the cameras.

Lomography Gallery Store *3 Newburgh Street, W1F 7RE (7434 1466, www.lomography.com).*

459

Appreciate the art of bathing

Whether by accident or design, the National Gallery has hung the world's two most famous paintings of bathers in adjacent rooms: Seurat's *Bathers at Asnières* in Room 44 and Cezanne's *Bathers* in Room 45. Both are large, immersive, and conveniently placed for benches. Dive in.

The National Gallery *Trafalgar Square, WC2N 5DN (7747 2885, www.nationalgallery.org.uk).*

Shop this street

460-477

Mayfair modern: Mount Street, W1

Significant swaths of W1 have always been known for their rather stuffy atmosphere. Doormen – that is, men who open doors for a living – are prone to sneer at potential customers who might rank below viscount. Mount Street, with its dignified Victorian terracotta façades and by-appointment-only art galleries, still harbours a superior Mayfair elite; consider, for example, traditional vendors such as master butcher Allens of Mayfair (no.117, 7499 5831, www.allensofmayfair. co.uk), cigar shop Sautter (no.106, 7499 4866, www.sauttercigars.com), with its dusty collection of antique crocodile-skin cigar cases, and Purdey (7499 1801, www.purdey. com), the traditional gunsmith that has stood aloof at 57-58 South Audley Street since 1882.

But Mount Street is now home to a raft of shops that have given the area's traditional luxury aesthetic a youthful, less exclusive twist – without compromising on quality. Towards the east end of the street, by the Connaught Hotel, sits the Balenciaga flagship (no.12, 7317 4400), its super-chic clothing set against a glowing sci-fi interior. Next door, you can splurge on a Moser wristwatch at Asprey offshoot William & Son (no.10, 7493 8385) – or buy a rifle at their branch at no.14.

Across the road, gentlemen's tailor Rubinacci (no.96, 7499 2299) sits near the Mount Street Galleries (no.94, 7493 1613, www.mountstreetgalleries.com), one of several fine art and antiques dealers in the area. Indeed, just round the corner on South Audley Street is Adrian Alan (nos.66-67, 7495

2324, www.adrianalan.com), selling some highly impressive items. It holds court with Thomas Goode & Co (no.19, 7499 2823, www.thomasgoode.com) and the serene Spa Illuminata (no.63, 7499 7777, www. spailluminata.com). But it's back on Mount Street where the new lease of life is most in evidence, with Marc Jacobs' first UK boutique (nos.24-25, 7399 1690) one of the first of the superbrands to appear. A stand-alone Marc by Marc Jacobs store opened at no.44 in spring 2009.

Another red-hot name is revered shoe designer Christian Louboutin (no.17, 7491 0033), whose eye-catching storefront displays are often the talk of the street. Parisian perfumer Annick Goutal has opened shop at no.109 (7629 8507), and you'll also find cult Australian skincare brand Aesop (no.91, 7409 2358) and the best highlights in town at Jo Hansford's salon (no.19, 7495 7774, www.johansford.com).

High-end fashion brands may have opened up on this previously sleepy stretch, but it's the deliberate absence of brash, ultra-luxe fashion houses like Louis Vuitton and Gucci that has given Mount Street its real cachet. The idea behind the renaissance was to source the best of everything – and not necessarily the most expensive or best known. Some of the biggest brands are conspicuous by their absence. So there's no chance of this becoming another Bond Street – at least for now. Other shops on or around the street include Lanvin (no.128, 7491 1839), bridal and cocktail dress shop Jenny Packham (3A Carlos Place, 7493 6295), and men's shoe store Harry's of London (59 South Audley Street, 7409 7988).

When the luxury gets too much, take time out in Mount Street Gardens, which snakes behind the south side of the street. You can sit and watch long-term residents of this history-loaded area puzzle over its new-found popularity with fashionable young upstarts.

478-486

Sip cocktails in the clouds

On clement summer evenings, head for a sundowner at one of the capital's rooftop bars.

Aqua Nueva & Aqua Kyoto

Visiting the ritzy roof terrace bars at either of the Aqua restaurants feels like walking into a set for a music video with a London skyline. Sip an exotic cocktail, or sample Kyoto's saké list.
5th floor, 240 Regent Street, W1B 3BR (7478 0540, www.aqua-london.com).

Boundary Rooftop

Ascend in the lift to emerge high above east London. Wicker chairs and sofas are surrounded by shrubbery; later on, heaters, a wood-burning fire and wool blankets keep chills at bay.
2-4 Boundary Street, E2 7DD (7729 1051, www.theboundary.co.uk).

Brera at Lyric Hammersmith

Overlooking hectic King Street, the Lyric's large terrace is a haven of planters, foliage and comfy seating, run by Italian pizza chain Brera.
Lyric Hammersmith, 2 King Street, W6 0QL (8741 6853, www.cafebrera.com).

Dalston Roof Park

An architect-designed, astroturfed haven, with beds of strawberries and herbs and a wooden shack dispensing the drinks: Pimms, draught beer and cocktails.
Print House, 18 Ashwin Street, E8 3DL (7275 0825, www.bootstrapcompany.co.uk).

No.5 Cavendish Square

Common folk are now welcome in some areas of this hitherto members-only club. Take the lift to the second floor, then walk up to the decked roof. A tiny bar serves a short menu of cocktails, including a mean mojito; there's also bottled beer, tapas and cigars.
5 Cavendish Square, W1G 0PG (7079 5000, www.no5ltd.com).

Proud Camden

The large roof terrace at this hip gallery, bar and club complex is ideal for supping cocktails and observing both the art and the arty crowd.
Stables Market, Chalk Farm Road, NW1 8AH (7482 3867, www.proudcamden.com).

Queen of Hoxton

The rooftop at this grungy bar and club is an unexpected delight, drawing Shoreditch sun-seekers with its deckchairs and wrought-iron furniture. A ramshackle 'rum shack' serves mojitos, bottled Beck's or Swedish Briska cider.
1 Curtain Road, EC2A 3JX (7422 0958, www.thequeenofhoxton.co.uk).

Sky Lounge Tower of London

The view from the Mint Hotel's swanky 12th-floor roof terrace takes in both the ancient majesty of the Tower of London and the brand-new Shard, piercing the skyline. City types populate the well-spaced tables, while drinks prices reflect the locality.
Mint Hotel, 7 Pepys Street, EC3N 4AF (7709 1043, www.minthotel.com).

Vista

Perched on top of the Trafalgar Hotel in Trafalgar Square, this smartened-up bar has impressive views – Nelson's Column looms large, plus there's the London Eye and Big Ben. A cocktail will set you back more than a tenner, though.
The Trafalgar, 2 Spring Gardens, SW1A 2TS (7870 2900, www.thetrafalgar.com).

Boundary Rooftop

487-490 *Celebrity-spot at London Zoo*

ZSL London Zoo has an illustrious history of famous residents. In 1850, for example, a hippo called Obaysch caused a sensation. A gift from the Viceroy of Egypt to the British Consul, he was transported from Alexandria via steamer, and was the first live hippopotamus seen in Britain. Even Queen Victoria viewed the celebrated pachyderm, while the *Times* ran endless coverage.

Another name to have gone down in zoo lore was Goldie the golden eagle, whose two-week escape in 1965 unleashed a media furore. Huge crowds gathered in Regent's Park to spot the fugitive; before being recaptured, he filched and ate a duck from the American Ambassador's garden. Special mention must also be made of Guy the gorilla, who arrived as a baby in 1947, clutching a tin hot-water bottle, and became one of the zoo's biggest ever crowd-pullers. He died in 1978, but is commemorated by a bronze statue at the centre of the zoo's Barclay Court.

While such stars are long gone, the zoo still has its fair share of personalities. Such is the popularity of Komodo dragon Raja, he even has his own Facebook page – though with razor-sharp teeth and 'virulently toxic' saliva, he's not the most approachable of idols. That's emphatically not the case with Polly, a Mexican red-kneed spider who helps arachnophobes face their fears as part of the zoo's Friendly Spider Programme – a hands-on course (£130) that aims to cure the phobia.

Lumpur the Sumatran tiger is one of the zoo's more familiar faces, thanks to his starring role as the face of the Tiger SOS campaign – an appeal that will raise funds for a new tiger conservation hub at the zoo. Meanwhile, Stan the African Blackfooted penguin is an inveterate show-off – and able to play to a worldwide audience, via the Penguin Beach webcam (www.zsl.org/penguins).

ZSL London Zoo *Regent's Park, NW1 4RY (7722 3333, www.zsl.org).*

Open House London

491

Unlock Open House weekend

On the third weekend in September, Open House London (www.londonopenhouse.org) allows visitors to see inside over 700 buildings normally out of bounds to the public. You might get to explore Jimi Hendrix's flat, snoop around Channel 4's glass and steel HQ or tour the Reform Club on Pall Mall. It's free to attend, though you need to book ahead for certain buildings.

492

Peruse the Monocle shop

Tracking down the ideal gift for a man-about-town can be painfully difficult, but help is at hand. Monocle's tiny retail outpost houses a cornucopia of delights for the sophisticated male: clothing, stationery, CDs, books and, of course, copies of the mannered magazine that launched the brand. The store also stocks Monocle's design collaborations, including fragrances in partnership with Comme des Garçons and Porter's luxury travel bags.
Monocle *2A George Street, W1U 3QS (7486 8770, www.monocle.com).*

493-495

Waste not, want not

Every year, hundreds of tonnes of edible food goes to waste in the UK, even though around four million Britons are affected by food poverty.

FoodCycle (www.foodcycle.org.uk) helps community groups and volunteers to collect surplus produce from food retailers and turn it into healthy, affordable meals. As well as providing food for those in need (volunteers are always welcome), FoodCycle has set up two community cafés, where everyone is welcome. Open for lunch on Fridays, from noon to 2.30pm, the Station Café (Station House, 73C Stapleton Hall Road, N4 3QF, 7377 8771) offers mains for £2.50, or three courses and a cup of tea for a mere £4. Its sister outpost, the Pie in the Sky Café (Bromley by Bow Centre, St Leonards Street, E3 3BT, 7377 8771), is open from Monday to Friday for breakfast and lunch, and there are more cafés in the pipeline.

Help out at the People's Kitchen at Passing Clouds (1 Richmond Road, E8 4AA, 07951 989897, www.thepeopleskitchen.org), meanwhile, and you can eat for free: every Sunday, spare food is used to create a slap-up meal for the volunteers who have helped to source and cook it.

496 *See a slice of shingle beach in Holloway*

Along Wheelwright Street, off Caledonian Road in N7, is an unexpected, charming stretch that resembles a Kent beach. A strip of shingle flanks the side of Pentonville prison, complete with rocks, driftwood, wildflowers and breakwaters. Inside the prison perimeter, and thus not accessible to the public, it provides a valuable sanctuary for urban wildlife. Its stony beauty is no accident; Islington's quietly visionary park planners based the design on film-maker Derek Jarman's famous shingle garden in Dungeness.

497

Wallow in childhood nostalgia

In a quiet corner of Fitzrovia, occupying two creaky Georgian townhouses, Pollock's Toy Museum (1 Scala Street, W1T 2HL, 7636 3452, www.pollockstoymuseum.com) comprises a warren of small, atmospheric rooms and twisting staircases. It's named after one Benjamin Pollock, last of the Victorian toy theatre printers: examples of his exquisite tiny tableaux are in room six. Elsewhere, you'll find all sorts of old familiars, from dapper lead soldiers to TV favourites Sooty, Sweep and Soo. Children frustrated by the glass cases and misty-eyed adults should make a beeline for the shop, with its animal masks, tin robots and reproduction cardboard theatres.

498-500
Catch an eco-friendly cab

Londoners now have the option to catch a greener cab. The following firms use hybrid electric and petrol engine cars, and also carbon-offset their emissions. The luxurious fleet of grey Toyota Prius cabs at Climate Cars (7350 5960, www.climatecars.com) come complete with newspapers and complimentary mineral water, while Ecoigo (0800 032 6446, www.ecoigo.com) runs a 24-hour service that promises to offset considerably more carbon than its fleet emits through the World Land Trust. Green Tomato Cars (8568 0022, www.greentomatocars.com), meanwhile, are branded with the trademark tomato, offering competitive prices and a dependable service.

501
Listen to a Pontic lyre

Looking to expand your musical horizons? Then head to the School of Oriental and African Studies, better known as SOAS (Brunei Gallery Lecture Theatre, Thornhaugh Street, WC1H 0XG, 7898 4500, www.soas.ac.uk/concerts). It runs a series of 12 world music and dance performances from October to May, with a programme that might feature Afro-Cuban batà drums, exorcistic salpuri dance from Korea, Pontic lyre sessions, Argentinian chacarera dances, and the maqam music of the Uyghurs. You can't book, so turn up in good time.

502
Have an epiphany in Neasden

Rising amid suburban Neasden is a miraculous vision in marble, topped by gleaming pinnacles and domes. The Shri Swaminarayan Mandir (105-119 Brentfield Road, NW10 8LD, 8965 2651, www.mandir.org) is the biggest Hindu temple outside India. Fascinating architecturally and culturally, the Mandir is open to people of all faiths and none; dress respectfully to enter.

Telling tales

Behind a monstrous east London shop lies a top-secret storytelling den. Emma Perry investigates.

At 159 Hoxton Street, the sign hanging on the shop door says: 'Official notice: the proprietor is hereby licensed to sell items including, but not limited to, malodorous gases, children's ears, gore, fear (tinned only), pencils, and other items as specified in the monster retailer's act of 1827, clause 14, subsection 5, revision (b).'

It's not kidding, either. Through the door is a shop full of freshly extracted nails, zombie mints, jars of thickest human snot, fang floss, neck bolt tighteners, tins of fear, unease and panic, an invisible cat, a monster hotline and a

door beyond which no one can venture without being in possession of a magic password.

The Hoxton Street Monster Supplies shop was set up by co-directors Lucy Macnab, who used to work in the Southbank's Learning and Participation Department, and theatre writer and director Ben Payne, with help from writer Nick Hornby. The model was based on a US project run by author Dave Eggers that offered underprivileged inner-city children a chance to explore their literary creativity: behind that secret door lies the Ministry of Stories, a writing centre for local kids, many of whom have no quiet space at home.

'A lot of people in London had heard about Dave Eggers' 826 Valencia project in San Francisco,' says Macnab. 'I was doing a course with Ben and we started talking about it over lunch. We applied for some funding and found a graphic designer, but it wasn't until Dave Eggers came to town and did a shout out for volunteers after a reading that it became concrete. It took us a long time to find the right premises in a suitable location. There were loads of empty shops, but not many landlords who were keen on what we were doing. Everything has been made by volunteer architects and designers, and most things, including the carpet, were donated for free.'

The Ministry of Stories offers a project room and a quiet study room for budding writers aged eight to 18, and aims to act as a drop-in centre for children after school and on Saturdays. Kids can bring in their own project and get one-to-one help from volunteer mentors, or be guided,

using the Ministry's prompts, exercises and workshops, to find literary inspiration.

'We consulted local children at the planning stage,' says Macnab, 'and what they said they wanted was exciting things to write with, to be able to write on the walls, and to have a space to call their own. Children of all ages responded really well to the idea of it being a secret place, hidden behind a shop.'

The Ministry's volunteers include writers, artists, designers, editors, teachers and locals who want to help out. 'The important thing for the children is to get individual help from an adult mentor, even if it's just someone who says: "Wow that's a great idea, what happened next?" But it has also proved to be a great experience and community for the volunteers,' says Macnab.

The Ministry of Stories *159 Hoxton Street, N1 6PJ (7729 4159, www.ministryofstories.org). Check the website for news of upcoming events open to all, or explore the shop.*

504-508

...Then seek out London's finest children's bookshops

London has some superb specialist children's bookshops, and this lot really go the extra mile, with book clubs, signings and storytelling sessions.

The Children's Bookshop

The likes of Michael Morpurgo, Mick Inkpen and Judith Kerr have dropped by this well-stocked specialist bookshop to meet their readers. Staff also run Thursday morning storytelling sessions for pre-schoolers.

29 Fortis Green Road, N10 3HP (8444 5500, www.childrensbookshoplondon.com).

Golden Treasury

London's largest independent children's bookshop houses an incredible array of titles, from picture books to teen fiction. Kids can also meet their literary heroes at author events; past extra-special guests have included the much-loved Lauren Child.

29 Replingham Road, SW18 5LT (8333 0167, www.thegoldentreasury.co.uk).

Lion & Unicorn

Opened in 1977 (Roald Dahl was the guest of honour), the Lion & Unicorn has kept up with the times. 'The Roar', its online newsletter, is terrific for the latest book reviews, and details of signings and events.

19 King Street, Richmond, Surrey TW9 1ND (8940 0483, www.lionunicornbooks.co.uk).

Tales on Moon Lane

Bright, airy premises and enthusiastic staff encourage long visits to this award-winning bookshop. Storytelling sessions, the odd puppet show and author events add to the appeal.

25 Half Moon Lane, SE24 9JU (7274 5759, www.talesonmoonlane.co.uk).

Victoria Park Books

With its book club and wall of book reviews written by local children, this place oozes community spirit. Reading material runs from buggy books to tomes on art and dinosaurs for older readers. Authors often visit, and there's a drop-in story session on Fridays.

174 Victoria Park Road, E9 7HD (8986 1124, www.victoriaparkbooks.co.uk).

509

See movies on the move

The Nomad inflatable cinema (www.whereis thenomad.com) pops up in the most unexpected of places, showing classic and cult movies. Atmospheric past screenings have included Wes Anderson's *The Life Aquatic* at Brockwell Lido, and the eerie *Pan's Labyrinth* at Brompton Cemetery; tickets cost from £8 to £12.50.

510 Catch big-name bands for free

Since Rough Trade East opened in 2007, few self-respecting up-and-coming bands (not to mention big names like Marianne Faithfull, Blur and Beirut) have passed up the opportunity of playing here, often at hush-hush 'secret' gigs. See the website for details of events, keep an eye on bands' Twitter accounts for any hints dropped, and be prepared to queue.

Rough Trade East *Old Truman Brewery, 91 Brick Lane, E1 6QL (7392 7788, www.roughtrade.com).*

511 Pay-as-you-go at the gym

Release yourself from the vortex of interminable monthly gym contracts and pay only for what you use. PayasUgym (www.payasugym.com) is a drop-in scheme that covers over 100 gyms in London – with prices from £3 per session, payable with an online pass. With the easy-to-search website (and accompanying phone app), you can zone in on a gym to suit, from no-frills leisure centres to state-of-the-art facilities.

512-515
Be at one with butterflies

Walk freely among brightly coloured beauties in London's butterfly houses.

Clissold Park
The new butterfly tunnel in Clissold Park is open Tuesday and Thursday (12.30-2.30pm). *Greenway Close, off Green Lanes, N4 2EY (8356 8428, www.hackney.gov.uk).*

Golder's Hill Park
Entry to the pretty little glass butterfly house is free. It's open daily during the summer and on weekends in September and October, but closed from November to March. *West Heath Avenue, NW11 7QP (7332 3511, www.cityoflondon.gov.uk).*

London Zoo
The Butterfly Paradise exhibit is home to hundreds of species from Africa, South-east Asia and Central and South America. *Regents Park, NW1 4RY (0844 225 1826, www.zsl.org).*

Natural History Museum
A regular but temporary summer installation, Sensational Butterflies hosts hundreds of moths and butterflies – giant birdwings among them. There's also a hatchery, where you can watch butterflies emerging from their chrysalises. *Cromwell Road, SW7 5BD (7942 5000, www.nhm.ac.uk).*

516
Count down to London 2012...

Keep track of how many days remain until the London 2012 Olympic Games and Paralympic Games begin with the official Countdown Clock. A sleek, four-tonne beauty standing in pride of place in Trafalgar Square, it was unveiled on 14 March 2011 – exactly 500 days before the Opening Ceremony of the 2012 Games.

517
... Then survey the Fourth Plinth

After admiring the Countdown Clock, have a look at the temporary art installation chosen to occupy the Fourth Plinth for 2012, Elmgreen and Dragset's *Powerless Structures, Fig.101.* Depicting a boy astride a rocking horse, it's a mischievous echo of the stately equestrian statues of Victorian military dignitaries that stand on the other three plinths.

518-530 *Find the hidden Wrens*

After the Great Fire of London in 1666, Sir Christopher Wren won a royal commission to rebuild the capital's religious monuments, creating 53 iconic churches – including his magnum opus, St Paul's Cathedral. More than 20 of the architect's other churches survive intact. They are generally quiet places, where Wren's genius can still be appreciated in peace – although many offer superb lunchtime organ recitals.

Start your exploration at Bank tube. South down Walbrook, just behind Mansion House, is one of Wren's most elegant constructions, St Stephen Walbrook (7626 9000, www.ststephenwalbrook.net, 10am-4pm Mon-Fri). It has a lovely domed ceiling, borrowed from the original design for St Paul's, and a rather incongruous-looking altar, sculpted by Henry Moore and unkindly dubbed 'the camembert' by its critics.

Returning to Bank, stroll north along Prince's Street, beside the Bank of England's blind wall. Look right along Lothbury to find St Margaret Lothbury (7726 4878, www.stml.org.uk, 7am-6pm Mon-Fri). The grand screen dividing the choir from the nave was designed by Wren, while the Grinling Gibbons woodcarvings were recovered from various churches damaged in World War II.

West along Gresham Street is St Lawrence Jewry (7600 9478, www.stlawrencejewry.org.uk, 8am-5pm Mon-Fri), which backs on to the Guildhall. In this, the City's official church, you can hear the renowned Klais organ and see the grand gilt ceiling during Tuesday lunchtime organ recitals.

Continuing west, glance north along Wood Street to see the isolated tower of St Alban, ruined in World War II and now an eccentric private home. At the end of the street is St Anne & St Agnes (7606 4986, www.stanneslutheranchurch.org, 10.30am-5pm Mon-Fri), with recitals on Monday and Friday lunchtimes.

Turn south down Foster Lane, passing another imposing Wren church, St Vedast-alias-Foster (7606 3998, 8am-5.30pm Mon-Fri, 11am-4pm Sat). From the end of Foster Lane, the cathedral is almost close enough to touch, but there are more fine churches to see before you get to explore Wren's crowning glory. Turn left into Cheapside. A brief walk east will take you to the corner of Bow Lane and St Mary-le-Bow (7248 5139, www.stmarylebow.co.uk, 7.30am-6pm Tue-Thur, 7.30am-4pm Fri), whose peals once defined anyone born within earshot as a true Cockney.

Grab a swift espresso along Bow Lane then continue south to St Mary Aldermary (7248 9902, 8.30am-5.30pm Mon-Fri), the only Gothic church by Wren to survive World War II. Inside are a fabulous moulded plaster ceiling and an original wooden sword rest (Londoners carried arms right up to the 19th century).

Head east along Cannon Street and turn south along College Hill to reach St Michael Paternoster Royal (7248 5202, 9am-5pm Mon-Fri). Dick Whittington, the first Lord Mayor of London, is depicted in its stained glass windows with his (possibly mythical) cat.

Now turn west along Skinners Lane to Garlick Hill and St James Garlickhythe (7236 1719, www.stjamesgarlickhythe.org.uk, 10.30am-4pm Mon-Fri), the official church of London's vintners and joiners, built in 1682. It was hit by bombs in both World Wars and partly ruined by a falling crane in 1991, but the interior has been convincingly restored.

Now you've earned St Paul's. Follow Trinity Lane to Queen Victoria Street and turn left, passing another stately Wren church: St Nicholas Cole Abbey. Finally, turn north along pedestrianised Peter's Hill, with St Paul's (7246 8350, www.stpauls.co.uk, 8.30am-4pm Mon-Sat) rising before you like a beacon.

Climb to the top of the dome to survey the City, with the spires of Wren's churches poking up between the office blocks, then pay your respects at Wren's humble tomb in the crypt. Finally, make one more detour to Paternoster Square to see another of his works: the Temple Bar archway, which once marked the boundary between the City and Westminster at the western end of Fleet Street.

531
Deep-clean the Thames

Declared a 'biologically dead' zone in 1957, the Thames has cleaned up its act considerably in recent years; these days, species found here include pike, carp and even the odd salmon. There's still plenty of work to be done, however, as the river is also home to a multitude of plastic bags and rubbish. Wade in and do your bit in the annual clean-up organised by Thames 21 (7248 7171, www.thames21.org.uk) on the lowest tide of the year – generally in late February to early March. Localised clean-ups take place year-round and are listed on the website, running from towpath-tidying to canal-clearing. All you need is enthusiasm – and a stout pair of wellington boots.

532-537
Get a full house

While many of London's iconic bingo houses have closed in recent years, Mecca Bingo Camden (180 Arlington Road, NW1 7HL, 7485 0144) and Mecca Bingo Hackney (211-227 Hackney Road, E2 8NA, 7739 7593) are still very much in business – legs eleven, anyone? For an equally dedicated eyes-down crowd, try your luck at the enormous London Palace (Elephant & Castle Shopping Centre, SE1 6TE, 7277 0001).

If you're less blue rinse, more blue dip-dye, the Underground Rebel Bingo Club (www.rebelbingo. com) always attracts a full house of revellers with its tongue-in-cheek compères, dancing, fancy dress and secret locations. Doing away with number-calling altogether is the itinerant Musical Bingo (www.musicalbingo.co.uk), which uses songs instead; its regular ports of call include Concrete (56 Shoreditch High Street, E1 6JJ, 7749 1883, www.concretespace.co.uk).

For a truly avant-garde, no-holds-barred take on bingo, though, no one does it quite like drag queen Jonny Woo, whose risqué Gay Bingo night (www.myspace.com/gay_bingo) has popped up everywhere from the ICA to the Soho Theatre. You've got to be in it to win it – just be prepared for all sorts of shenanigans when number 69 is called.

538
Test-drive a recumbent

Compared to a standard upright, a recumbent trike is quite literally a more laid-back experience – perfect for a few laps of Dulwich Park's green and near gradient-free pathways. London Recumbents (Ranger's Yard, Dulwich Park, SE21 7BQ, 8299 6636, www.londonrecumbents.com) also hire out a side-by-side tandem trike – ideal for chatting while you pedal, while families can strap the kids in a front-running trailer. There's also an outpost in Battersea Park.

539
Drink soup from a dumpling at Leong's

With their characteristic rippled surface at the crown, *Xiao long baos* ('mini-basket dumplings') are traditional Chinese dumplings, steamed in a small bamboo basket – hence the name. There's hot soup inside, so consume them with due care and concentration. The pork- and crab-filled beauties at Leong's Legends in Chinatown are among London's finest: dip them in the black vinegar sauce and arrange a few strips of ginger on top, then bite off the crown and slurp away.

Leong's Legends *4 Macclesfield Street, W1D 6AX (7287 0288).*

540
Hear a 1,000-year-long song

Former ship and buoy maintenance depot and home to London's only lighthouse, Trinity Buoy Wharf is now a thriving centre for the arts with spectacular, semi-industrial riverside views. Up in the lighthouse's lamp room you'll find the Longplayer Tibetan Bell Sound installation: Jem Finer's 1,000-year-long musical composition that should continue, without repetition, until the year 3,000. It's open to the public at weekends.

Trinity Buoy Wharf *64 Orchard Place, E14 0JY (7515 7153, www.trinitybuoywharf.com).*

541 *Cheer on the Goat Race*

While the traditional boat rowing race between the Universities of Oxford and Cambridge takes place on the Thames, two goats – one named Oxford, the other Cambridge – take part in a madcap dash around Spitalfields City Farm. There's an official bookie and sweepstake, as well as goat-themed stalls and entertainment. In 2011, Cambridge sprinted to victory in a record-breaking 56.9 seconds, scoring a hat trick: will this year be Oxford's turn?
Spitalfields City Farm *Buxton Street, E1 5AR (7247 8762, www.thegoatrace.org).*

542 *Switch to tap*

It's a simple idea, but a good one: a website and iPhone app that pinpoints places where you can refill re-usable water bottles, saving money and doing the environment a favour. Restaurants, cafés and pubs across London have signed up: see www.tapwater.org for details.

543 *Feel the power*

If you harbour a secret passion for power ballads, you're not alone. Held at Scala at Kings Cross, Ultimate Power (www.ultimatepowerclub.com) is invariably a sell-out, thanks to a playlist that might take in Bon Jovi's *Always*, Whitney Houston's *I Will Always Love You*, Jennifer Rush's *The Power of Love* and GNR's *November Rain*. Bring your air guitar.

544 *Crown a king of comedy*

Those who like their comedy with a whiff of terror will relish the Comedy Store's King Gong night, held on the last Monday of the month. Would-be comics and foolhardy volunteers are given as much time on the stage as the rowdy audience will allow – barely time for a one-liner for some sorry souls.
Comedy Store *14 Oxendon Street, SW1Y 4EE (0844 871 7699, www.thecomedystore.co.uk).*

545
Find a free court

The good people at Tennis for Free believe everyone should be able to play a game of tennis in their local park, without being put off by the price. Visit www.tennisforfree.com for a list of courts where you can play without paying a penny; free coaching is offered at one or two.

546 *Stroll the pergola on Hampstead Heath*

Hidden away at the west side of Hampstead Heath (www.cityoflondon.gov.uk), near Golders Hill Park, this elaborate Edwardian garden is one of the Heath's lesser-known treasures. Herbs, honeysuckle, jasmine and roses line the shady walkways and crawl over the restored wooden pergola and stone colonnades, designed by celebrated landscape architect Thomas Mawson: think of it as a free aromatherapy session.

547
Attend the Poetry Parnassus

Spearheaded by the Southbank Centre's poet in residence, Simon Armitage, the week-long Poetry Parnassus is an intriguing strand of the London 2012 Cultural Olympiad. Taking place in summer 2012, its aim is to bring together poets from every participating Olympic nation – some 205 wordsmiths – for readings, workshops and a gala event. 'It's crazily ambitious, but I think that's one of the reasons why we're doing it: the Olympics feels like a time for making extravagant and bold gestures,' says Armitage.
Southbank Centre *Belvedere Road, SE1 8XX (7960 4200, www.southbankcentre.co.uk).*

548-550
Chew bubbles

Love it or hate it, Taiwanese bubble tea is certainly an experience. The milk- or fruit-based drink is named for the plump, bubble-like tapioca pearls that sit at the bottom, which you suck up through the wide straw and chew as you drink the sweet tea. HK Diner (22 Wardour Street, W1D 6QQ, 7434 9544) serves a fine rendition, while specialist café Bubbleology (49 Rupert Street, W1D 7PF, 7494 4231, www.bubbleology. co.uk) promises an authentic blend. Meanwhile, Camden's Chaboba (8 East Yard, NW1 8AL, 7267 4719, www.chaboba.co.uk) adds an extra burst of flavour with its popping, fruity *boba* (pearls).

551 *Find your dream denims*

Banish ill-fitting jeans by stepping inside the Bodymetric 3-D scanner at Selfridges (400 Oxford Street, W1A 1AB, 0800 123400, www.selfridges. com). After the high-tech body scan, a consultant suggests the styles that'll suit your shape. Genius.

552 *Mind your Ps and Qs*

Ragged schools were a Victorian experiment in public education, providing schooling for neglected children – and this East End school was London's largest, set up in 1877 by social reformer Dr Barnardo. On the first Sunday of the month, at 2.15pm and 3.30pm, visitors are invited to attend a class in its reconstructed 19th-century classroom. Leading the lesson is Miss Perkins – armed with a pointer stick, blackboard and strictly 'seen and not heard' pupil policy.
Ragged School Museum *46-50 Copperfield Road, E3 4RR (8980 6405, www.raggedschoolmuseum. org.uk).*

553-554
Get a sneak preview

Sign up to sites like www.seefilmfirst.com and www.momentumscreenings.co.uk for invites to preview screenings; what's more, tickets are free.

555 *Peruse the papers at Shepherds Falkiners*

Lined with wooden shelves, this fine paper and bookbinding materials shop is a delight. The range of papers is superb, from intricate, Japanese silk-screen designs to 1930s prints with designs by the likes of Eric Ravilious. For bookbinding, head to the bindery on Rochester Row in Victoria, where you can get a photograph album bound in one of 100 choices of material (from £45).
Shepherds Falkiners *76 Southampton Row, WC1B 4AR (7831 1151, www.falkiners.com).*

556
Hear the screech of tyres on tarmac

Every Sunday from October to March, bangers, hot rods and stock cars come together at Wimbledon Stadium (01252 322920, www. spedeworth.co.uk) for some pedal-to-the-metal, family-oriented mayhem.

A few of my favourite things

557-564

Audrey Niffenegger,
writer

Back in Chicago, I read the *London Review of Books* avidly, so going into the London Review Bookshop (14 Bury Place, WC1A 2JL, 7269 9030, www.lrbshop. co.uk) feels like crawling inside the periodical. Sometimes I see things that I've already got but with a different cover, and I get all excited and buy them again. I like to buy a few books, then have a cake in the little café.

Years back, my sister and I won tickets to anywhere in the world and we chose London. For this first of many visits, the Sir John Soane's Museum (13 Lincoln's Inn Fields, WC2A 3BP, 7405 2107, www.soane.org) was near the top of our to do list. It's immensely personal and claustrophobic – the reverse of the big museums. If you stand at the bottom and look up you can see the balconies of the higher storeys all encrusted with stuff, and you feel like Alice looking down the rabbit hole. The Hogarth Room has a gallery of paintings that are actually shutters; you open them and there are more paintings within.

I had permission to hang around Highgate Cemetery (Swains Lane, N6 6PJ, www. highgate-cemetery.org) to research *Her Fearful Symmetry*, and really got to know and love it. I come to London regularly and always try and give a few tours. My favourite places are on the west side. The Circle of Lebanon is a circular avenue of mausoleums, topped by a spectacular cedar tree. The inner side is Egyptian style, the outer Gothic. When the weather's bad it's one of the gloomiest spots ever, which I like. There's also the tomb of George Wombwell, which is guarded by a beautiful lion sitting on it – it's meant to be his favourite, called Nero. Wombwell started his career as a menagerist by buying two boa constrictors from some sailors, then worked his way up to elephants, bears and lions.

From afar the Watts Memorial (Postman's Park, King Edward Street, EC1A 7BX) looks like a little hut, but get closer and you see the beautiful blue and white tiles. The painter, George Watts, wanted memorials to the heroic acts of ordinary people. Each tile commemorates someone who lost their life in an act of bravery – there's one of an actress whose dress caught fire backstage, and the person who leapt on her to try to put it out. They're very succinct and vivid; read too many, and you feel quite woozy.

Secretly I'm a clotheshorse. I like to go to Philip Treacy (69 Elizabeth Street, SW1W 9PJ, 7730 3992, www.philiptreacy.co.uk) and look at the super-extravagant hats. I only own one, but I'm a big fan. Mine is made from rust coloured velvet, and is like a top hat with an enormous spray of feathers. When I wear it on the tube, people give me their seat.

There's a great restaurant near Kew called the Glasshouse (14 Station Parade, TW9 3PZ, 8940 6777, www.glasshouse restaurant.co.uk). I remember ordering the black pudding, and it was fantastic – as an American, it's not a natural thing to gravitate to, but you know if the black pudding is good, everything's good. There are always things on the menu that I would never normally touch, but I'm willing to be more experimental with them.

I did a lot of research for *Her Fearful Symmetry* in the Humanities Reading Rooms of the British Library (96 Euston Road, NW1 2BD, 0843 208 1144, www.bl.uk). You can do some research, wander round and look at the Magna Carta, then carry on with your work. You need to apply for a reader's card, and I didn't have a formal letter with me when I went. I needed to prove I was a writer, so I showed them *The Time Traveller's Wife* on Amazon and my ID and they let me have a card, which I thought was really nice of them.

The illustrator Aubrey Beardsley is an enduring influence – I first found his work when I was 14, and it took over my brain. So seeing the blue plaque where he lived on Cambridge Street in Pimlico is special to me. He was the bad boy of 1890s London, and a lot of his stuff is either naughty or just plain strange. You can see his work in the Prints and Drawings Study Room at the Victoria & Albert Museum (Cromwell Road, SW7 2RL, 7942 2563, www.vam.ac.uk). They bring it out to you in boxes, and you can sit and look at one drawing after another. I spent my 30th birthday doing that.

565-569

Run away to join the circus

Fancy yourself as an aerial artiste, flying through the air with the greatest of ease? Then swing by Circus Space (Coronet Street, N1 6HD, 7613 4141, www.thecircusspace.co.uk). Its experience days instruct novices in the static and flying trapeze, along with unicycling, tightwire walking, juggling and other circus essentials.

The Gorilla Circus (8144 5329, www.gorilla circus.com), meanwhile, travels around various London parks, inducting six-and-overs into the art of the flying trapeze. You'll end the two-hour taster by swooping towards a 'catcher' on a swinging bar – with a safety belt and net in place, mind. Daredevils will also relish the range of classes at AirCraft Circus (Hangar Arts Trust, Harrington Way, SE18 5NR, 8317 8401, www. aircraftcircus.com): chinese pole, silks, rope work and the terrifying-sounding bungee trapeze.

Albert & Friends Instant Circus (8237 1170, www.albertandfriendsinstantcircus.co.uk) runs termly workshops for children and families in several west London venues. It has classes for all abilities, from relatively simple stilt-walking to the acrobatically challenging corde lisse.

Over in Covent Garden, finally, there are all manner of circus-related shenanigans at City Lit (Keeley Street, WC2B 4BA, 7492 2600, www. citylit.ac.uk). Its clown summer school promises a focus on the all-important red nose, while the circus skills course explores everything from escapology to unicycling.

570 *Pay what you can at the Arcola*

Dalston's theatrical success story moved into its new home on Ashwin Street in 2011. Many of the fittings and furnishings are salvaged finds, in keeping with the Arcola's focus on sustainability: it hopes to become the world's first carbon-neutral theatre. The programming is a mix of socially relevant pieces and reworked classics, often with impressively innovative staging. On Tuesday nights, a limited number of tickets are sold on a pay-what-you-can basis; see online for details.

Arcola Theatre *24 Ashwin Street, E8 3DL (7503 1646, www.arcolatheatre.com).*

571-578

Upgrade your undies

Agent Provocateur

London's original luxury lingerie emporium is still going strong. Tantalising cuts, luxe fabrics and friendly assistants – clad in pink, Vivienne Westwood-designed uniforms – are its hallmarks. *6 Broadwick Street, W1F 8HL (7439 0229, www.agentprovocateur.com).*

Bordello

From Ayten Gasson's silky little somethings to Nichole de Carle's bondage-influenced briefs, Bordello has something for all tastes. *55 Great Eastern Street, EC2A 3HP (7503 3334, www.bordello-london.com).*

Coco de Mer

Styled like a glamorous boudoir, and with cheeky peek-a-boo cameras in the velvet changing rooms, this place exudes a seductive glamour. Brands include Stella McCartney, Damaris and La Perla. *23 Monmouth Street, WC2H 9DD (7836 8882, www.coco-de-mer.com).*

The Lingerie Collective

Having started life as a pop-up shop, this shrine to luxury smalls is now a permanent fixture. Of its heady array of designers, highlights include Ell & Cee, Modern Courtesan and Lascivious. *8 Ganton Street, W1F 7QP (07894 906871, www.thelingeriecollective.com).*

Myla

Despite some serious expansion, this upmarket lingerie label retains its cachet. The silk, satin and lace designs are sexy but subtle, and updated every season. *74 Duke of York Square, SW3 4LY (7730 0700, www.myla.com).*

Rigby & Peller

Rigby & Peller is famed for its fitting service, so be sure to book ahead. The Knightsbridge outpost is a vision of old-fashioned opulence, with its art nouveau shopfront and chandeliers. *2 Hans Road, SW3 1RX (0845 076 5545 (www.rigbyandpeller.com).*

Tallulah Lingerie

Silky slips, frilled knickers and bras from the likes of Lejaby, Fleur and Huit are beautifully arrayed at this elegant little boudoir, set on one of Islington's prettiest sidestreets *65 Cross Street, N1 2BB (7704 0066, www.tallulah-lingerie.co.uk).*

What Katie Did

Wasp waists, bullet bras and authentic seamed nylons are the stock in trade at What Katie Did, purveyors of 1940s and '50s inspired lingerie. You'll feel super-glamorous in a peach satin Harlow, or a jet-black, spiral-stitched Maitresse. *26 Portobello Green, 281 Portobello Road, W10 5TZ (0845 430 8743, www.whatkatiedid.com).*

579 *Sup a secret cuppa*

Stowed away above the Coach & Horses, the Soho's Secret Tea Room serves afternoon tea in a '50s-themed room, with lace curtains, floral crockery and gramophone records crackling away in the background. There's the full complement of fairy cakes, scones and sandwiches with the crusts cut off, plus 16 leaf teas. Watch out for the owner's collection of vintage aprons in action. **Soho's Secret Tea Room** *29 Greek Street, W1D 5DH (7437 5920, www.sohossecrettearoom.co.uk).*

Bates the Hatters

582-587
Meet London's milliners

Philip Treacy (69 Elizabeth Street, SW1W 9PJ, 7730 3992, www.philiptreacy.co.uk) remains the capital's most high-profile hatter: his creations have been worn by everyone from Lady Gaga to the Duchess of Cornwall. His rival for the title of London's most fashionable milliner is Stephen Jones (36 Great Queen Street, WC2B 5AA, 7242 0770, www.stephenjonesmillinery.com), famed for his surrealist flights of fancy.

If you're on a more restricted budget, try Bernstock Speirs (234 Brick Lane, E2 7EB, 7739 7385, www.bernstockspeirs.com). From ribbon trimmed gentlemen's panamas to playful bunny-ear caps, there's something to suit most tastes.

Traditionalists favour Bates the Hatters (73 Jermyn Street, SW1Y 6JD, 7734 2722, www.bates-hats.co.uk), which has plied gents' hats on Jermyn Street for over a century. It covers all eventualities, from summer boaters to winter deerstalkers and classic top hats. Another venerable establishment is James Lock & Co (6 St James's Street, SW1A 1EF, 7930 8874, www.lockhatters.co.uk), founded in 1696: look no further for splendid felt trilbies and dapper tweed caps.

Keeping the tradition of classic hats alive in a very different way is Moody & Farrell (07906 990390). From her Hackney studio, Eloise Moody concocts antique-inspired, thoroughly modern headgear of the highest order, from powder-blue pigskin boaters to oak-veneer cowboy hats; consult www.moodyandfarrell.co.uk for stockist details and bespoke commissions.

580
Pick your own breakfast

Once a year, mushroom expert Andy Overall (07958 786 374, www.fungitobewith.org) organises a Breakfast Foray on Hampstead Heath, helping participants identify and pick different sorts of fungi. Breakfast is served at a nearby pub, where scrambled eggs, risotto and stews – containing mushrooms gathered by Andy – await the hungry hunters. For dates and details of Andy's other fungi forays and workshops, check the website.

581 *Get feathers flying*

International Pillow Fight Day (www.pillow fightday.com) takes place every spring in cities around the world, from Berlin to Bangalore. Pillow-wielding Londoners have eagerly entered the fray, with past events held at Leicester Square, St Paul's and Trafalgar Square – much to the bemusement of passers-by.

588 *Spot the difference in Bayswater*

As you're strolling down Bayswater's Leinster Gardens, admiring the grand stuccoed terraces, you may notice that the windows of nos.23 and 24 look rather peculiar. That's because they're trompe l'oeil fakes, made from plaster and paint. The original houses were demolished in the mid 19th century to make way for the underground; walk round to the rear, on Porchester Terrace to see the iron struts supporting the fake façades, and the District line trains thundering through.

589 *Believe your ears*

'In the Dark' events (www.inthedarkradio.org) are all about listening in new ways. The monthly salons are for alternative audio lovers, allowing audiences to indulge their ears – and rest their eyes – in dark, cinema-like surrounds. The pieces range from abstract soundscapes to in-depth radio documentaries, with each session programmed by a guest curator. Past venues have included the Pleasance Theatre, Toynbee Hall and Passing Clouds; check online for the next installment.

590
Snack on seafood at Tubby Isaacs

Stop by Tubby Isaacs' stand, which has been trading since 1919, to partake of a tub of winkles, whelks, cockles, prawns or crab claws – or treat yourself to a tasty lobster tail (£1.50 apiece). Still run by one of Tubby's descendents, it's a unique slice of East End history – and one that needs your support.

Tubby Isaacs *Outside the Aldgate Exchange pub, Petticoat Lane Market, Goulston Street, E1 7TP (07846 848813, www.tubbyisaacs.co.uk).*

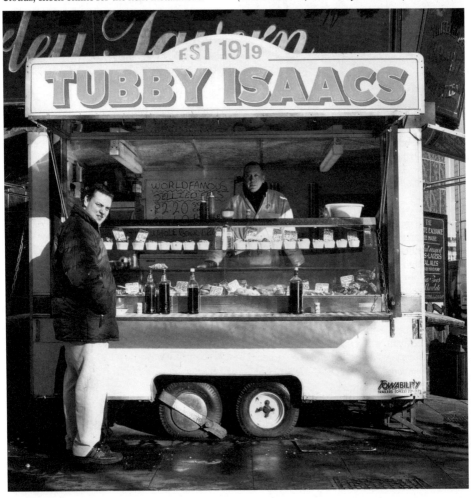

Discover London's secret gardens

Camley Street

London has a wealth of grand parks and well-known squares, which can get rather crowded. But the city has its secret gardens too, found in the most unexpected of locales.

Bonnington Square
Planted on a patch of wasteland by local residents, this square in the backstreets of Vauxhall is a sanctuary for people and wildlife. Fringed by magnificent palms, at night it is romantically lit with fairy lights.
*Bonnington Square, SW8
(http://bonningtonsquaregarden.org.uk).*

Camley Street Natural Park
Once a coal drop yard, on the banks of the Regent's Canal at King's Cross, this two-acre site has been transformed into a glorious wilderness, home to kingfishers, newts, reed warblers and bats.
12 Camley Street, N1C 4PW (7833 2311, www.wildlondon.org.uk).

Centre for Wildlife Gardening
A gorgeous cottage garden found on a suburban street in Peckham, with a summer meadow, stag beetle sanctuary, wildlife pond and bog garden.
28 Marsden Road, SE15 4EE (7252 9186, www.wildlondon.org.uk).

Culpepper Community Garden
An organic garden in the middle of Angel, with ponds, rose pergolas, ornamental beds, vegetable plots and a drought-resistant dry garden.
1 Cloudesley Road, N1 0EG (7833 3951, www.culpeper.org.uk).

Gillespie Park
A tiny wilderness sandwiched between the Finsbury Park rail tracks and gigantic Arsenal stadium. Get lost in the long grass and twisting woodland.
191 Drayton Park, N5 1PH (7527 4462, www.islington.gov.uk).

Inner Temple Gardens
Within the venerable precincts of Inner Temple is a delightful three-acre garden, with peaceful lawns, fragrant herbaceous borders and a centuries-old sundial. It's generally open to the public from 12.30 to 3pm on weekdays; entry is via the north gate, opposite Crown Office Row.
Inner Temple, EC4Y 7HL (7797 8250, www.innertemple.org.uk).

Phoenix Garden
A central London paradise, moments from the hell of Tottenham Court Road tube. It's managed by volunteers with urban wildlife in mind.
*21 Stacey Street, WC2H 8DG
(www.phoenixgarden.btck.co.uk).*

Redcross Garden
Set up in 1888 by the co-founder of the National Trust, Octavia Hill, this now restored garden boasts a historical (but private) hall and cottages, alongside wildlife-friendly flowers and plants.
50 Redcross Way, SE1 1HA (7403 3393, www.bost.org.uk).

St Mary's Secret Garden
This Hackney green space has woodland, vegetable beds, fruit trees, a greenhouse and a sensory garden, all cared for in an organic and eco-aware way.
50 Pearson Street, E2 8EL (7739 2965, www.stmaryssecretgarden.org.uk).

York House Gardens
Formal gardens attached to a 17th-century house on the banks of the Thames, with a sunken lawn, sea-nymph statuary and a Japanese garden.
*Sion Court, Sion Road, Twickenham TW1 3DD
(0845 612 2660, www.richmond.gov.uk).*

601

Be an urban vintner

Thanks to London's benign micro-climate, it's not that tricky to cultivate a vine or two in a sunny garden, allotment or roof terrace. Put the fruits of your labour to good use by joining the Urban Wine Company – a Tooting-based collective of small-scale growers in London and the South-east.

By pooling their harvests (contributions range from a 'modest bucketful' up to 100kg), its members produce enough grapes for a professional pressing at Booker's Vineyard in West Sussex. The following March, each person receives a share of the booty. For more on the scheme and its membership costs, see www.urbanwineco.com.

602-603

Pray silence for the Paralympics...

Of the many impressive sports on the programme for the Paralympic Games, Goalball (30 Aug-7 Sept 2012) and 5-a-side Football (31 Aug-8 Sept 2012) offer a very unusual experience: spectators watch in silence. Designed for visually impaired athletes (all competitors wear blindfolds to ensure absolute equality), both sports are played with balls that contain noise-making devices, so the crowd has to keep shtum until the game is over.

604 *... Or hear titans clash in 'murderball'*

At the opposite end of the noise spectrum is the intensely physical Wheelchair Rugby (5-9 Sept), originally called 'murderball' due to the ferocity of the clashes between competitors.

If you don't manage to get tickets for Goalball, 5-a-side Football or Wheelchair Rugby, settle in to watch the action at one of the several Live Sites that will be scattered across the city for the duration of the Games (www.london2012.com).

605-609

Forget Hollywood, go Bollywood

The biggest Bollywood blockbusters can be found playing in cinemas across London, including the Vue Acton (Royale Leisure Park, W3 0PA, 0871 224 0240, www.myvue.com) and Cineworld Feltham (Air Park Way, TW13 7LX, 0871 200 2000, www.cineworld.co.uk).

For a more traditional Bollywood viewing experience, watch a film at the Safari (Station Road, HA1 2TU, 8426 0303, www.safaricinema.com) in Harrow. Samosas and other Indian snacks are sold in the foyer and the audience are far from shy – don't be surprised if people sing along to well-known songs or talk over the dialogue. For a not too dissimilar experience in east London, visit Upton Park's Boleyn Cinema (7-11 Barking Road, E6 1PW, 8471 4884, www.boleyncinema.com).

Screenings are notoriously long (usually three hours plus), but a 15-minute interval is standard. Unsurprisingly, there's often a stampede for the loos, so bag a seat near the back if you want to avoid the crush. Screenings generally have English subtitles, but phone ahead to be sure.

For independent Indian film not of the Bollywood school, attend a screening or two at the London Asian Film Festival (www.tongues onfire.com), held in the spring across various arthouse venues.

610 *Visit an unusual urban farm*

FARM Shop in Dalston is a must-visit for anyone keen on urban agriculture and self-sufficiency. Once derelict, the building is now literally alive, taking in an indoor allotment, a polytunnel, a rooftop chicken coop and an aquaponic fish farm, which casts a spooky glow at night. Focused more on education and experimentation than mass production, this design-led project isn't going to feed London, but will definitely inspire you to grow your own. It's generally open Monday to Saturday; if you're making a special trip, call ahead to check they'll be open.

FARM Shop *20 Dalston Lane, E8 3AZ (07855 027876, http://farmlondon.weebly.com/ farmshop.html).*

611-616

Book a bike event into your diary

Critical Mass

Critical Mass (www.criticalmasslondon.org.uk) sets out from under Waterloo Bridge on the last Friday of the month, to reclaim the road. Human-powered vehicles (bikes, skateboards, Rollerblades and other things self-propelled) take en masse to the streets in a noisy, joyous throng.

London Bicycle Film Festival

The Bicycle Film Festival (www.bicyclefilm festival.com/london) started in New York in 2001. Events now take place worldwide, showing a terrific selection of bike-related movies.

London Nocturne

Smithfield market becomes a race circuit once a year for the Nocturne (www.londonnocturne. com). Amateurs can take part in the folding-bike races or longest skid competition, but simply watching proceedings, cold beer in hand, is

enjoyable enough. Later on comes the floodlit, furious-paced men's elite road race; arrive by late afternoon to secure a prime spot by the barriers.

Mayor of London's Sky Ride

Held in September, this central London ride (www.goskyride.com) is geared towards families – operated on closed roads, and taking in such sights as Buckingham Palace and Big Ben along its 15-kilometre route. In 2010, it attracted a whopping 85,000 riders.

Tour of Britain

The world's top pros compete in Britain's biggest and best bike race, the Tour of Britain (www.tourofbritain.com). London hosts the final stage of the eight-day epic, so there's everything to pedal for. Held in September, it's free to watch.

World Naked Bike Ride

Help expose the problem of pollution caused by motor vehicles by exposing yourself in honour of the World Naked Bike Ride (www.worldnaked bikeride.org). Cyclists across the globe strip off and saddle up to mark the occassion, and London has hosted an event every year since 2004. Dare you bare? Many do, but scantily clad will suffice.

617-623 *Dress up!*

Angels (119 Shaftesbury Avenue, WC2H 8AE, 7836 5678, www.fancydress.com) has long been the doyenne of London's fancy dress emporiums. From two-person horse suits to lavish period pieces, this place has it all: if you've ever wanted to dress up as a brussels sprout or a Christmas bauble, this is your big chance.

In east London, investigate Mad World (69-85 Tabernacle Street, EC2A 4BA, 7253 1003, www.madworld.co.uk), an Old Street basement crammed with thousands of costumes. Another well-stocked specialist is Camden's Escapade (45-46 Chalk Farm Road, NW1 8AJ, 7485 7384, www.escapade.co.uk), which also has masks, wigs and accessories. Other finishing touches can be found at Charles H Fox (22 Tavistock Street, WC2E 7PY, 0870 200 0369, www.charlesfox. co.uk), the place film and theatre professionals shop for make-up, wigs, latex and lashes.

For a showstopping outfit, visit the National Theatre Costume Hire Department (Chichester House, Kennington Park Business Centre, 1-3 Brixton Road, SW9 6DE, 7735 4774, www. nationaltheatre.org.uk), open by appointment Monday to Thursday. Used in past productions, costumes range from military apparel to mermaid suits. The Costume Studio (159-161 Balls Pond Road, N1 4BG, 7923 9472, www.costumestudio. co.uk) is another good bet for authentic-looking clobber, charging from £65 for a week's hire.

For bespoke fancy dress, call Prangsta Costumiers (304 New Cross Road, SE14 6AF, 8694 9869, www.prangsta.co.uk), whose extraordinary creations run from ogres and twisted harlequins to resplendent animal heads. Hire prices start at £50 per week for a full outfit, while bespoke costumes cost £150 labour, plus materials.

624 *Sing with a ukulele band*

KaraUke (www.karauke.net) is a 14-strong band of ukulele players, who'll strum along as you sing your favourite songs. Playing one Thursday a month (venues vary), their repertoire includes *Crazy Little Thing Called Love, Don't Look Back in Anger* and *Sweet Child o' Mine*. If you have a song request, email ahead and they'll prepare it for you – and provide backing vocals.

Prangsta

625-630
Have a close shave

Wet shaves take around half an hour, with hot towels used to soften hairs and open pores, allowing the barber's single blade to get super-close to the root – first shaving with the grain, then against. The result? A finish that disposables can only dream of.

Geo F Trumper
The original Geo F Trumper (est. 1875) has cubicles with red velvet curtains and mahogany-panelled walls. A wet shave costs £38.
9 Curzon Street, W1J 5HQ (7499 1850, www.trumpers.com).

F Flittner
Warm service awaits behind a tiny shopfront, stacked with pomades, brushes and unguents. Flittner has smoothed the cheeks of City gents for over a century, charging £23 for a wet shave.
86 Moorgate, EC2M 6SE (7606 4750, www.fflittner.com).

Mesut Barber
Venture east for a Turkish wet shave in Dalston. Even with the additional singeing off of stray ear and nose hairs, wet shaves cost the princely sum of £10. And the banter's absolutely free.
36 Stoke Newington High Street, N16 7PL (7503 8840).

Murdock Covent Garden
Murdock's luxurious shave (£45) mixes old-fashioned techniques with modern pampering – including a detoxing clay mask.
18 Monmouth Street, WC2H 9HB (3393 7946, www.murdocklondon.com).

Pall Mall Barbers
Pall Mall's is compact, bustling and hidden away, with black and white prints adorning the walls and wet shaves at £32.50.
27 Whitcomb Street, WC2H 7EP (7930 7787, www.pallmallbarbers.com).

Truefitt & Hill
Operating since 1805, this place elevates the traditional shave to an art form. A wet shave will set you back £39; shoeshines are complimentary.
71 St James's Street, SW1A 1PH (7493 2961, www.truefittandhill.co.uk).

631
Let Herb Lester be your guide

See London in a new light, armed with one of Herb Lester Associates' themed maps, which chart the city's curiosities, quirks and lesser-trodden corners. *An Uncle's guide to London* is essential reading for those entertaining a youthful relative for the day, while *May We Help You?* uncovers some unusual shops, whose specialisms run from taxidermy to covered buttons. At £3 a throw (plus postage), we'd consider them money well spent. For details, visit www.herblester.com.

632
See avant-garde art in Leicester Square

Founded in 1865 for London's French Catholic community and completely rebuilt after World War II, Notre Dame de France (5 Leicester Place, WC2H 7BX, 7437 9363, www.ndfchurch.org) is a little-known gem, just off Leicester Square. Inside are a series of bold, linear murals, created over a week in 1960 by writer, filmmaker and avant-garde polymath Jean Cocteau. The sharp of eye will spot his troubled-looking self-portrait, in yellow, to the left of the altar.

633
Pick up a Penguin in Wimbledon

Seek solace for tedious commuting at the Waiting Room on platform 5 at Wimbledon Station – home to an enterprising bookswap scheme. A motley but enticing array of reading material is propped along the windowsill, from ancient editions of *Reader's Digest* to contemporary classics. Note that bookswap etiquette is to bring in a book for each that you take, so that there's plenty of stock for other bored commuters. For more on the scheme, search for 'Wimbledon Station Bookswap' on Facebook.

634-635
Get a sugar rush in Knightsbridge

For years, Ladurée's outpost in Harrods
(87-135 Brompton Road, SW1X 7XL, 3155 0111,
www.laduree.fr) was *the* place to go for macarons.
Then, in 2010, legendary French pastry chef
Pierre Hermé – dubbed the 'Picasso of Pastry'
by French *Vogue*, and renowned across the globe
for his exquisite confections – opened a flagship
shop and café, some five minutes' walk away (13
Lowndes Street, SW1X 9EX, 7245 0317, www.
pierreherme.com). Ladurée addicts praise the
intense flavour hits and perfect crunch of the
bite-sized macarons, while Hermé's followers cite
a chewier texture and more outré combinations;
olive oil and vanilla, say, or peach, saffron and
apricot. We'd advise a trip to both, to come to
your own conclusions.

636-638
Find Freud

Forced into exile by the Nazis, Freud came to
London in 1938. He moved into a handsome red-
brick Hampstead pile, now the Freud Museum
(20 Maresfield Gardens, NW3 5SX, 7435 2002,
www.freud.org.uk).

Before leaving Vienna, the good doctor had the
position of everything in his study written down,
so that it could be exactly recreated in London –
no mean feat, considering his magpie eye for
antiquities. From an Egyptian mummified falcon
to a small jade lion paperweight, it's an endlessly
intriguing collection, taking in some 2,000 items.
Along with his vases, statues, prints and books,
Freud also brought his famous couch – an
unexpectedly inviting affair, piled with cushions
and swathed in an Oriental throw.

A short stroll away, in front of the Tavistock
Centre and on the junction of Fitzjohn's Avenue
and Maresfield Gardens, is Oscar Nemon's
contemplative seated statue of Freud, sculpted
in the 1930s. His ashes, meanwhile, reside in a
Greek urn at Golders Green Crematorium (Hoop
Lane, NW11 7NL, 8455 2374). To see them,
you'll need a member of staff to unlock the
columbarium, so it must be in office hours.

639
Become a Blue Badge guide

The Blue Badge is the acme of guiding standards
in the UK. To qualify as a Blue Badge guide
for London, you need to attend a near-two year
part-time course. It's for people planning to work
as a guide, but also a fantastic way of getting to
know London's every nook and cranny. For more
details, see www.blue-badge-guides.com/training.

640
Reduce and reuse at Unpackaged

Catherine Conway's Islington food shop,
Unpackaged (42 Amwell Street, EC1R 1XT,
7713 8368, www.beunpackaged.com), is filled
with organic, Fairtrade and/or locally sourced
loose teas, grains, nuts, chocolate, superfoods,
fruit, veg, cheese, toiletries and much more, all
beautifully arranged in square containers. Bring
in your own jars, Tupperware and bags, and fill
'em up to avoid the use of disposable packaging.
The concept has been so popular that Conway
is seeking to expand to larger premises.

641-646

Make some feathered friends...

Herons, Regent's Park

By the boating lake in Regent's Park (0300 061 2300, www.royalparks.org.uk), one of the biggest urban heron colonies in Europe nests in the treetops. On selected spring afternoons, the RSPB (7808 1241, www.rspb.org.uk) sets up a manned viewpoint by Clarence Gate; borrow a pair of binoculars and have a gander at the baby grey herons, sporting spectacular feathery mohawks.

Peacocks, Holland Park

The jewel in the crown of this manicured park (7361 3003, www.rbkc.gov.uk) are its magnificent peacocks. You'll probably hear their eerie, miaow-like cries before you glimpse their gorgeous tail feathers and irridescent plumage: they're generally to be found strutting on the Peacock Lawn, south of the Kyoto Garden, or in the formal gardens by Holland House.

Pelicans, St James's Park

The waterfowl lake at St James's Park (7930 1793, www.royalparks.org.uk) is a source of endless delight, with its splay-footed coots, equable mallards and tufted ducks. The scene-stealers, though, are the five mischievous pelicans. A few years ago, one was caught on camera as it swallowed a passing pigeon; in general, though, the birds stick to a diet of fresh fish. If you want to see them gulping their lunch down, feeding time is at around 2.30pm daily.

Penguins, London Zoo

With their waddling gait and graceful dives, the penguins have long been a star turn at London Zoo (Regent's Park, NW1 4RY, 7722 3333, www.zsl.org). Formerly housed in Berthold Lubetkin's iconic 1930s pool, the penguins moved to Penguin Beach in 2011. It's four times bigger, three times as deep and has underwater viewing areas: happily, the crowd-pleasing tradition of feeding time (from 2pm) remains unchanged.

Peregrines, Tate Modern

The capital's peregrine falcons seem to favour high-profile sites for their roosts, among them Parliament and Tate Modern – lofty vantage points from which they can scope out prey. The fastest birds in the sky, peregrines are remarkable to watch in action. From mid July to September, the RSPB (7808 1241, www.rspb.org.uk) runs a stand by the Millennium Bridge, from noon until 7pm daily, where staff will help you train a powerful telescope on the birds.

Ravens, Tower of London

Will the kingdom really fall if the ravens ever leave the Tower of London (Tower Hill, EC3N 4AB, 0844 482 7777, www.hrp.org.uk)? The powers-that-be aren't taking any chances, and there are six birds, 'plus reserves', in residence. The birds are fed on six ounces of raw meat a day, plus boiled eggs, bird biscuits soaked in blood and the odd rabbit. Although they come at the Ravenmaster's whistle, they're far from tame: heed official advice and don't get too close.

647 *... Or read the diary of a London pigeon*

Discover what's ruffling the feathers of a typical London pigeon at the Pigeon Blog (http://pigeon blog.wordpress.com) – the ban on pigeon-feeding in Trafalgar Square, for starters.

648-656 *Sip a sherry*

Fino, manzanilla and amontillado (which is sometimes sweetened) are the lighter, drier styles, while darker, richer sherries include the fragrant – and potent – olorosos. Here are some of our favourite stop-offs for a tipple.

Bar Pepito
Small is beautiful at this cosy specialist bar. There are just five tables, but 15 choices of fortified wine, plus taster 'sherry flights'.
Varnisher's Yard, The Regent Quarter, N1 9DF (7841 7331, www.camino.uk.com/pepito).

Barrica
Barrica's list boasts around 20 sherries in every style, from the driest fino to the nutty, rare palo cortado and syrupy sweet pedro ximénez (PX).
62 Goodge Street, W1T 4NE (7436 9448, www.barrica.co.uk).

Barrafina
There's more of a focus on food at this small but slick tapas bar, but the sherry on offer is perfectly matched to it.
54 Frith Street, W1D 4SL (7813 8016, www.barrafina.co.uk).

Capote y Toros
Over 40 varieties of sherry are sold by the glass; it also pops up on the menu, in dishes such as Iberico pork cheeks cooked with oloroso dulce.
157 Old Brompton Road, SW5 0LJ (7373 0567, www.cambiodetercio.co.uk).

Cigala
A sophisticated Spanish restaurant, with an emphasis on drier sherry styles.
54 Lamb's Conduit Street, WC1N 3LW (7405 1717, www.cigala.co.uk).

Fino
Barrafina's more formal sister establishment has a comprehensive sherry list; look out for limited runs from revered producer Equipo Navazos.
33 Charlotte Street, entrance on Rathbone Street, W1T 1RR (7813 8010, www.finorestaurant.com).

José
A new arrival on the scene, José Pizarro's small, informal eaterie has a daily-changing tapas list and a sterling selection of sherries.
104 Bermondsey Street, SE1 3UB (7403 4902, www.josepizarro.com).

Morito
Moro's little brother (*see below*) has a fine array of sherries to accompany its superb (though tiny) tapas. Finish with a scoop of Malaga raisin ice-cream served in a shot of pedro ximénez.
32 Exmouth Market, EC1R 4QL (7278 7007).

Moro
The wine list at Sam and Sam Clark's acclaimed southern Mediterranean eaterie includes over 20 sherries by the glass, with handy tasting notes.
34-36 Exmouth Market, EC1R 4QE (7833 8336, www.moro.co.uk).

657-660
Catch a double bill

Riverside Studios (Crisp Road, W6 9RL, 8237 1111, www.riversidestudios.co.uk) is the doyenne of the double bill. Its pairings often showcase the work of particular directors, from rising talents to cinematic legends. Down in Brixton, the Ritzy (Brixton Oval, Coldharbour Lane, SW2 1JG, 0871 902 5739, www.picturehouses.co.uk) also peppers its programme with thought-provoking double bills, often paired by theme. Sunday mornings double bills at East Finchley's Phoenix Cinema (52 High Road, N2 9PJ, 8444 6789, www.phoenix cinema.co.uk) are geared towards sophisticated cinephiles too: a two-for-one Truffaut screening, say, or a bittersweet exploration of relationships, courtesy of *Norwegian Wood* and *Blue Valentine*. Double bills at the Prince Charles (7 Leicester Place, WC2H 7BY, 7494 3654, www.prince charlescinema.com), meanwhile, cater to all tastes, running from the titillating (*Showgirls* and *Striptease*) to the terrifying (*The Evil Dead* and *Army of Darkness*). Sit back, relax, and make sure you've got plenty of popcorn.

661-663
Pick your own

Londoners, get back to the land! Instead of relying on limp supermarket offerings, select your own fruit and veg fresh from the soil, getting a lungful of fresh air in the process. The closest pick-your-own is Heathfield Farm (Coombe Lane, CR0 5RH, 01883 743636) – a slice of country life in Croydon, whose bounty includes plums, berries and enormous ears of sweetcorn. Set in the rolling hills of Enfield, the award-winning Parkside Farm (Hadley Road, Middlesex, EN2 8LA, 8367 2035, www.parksidefarmpyo.co.uk) cultivates around 20 different crops, running from beets to blackcurrants; check the online calendar to see what's in season. On the fringes of London, meanwhile, Garsons at Esher (Winterdown Road, Esher, Surrey, KT10 8LS, 01372 464389, www.garsons.co.uk) is a 100-acre land of pick-your-own plenty; among the crops are delicious but tricky to cultivate cherries.

664
Eat carrot cake with the fashionable set

On the top floor of Dover Street Market 17-18 Dover Street, W1S 4LT, 7518 0680, www.dover streetmarket.com), London's shrine to high fashion, is an outpost of Rose Bakery – the British café that charmed *le tout Paris* when it opened on rue des Martyrs in 2002. The low-key London branch is frequented by fashionistas and French food-lovers, drawn by its sterling quiches and comforting cakes; don't miss the famed carrot cake, or very superior crumbles.

665
Join the Freemasons

For a tour, that is. Although the austere, art deco Freemasons Hall may look rather impenetrable (so much so that it stood in for Thames House, MI5's headquarters, in TV series *Spooks*), it actually welcomes visitors, running regular free tours. You don't get to see all the temples – which cover over two acres in total – but you can poke about in the museum (collections include various regalia, elaborately embroidered Masonic aprons and symbol-heavy silverware) and see the 2,000-seater Grand Temple, with its zodiacal signs, gilt throne, enormous bronze doors and all-seeing eyes.
Freemasons Hall *60 Great Queen Street, WC2B 5AZ (7831 9811, www.ugle.org.uk).*

666
Escape the city in Brockwell Park

In green and pleasant Brockwell Park, south-east London comes over all bucolic for a weekend in July for the Country Show (www.lambeth.gov.uk/Country-Show). There is quaint village green activity in the Flower Zone, with the eagerly anticipated vegetable character competition, flower shows, scarecrow making contests, and the fluffiest sponge cakes battling it out in the baking contest. Elsewhere, there are displays of sheep herding and shearing, knights jousting, livestock competitions, a giant tug of war, and visiting animals from Vauxhall City Farm.

667-671

Get inked

The Family Business
Owner Mo Coppoletta runs a tight ship at the Family Business, and you're in safe hands with his suited and booted team. Its custom tattoos often mix western and oriental iconography, with sharp colours and precision lines.
58 Exmouth Market, EC1R 4QE (7278 9526, www.thefamilybusinesstattoo.com).

Frith Street Tattoo
Frith Street draws a young, punky crowd to its Soho premises. Its six resident artists are much in demand: for a curvaceous pin-up girl or superb script lettering, check out Emiliano's work. Appointments are few and far between, so keep an eye out for last-minute cancellations on Twitter.
18 Frith Street, W1D 4RQ (7734 8180, www.frithstreettattoo.co.uk).

Good Times
This antiques- and kitsch-filled hideaway isn't your average parlour. The team takes in some of London's finest female tattoo artists, including Saira Hunjan (who has worked on designs for Kate Moss and Katy England) and Nikole Lowe, known for her intricate Japanese-influenced work. Both have serious waiting lists.
147 Curtain Road, EC2A 3QE (7739 2438, www.ilovegoodtimes.co.uk).

Into You
This Clerkenwell establishment is one of the most sought after studios in London, and some of the capital's best tattoo artists have worked under its steer. Tribal designs are a forte: check out owner Alex Binnie's bold designs, or Tomas Tomas' intricate geometric patterns.
144 St John Street, EC1V 4UA (7253 5085, www.into-you.co.uk).

New Wave Tattoo
Lal Hardy's Muswell Hill studio is London's most famous, offering a wide range of styles, from mechanical to Japanese. Past customers include Dave Grohl, who had the Foo Fighters' logo inked on his neck.
157 Sydney Road, N10 2NL (8444 8779, www.newwavetattoo.co.uk).

672-677 *Attend evensong*

At the close of day, attending daily evensong, with the choir in residence, is a timelessly lovely, meditative experience. Check online to make sure it is a sung evensong, not a spoken one, then turn up on the day. Most services start at 5pm, and last under an hour. The Catholic Westminster Cathedral, meanwhile, has a choral mass in place of evensong – and a wonderful choir, courtesy of the Westminster Cathedral Choir School.

King's College London Chapel *Strand, WC2R 2LS (7836 5454, www.kcl.ac.uk). 5.30pm Tue, term-time (late Sept-May).*
St Martins in the Fields *Trafalgar Square, SW1P 3HA (7766 1100, www2.stmartin-in-the-fields.org). 5pm Wed.*
St Paul's Cathedral *Ludgate Hill, EC4M 8AD (7236 4128, www.stpauls.co.uk). 5pm Tue-Sat; 3.15pm Sun.*
Southwark Cathedral *London Bridge, SE1 9DA (7367 6700, http://cathedral.southwark.anglican.org). 5.30pm Tue, Thur, Fri; 4pm Sat; 3pm Sun.*
Westminster Abbey *20 Dean's Yard, SW1P 3PA (7222 5152, www.westminster-abbey.org). 5pm Mon, Tue, Thur-Sat; 3pm Sun.*
Westminster Cathedral *42 Francis Street, SW1P 1QW (7798 9055, www.westminstercathedral. org.uk). 5pm Mon-Fri.*

678

Gaze up at the UK's biggest work of art

Towering over the Olympic Park, Turner Prize-winning sculptor Anish Kapoor's 115m-high ArcelorMittal Orbit will be the tallest sculpture in the UK. Made from one continuous loop of steel, the dramatic, coiling design, which incorporates the five Olympic Rings, has been compared to a rollercoaster. When it's complete, you'll be able to see it from across town – and the viewing platforms will offer a panoramic perspective of the city. It will remain in the Olympic Park after the 2012 Games, as a key part of the Legacy – London's answer to the Eiffel Tower, if you will.

679-687

Take a taxidermic tour of London

You can spot some extraordinary – and ancient – examples of the taxidermist's art around London: here are a few that have caught our eye.

Athena the Owl

The Lady with the Lamp was partial to unusual pets – among them two chameleons, a cicada and a pair of tortoises. Perhaps her favourite, though, was an owlet named Athena, who habitually travelled in her pocket. When Athena died in 1854, Florence Nightingale delayed her departure to the Crimea to get the 'poor little beastie' embalmed; the bird's remains are now one of the highlights of the Florence Nightingale Museum.

Florence Nightingale Museum *2 Lambeth Palace Road, SE1 7EW (7620 0374, www. florence-nightingale.co.uk).*

Bulldog, Les Trois Garçons

Numerous antique specimans lurk among the high-camp interior of this east London eaterie. Most are bedecked with costume jewels – not least the winged, tiara-wearing bulldog. Despite such surface frivolity, food is taken seriously, with polished renditions of classical French cuisine.

Les Trois Garçons *1 Club Road, E1 6JX (7613 1924, www.lestroisgarcons.com).*

The Duchess of Richmond's parrot

Amid the ecclesiastical treasures of Westminster Abbey Museum, a 310-year-old African grey parrot comes as an unexpected find. You'll find him perched next to a life-sized wax effigy of his former mistress, Frances Teresa Stuart, Duchess of Richmond and Lennox. The two were boon companions for 40 years; it's said the faithful bird died just four days after his mistress.

Westminster Abbey Museum *20 Deans Yard, SW1P 3PA (7222 5152, www.westminster-abbey.org).*

Get Stuffed

You'll generally find a couple of passers-by transfixed by this Essex Road emporium, noses pressed to the glass. Although the shop is open by appointment only, the window display is a sight to behold, brimming with antique birds and beasts: stop for a look and you'll find a host of glassy eyes staring back at you.

Get Stuffed *103 Essex Road, N1 2SL (7226 1384, www.thegetstuffed.co.uk).*

The Grant Museum's moles

A venerable repository of zoological specimens, founded in 1827, the Grant Museum's collections take in skeletons, mounted animals and embalmed remains. While many of its exhibits are memorable, the baby moles are particularly poignant – crammed into a jar, their paws pressed against the glass.

Grant Museum *21 University Street, WC1 E6DE (3108 2052, www.ucl.ac.uk/museums/zoology).*

Guy the Gorilla

Guy arrived at London Zoo in 1947, holding tight to his hot-water bottle, and became a sensation. A gentle giant, with a neck circumference of almost a metre, he died in 1978; now, he has become a posthumous crowd-puller at the Natural History Museum. He sometimes appears in temporary exhibitions, so enquire at the front desk for his current whereabouts.

Natural History Museum *Cromwell Road, SW7 5BD (7942 5011, www.nhm.ac.uk).*

Bulldog, Les Trois Garçons

The Horniman's walrus

Of this anthropological museum's menagerie, the standout has to be the walrus. Back in the 1870s, little was known about walrus anatomy – and instead of leaving the skin to hang in folds, the over-zealous taxidermist stuffed it to the hilt, resulting in a strangely smooth, oversized beast.
The Horniman Museum *100 London Road, SE23 3PQ (8699 1872, www.horniman.ac.uk).*

The Lord's sparrow

Amid the cricket kits, busts of great batsmen and assorted memorabilia of the museum at Lord's is a stuffed sparrow, attached to the ball that killed it. It dates back to July 1936, when the match took place: the fatal ball was struck by Jehangir Khan, as a small plaque relates.
MCC Cricket Museum *St John's Wood Road, NW8 8QN (7616 8595, www.lords.org).*

The Zetter Townhouse's cat

The decor at this Clerkenwell hotel and cocktail lounge is a visual feast of rich fabrics and colours, with some unusual finishing touches. The lounge is home to a crinoline-wearing cat; peek into the private dining room to see the stuffed kangaroo.
The Zetter *49-50 St John's Square, EC1M 5RJ (7324 4545, www.thezettertownhouse.com).*

688
Take tea in the Long Room at Lord's

Cricket and afternoon tea go together like, well, leather thwacking against willow – and you can now take tea in Lord's historic Pavilion Long Room on irregular dates through the year. Tea costs £38 (£47 with champagne) and includes a blazer-busting array of neat finger sandwiches, jam-and-cream filled scones and dainties from the ground's pâtissier, Thierry Besselievre, served to the soothing accompaniment of a string quartet.

The Long Room is hung with evocative cricketing paintings, but most eyes will be drawn to the views over the verdant green outfield of cricket's spiritual home. A tour of the Lord's Museum (usually £15) is part of the entertainment. You'll need to book ahead: last year's inaugural tea sold out in 24 hours.
Lord's Cricket Ground *St John's Wood Road, NW8 8QN (7432 1000, www.lords.org).*

A few of my favourite things

689-695

Sebastian Coe
Olympian & Chair of the London 2012 Organising Committee

I've been a lifelong Chelsea Football Club supporter, so for years the Shed End of Stamford Bridge (Fulham Road, SW6 1HS, 0871 984 1955, www.chelseafc.com) has been my home on match days. Recent seasons have seen great successes – though I try to tell my children that despite this, winning the double is not a regular occurrence. I was there for the 27 years between winning FA Cups, so it's great to be back to winning ways.

While on the topic of Stamford Bridge, it would be wrong of me not to mention L'Antico (564 Kings Road, SW6 2DY, 7371 9536), a family-run Italian café a short walk from the ground. It's perfect for a quick bite to eat or post-match drink. I was born in Chiswick and my grandparents and father were brought up in Fulham, so I feel very at home in the area. It seems that the penne all'arrabiata is a lucky dish as when I eat it, Chelsea always win.

Throughout my athletics career, hill training was an integral part of conditioning, and I spent many hours running up and down Richmond Hill (www.visitrichmond.co.uk) working on my speed, strength and fitness. Despite the exertions, it was the view that made it that little bit more bearable. Many artists and writers have been inspired by its beauty; it appears in a Sir Walter Scott novel and has a mention in a Wordsworth sonnet. Whether I'm at a flat-out pace at 6am or with the family for a Sunday stroll, the views are breathtaking.

The sheer size and scale of the Turbine Hall at Tate Modern (Park Street, Bankside, SE1 9TG, 7887 8888, www.tate.org.uk/modern) always fills me with awe. I am honoured that we will be taking a London 2012-inspired installation there as part of the London 2012 Festival, the finale of the summer's Cultural Olympiad. All we know about British-born artist Tino Sehgal's commission for the space is that it will involve conversation, dance, sound, movement and debate. His work always engages with people, and I can't wait to join the thousands who will visit the Hall to participate. We wanted the Cultural Olympiad to celebrate Pierre de Coubertin's original vision of a global Olympic movement combining sport, culture and education, and I think we have achieved that.

The 606 Club (90 Lots Road, SW10 0QD, 7352 5953, www.606club.co.uk) is, for me, the best jazz club east of Greenwich Village. Jazz has been a lifelong passion, and their regular line-up supports the growth of the local scene, giving British-based musicians the opportunity to showcase their talents. If you're lucky you'll find yourself in the midst of an informal jam session.

I have many fond memories of days spent watching Test matches at Lord's Cricket Ground (St John's Wood Road NW8 8QN, 7432 1000, www.lords.org). Lovingly referred to as the 'home of cricket', Lord's is steeped in history. You don't even need the excuse of a match to draw you there; the MCC Museum, the oldest sports museum in the world, contains an absolutely amazing collection of cricket memorabilia. What makes the venue even more special for 2012 is that we will be using it as a backdrop for the Olympic Games Archery competition.

The capital's ethnic and religious diversity was key to helping us win the hosting bid. When the IOC Coordination Commission came to see our progress on delivering the Games, we took them to the Brady Centre (192-196 Hanbury Street, E1 5HU, 7364 7900, www.towerhamletsarts.org.uk) in Banglatown. Rather than going to one Brick Lane curry house, we got together lots of different chefs and showcased the area's cuisine in one place. The Centre serves the community by providing art courses and workshops, including dance, drama, music and singing.

696
Enjoy global sounds by the Thames

On 26 July 2012, the eve of the Opening Ceremony, the London 2012 Festival will culminate in the River of Music (www.london2012.com/music). Some 500,000 spectators are expected to attend free gigs and performances at key sites along the Thames, with a series of open-air stages devoted to different continents.

697-703
Take a curry tour

Curry is often cited as the UK's national dish, but most of us are oblivious to the difference between the subcontinent's many and dramatically varied cuisines. Fortunately, London is home to some fine exponents of most of the major styles.

Bangladeshi
Much of what we think of as 'Indian' food is in fact a colonial pastiche of Bangladeshi dishes. Real Bangladeshi cooking is less immediately appealing to Brits, perhaps because it's fish-heavy and quite plain. Best for sampling it in the raw is to wander down Brick Lane, E1, and look for basic cafés and sweet shops, with menus written in Bengali, serving locals. Gram Bangla (no.68, E1 6RL, 7377 6116) was the first.

Gujarati
Crispy street snacks such as bhel poori and bhajis are native to Gujarat. A great place to try them is the utilitarian Sakonis (129 Ealing Road, Middx HA0 4BP, 8903 1058, www.sakonis.co.uk) in Wembley.

Modern
At the Cinnamon Club (Old Westminster Library, 30-32 Great Smith Street, SW1P 3BU, 7222 2555, www.cinnamonclub.com), Vivek Singh and Hari Nagaraj evolve Indian flavours into innovative dishes using contemporary haute-cuisine techniques and presentation.

North Indian
You'll find dishes originating in north India (tandooris, kofta, korma and biriani) ubiquitous on pan-Indian menus, but the upmarket Red Fort (77 Dean Street, W1D 3SH, 7437 2525, www.

redfort.co.uk) specialises in in the cuisine of the Mughal empire, which at one time had its capital in Delhi. Prices are high, but so's the quality.

Pakistani
Pakistani cooking is diverse and overlaps to a degree with North Indian. Typical are the earthy dahls, fiery Punjabi meat curries, seekh kebabs and fluffy breads served at Tayyabs (83-89 Fieldgate Street, E1 1JU, 7247 9543, www.tayyabs.co.uk). This BYO grill and canteen has a huge following, so best go off-peak.

Pan-Indian
This term is self-explanatory, and covers the menus of most non-denominational curryhouses. We've included it here as a way of mentioning Dishoom (12 Upper St Martin's Lane, WC2H 9FB, 7420 9320, www.dishoom.com), which bases its style on Mumbai's cheap, cosmopolitan 'Irani' cafés. Its diverse menu includes standards and happy surprises: chilli cheese toast is a standout.

South Indian
South Indian cooking is largely vegetarian, with lots of gently spiced potato and pulses, plus dosa pancakes – usually made from fermented rice and lentil batter. Near Euston station, Drummond Street is good for dosas; for Keralan specialities and fish, try Rasa Samudra (5 Charlotte Street, W1T 1RE, 7637 0222, www.rasarestaurants.com).

Tayyabs

704-708

Attend a village fête

There's nothing quite like a village fête – sipping warm beer in the sunshine, taking a punt on the tombola and browsing trestle tables of home-made cakes, dog-eared books and illegibly labelled jams. Happily, you can sample these pleasures without leaving the city; look out for posters touting smaller events, or head for one of the following shindigs.

Primrose Hill's May fête (Primrose Hill Road, NW1 3NA) is an upmarket take on tradition, with rides, face-painting, stalls and some decidedly superior raffle prizes and auction lots; see www.primrosehillca.org.uk for details. Well-heeled Marylebone Village also closes its streets to traffic for an annual Summer Fayre (Marylebone High Street, W1U 5HD, www.marylebonesummerfayre.com) – more like a mini festival, where different zones offer music, food, dance, children's activities and more. In late September, meanwhile, the Bermondsey Street Festival (www.bermondseystreetfestival.org.uk) is a truly 21st-century fête, mixing craft stalls, hog roasts, dog shows and maypole dancing with contemporary music and fashion (the festival's patron is Zandra Rhodes). Far smaller in scale is the delightful Alma Street Summer Fair, held in the backstreets of Kentish Town in July. On the appointed Sunday afternoon, the length of the road is closed to traffic and taken over by gymnastic displays, local bands and stalls selling cakes, plants, beers and bric-a-brac; for details, see www.inkermanresidents.org.uk.

For a more bucolic feel, head for leafy Kew Green and the the Kew Midsummer Fete (Kew Green, Surrey TW9 3AA, www.kewfete.org). A dog show, fairground rides and some 70 stalls featured in 2011; this being Kew, there was a Pimms stall as well as a beer tent.

709

Brush with genius

Labour & Wait is the Spitalfields shop that elevated enamel milk pans, balls of twine and humble household wares into objects of desire. Just above the shop's staircase is the recently installed 'Brush Museum' – a 30-strong collection, amassed on the owners' travels over the past decade. Ponder the ingenious travelling clothes brush-come-coat hanger, admire the skunk-bristled cobweb brush, and consider upgrading your own domestic dustpan and brush.
Labour & Wait *85 Redchurch Street, E2 7DJ (7729 6253, www.labourandwait.co.uk).*

Marylebone Summer Fayre

Proud2

710-719

Dance the night away...

For a while it felt as if the lights had gone out on the capital's big nightclubs, as one by one stalwarts like Turnmills and the End closed their doors. Mercifully, the fortunes of those that remain seem once again to be on the rise, and there are even a few newcomers feeding the fever.

Of the old guard, Fabric (77A Charterhouse Street, EC1M 3HN, 7336 8898, www.fabriclondon. com) remains the standard-bearer: located in a former meatpacking warehouse, its line-ups are as legendary as its queues. Ministry of Sound (103 Gaunt Street, SE1 6DP, 0870 060 0010, www. ministryofsound.com), set in a former bus depot, is possibly the UK's best-known clubbing venue, and continues to lead from the front thanks to long-running Friday trance night, the Gallery.

More alternative is Corsica Studios (Unit 5, Elephant Road, SE17 1LB, 7703 4760, www. corsicastudios.com), an independent arts complex in Elephant & Castle with an innovative array of nights. Meanwhile, Egg (200 York Way, N7 9AX, 7871 7111, www.egglondon.net) caters to house fanatics looking to large it in luxury over three floors, a multi-level garden and a terrace.

Of the newer establishments, Shoreditch's 800-capacity XOYO (32-37 Cowper Street, EC2A 4AP, 7729 5959, www.xoyo.co.uk) lays on cutting-edge nights in association with labels like Kitsuné; Cable (33A Bermondsey Street Tunnel, SE1 3JW, 7403 7730, www.cable-london.com) brings hard-edged dance nights like Basslaced to a moody, under-the-arches location near London Bridge; and Barden's Boudoir has become the Nest (36 Stoke Newington Road, N16 7XJ, 7354 9993, www.ilovethenest.com), a champion of emerging indie and electronic music through nights like Scandalism. On a larger scale, Proud2 (The O2, Peninsula Square, SE10 0DY, 8463 3070, www. proud2.com) is doing a commendable job of filling the enormous boots of 2,600-capacity superclub Matter at the O2 Arena.

Of the smaller clubs that nonetheless make their presence felt, Plastic People (147-149 Curtain Road, EC2A 3QE, 7739 6471, www.plasticpeople. co.uk) and the *Vice* magazine-operated Old Blue Last (38 Great Eastern Street, EC2A 3ES, 7739 7033, www.theoldbluelast.com) offer the most eclectic programming; the former is home to pioneering dubstep and grime night FWD>>, while the latter has hosted shows by everyone from Simian Mobile Disco to Diplo.

720 *... Or start first thing*

Clubbers senior or sensible enough not to want to lose a night's sleep have long opted for Sunday afterparty events that start as the sun rises and run until noon or thereafter. It's not just the extra sleep that helps: there's a notable absence of weekend warriors, reduced door prices and the chance of a good breakfast before the dancing starts. One of the best is Jaded, currently held at Cable (*see left*) between 5am and 1pm on Sundays.

Prospect of Whitby

721-731
Drink in a beer garden

Albion
This Georgian boozer offers traditional charm, terrific food and a walled, wisteria-draped beer garden. Book well ahead.
10 Thornhill Road, N1 1HW
(7607 7450, www.the-albion.co.uk).

Avalon
The alfresco options comprise front and side terraces and, at the rear, a proper garden – huge and beautifully landscaped.
16 Balham Hill, SW12 9EB
(8675 8613, www.theavalonlondon.com).

Crabtree
This riverbank Victorian hostelry has a gorgeous garden, and a terrace overlooking the Thames.
4 Rainville Road, W6 9HA
(7385 3929, www.thecrabtreew6.co.uk).

Dolphin
A formal pattern of box hedges, privet and gravel surround a central water sculpture, edged by apple trees.
121 Sydenham Road, SE26 5HB
(8778 8101, www.thedolphinsydenham.com).

Florence
The beer garden has its own dedicated bar (with taps), a children's 'playroom' and plenty of tables.
133 Dulwich Road, SE24 0NG
(7326 4987, www.florencehernehill.com).

Garden Gate
On the edge of Hampstead Heath, this lively local has an expansive garden and weekend barbecue.
14 South End Road, NW3 2QE (7435 4938, www.thegardengatehampstead.co.uk).

Marlborough
Beyond the decked area and umbrella-shaded tables is a verdant, grassy expanse; the resident rabbits and guinea pigs delight visiting children.
46 Friars Stile Road, TW10 6NQ (8940 8513, www.themarlboroughrichmond.co.uk).

Prospect of Whitby
A scenic beer garden under a huge weeping willow, right beside the Thames.
57 Wapping Wall, E1W 3SH (7481 1095).

Stein's
This leafy, stein-swaying, pretzel-munching Bavarian beer garden is perched right on the riverside in Richmond.
55 Petersham Road, Richmond Towpath, TW10 6UX (8948 8189, www.stein-s.com).

Swan
The Swan's lush, sun-dappled garden has 30 tables, and is set in the heart of Chiswick.
Evershed Walk, 119 Acton Lane, W4 5HH (8994 8262, www.theswanchiswick.co.uk).

Windsor Castle
This ivy-clad walled garden is an inviting spot to sample some well-kept real ales and ciders.
114 Campden Hill Road, W8 7AR (7243 8797, www.thewindsorcastlekensington.co.uk).

732 *Seek out the pagan heart of the City*

Set low in the wall of the Bank of China, opposite Cannon Street Station, is a strange glass case, protected by an ornate wrought-iron grille. It contains the bare stump of a stone reputed to be a pagan menhir that once stood at the centre of the Roman city, from which all measurements in the land were taken. It's said that if the stone ever leaves London, the city will fall.

733
Discover a shrine to Super-8

The signs in the windows of Umit & Son (35 Lower Clapton Road, E5 0LN, 8985 1766) should give some idea of the bias of its 'completely film-nuts' owner, Umit Mesut, with customers warned 'THIS IS SUPER 8, NOT VIDEO OR DVD RUBBISH' and 'SUPER 8 IS SILVER, DIGITAL IS RUST!' Inside, the walls are stacked high with Super-8 and Super-16 reels, a mix of old, classic, cult and blockbuster films, from *Bond* to *Teen Wolf*. You can buy collectors' projectors, cameras and the films themselves – ranging in price from £50 to £1,000-plus. If you fancy hosting a private screening, Umit will come round with a projector and screen for a very reasonable £200 all-in.

734
Appreciate an LP

In this age of iPod playlists, impulse-buy downloads and music on the move, listening to an album from beginning to end, paying it proper attention, is something of a lost art. Classic Album Sundays (www.classicalbumsundays.tumblr.com) aims to change all that, meeting at the Hanbury Arms in Islington (33 Linton Street, N1 7DU, 7288 2222) to stage weekly listening sessions devoted to classic albums (Love's *Forever Changes*, Bob Marley's *Exodus*). Albums are played on vinyl, with no phones, talking or texting allowed; instead, the assembled audiophiles listen to the record in its entirety, then discuss it in the bar afterwards.

735
Watch pomp and pageantry on the Mall

Taking place on the second Saturday in June, Trooping the Colour celebrates the sovereign's official birthday, and is perhaps the most spectacular of London's archaic annual traditions. It's a spectacular sight, with foot guards and mounted cavalry, military bands, gun salutes and a Royal Air Force fly-past. Join the crowds lining the Mall, or apply to the ticket ballot in January or February for a seat in the stands; call 7414 2479 for details of how to apply.

736-739
Pitch your tent

To dip into the camping craze without a costly trip, pitch up at one of the campsites that lie within the Oystercard zone. They can't compete with a Devon cliffside or Suffolk field in terms of scenery, it's true, but still afford a chance to breathe some fresh air and sleep under the stars.

On the fringes of Epping Forest are Debden House (8508 3008, www.debdenhouse.com), a Newham Council operation with a shop, laundry, fire field, farm animals and play areas, and the family-run Elms (8502 5652, www.theelms campsite.co.uk), provided with log cabins, Wi-Fi internet and a handy pub. Lee Valley Park (8803 6900, 8529 5689, www.leevalleypark.org.uk) runs two sites at Edmonton and Sewardstone, both with snug woodland cabins, two-person 'cocoons' and easy access to the greenery and sports facilities of the park.

That's pretty much it for legal camping opportunities – except during Wimbledon (www.wimbledon.com), when diehard tennis fans are permitted to put up their tents in Wimbledon Park in a ticketed queuing system, rather than pitching on the pavement.

740-741
Watch a film in peace

Rustling sweet wrappers, the bovine chomp of popcorn addicts, smooching teens and the disgruntled tutting of everyone else will all be distant memories when you attend a Silent Cinema (www.silent-cinema.co.uk) screening. Thanks to the wireless headphones, you can immerse yourself completely in the film – or nip to the loo without missing out on the action. Events take place sporadically, in unusual venues all over town, so check the website for the latest.

Wireless headphones are also a feature at the Rooftop Film Club, perched above the Queen of Hoxton pub (1-5 Curtain Road, EC2A 3JX, 7422 0958, www.rooftopfilmclub.com). In its inaugural season in summer 2011, sell-out screenings ran from *Scarface* to *Spinal Tap*.

Up the creek

Elizabeth Winding **wades in to an unusual urban oasis.**

Set on an unremarkable south-east London street, the entrance to Deptford Creekside Centre comes as something of a surprise. Reeds, butterflies and sycamore spinners lend a fairytale feel to its high steel gates; beyond them, the centre itself is a handsome wooden eco-build, with sheep's wool insulation and a wildlife-friendly brown roof. Inside and out, wooden shelves are stacked with a Womble-ish assortment of treasures fished from the creek's muddy depths: mobile phones, china tea cups, old shoes, stopped watches and even a forlorn-looking typewriter, with gravel and moss wedged between its keys.

Other finds have been incorporated into the centre's design. A flock of antiquated shopping trolleys rescued from the river have been beautified with spring bulbs, while fences made from old railway sleepers line the garden's wooden walkways. To the rear of the building, a meandering, wildflower-lined path leads down to the creek – which is exactly where we're heading.

Inconspicuous from street level, this half-mile tidal stretch of the River Ravensbourne, which flows into the Thames at Greenwich Reach, is rich in history and wildlife – and the Centre's speciality is two-hour, low-tide 'expeditions' along its bed. Our leader is Nick Bertrand – an affable chap with a biblical beard, and an expert raconteur. Before venturing in, he kits us out with the necessary gear: thigh-high waders (wear thick socks and old jeans), long wooden poles and, for drizzly days like today, a rail of ancient yellow oilskins, in various states of disrepair.

Once we're in the creek, the pole comes into its own: for balance, testing the way ahead, and prodding the viscous, treacherous expanse of mud that lines the river. It's perfectly easy to avoid sinking into the mudflats, if you follow Nick's instructions, although he has had to fish the odd malefactor out over the years – no surprise that it's mostly boys. 'If they're really stuck I have to pull them out, put them down in the river and then go back and pull their waders out,' he says cheerfully. 'It's a messy, wet experience.'

Messy and wet is just how most of the creek's inhabitants like it, though. Seen up close, it is teeming with life, from the self-seeded wildflowers growing in nooks on the walls to dragonflies, crabs, grey wagtails and the odd kingfisher.

Nick has come equipped with a net and tray, and our muddy sweeps through the water turn up flounders, wriggling goby and tiny, translucent gammarus shrimp.

Along the way, we also discover all manner of flotsam and jetsam, from discarded Chinese mitten-crab carapaces to shards of willoware pottery, half buried in mud. Another find is a cache of weighty old ships' nails, discarded by boat-breakers working along the creek. From 1513 until the mid 19th century, Deptford was home to the Royal Naval Dockyard, founded by Henry VIII – but its days were numbered when the river silted up and newfangled iron ships began to replace wooden ones. The site then became the City of London's foreign cattle market and slaughterhouse, which means fragments of bone are another common find. That's about as sinister as our discoveries get for today – although some years ago, the bomb squad had to be summoned when one group found an unexploded shell.

We also spot the odd shopping trolley, jutting out of the water and festooned with weed. Unexpectedly, it turns out that they have a beneficial effect on wildlife – in moderation, at least. Over the centuries, the creek has grown narrower and the sides steeper, which means there are no reed beds or wildlife-accommodating crevices. 'By accumulating leaves and debris, the trolleys create places where invertebrates and small fish can hide,' says Nick. 'We've tried putting in alternative features, such as bundles of branches, but shopping trolleys are hard to beat.'

Looking up from the creek's depths, meanwhile, affords a novel perspective on London. On one bank stands Joseph Bazalgette's 19th-century pumping station, hidden behind a grandly Italianate façade, while Herzog & de Meuron's Laban Dance Centre, built in 2003, is a more glamorous newcomer, its translucent, colour-washed cladding shimmering in the sunshine.

The skyline is also bisected by cranes: in recent years, Deptford has been earmarked as a prime site for new residential housing. Along with the impact of shading from tall buildings, light pollution and increased levels of disturbance, says Nick, the big worry is the developers' 'overwhelming urge to tidy everything up'. With that in mind, best get down here while you can, to celebrate the Creek's shopping trolleys, wildlife and fecund disarray.

Creekside Centre *14 Creekside, SE8 4SA (8692 9922, www.creeksidecentre.org.uk). Walks are seasonal, and must be booked in advance.*

743-748

Sew your own

City Lit

This adult education centre has a huge variety of modestly priced courses – including textiles courses for beginners, novices and experts. After the three-week intensive course (£160) you'll be a whizz on the Bernina, and able to tackle zips, seams, waist facings and hems.

Venues and prices vary (7831 7831, www.citylit.ac.uk).

Hackney City Farm

The good people of Hackney City Farm offer a wholesome range of life skills courses, from soap making to chicken rearing. Keep an eye on the website, as clothes making and adapting often crops up – the idea being to re-imagine old clothes in new ways, rather than lobbing them in landfill. Courses are basic but very cheap, and the classes are held at various venues around Hackney.

1A Goldsmiths Row, E2 8QA (7729 6381, www.hackneycityfarm.co.uk).

Homemade London

Located on a dapper little street in Mayfair, Homemade London run short textiles courses with a simple premise: take along some fabric and a pattern you like, and they'll teach you to follow it. They also offer a rolling programme of crafty activities, from perfume-making to book binding. Classes are fun and sociable, and you can sip a glass of wine while you stitch. Courses cost from £10 per hour.

21 Seymour Place, Portman Village, W1H 5BH (8616 0771, www.homemadelondon.com).

The Make Lounge

The Make Lounge hosts champagne-fuelled workshops and parties where ladies (and the occasional gent) gather to learn how to sew, make or adapt clothes. Whether you're a novice who can't thread a needle, or a long out of practice machinist, there is a class to suit – not least the three-and-a-half-hour Knockout Knickers session (£59).

49-51 Barnsbury Street, N1 1TP (7609 0275, www.themakelounge.com).

The Make Lounge

Our Patterned Hand

This haberdashery shop on Broadway Market has a downstairs workshop, where you can learn what to do with all the rolls of fabric and ribbons up on the shop floor, following basic patterns or copying pieces of clothing you've brought in. Courses run from three-hour Saturday morning sessions (from £40) to six-week stints (£225) consisting of weekly three-hour tutorials in small groups – in hours friendly to those with full-time jobs.

49 Broadway Market, E8 4PH (7812 9912, www.ourpatternedhand.co.uk).

The Papered Parlour

The Parlour's one-day dressmaking course promises to turn butter-fingered beginners into domestic sewing goddesses; you can bring your own machine, or borrow one of the vintage Singers. Sessions are geared towards revamping and altering old clothes, and a recuperative afternoon tea is included in the price (£77.50).

7 Prescott Place, SW4 6BS (7627 8703, www.thepaperedparlour.co.uk).

749-751
Be in a TV audience

See TV and radio shows for free by offering your services as an audience member at shows filmed around London. Try www.sroaudiences.com for a good range of comedy shows (*Mock the Week, Live at the Apollo, 8 out of 10 Cats*); for more of a starring role, you can apply to be a contestant on various quiz shows. Alternatively, highlights of the line-up at www.applausestore.com include Stephen Fry's know-it-all quiz *QI*, and, for music buffs, *Never Mind the Buzzcocks*. There are also some choice pickings to be had at www.bbc.co.uk/tickets, whose radio and TV offerings range from *Just a Minute* to *The Now Show*.

752
Star in a Sunday Shoot

Every Sunday, photographer Seamus Ryan opens up his Columbia Road Studio from 11am to 2pm, and takes a portrait of anyone who wanders in – from bemused-looking Yorkshire terriers and kids in Superman capes to tattooed gents, pregnant ladies and loved-up couples. The project has been running since 2006, with Ryan announcing the week's theme on his website the Friday before – 'Windswept and Interesting', perhaps, or 'Mugshots' (shot in profile and front on, with a board proclaiming the holder to be GUILTY OF SOMETHING). One Sunday Tom Stoppard wandered in, and the shot was later purchased by the National Portrait Gallery. Each volunteer gets four or five shots, which are posted up in the online gallery; if you like the results, you can buy an A4 print for £45. And if Ryan likes the results, you could end up with the ultimate accolade: a place in his professional portfolio.
Sunday Shoots *7 Ezra Street, E2 7RH (7613 1560, www.sundayshoots.com).*

753
Meet Bompas & Parr

London-based duo Bompas & Parr are culinary creatives of the first order – think Willy Wonka, with a dash of Heston Blumenthal. Their past flights of fancy have run from a breathable cloud of gin and tonic to 'scratch and sniff' cinema and a walk-through chocolate waterfall. Their forte, however, are resplendent jellies – quivering things of beauty, sculpted into all sorts of outré shapes. While some events are privately commissioned, others are open to the public: www.jellymongers.co.uk has details of the duo's latest schemes.

754
Snap up a London 2012 Games souvenir

If you want something to help you remember the 2012 Games, browse the shelves at an official London 2012 Shop (http://shop.london2012.com). Perhaps the handiest is the stand-alone shop in St Pancras International station (Pancras Road, NW1 2QP, 7837 8558), but there are also outlets at Paddington station, Stansted Airport and airside at Heathrow's Terminals 3 and 5. Further London 2012 Shops are to be found in the John Lewis stores on Oxford Street (300 Oxford Street, W1A 1EX, 7629 7711, www.johnlewis.com) and in Stratford City Shopping Centre. You'll find everything from collectable pin badges, mugs and die-cast models of double-decker buses to Stella McCartney-designed sportswear.

755-770
See London through Hogarth's eyes

Born in 1697, artist William Hogarth became synonymous with the seedy side of London life, thanks to his paintings and engravings of its slums, drinking dens and debauchery.

His birthplace on Bartholomew Close is hidden in the now rather undistinguished alleys to the east of Smithfield Market, but he was baptised in the wonderfully atmospheric St Bartholomew-the-Great (West Smithfield, EC1A 9DS, 7606 5171, www.greatstbarts.com). If you're in the area on Friday, grab a place on one of the 2pm tours from the Museum of St Bartholomew's Hospital (North Wing, St Bartholomew's Hospital, EC1A 7BE, 3465 5798, www.barts andthelondon.nhs.uk/museums) to see the two huge pictures of Bible stories he donated to the hospital, gazumping a Venetian painter the hospital had planned to pay to do the same work.

On the other side of the market, the refurbished Museum of the Order of St John (St John's Gate, St John's Lane, EC1M 4DA, 7324 4005, www.museumstjohn.org.uk) was once a coffee house run by Hogarth's father.

Further west, Sir John Soane's Museum (13 Lincoln's Inn Fields, WC2A 3BP, 7405 2107, www.soane.org) has several Hogarths among its eccentric holdings: the paintings of *A Rake's Progress* (1733) and *An Election* (1754-5) are scabrous masterpieces. You're now close to Dr Johnson's House (17 Gough Square, EC4A 3DE, 7353 3745, www.dr johnsonshouse.org), a fine example of a residential Georgian house – and, given Johnson's intellectual milieu, possibly visited by Hogarth. The artist's relationship with the Foundling Museum (40 Brunswick Square, WC1N 1AZ, 7841 3600, www.foundling museum.org.uk) is more certain. In his role as a governor of Captain Thomas Coram's Foundling Hospital, Hogarth not only designed the coat of arms, but also established – as a fundraising wheeze – Britain's first permanent art collection here, gathering work from such masters as Gainsborough and Reynolds. The museum's displays also include Hogarth's portrait of Coram and the *March of the Guards to Finchley*.

One of Hogarth's most notorious works is *Gin Lane* – a vigorously grotesque engraving, issued in 1751. The picture is set in St Giles (the area where Centre Point now stands) and the weird ziggurat-shaped steeple in the background is no invention: it still adorns St George's Bloomsbury (Bloomsbury Way, WC1A 2HR, 7242 1979, www.stgeorges bloomsbury.org.uk). The print is among the holdings of the British Museum (Great Russell Street, WC1B 3DG, 7323 8299, www.britishmuseum.org), but is rarely out on display.

Head instead to Room 46 (Europe 1400-1800), which contains Hogarth's gold ticket for lifelong admission to the music, dancing and illicit liaisons of Vauxhall Pleasure Gardens. Downstairs at the Museum of London (150 London Wall, EC2Y 5HN, 7001 9844, www.museumoflondon.org.uk) you can stroll through a reconstruction of the selfsame Pleasure Gardens – given a playful twist with

Philip Treacy hats popped on to mannequins in 18th-century gowns. Other stunning exhibits from the period include the golden Lord Mayor's Coach, built in 1757, and a cell salvaged from the debtors' prison that used to stand on Wellclose Square.

In the background of *Gin Lane*'s less well-known counterpart, the contrastingly cheerful and orderly *Beer Street*, you can see the steeple of St Martin-in-the-Fields (Trafalgar Square, WC2N 4JJ, 7766 1100, www.smitf.org) – where a candle-lit concert of Handel or Bach will provide beautiful musical context. This is another corner of London rich in Hogarthian connections.

The artist was apprenticed at a house now buried under the substantial foundations of the Royal Opera House, and had studios on Leicester Square. Ignored by the masses who congregate at the Chaplin statue in the middle of the square, Hogarth's bust (in one corner) has much more right to be here.

South of the square, the National Gallery (Trafalgar Square, WC2N 5DN, 7747 2885, www.nationalgallery.org.uk) has several of Hogarth's works: the *Marriage A-la-Mode* sequence (c1743) and a salty-fresh, lively *Shrimp Girl* (c1740-5) are in Room 35.

Next door, in the National Portrait Gallery (St Martin's Place, WC2H OHE, 7306 0055, www.npg.org.uk), check out the portrait of Hogarth attributed to Jean André Rouquet (c1740-45; Room 11) and a later self-portrait (c1757; Room 10). Perhaps the most famous depiction of Hogarth, though, is another self-portrait. *The Painter & his Pug* (1745) is on display at Tate Britain (Millbank, SW1P 4RG, 7887 8888, www.tate.org.uk) in the room of British Art: 1550-1880; both man and dog have a certain pugnacious set to their jaw.

Two final destinations are in Chiswick. The artist's summer retreat, Hogarth's House (Hogarth Lane, Great West Road, W4 2QN, 8994 6757, www.hounslow.info/arts/hogarthshouse), should reopen to the public by late 2011. When it does, you'll be able to see the best permanent display of his engravings – and the mulberry tree he used to sit beneath.

Nearby, the graveyard of St Nicholas Chiswick (Church Street, W4 2PH, 8995 7876, www.stnicholaschiswick.org) contains the tomb of Hogarth and his wife; look on the south side of the church. Hogarth was buried here in 1764, acknowledged by his epitaph – written by the actor David Garrick – as the 'great Painter of Mankind'.

Be quick on the draw at the Cartoon Museum

From satirical swipes by the likes of Steve Bell and Ralph Steadman to classic *Desperate Dan* strips, the Cartoon Museum is the capital's reliquary of classic British cartoon art. If you're inspired to put pen to paper, hands-on events run from cartooning masterclasses to monthly family fun days, when artists of all ages can spend the day drawing alongside the museum's cartoonist in residence. The school holiday programme of animation and cartooning workshops is also superb; past sessions have included creating your own superhero, making manga T-shirts and producing a mini-comic, all under the tutelage of a master draughtsman.

Cartoon Museum *35 Little Russell Street, WC1A 2HH (7580 8155, www.cartoonmuseum.org).*

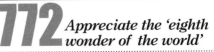

Appreciate the 'eighth wonder of the world'

One of Victorian engineer Isambard Kingdom Brunel's most impressive feats is buried below the Thames. Catch a train from Wapping to Rotherhithe – part of the underground section of the Overground line – and you'll be passing through the world's first tunnel built beneath a river. It opened in 1843 to great fanfare, and was dubbed the 'eighth wonder of the world': although it was never used for carriages, as intended, the gas-lit tunnel was lined with shops and entertainers, 'from Egyptian necromancers and fortune-tellers to dancing monkeys', according to one visitor. Alas, these exotic pleasures came to an end in the 1860s, when it was bought by a railway consortium.

Rotherhithe's little Brunel Museum (Brunel Engine House, Railway Avenue, SE16 4LF, 7231 3840, www.brunel-museum.org.uk) tells the extraordinary tale of technological innovation and perseverance that lies behind the tunnel's construction. You can visit the Grand Entrance Hall as part of a weekly guided walk from Bermondsey station (6.15pm Tue), and tunnel tours on floodlit trains are currently being negotiated with Transport for London.

Mahiki

773–777

Set your watch to Tiki time

The modern tiki culture of Hawaiian shirts and hula girls took shape after World War II, when GIs returned home from the South Pacific with memories of beach shacks, rum and beautiful women. In London, it reached the height of fashion in the '60s – the Beachcomber bar at the Mayfair Hotel was a glamorous celebrity haunt – before falling from favour with all but the staunchest of fans.

Now, a rise in rum drinking is putting tiki back on the radar. The kitsch Trailer Happiness (177 Portobello Road, W11 2DY, 7065 6821, www.trailerhappiness.com) has been a hit in Notting Hill; South London Pacific (340 Kennington Road, SE11 4LD, 7820 9189, www.southlondonpacific.com) is teaching Kennington to embrace the Hawaiian shirt; and Kanaloa (18 Lime Office Court, Hill House, Shoe Lane, EC4A 3BQ, 7842 0620, www.kanaloaclub.com) is persuading city types to lighten up with its heady rum cocktails and outré interior. For the chance of spotting a tipsy young royal over your pina colada, head for Mahiki (1 Dover Street, W1S 4LD, 7493 9529,

www.mahiki.com) – a mock Polynesian palace in Mayfair that draws a monied crowd. For a flashback to the scene's 1960s heyday, though, there's only one address: the inimitable Trader Vic's (London Hilton, Park Lane, W1K 1BE, 7208 4113, www.tradervicslondon.com), which has been plying cocktails and kitsch from the Park Lane Hilton's basement since 1963.

778

See a temporary architectural icon

With its thought-provoking exhibitions of modern and contemporary art, the Serpentine Gallery (Kensington Gardens, W2 3XA, 7402 6075, www.serpentinegallery.org) has long been a great pit-stop on a leisurely stroll around Hyde Park. The annual highlight, though, is the annual pavilion commission. Each year, a high-profile architect or designer is asked to design a pavilion, which then occupies the gallery's lawns for the summer. From Jean Nouvel's edgy, bright red design (2010) to Swiss architect Peter Zumthor's quietly contemplative secret garden (2011), the results are always surprising.

779

Experience dawn from the sky

Adventure Balloons (01252 844222, www. adventureballoons.co.uk) operate hour-long hot air balloon flights from a number of London take-off sites, affording spirit-soaring views across the capital. Air traffic restrictions mean that flights can only take place at dawn, on weekdays between late April and the middle of August. Flights are also reliant on suitable weather conditions; see the website for details.

780-784

Place your bid

If you're not already an initiate, you'll find the world of auctions revelatory. There's the serendipitous excitement of going to a viewing, the tension of the auction itself, and (hopefully) the satisfaction of snaffling a unique piece at an advantageous price. Even if you don't intend to buy, the viewings at Bonhams, Christie's and Sotheby's can be on a par with major gallery shows – and even here there are some eclectic smaller items you might have the funds for, especially if no one else is interested.

The golden rule is to set yourself a maximum price and stick by it rather than getting carried away by the bidding. The adrenaline will pump when your lot comes up, but the general mood (unless there's a Van Gogh under the hammer) is very civilised, even workaday.

Make sure you know the etiquette: some houses will give you a paddle to bid with, and all require you to register in advance. But don't worry about accidentally purchasing a Picasso with a cough: auctioneers will always check the intention of an ambiguous gesture. If you simply don't trust yourself, put in an advance bid; the same goes if you can't attend in person (the catalogues are generally online).

Bonhams
*101 New Bond Street, W1S 1SR
(7447 7447, www.bonhams.com).*

Christie's
*85 Old Brompton Road, SW7 3LD
(7930 6074, www.christies.com).*

Criterion Auctions
*41-47 Chatfield Road, SW11 3SE (7228 5563,
www.criterionauctions.co.uk); 53 Essex Road,
N1 2SF (7359 5707).*

Lots Road Auctions
*71 Lots Road, SW10 0RN (7376 6800,
www.lotsroad.com).*

Sotheby's
*34-35 New Bond Street, W1A 2AA
(7293 5000, www.sothebys.com).*

785-805
Whoop it up in the city's best playgrounds

**Diana, Princess of Wales'
Memorial Playground**

Sometimes children want something a bit more exciting than a set of swings and a slide – and the following playgrounds exercise the imagination as well as the body.

The grandaddy of them all is the seven-acre Coram's Fields (93 Guilford Street, WC1N 1DN, 7837 6138, www.coramsfields.org). In a neat reversal of normal rules, adults are only allowed in when accompanied by a child: beyond its gates lie an enormous sandpit, a small farm area, climbing frames, slides, swings and a zip wire.

Perhaps London's best-known playground, though, is Diana, Princess of Wales' Memorial Playground (Broad Walk, Kensington Gardens, W8 2UH, 7298 2117, www.royalparks.org.uk). A huge pirate ship on its own beach takes centre stage; beyond it are three wigwams and a tree-house encampment with walkways, ladders, slides and 'tree phones'.

Over in Regent's Park (7298 2117, www.royalparks.org.uk), the most interesting play area is at Hanover Gate. In 2010, a new timber treehouse area was built within a large sandpit, by the boating lake and traditional playground. North of here, Parliament Hill sports a state-of-the-art playground (Parliament Hill, Highgate Road, NW5 1QR, 7433 1917, www.cityoflondon.gov.uk) with challenging equipment and a huge paddling pool.

The excellent playground in Highgate Woods (Muswell Hill Road, N10 3JN, 8444 6129, www.cityoflondon.gov.uk) sports all the old favourites, including a zip wire, swings and sandpit. For a 21st century take on play, head for the architect-designed Kilburn Grange Park (Messina Avenue, NW6 4LD, 7974 1693, www.camden.gov.uk). Half hidden among the trees and built from sustainable materials, its design won a RIBA award; kids adore its treacherous-looking log stepladder, rope swings and wooden walkways.

The playground by the café in Finsbury Park (Endymion Road, N4 1EE, 8489 1000, www.haringey.gov.uk) has fast slides going into the sandpit and really tricky climbing equipment. Look out too for the new adventure playground in nearby Clissold Park (Stoke Newington Church Street, N16 9HJ, 8800 1021, www.clissoldpark.com), still a work in progress as we went to press. Highbury Fields (Highbury Crescent, 7527 2000, www.islington.gov.uk) combines old-fashioned thrills (an excitingly long, steep slide) with more recent additions, such as the flying fox and web-like climbing frames.

In west London, the adventure playground at Ravenscourt Park (Ravenscourt Road, W6 0UL, 8748 3020, www.lbhf.gov.uk) boasts fort-style climbing frames, slides and a popular basket swing. Dukes Meadows (Promenade Approach Road, W4 2RX, 8742 2225, www.dukesmeadowstrust.org) is a great local addition to Chiswick, with a water play area and some terrific climbing and adventure play equipment, including a spectacular slide. Also not to be missed is the playground in Holland Park (Ilchester Place, W8 6LU, 7602 2226, www.rbkc. gov.uk) with its giant see-saw, zip wire, climbing frames and tyre swing.

South London families favour Brockwell Park (Herne Hill, SE24 0NG, www.brockwell park.com), with its tastefully landscaped water features (a fine array of jets, pumps and dams), while the new play space at Goose Green (East Dulwich Road, SE22 9AT, www.friendsofgoosegreen.org.uk) is a hit with all ages. The tunnels, climbing tower reaching into the treetops and high-level rope nets may give parents a fright, but kids love them. Meanwhile, Horniman's

Brockwell Park

Triangle (London Road, SE23 3PH, www. lewisham.gov.uk) was completely revamped in 2009 with a massive circular sandpit, a climbing boulder and a spider's web climbing frame.

Battersea Park's adventure playground (Sun Gate Entrance, Albert Bridge Road, SW11 4PY, 8871 7539, www.wandsworth. gov.uk) is superb. Its imaginative climbing structures, slides and high climbing nets present real challenges for children aged five and over. The council is threatening to charge admission at weekends from autumn 2011, though, so check before you visit. Meanwhile, a brilliant BMX track and five-ramp skateboard park are key attractions at Kimber Adventure Playground (King George's Park, Kimber Road, SW18 4NY, 8870 2168, www.wandsworth.gov.uk), along with monkey bars, climbing frames, big swings, tyres and ropes.

Out east, Mile End Children's Park and Adventure Park (Locksley Street, E14 7EJ, www.towerhamlets.gov.uk) are both colourful, imaginative spaces, whose features include a scrambling wall, rope slide, complicated climbing frame and skateboard park. Glamis Adventure Playground (10 Glamis Road, E1W 3DQ, 7702 8301, www.glamis adventure.org.uk) enables kids to take controlled risks while they are playing – and must be one of the few places in the country where children are actively encouraged to build and light a bonfire (under supervision). There's also a beached boat to play on, plus a sprawling, thrilling climbing structure, daubed with colour, cheery slogans and psychedelic patterns.

Digging, climbing, water fights, go-kart making and den building are some of the possibilities at Whitehorse Adventure Playground (Whitehorse Road, E1 0ND, 7790 5984). Also this side of town is Victoria Park (Old Ford Road, E3 5DS, 7364 2494, www.towerhamlets.gov.uk), which is seeing multi-million pound improvements in preparation for London 2012: a skate and BMX park is planned on the east side, and the Pools Play area will include unusual wooden climbing structures, as well as fantastic water features.

806

Buy a bargain bike

What goes around, comes around – which means no self-respecting cyclist would buy a bike from the street sellers around Brick Lane, notorious for their freshly nicked stock. Far better to head to Frank G Bowen's auction house (253 Joseph Ray Road, E11 4RA, 8556 7930). Here, stolen bikes recovered by the police, whose owners couldn't be traced, are auctioned off every other Thursday. Proceedings kick off at 11am, while viewing is the day before. Bikes go for anywhere from £10 to £5,000 depending on their condition.

807 Get spirited away in South Kensington

The Spirit Collection tour at the Natural History Museum has nothing to do with ghosts, ghouls or partaking of strong liquor. Instead, it offers an intriguing opportunity to watch the museum's research scientists at work in the Darwin Centre's Zoology Spirit building – and a glimpse of some of the 22 million specimens housed here, which aren't otherwise on display. Among them is Archie the giant squid, caught off the coast of the Falkland Islands in 2004. Measuring over eight metres, he can be examined from all angles in a specially constructed case in the tank room. Tours are free, but advance booking is required. **Natural History Museum** *Cromwell Road, SW7 5BD (7942 5000, www.nhm.ac.uk).*

808 Eat 'shaking beef' at Loong Kee

Don't worry: it's calmed down by the time it's reached your plate. The northernmost of a strip of excellent Vietnamese restaurants, Loong Kee (134G Kingsland Road, E2 8DY, 7729 8344) is the place other chefs from the area choose to eat at. Marinated in black bean sauce, tossed in a pan (hence the name) and served on salad, its speciality 'shaking beef' is a standout.

809 Open your eyes to Unseen London

Unseen Tours' walks are led by homeless guides, who bring their own stories and perspectives to well-known landmarks and quirkier nooks and crannies around Mayfair, Covent Garden, Brick Lane, Shoreditch and London Bridge. Run by Sock Mob, a volunteer network that provides socks, food and a friendly ear to London's homeless, the tours have drawn a steady stream of locals, tourists and school groups since they started in 2010. Check www.sockmobevents.org.uk to see when the next tour is taking place.

810 Go down to the woods today

At 726 acres, Ruislip Woods National Nature Reserve is the largest area of woodland in Greater London. The four main areas are Bayhurst Wood, Park Wood, Copse Wood and Mad Bess Wood – said to be named after the eccentric wife of an 18th-century gamekeeper, who prowled among the trees at night, on the lookout for poachers. Oak and hornbeam coppice dominate, though you'll also find birch, aspen, beech and sweet chestnut. There's a list of easy rambles and guided walks at www.ruislipwoodstrust.org.uk, plus details of the annual Woodland Festival – a joyous shindig involving charcoal burning, morris dancing, woodland crafts and more.

811

Look out for ghost wall hoardings

High on walls and at the end of terraces are hundreds of gradually fading painted advertising signs from the 19th and early 20th centuries, usually vaunting the wares and prowess of resident businesses. They're all around town, but easy to miss: it's worth keeping an eye out from the top deck of the bus. Visit http://faded-london.blogspot.com for pictures of some particularly fine examples, from a sign touting Nettle's Tonic ('The Best Pick-Me-Up') in Balham to a beauty of a Boots the Chemist sign on Camden High Street, in curling, elegant script.

Road. The maze-like entrance adds to the illicit thrill of the place, whose stock runs from out-of-print David Bailey books to lesser-spotted style mags like *Nico* or *Dapper Dan*.
121-125 Charing Cross Road, WC2H 0EW (7287 1813, www.clairederouenbooks.com).

Forbidden Planet
Self-confessed geeks (and otherwise) get together at London's sci-fi, fantasy and graphic novel superstore, scene of myriad book signings.
179 Shaftesbury Avenue, WC2H 8JR (7420 3666, www.forbiddenplanet.com).

Gay's the Word
As well as running a monthly bookgroup, this gay and lesbian bookshop hosts some impressive author events: Alan Hollinghurst, Armistead Maupin and Stella Duffy have all held court here.
66 Marchmont Street, WC1N 1AB (7278 7654, www.gaystheword.co.uk).

Magma
You'll find a creative crowd perusing the shelves at Magma, in search of design, art, fashion and architecture-focused reading material. There are some inspired un-bookish items too, not least the terrific T-shirts.
117-119 Clerkenwell Road, EC1R 5BY (7242 9503, www.magmabooks.com).

Persephone Books
This Bloomsbury publisher reprints works by female (mainly interwar) writers. Some are familiar names (Katherine Mansfield, Virginia Woolf), others undeservedly obscure. The elegant editions feature dove grey jackets and glorious endpapers, printed with vintage pattern designs.
59 Lamb's Conduit Street, WC1N 3NB (7242 9292, www.persephonebooks.co.uk).

Stanfords
Whether you're off tramping in the Lake District or voyaging to Belize, this venerable travel and maps specialist is the place to go.
12-14 Long Acre, WC2E 9LP (7836 1321, www.stanfords.co.uk).

Treadwell's
Speciality subjects at this incense-scented bookshop include Wicca, paganism and the history of Western magic. The noticeboard is enthralling, detailing pagan ceremonies, tarot reading services and occult goings-on.
33 Store Street, WC1E 7BS (7419 8507, www.treadwells-london.com).

812-820
Browse the shelves at a specialist bookstore

Bookmarks
London's socialist bookshop (there's almost a pun in the name) stocks a superlative selection of left-wing literature. It's not just history and politics: there's fiction, and even a children's section.
1 Bloomsbury Street, WC1B 3QE (7637 1848, www.bookmarks.uk.com).

Books for Cooks
This fragrant establishment practises what it preaches. It has a tiny kitchen at the back, where recipes from the massive stock of cookery books are put to the test and sold from midday (no reservations); you can also sign up for workshops.
4 Blenheim Crescent, W11 1NN (7221 1992, www.booksforcooks.com).

Claire de Rouen
A shrine to fashion and photography books, tucked away above a sex shop on Charing Cross

821-823
Celebrate carnival

With its steel bands, pounding sound systems, shimmying dancers and exotic parades, Notting Hill Carnival (www.thenottinghillcarnival.com) is firmly on the map – and attended by over a million revellers. It's not the only fiesta in town, though. In early August, the Hackney One Carnival (www.hackney.gov.uk/onecarnival.htm) sees around 1,000 performers from 20 carnival and community groups take to the streets, while south London's Carnaval del Pueblo (www. carnavaldelpueblo.co.uk) is the largest outdoor Latin-American festival in Europe; scoff an empanada, quaff a rum and be swept into a salsa.

824
Attend a knees-up in a cemetery

Once a year, the Friends of Kensal Green Cemetery organise a day of festivities to raise awareness for the cemetery, attracting curious locals and funereal goths in equal numbers. In past years, demonstrations of coffin furnishing, a motorcade of hearses, and face painting and fancy dress in the style of Victorian mutes and mourners have all featured, alongside more conventional distractions (jam vendors, the Friends' bookstall and assorted craft stalls). The organisers recommend buying tickets for cemetery and catacombs tours on arrival, as these generally sell out by early afternoon.
Kensal Green Cemetery *Harrow Road, W10 4RA (8969 0152, www.kensalgreen.co.uk).*

825 Stand at the old centre of the world

Heard of Greenwich Mean Time? It could so easily have been Kew Mean Time. The meridian was once adjudged to pass through what is now called the King's Observatory, in the heart of the Old Deer Park in Richmond (now sports grounds), and London time was set from here. The king in question was George III, a keen astronomer, who had the observatory built to watch the rare transit of Venus. Three obelisks mark the north, east and west compass points used to line the instruments up. The King's Observatory is also famously the site of the discovery of a body beneath an iron vice. Former curator John Little was suspected of the murder, and executed in 1795 for two others.

826
Try a truffle at Paul A Young's

Master chocolatier Paul A Young's delectable truffles include an award-winning raspberry ganache and addictive sea salted caramel. If you're feeling a little braver, the Marmite truffle has divided chocolate-lovers across London.
Paul A Young *33 Camden Passage, N1 8EA (7424 5750, www.paulayoung.co.uk).*

The capital's parks present ample opportunity for messing about on the water. Most boating lakes are open from Easter to autumn, closing by sundown; prices given below are for adults, but there are discounts for children and families.

London's biggest boating lake, the Serpentine (Hyde Park, Serpentine Road, W2 2UH, 7262 1330, www.royalparks.org.uk) offers plenty of room for manoeuvre, and has over 100 rowboats and pedalos for hire; it's more expensive than most, though, charging £8 for 30 minutes or £10 an hour.

In Regent's Park (Outer Circle, NW1 4NR, 0300 061 2300, www.royalparks.org.uk) boaters share the water with more than 650 wildfowl, including 260 pairs of resident ducks. Twenty pedalos and 30 rowing boats are available for £4.85 per half hour or £6.50 per hour: a £5 deposit is required.

The lake at Alexandra Park (Alexandra Palace Way, N22 7AY, 8365 2121, www.alexandrapalace. com), meanwhile, is populated by irresistibly kitsch, antique-looking, swan-shaped pedalos, yours for £5 per half hour (50p more than the more conventional craft, but worth every penny).

A Lottery grant has restored the once-neglected boating lake at Finsbury Park (Seven Sisters Road, N4 2NQ, 07905 924282, www.finsbury parkboats.co.uk) to its former glory, and you can row alongside the ducks and swans for £6 per half hour.

Although the concrete pond at Greenwich Park (Romney Road, SE10 9NF, 7262 1330, www. royalparks.org.uk) might not have the verdant appeal of its rivals, it remains a popular choice at just £4 for half an hour of boating. Situated near the St Mary's Gate entrance, the lake often stays open late on summer evenings.

In Battersea Park (Albert Bridge Road, SW11 4NJ, 7262 1330, www.batterseapark.org), pedalos and rowing boats are a reasonable £5 per half hour, or £7 an hour. Ringed by ancient trees, the lake is quite a looker: its two islands, off-bounds to boaters, shelter herons, cormorants and grebes.

833

Cycle a secret railway... Tree-canopied and almost invisible from the surrounding streets, the Parkland Walk (www.parkland-walk.org.uk) cuts an east–west swathe across north London. Running four and a half miles from Finsbury Park to Highgate, along a disused railway line, it makes for a delightful off-road ride. A sign at the Highgate end lists the resident flora and fauna, including foxes, hedgehogs, butterflies and even muntjac deer (though we've never spotted one).

834-840

... Then discover seven more places to go off-road

For the traffic-averse, London has several areas where you can cycle without having to look over your shoulder. (Just because there are no cars doesn't mean you own the trail, though: always be considerate towards pedestrians, and give way if necessary.) The most picturesque are often by the water: we're thinking of the Thames Path along the South Bank, the towpaths of the Regent's and Grand Union Canals, the 12-mile Wandle Trail and the miles of cycle paths that criss-cross Lee Valley Regional Park.

The larger parks, meanwhile, offer tranquil, leafy lanes. Centrally, Hyde Park is the best, both because of its beauty and because there are plentiful London Cycle Hire docking stations around the perimeter. Cyclists and pedestrians have broad esplanades such as Rotten Row and Serpentine Road all to themselves. Richmond Park's roads are much used by sports cyclists, but runners, walkers and cyclists have exclusive use of the seven-and-a-half-mile circular Tamsin Trail. For more ideas and details of the routes mentioned, see www.sustrans.org.uk.

841-845

Hit the beach (and be back by teatime)

It's perfectly possible to go on a morning or afternoon excursion to the seaside from London. Forget the car, though; you'll need a fast train to cut through the suburbs. The league table of the quickest station-to-beach journey is headed by Leigh-on-Sea, just 45 minutes from Fenchurch Street, with Southend eight minutes further on. Leigh is small and quirky, with a folk music tradition, a tiny mud-and-sand beach beloved more of children than adults, and good seafood; Southend has the world's longest pleasure pier and mainly sandy beaches.

At 51 minutes from Victoria, Brighton comes in a close second to Leigh, enticing daytrippers with its pebbly beach, offbeat boutiques, dome-topped Pavillion and thriving café society.

Whitstable

We had hoped that the new fast service to Kent would speed Londoners out to the east and south Kent beaches. Sadly not yet. But it does make the journey to Faversham more pleasant (albeit more pricey), and adds the option of travelling from King's Cross. And from Faversham, an intriguing creekside destination in its own right, it's just eight minutes to the harbourside charms of Whitstable, with its oysters and shingle strands.

846

Take part in a BioBlitz

Science: slow and methodical. BioBlitz: fast, frantic and a lot of fun. Co-ordinated by the Natural History Museum, a BioBlitz (www.gigl.org.uk) is a down and dirty 24-hour biological survey that brings valuable knowledge to our understanding of London's biodiversity. Organisers describe it as a 'collaborative race to discover as many types of wildlife as possible within a set location'; in June 2011 that location was Alexandra Palace, when an astonishing 8,000 members of the public turned up, 4,000 of whom joined the survey. Check the website for news of the 2012 event.

847-855

See some great Scotts

One of the great 20th-century British architects, Sir Giles Gilbert Scott (1880-1960) has left icons all over London – some small, some vast and several rarely recognised as his work. Scott came to prominence in the 1920s with his design for the classic red K2 phonebox. Good examples are lined up on Broad Court, just opposite the Royal Opera House (Covent Garden, WC2E 9DD, 7304 4000, www.roh.org.uk). The phonebox's classic dome roof was inspired by Sir John Soane's mausoleum, which can still be seen in the cemetery of St Pancras Old Church (St Pancras Road, NW1 1UL, 7387 4193).

On a monumental scale, Scott was behind London's two most recognisable industrial buildings: Battersea Power Station (www. battersea-powerstation.com), with its four distinctive corner chimneys, and Bankside Power Station, topped by a single square chimney. In 2000, of course, the latter became Tate Modern (Bankside, SE1 9TG, 7887 8888, www.tate.org. uk). While you're on the South Bank, pay your respects at Waterloo Bridge – it's another Scott design. Even more surprising, the sensitive post-war rebuild of the House of Commons (Parliament Square, SW1A 0AA, 7219 4272, www.parliament.uk) is also down to Scott.

Confusingly, Sir Giles's father was also a prodigious architect. Pioneer of the High Gothic style, George Gilbert Scott's key works are also in London. So to complete your Scott-spotting with some stunning Victoriana, head to the Albert Memorial in Kensington Gardens (Hyde Park Gate, W2 2UH, 7298 2141, www.royalparks. gov.uk), the Foreign Office (King Charles Street, SW1A 2AH) and the Midland Railways Terminus Hotel, reopened in 2011 as the magnificently refurbished St Pancras Renaissance (Euston Road, NW1 2AR, 7841 3540, www.marriott.com).

Tate Modern

856-861

Pay tribute to London's great trees

Having survived centuries of disease and development, London's ancient trees deserve some appreciation. Here are six of our all-time favourites. For more on the city's trees, visit www.treesforcities.org.

The Amwell Fig

Standing next to Clerkenwell Primary School (Amwell Street, EC1R 1UN), this bountiful fig tree is actually made up of three trees, whose branches and foliage have grown together to form one crown. Gratefully resting its limbs on four A-shaped supports (it is around 200 years old, after all), it produces an abundance of fruit, which litters the pavement below.

The Forty Hall Cedar of Lebanon

Soaring over the Grade II-listed grounds of Forty Hall, Enfield (Forty Hill, EN2 9HA), this beauty is one of the oldest cedars of Lebanon in the country, planted around the turn of the 18th century. Its huge girth and massive branches are undeniably impressive; afterwards, stroll the serene park and have a cup of tea in the café.

The Ravenscourt Plane

There's something strangely human about this bulbous plane tree. Standing at the southern end of Ravenscourt Park, halfway down the path that runs through the central open area, it appears to have grown outwards rather than upwards. The two lowest branches look like feeble, skinny arms, waving in indignation; the overall effect is of a querulous but lovable old eccentric.

The Richmond Royal Oak

Looking for one particular tree in leafy Richmond Park might seem crazy – but once you get near the right area, there's no missing this squat oak, set in a ferny clearing. Thought to be around 750 years old, its gnarled trunk exudes a fairytale quality, with a huge split that looks like the door to another world. To find the tree from the park's Richmond Gate entrance, follow Sawyer's Hill then take the footpath by the north-eastern side of Sidmouth Wood and head round the wood's eastern flank, near

The Amwell Fig

The Totteridge Yew

Queen Elizabeth's Plantation to the north-west of Pen Ponds. Here you'll find the oak.

The St Pancras Churchyard Ash

Ringed by a low privet hedge, the ash tree that stands in Old St Pancras Churchyard (Old Church, Pancras Road, NW1 1UL) looks unremarkable at first. Get closer, though, and you'll see that its vast trunk is in the process of swallowing up the crazily tilted welter of tombstones that surround it.

The Totteridge Yew

In 1796, Dr S Lyons wrote of 'a yew tree of a very remarkable size, its girth, at three feet from the ground, being 26 feet'. The yew is still there – and, at around 2,000 years old, is London's oldest tree. It's a spritely ancient, with vigorous new growth, set in the churchyard of St Andrew's Church (Totteridge, Barnet, Herts N20 8PR). It generally stands guard over the dead – but in 1722, a baby was abandoned in its shelter, and named Henry Totteridge. Creep under the wide, low limbs and shaggy branches to admire its ancient heart and incredible textured trunk.

The Forty Cedar of Lebanon

The Ravenscourt Plane

Richmond Royal Oak

St Pancras Churchyard Ash

873
Meet London's maverick knitters

Founded by four fearless guerrilla knitters, I Knit the City (http://knitthecity.com) stages stunts across the capital. Past exploits include installing a patchwork 'phonebox cosy' near Parliament Square (attracting the attentions of a passing policeman in the process), dangling a knitted Hubbub of Hearts from Eros' bow in Piccadilly Circus and weaving a 13-foot spider's web in a tunnel near Waterloo Station. Follow their latest projects on Twitter or Facebook.

874-879
Get fighting fit

Anyone can learn to pack a punch at former super-middleweight contender Enzo Giordano's excellent Boxing London (1 Martha Street, E1 2PX, 07956 293768, www.boxinglondon.co.uk), which runs beginner-friendly sessions three times a week. No experience is required, and the aims are control, focus and fitness rather than beating your opponent to a pulp. Novices are also welcome at Rooney's Gym in London Bridge (895-896 Railway Arch, Holyrood Street, SE1 2EL, 7403 6113, www.rooneysgym.com), whose schedule includes intensive workout sessions with no sparring involved, as well as boxing training.

In East London, the schedule at the Real Fight Club (2-6 Curtain Road, EC2A 3NQ, 7247 2358, www.therealfightclub.co.uk) takes in kickboxing, fitness-focused 'Cardio Box' sessions, beginners' tuition and more: if you want to see advanced part-time pugilists in action, the club also runs white collar boxing events at York Hall.

Plenty of pro boxers train at TKO Ultrachem Gym (Gillian House, Stephenson Street, E16 4SA, 7474 3199, www.ultrachemtkogym.co.uk), but its coaches also offer beginners' classes and non-contact sessions for over-eights. Women's training here is led by pro boxer Marianne 'Golden Girl' Marston, who also teaches at Ringtone Gym (141-153 Drummond Street, NW1 2PB, 07816 823586, www.ringtonehealthandfitness.com) and Tokei Martial Arts & Fitness Centre (28 Magdalen Street, SE1 2EN, 7403 5979, www.tokeicentre.org).

862-872
See Olympians in action – for free

Eleven Olympic events offer great roadside spectating opportunities, with no need to buy a ticket for long sections of the route.

The Cycling Road Race events take place on 28 and 29 July; the route heads south-west from the Mall via Richmond and Hampton Court to Surrey's Box Hill before looping back to town. Time Trials for both men and women are at Hampton Court on 1 August. Team GB have a real chance to be among the medals in both these events, so expect the mood to be electric. The cycling element of the Triathlon (women's 4 August, men's 7 August), a 40km course that passes several of London's iconic sights, can also be viewed by all.

Road-based Athletics events, in and around central London, are the Marathon (women's 5 August, men's 12 August) and Race Walk (men's 20km 4 August, men's 50km and women's 20km 11 August). For details, see www.london2012.com.

880-883 *Follow the seasons*

Some complain that city dwellers are cut off from the changing seasons; we beg to differ.

Spring announces itself with blooming bulbs and bleating lambs. Kew Gardens (Kew Road, Surrey W9 3AB, 8332 5655, www.kew.org) is stuffed with the former, while the Chelsea Physic Garden (66 Royal Hospital Road, SW3 4HS, 7352 5646, www.chelseaphysic garden.co.uk) opens specially to show off its gorgeous snowdrop collection. Several of London's city farms have sheep-breeding programmes, of which we will single out Vauxhall (165 Tyers Street, SE11 5HS, 7582 4204, www.vauxhallcityfarm.org), mainly just because it's in Lamb-beth – but also for its rare breeds.

Summer invites us outside, to loll in deckchairs (Hyde Park, W2 2UH, 7298 2100, www.royalparks.gov.uk; £1.50 an hour), go to fetes and festivals and outdoor events (ubiquitous: consult *Time Out*'s listings), and picnic in parks. For some reason, London Fields (Westgate Street, E8 3EU, 8356 8428, www.hackney.gov.uk) has become the centre of picnic-swarming. It must be because of the ready supply of great takeaway food at the adjoining Broadway Market (www.broadwaymarket. co.uk), but it's not a particularly distinguished scrap of land, and is suffering badly from overcrowding. We suggest going somewhere prettier and quieter, such as Springfield Park, Brockwell Park, Highgate Woods, Battersea Park and, of course, the more central favourites, notably Primrose Hill and Holland Park. London Fields does ace it for its Olympic-sized heated lido (London Fields Westside, E8 3EU, 7254 9038, www.gll.org), though, for the other summer prerequisite of inadvisably getting one's kit off in public.

Autumn calls us to admire blazing foliage. You can see this in rolling swathes at Hampstead Heath (Highgate Road, NW5 1QR, 7332 3322, www.cityoflondon.gov.uk); if you have an arboreal interest, make a pilgrimage to Regent's Park (Outer Circle, NW1 4NR, 7486 7905, www.royalparks.gov.uk) or Abney Park Cemetery in Stoke Newington (Stoke Newington High Street, N16 0LH, 7275 7557, www.abney-park.org.uk), both of which harbour many tree species (along with Kew Gardens again, of course). To combine breathtaking

leaf landscapes with snuffling out fungi (no picking) and watching rutting deer, go to Richmond Park (Queen's Road, Surrey TW10 5HS, 8948 3209, www.royalparks. gov.uk) or Epping Forest (High Beech, Loughton, Essex IG10 4AF).

This is also the season for firework displays. *Time Out* (www.timeout.com/ london) always lists these and they do vary from year to year, though Victoria Park and Clapham Common are reliably spectacular.

Winter, at its best, lures us out on clear, frosty days. Greenwich is a good place to head for – you can contemplate the 1653 freeze, when you could get here by sleigh along the frozen river, and clutch a spiced punch while fossicking for Christmas presents in the market (King William Walk, SE10 9HZ, www.greenwichmarket.net). If it's snowing, you can sledge in the park.

At its worst, winter requires hot toddies in fire-warmed pubs, preferably your local, or somewhere near a bracing walk. Down the road from Hampstead Heath, the back-to-basics, real-ales-and-fire Southampton Arms (139 Highgate Road, NW5 1LE, no phone, www.thesouthamptonarms.co.uk) in Gospel Oak is a good bet. It doesn't accept cards, so bring sufficient cash.

884

Peek at a pet cemetery

Next time you're sitting on the top deck of the 148 or 390 bus as it passes Lancaster Gate tube station, pay close attention to Hyde Park. If you're lucky, you might get a glimpse of the pint-sized Pet Cemetery, by Victoria Gate Lodge on the Bayswater Road. It was founded in 1881 by the lodge-keeper, Mr Winbridge, when Cherry the Maltese terrier, a regular visitor to the park, was laid to rest. 'Poor Cherry' turned out to be the first of many, and by the time the cemetery closed in 1903, it contained over 300 tiny graves – including those of Wee Bobbit, Dolly, Pupsey, Smut, Chin Chin and Chips. As well as having plenty of imagination when it came to pet names, the Victorians were masters of the heart-rending inscription: Jim (1883-96) was 'a little dog with a big heart', while Ba-Ba (dates unknown) was 'Never forgotten, never replaced'. It isn't open to visitors, but you can also steal a glimpse if you're walking past, peering though the iron railings and dense undergrowth.

885-896

Saddle up

Prices at London's riding stables vary considerably, but expect to pay around £30 an hour for a group lesson, and £40 to £50 for a one-on-one session. Riders must wear a BSI-approved hard hat (establishments usually lend or hire out) and boots with a small heel rather than trainers or wellies; lessons must be booked in advance. Many stables cater for riders with disabilities, though not all have equipment to winch riders on to horses or ponies. All the establishments listed below are British Horse Society-approved (www.bhs.org.uk).

Deen City Farm & Riding School

A friendly yard that offers private lessons, lunge lessons and stable management classes.
39 Windsor Avenue, SW19 2RR (8543 5858, www.deencityfarm.co.uk).

Ealing Riding School

Individual and group lessons for all abilities are offered, while children can attend pony days.
17-19 Gunnersbury Avenue, W5 3XD (8992 3808, www.ealingridingschool.biz).

Hyde Park & Kensington Stables
Riding lessons for five-and-overs are conducted along Rotten Row in Hyde Park, London's most famous bridleway; prices reflect the smart setting
63 Bathurst Mews, W2 2SB (7723 2813, www.hydeparkstables.com).

Kingston Riding Centre
Kingston's facilities include a floodlit indoor school, outdoor arena and cross-country course.
38 Crescent Road, Kingston-upon-Thames, Surrey KT2 7RG (8546 6361, www.kingston ridingcentre.com).

Lee Valley Riding Centre
This busy east London school boasts one indoor and two floodlit outdoor arenas. 'Have-a-Go' sessions are a good entry point for newcomers.
71 Lea Bridge Road, E10 7QL (8556 2629, www.leevalleypark.org.uk).

London Equestrian Centre
There are 50 horses and ponies at this yard, which accommodates all ages and levels of experience.
Lullington Garth, N12 7BP (8349 1345, www.londonridingschool.com).

Mount Mascal Stables
More experienced riders can hack out in Joydens Wood, while the centre itself is the largest within the M25, and charges very reasonable rates.
Vicarage Road, Bexley, Kent DA5 2AW (8300 3947, www.mountmascalstables.com).

Mudchute Equestrian Centre
New riders are given a warm welcome, and lessons are some of the most affordable in town.
Mudchute Park & Farm, Pier Street, E14 3HP (7515 0749, www.mudchute.org).

Ross Nye's Riding Stables
At the more expensive end of the spectrum – tuition is £60 per hour – this stable's lessons take place in Hyde Park.
8 Bathurst Mews, W2 2SB (7262 3791, www.rossnyestables.co.uk).

Stag Lodge Stables
Jumping or flatwork lessons for all abilities are held in one of two outdoor manèges, and there's hacking in Richmond Park.
Robin Hood Gate, Richmond Park, SW15 3RS (8974 6066, www.ridinginlondon.com).

Trent Park Equestrian Centre
Lessons are available for four-and-overs. Those with more experience can canter cross-country.
Bramley Road, N14 4UW (8363 8630, www.trentpark.com).

Willowtree Riding Establishment
Lessons (flatwork only) take place in a full-size indoor arena; young or nervous riders are welcome.
The Stables, Ronver Road, SE12 0NL (8857 6438, www.willowtreeridinglondon.co.uk).

Hyde Park & Kensington Stables

Dear diary...

Cringe nights turn teenage angst into toe-curling comedy.
*Candice Pires **takes a deep breath and steps up to the mike.***

My 13-year-old self would be horrified. I am sitting in a room watching other people read extracts from their teenage diaries to an audience, waiting my turn. I was a seriously shy teen, which makes it all the more cruel that I'm about to share my innermost thoughts with a roomful of sniggering strangers. Albeit thoughts mainly consisting of 'I love Neil,' 'I know Michael Jackson is innocent,' and, 'I still love Neil'.

There are six other readers at tonight's Cringe London event, held above a pub near Temple. First up is the night's host, Ana Sampson, who assures me that it's quite normal to be terrified. 'Once you get up there, though, you'll love it,' she tells me. I try my best to believe her, and take another swig of wine.

Cringe was founded in 2005 by New Yorker Sarah Brown, in the back room of a Brooklyn bar. She came up with the idea after rediscovering her teenage diaries at her parents' house and emailing 'the most painful excerpts' to close friends, to much hilarity. Sure enough, the night became an instant hit, with stylish New Yorkers queuing round the block to share their teenage angst.

Sarah brought the night to London in 2007. 'I was pretty confident it would work here – in all honesty, it's a little funnier than New York, because there is some truth in the repressed English stereotype. It's that much more painful when an English person shares their shame – which in Cringe terms means more hilarious.'

Most readers at Cringe London's events volunteer in advance, but a plucky few turn up on the night, diary in hand. I'm in the former

camp, having dug out my diaries from my old bedroom, in the suburbs of north west London. My diary writing habits were sporadic, provoked mainly by crushes and seemingly insurmountable grudges against my mother over not being allowed to go to sleepovers. I scrawled a succession of diaries: this one, the longest running and most faithfully kept, had the advantage of a padlock.

Secrecy, of course, was paramount – which begs the question, why would anyone volunteer to read their embarrassing teenage diaries in public? 'It's a way to make fun of yourself,' says fellow first-timer Kate Sherriff, whose stories of shopping trips to buy Rimmel make-up and being asked out by a boy, but not being sure if it was a joke, also have a comfortingly familiar ring. 'It makes other people feel better about their own adolescence,' says Kate. 'Even though we didn't know it at the time, we were all worried about the same things.'

Other readers regale us with entries about spending hours on Teletext, disastrous French exchanges, trips to the Body Shop to stock up on White Musk and the curious enjoyment gained from hours of blubbing uncontrollably while watching *Titanic*. Although it makes for toe-curling listening, it's more therapeutic than cruel, for the audience and participants alike. 'You're laughing at yourself, but not at yourself *now*,' says Ana. 'You're saying, Look how silly I was – I'm not anymore.'

My biggest fear is that when I get up on stage, people will think I'm not so different to the supremely awkward teen I was, and feel sorry for me instead of laughing. 'Every single person who has read has been funny,' says Ana. 'And some of the most miserable writing gets the

biggest laughs.'
A case in point is Tim Jones, whose laconic delivery has the room in stitches: '21/5/81: Dead bored. Watched *Miss UK*. Feel a bit better now.' And, '19/12/81: 56 people killed by army in Poland... Had a hairwash.'

Tim finishes his piece, and I'm next up. I suddenly remember how, in my early teens, I would feign illness to get out of public speaking at school, and I'm suddenly not sure how I got to be here. Heart pounding, clutching my wine in one hand and padlocked gold and turquoise diary in the other, I walk towards the stage.

'Nice diary,' says a girl sitting on the floor at the front, triggering a ripple of laughter. The relief is immediate. I set my glass down, open the closely-written pages and look out on a sea of expectant faces. 'April 3rd, 1993. Weather, warm,' I begin. 'I heart Neil. I don't think he's good looking or anything, but I think he's got a really nice personality.'

As I chart the progression of my unrequited love for a skinny, shy 13-year-old classmate, whose tie was too short and who could barely look a girl in the eye, I realise I'm enjoying myself. Sharing experiences that were once hugely traumatic puts them back in their proper perspective: at points, I have to compose myself to get the words out through my own laughter. I leave the stage in a state of euphoria: for ten minutes of my life, I felt like a stand-up comedian. Ana was right, I did love it – and I think my 13-year-old self would have secretly been proud.

For Cringe London dates, join the Facebook group by searching for 'Cringe London: Teenage Diary Writers Unite'. Readings are held every two to three months, and entry is free.

898

Pay your respects to London's radicals

Just off City Road, near Old Street, Bunhill Fields is a popular place for lunching office workers, trying to escape the frenzy of the City. It's also a former dissenters' cemetery that contains over 2,000 monuments, including dedications to three of Britain's most notable nonconformists: artist, poet and visionary William Blake; John Bunyan, author of *The Pilgrim's Progress*; and *Robinson Crusoe* writer Daniel Defoe. In the 17th century, the site was managed by a Mr Tindal, who granted burial permits to anyone able to afford them, regardless of religion. As a result, Bunhill Fields became the final resting place of choice for Britain's radical thinkers and religious rebels until its closure in 1855. For a detailed account of the cemetery's history, join one of the guided tours held on Wednesdays throughout the summer (£5, no booking required).
Bunhill Fields *City Road, EC1Y 2BG (7247 8548, www.cityoflondon.gov.uk).*

899

Hear world-class DJs spin in your living room

Few recent innovations in London's club scene have captured the zeitgeist in the same way as the Boiler Room (www.boilerroom.tv), which occupies an uncharted space somewhere between a club night, a podcast and a pirate radio station, and has gained itself a cult following. Taking place at Corsica Studios, its events feature hot names on the musical underground – the likes of James Blake, Jamie Woon and Seb Chew – performing to camera, with a select group of clubbers bopping behind them. If you're lucky, you might blag a ticket, but don't get your hopes up: you're more likely to watch the sets as they're broadcast online, joining the international Twitter debate and desperately trying to ID tracks. It's unlikely to spell the end of clubbing as we know it, but it's the closest the social networking generation has come to online raving.

900 Become a bell ringer

Coaxing a ton of metal to take its place in a delicate pattern that rings out from an ancient church can be an awe-inspiring experience. Bell-ringing isn't easy – the old saw about being hauled up to the ceiling at the end of a rope is not an impossible scenario for intemperate beginners – and takes many months to learn, especially to a standard that ensures you'll be welcome at the more prestigious towers. But it's extremely rewarding, especially for those of a mathematical, beer-drinking or folkloric bent. Local parishes welcome committed learners; get in touch with the Middlesex County Association and London Diocesan Guild (www.mcaldg.org.uk) to find a church near you, or just follow the sound of the bells.

901

Appreciate art on an epic scale

Giant spiders, spiralling slides and 100 million porcelain sunflower seeds have all memorably featured among Tate Modern's Turbine Hall installations. Next up is Tacita Dean, whose site-specific piece, due to be unveiled in October 2011, will become the 12th commission in the Unilever Series. Dean is renowned for her work with film, but what she'll come up with is anyone's guess: you've got until 9 April 2012 to find out.
Tate Modern *Bankside, SE1 9TG (7887 8888, www.tate.org.uk).*

902 Peek inside a garden square

Every June, over 100 private gardens open their gates to the public for Open Garden Squares Weekend (www.opensquares.org). It's a fantastic opportunity to see into the gracious residents-only squares of London's posher postcodes, and also the grassroots plots of community projects, plus the gardens of academic institutions, almshouses, shops and even prisons. All sorts of events are organised, from music to wine-tasting.

903

Hear heavenly music at the Union Chapel

What do churches do when it's not Sunday? Well, Islington's Union Chapel turns into a venue for secular music: celestial choirs get replaced by the likes of Athlete and Laura Marling. Not your standard nave-and-transept church, the gorgeous round galleried auditorium lends itself well to gigs: think sunlight filtering in through stained glass during the free Saturday lunchtime concerts and soft, atmospheric lighting at night. The pews can be a bit hard on the backside, but that's a small price to pay for so divine an experience.

Union Chapel *Compton Terrace, N1 2UN (7226 3750, www.unionchapel.org.uk).*

904

Get your hair cut at Kennaland

Sought-after hair salons, however luxurious, can have something of a conveyor-belt feel, expecially on busy weekends. Those seeking a one-on-one experience would do well to seek out Kennaland (7254 2416, http://kennaland.com) – a tiny, semi-secret East End hairdressers, perched high above a pub. The atmospheric warren of bric-a-brac-filled rooms is presided over by session stylist and *Vogue* regular Kenna (fresh from cutting Keira Knightly's locks last time we visited), who works alongside just one other stylist: no queues at the hair-washing basins here. Highlights, meanwhile, come courtesy of Sophia Heffer – a precision colourist who's one of London's best. Order a beer from the bar below, curl up on the sofa and make yourself at home – everyone else does.

905

See a pickled shark...

Damien Hirst's best-known works define the 1990s generation that became known as the Young British Artists, so it's surprising the forthcoming retrospective of his career at Tate Modern (Bankside, SE1 9TG, 7887 8888, www.tate.org.uk) will be the first on this scale to be held in Britain. Running from 5 April to 9 September 2012, it's part of the London 2012 Festival. The exhibition draws work from across his 25-year career, including, yes, *The Physical Impossibility of Death in the Mind of Someone Living* – Hirst's notorious shark, preserved as if swimming through a vitrine of formaldehyde.

906-908

... Then appreciate art by three other key Brit artists

Hirst's retrospective is just one of several art events being organised for the London 2012 Festival that will showcase the best of British contemporary art. Other highlights include:

Lucian Freud Portraits
An exhibition of realist paintings of people by the late Lucian Freud, including acutely observed pictures of his family, friends and lovers. It runs from 9 February to 27 May 2012.
National Portrait Gallery *St Martin's Place, WC2H 0HE (7306 0055, www.npg.org.uk).*

David Hockney: A Bigger Picture
From 21 January to 9 April 2012, the Royal Academy is hosting a David Hockney exhibition, with a focus on his landscapes – many of them large, new works created especially for this show.
Royal Academy *Burlington House, Piccadilly, W1J 0BD (7300 8000, www.royalacademy.org.uk).*

Rachel Whiteread
Rather than gathering work for an exhibition, this Turner Prize-winning artist has been commissioned to create a permanent artwork. Due to be unveiled in summer 2012, her piece will occupy a blank frieze that has been on the façade of the Whitechapel Gallery since it was built in 1901.
Whitechapel Gallery *77-82 Whitechapel High Street, E1 7QX (7522 7888, www.whitechapelgallery.org).*

909

Chuck a cheese

In the cellar at the Freemason's Arms in Hampstead is a traditional English skittle alley. To play, you throw a 'cheese' – of the inedible, wooden variety – from 21 feet away, and try to clear a frame of nine pins in four throws or less. Cheeses average about ten pounds in weight, which may go some way towards explaining the difficulty. That, and the time-honoured accompaniment of several pints of beer (real ales, naturally). Staff recommend public transport for your journey home. Get a slice of the action on Tuesday evenings, by attending one of the sessions run by London Skittles (07867 822125, www.londonskittles.co.uk); you need to call ahead to arrange a place.
Freemason's Arms *Downshire Hill, NW3 1NT (7433 6811, www.freemasonsarms.co.uk).*

910

Take a steam train to the past

Before the mechanisation of the hop harvest in the 1960s, crowds of East Enders (including whole families) would decamp to Kent for their annual working holiday to pick the crop; it was such a popular activity that special trains were laid on for the workers.

On the first weekend of September, as part of the Faversham Hop Festival (www.faversham hopfestival.org), local brewery Shepherd Neame (www.shepherdneame.co.uk) arranges a day trip from Victoria station on a steam train pulling period carriages. It travels out via the Medway towns, including Rochester and Chatham, and back via a scenic tour of Kent, giving the engine a chance to get up steam. Return tickets started at £64.50 in 2011.

911 *Sharpen up your knife skills*

Who doesn't envy the ability of TV chefs to micro-slice a carrot with a whirring blade while promoting their latest recipe book straight to camera? To kitchen mortals, there's no more desirable skill, not only for the flash factor but also because pretty much all food preparation calls for chopping-board work, and inexpert slicing is both laborious and accident prone. So a knife-skills course should be the most life-changing investment an amateur cook can make.

But surely a single evening can't change the ham-fistedness of a lifetime? I'm an amateur cook in the strictest sense of the word, and bear several culinary scars, physical and emotional, to prove it. My chunks are uneven, my slices inseparable, my dice fluffy. Call me Disasterchef.

When your fingers are at stake, you go to someone with a rock-solid reputation. Hence my participation at an evening knife-skills 'hands-on masterclass' at renowned kitchenware retailer and cookery school Divertimenti on Marylebone Road. The basement classroom is handsomely outfitted, with a raised kitchen overlooking the students' work and seating area. Our instructor, Gloria Ford, works at the counter that separates the two; an angled mirror provides an overhead view and TV screens relay close-ups to the class.

Gloria is young, authoritative, friendly and inspirationally enthusiastic. She's also built nothing like James Martin, which is reassuring – the knife, rather than the muscle, must be doing the talking. She starts by outlining some basic techniques. It turns out that the whirring blade thing is a bit of a distraction, fortunately. If the knife is sharp enough and the object approached correctly, the slicing part follows naturally, and speed will come in its own time.

We are told about knives (forget fancy sets, you just need a paring knife, 20cm cook's knife and possibly a serrated tomato knife) and knife sharpeners (a steel is essential). And we're told about basic precepts: a large and stable chopping board; a grip that extends to the blade; using the first slices to create a firm base for further cutting. Then it's straight to watching Gloria joint a chicken – wishbone out, legs off and separated into thighs and drumsticks, breasts lifted and separated and divested of wings. And, precipitously, we are all issued with chickens and our own workstations.

This is somewhat nervous-making. First, and not least, I have to share a workbench with another knife-skills novice with a slippery chicken. Fortunately he (the novice, not the chicken) turns out to be left-handed, and I'm a rightie, so we position ourselves with cutting arms diametrically opposed. Second, the chicken is not co-operating, and I can't find its oysters. But the down-shaft grip Gloria taught us is very controllable, so my inexpert swipes and slashes damage only the animal. Still, I manage to reduce it, albeit more mad-axeman than precision-cutting, to eight joints and a carcass.

Then it's on to fruit and veg. Gloria slices an onion (slice it sideways for even-sized pieces), pepper, cucumber, tomato, radish and kiwi fruit; chops parsley and coriander; purées a garlic clove; chunks a pineapple; dices a mango and papaya; segments an orange; and chiffonades lettuce and mint. Again, it's over to us, and this is child's play compared to the chicken. That or I'm growing into the knife grip, the guide fingers and the rocking technique. A more relaxed mood spreads.

After a break, we return to find the classroom transformed into a dining room. What's more, dinner – gazpacho, pomegranate chicken, fatoush and fruit salad – has been prepared from our combined choppings. We have a chance to chat to Gloria and each other, and I find the students have various motivations for attending. There's a food-pub owner from Bath; a business traveller with time to fill; two friends on a birthday treat; and some keen young amateur cooks.

I leave with an agile wrist, a satisfied appetite and 12 chicken carcasses for stock – 11 of them cleanly de-fleshed. *Ruth Jarvis.*
Divertimenti Cookery School *33/34 Marylebone High Street, W14 4PT; 227-229 Brompton Road, SW3 2EP (7581 8065, www.divertimenti.co.uk). Masterclasses are held regularly at both locations. They last three-and-a-half hours and cost £105. Book ahead.*

912

Nose out Admirality Arch's strangest feature...

Hidden on an internal wall of the grandiose gateway from Trafalgar Square to the Mall, about seven feet off the ground, is a small and curious protrusion. With the application of a little imagination, you can make out a vaguely nasal aspect: this, traditionally, is considered to be a rendering of the Duke of Wellington's nose. The riders of the Household Cavalry supposedly touch it for luck as they pass – which could be why it looks a little worn around the edges.

913-919

... Then find the seven noses of Soho

Dotted around Soho are seven – or perhaps six or eight or nine (depending on which urban myth you believe) life-size noses. Adorning walls and buildings, they're said to be casts of sculptor Rick Buckley's honker, mounted from 1996 to 2005. Set yourself the challenge of sniffing out all seven (we'll kick you off by suggesting you start at Great Windmill Street). If you tire of the chase, sign up for a guided walk with Peter Berthoud (http://exploringwestminster.blogspot.com), who will take you to see all seven. Anyone who finds the seven can expect to attain 'infinite wealth' – though Peter's not offering any guarantees on that score.

920-922

Join a pub singalong

Lend your voice to the crowd gathered around the piano at the Golden Eagle (59 Marylebone Lane, W1U 2NY, 7935 3228) on Tuesdays, Thursdays and Fridays; the Coach & Horses (29 Greek Street, W1D 5DH, 7437 5920) on Wednesdays and Saturdays; and the Palm Tree (127 Grove Road, E3 5RP, 8980 2918) in Mile End (Friday to Sunday, after a jazz band). Expect Cockney standards and other belters.

923-963

Succumb to a caffeine craving

Allpress Espresso
The New Zealand roaster's first outlet in Europe is an impressive one.
58 Redchurch Street, E2 7DP (7749 1780).

Bea's of Bloomsbury
The formula of La Marzocco machine, Square Mile beans and spectacular cakes works a treat.
44 Theobald's Road, WC1X 8NW (7242 8330, www.beasofbloomsbury.com).

Brill
Superior coffees – Union Hand Roasted's Revelation espresso blend – plus CDs and Brick Lane bagels.
27 Exmouth Market, EC1R 4QL (7833 9757).

Browns of Brockley
A funky coffee bar/deli run by friendly twentysomethings (and their popular pug, Ludd).
5 Coulgate Street, SE4 2RW (no phone).

Cà Phê VN
Vietnam's finest coffee, made using the drip-filter method; lighten the espresso with condensed milk.
149b Upper Street, N1 1RA (7359 1400, www.caphevn.co.uk).

Caravan
The in-house coffee roastery at this New Zealand-owned eaterie guarantees excellence.
11-13 Exmouth Market, EC1R 4QD (7833 8115, www.caravanonexmouth.co.uk).

Climpson & Sons
Macchiato, piccolo, zola, gibraltar... you can have it all in this charming coffee-geek haven.
67 Broadway Market, E8 4PH (7812 9829, www.climpsonandsons.com).

Coffee Circus
A homely Crouch End café where Union Hand Roasted coffee is made with care.
136 Crouch Hill, N8 9DX (no phone, www.coffeecircus.co.uk).

Coffee Plant
Around for 15 years, Coffee Plant has a range of own-roasted beans.
180 Portobello Road, W11 2EB (7221 8137, www.coffee.uk.com).

Container Café

Top-notch coffee overlooking the Olympic Park.
*The View Tube, The Greenway, Marshgate Lane,
E15 2PJ (07834 275687, www.theviewtube.co.uk).*

Counter Café

Sister to the Container Café, now based within
Stour Space gallery; try the smooth flat white.
*Roach Road, E3 2PA (07952 696388,
www.thecountercafe.co.uk).*

Department of Coffee and Social Affairs

Serious espresso, made using seasonal blends.
*14-16 Leather Lane, EC1N 7SU
(no phone, www.departmentofcoffee.co.uk).*

Dose Espresso

James Phillips' quirky little coffee shop punches
above its weight, using ethically sourced beans.
*70 Long Lane, EC1A 9EJ (7600 0382,
www.dose-espresso.com).*

Espresso Room

This tiny coffee bar won Best New Coffee Bar in
the 2010 Time Out Eating & Drinking Awards.
*31-31 Great Ormond Street, WC1N 3HZ
(07760 714883, www.theespressoroom.com).*

Federation Coffee

A groovy little coffee shop serving a range of
coffees from Nude Espresso.
*Unit 46, Brixton Village Market, Coldharbour Lane,
SW9 8PS (no phone, www.federationcoffee.com).*

Fernandez & Wells

Invigorating triple ristretto shots are served at
the 'espresso bar' branch of Fernandez & Wells.
*16a St Anne's Court, W1F 0BG (7494 4242,
www.fernandezandwells.com).*

Flat White

Flat White's shabby chic looks resemble cafés
found all over the central New South Wales coast;
its namesake coffee is good and strong.
*17 Berwick Street, W1F 0PT (7734 0370,
www.flatwhitecafe.com).*

Ginger & White

Commendable coffee and cakes from a self-
proclaimed Brit-style café.
*4a-5a Perrins Court, NW3 1QS (7431 9098,
www.gingerandwhite.com).*

Hackney Pearl

Sublime coffee and cakes in a thrift shop setting.
*11 Prince Edward Road, E9 5LX (8510 3605,
www.thehackneypearl.com).*

Kaffeine

A good-looking Aussie-owned venture,
with skilled baristas.
*66 Great Titchfield Street, W1W 7QJ
(7580 6755, www.kaffeine.co.uk).*

Kipferl

Stop by Kipferl for Austrian coffees (melange,
grosser brauner and so on) and some truly
splendid cakes.
*20 Camden Passage, N1 8ED (7704 1555,
www.kipferl.co.uk).*

Lantana

Australian proprietress Shelagh Ryan swears
by the 'coffee super-couple' of Square Mile beans
and a La Marzocco espresso machine.
13 Charlotte Place, W1T 1SN (7637 3347).

Climpson & Sons

Leila's Shop
Leila McAlister's eclectic deli-café is a long-time favourite for consistently excellent coffee.
15-17 Calvert Avenue, E2 7JP (7729 9789).

London Particular
Higgins Coffee have created a bespoke 'Particular' blend for this fine neighbourhood café.
399 New Cross Road, SE14 6LA (8692 6149).

Milk Bar
In a city of crappuccinos, effortlessly cool Milk Bar (sister to Flat White) gets it right.
3 Bateman Street, W1D 4AG (7287 4796).

Monmouth Coffee
This classic coffee company – supplier to many other cafés – has been roasting since 1978.
27 Monmouth Street, WC2H 9EU (7379 3516, www.monmouthcoffee.co.uk).

Notes Music & Coffee
Music, film and coffee, from the men behind the Flat Cap Coffee Company coffee cart in Victoria.
31 St Martin's Lane, WC2N 4ER (7240 0424, www.notesmusiccoffee.com).

No 67
The café serves (in their own words, and we'd agree) 'really good food and really good coffees'.
South London Gallery, 67 Peckham Road, SE5 8UH (7252 7649, www.southlondongallery.org).

Nude Espresso
Kiwi-run café with textbook-perfect flat whites.
26 Hanbury Street, E1 6QR (07804 223590, www.nudeespresso.com).

Pavilion Café
Flat whites, constructed with Square Mile coffee and creamy Ivy House Farm organic milk.
Victoria Park, Crown Gate West, E9 7DE (8980 0030, www.the-pavilion-cafe.com).

Prufrock
Gwilym Davies is a demi-god among those who take their cup of joe seriously; test his wares here.
23-25 Leather Lane, EC1N 7TE (07852 243470, www.prufrockcoffee.com).

Railroad
Excellent coffee in hand-made cups, matched by great *banh mi* (Vietnamese baguettes).
120-122 Morning Lane, E9 6LH (8985 2858, www.railroadhackney.co.uk).

Roastery
The beans are roasted in-store at this café, which is run by New Zealanders.
789 Wandsworth Road, SW8 3JQ (7350 1961).

St Ali
The London branch of an esteemed, coffee-focused café in Melbourne.
27 Clerkenwell Road, EC1M 5RN (7253 5754).

St David Coffee House
The best coffee in the area, perfectly frothed and served in mismatched crockery.
5 David's Road, SE23 3EP (8291 6646).

Scootercaffè
A coffee shop in a former Vespa repair garage, employing a vintage Faema espresso machine.
132 Lower Marsh, SE1 7AE (7620 1421).

Store Street Espresso
Good, strong coffee, with beans from Square Mile.
40 Store Street, WC1E 7DB (no phone).

Tapped & Packed
Choose your method – siphon, Aeropress, cafetiere – as well as your bean.
26 Rathbone Place, W1T 1JD (7580 2163, www.tappedandpacked.co.uk).

Tina, We Salute You
One for Dalston-based coffee connoisseurs, this always interesting café is a Square Mile devotee.
47 King Henry's Walk, N1 4NH (3119 0047, www.tinawesaluteyou.com).

Towpath
Sip gourmet Florentine coffee overlooking the Regent's Canal at this whimsical one-off.
42 De Beauvoir Crescent, N1 5SB (no phone).

Wilton's
A small, fashionable café, using beans roasted by locals Climpson & Sons.
63 Wilton Way, E8 1BG (7249 0444).

Shop this street

964-976

Boho boutiques:
Ledbury Road, W11

As fantasy high streets go, swankily bohemian Ledbury Road is up there with the best of them. Even for Notting Hill's most pampered, spoilt and well-heeled residents, shopping here is an unalloyed indulgence. With an impressive choice of high-end independents and a smart yet laid-back vibe, the street is made for unhurried browsing. Accessorise with a cappuccino, a cherubic child and someone else's credit card, and you'll fit right in. Passing elegantly refined residences and starting from the Westbourne Park end of the road, make Matches (nos.60-64, 7221 0255, www.matchesfashion.com) your first stop for assorted luxe labels by Chloé, Balenciaga and Lanvin. Or, for sharply dressed guys, Matches Menswear has a host of brands including Marc Jacobs, Miu Miu, Paul Smith and Prada. A bit further along, classy kids (or, rather, their mums) will be happy at chic Caramel (no.77, 7727 0906, www.caramel-shop.co.uk) and classic Petit Bateau (no.73, 7243 6331, www.petit-bateau.co.uk); the former also has its own range of shoes and accessories and a hair salon in the basement.

On the other side of the road is the quirky and undefinable JW Beeton (nos.48-50, 7229 8874, www.jwbeeton.co.uk), one of the longest-serving boutiques in this now-crowded patch of town. Owner Debbie Potts buys up small quantities of international labels and sells them on at non-extravagant (for these parts) prices. Ottolenghi (7727 1121, www.ottolenghi.co.uk) is next, at no.63; a quick glance at the window display and you can see why it's a winner when it comes to interior deli

design. There's a selection of colourful Mediterranean, Middle Eastern and oriental dishes on offer alongside tempting pastries and salads.

The bag designs next door come by way of Anya Hindmarch (no.63a, 7792 4427, www.anyahindmarch.com), while opposite, on the corner of Westbourne Grove, is the shop of swimwear designer Melissa Odabash (no.48b, 7229 4299, www.odabash.com); her bikinis and one-piece swimsuits don't come cheap, but you may decide that it's worth the splurge for amazingly flattering cuts in gorgeous materials.

The road is also host to a clutch of top Gallic boutiques. Aimé (no.32, 7221 7070, www.aimelondon.com), founded by French-Cambodian sisters, has simple pieces from the étoile range by Isabel Marant, cute dresses by Antik Batik and Bardot-style ballet shoes by Repetto. Next door, at Petit Aimé (no.34, 7221 3123), you'll find equally desirable children's garb.

For a one-stop shop for gorgeous shoes, head to Joseph (no.61, 7229 1870, www.joseph.co.uk). The Milan-based boutique houses so many top designers – among them Chloé, John Galliano, Marc Jacobs, Victor & Rolf and Paul Smith, to name but a choice few – that you should find something that matches your newly purchased Ledbury Road designer outfit.

Next door at no.59, there's more edible indulgence at Melt (7727 5030, www.melt chocolates.com) in the form of some mouth-watering chocolates, all lovingly handcrafted on the premises. On the other side of the road at Bodas (no.38b, 7229 4464, www.bodas.co.uk) you'll find a simple and sexy line in underwear, all made with high-quality fabrics.

Where once antiques shops lorded it over the road, nowadays you'll have to walk further up the block to see them; don't miss art deco specialist B&T Antiques (no.47, 7229 7001, www.bntantiques.co.uk), which has a near-cult following.

977-978

Be inspired by tales of gallantry

Opened in 2010, the Lord Ashcroft Gallery at the Imperial War Museum (Lambeth Road, SE1 6HZ , 7416 5320, www.iwm.org.uk) is home to the world's largest collection of Victoria Cross medals – 210 of them – awarded to servicemen and women for acts of extreme gallantry. There are also 31 George Crosses, the civilian equivalent. Alongside are exhibits such as the badly-damaged backpack worn by Lance Corporal Matt Croucher, GC, in Afghanistan in 2008. Croucher smothered an exploding grenade with his body, saving the life of his colleagues and – thanks to his quick-thinking in using the backpack – sustaining little injury himself.

For quieter contemplation of everyday heroes, visit Postman's Park (between King Edward Street & Aldersgate Street, EC2Y 5HN), a tranquil slice of hidden greenery near the Museum of London. Here, you'll find the Watts Memorial to Heroic Sacrifice: a series of Victorian ceramic plaques that pay tribute to ordinary people who died trying to save others. Many of the dead were children – among them 11-year-old Solomon Galaman, who 'died of injuries September 6 1901 after saving his little brother from being run over in Commercial Street'. Sit on a bench and pay a moment's tribute.

979-981

Get wheels

Full-time car ownership being a notoriously pricey business, Londoners have embraced car clubs with great enthusiasm: no parking permits, no MOT-induced anxiety, and no whopping insurance bill. Instead, with clubs like City Car Club (0845 330 1234, www.citycarclub.co.uk) and Streetcar (0845 644 8475, www.streetcar.co.uk), you pay an annual membership fee of around £50 to £60, get a smartcard and PIN, then pay by the hour when you borrow a car.

A more unusual option is offered by Hackney 2 Horse (www.2hutilitycar.co.uk), a small and charming Citroën 2CV specialist. As well as offering repairs and servicing, its owner Ted Sawyer runs a Utility Club Car Co-operative that enables members to borrow the iconic little motors on a temporary basis. After buying a share in the co-operative (generally £250 minimum), you'll pay a quarterly fee, depending on usage; the entry-level cost would work out at around £160 annually, which equates to three months' driving. It's really for locals (you need to pick up and drop off the car at Ted's garage in Hackney Marshes) and is more a labour of love than a polished commercial operation – so don't expect automated booking systems and suchlike.

Camley Street Natural Park

982

Stand astride the Greenwich Meridian Line (for free)

There are many fabulous astronomical things to do at the Royal Greenwich Observatory's Flamsteed House and Meridian Courtyard (Greenwich Park, SE10 9NF, 8312 6565, www.rog.nmm.ac.uk), but buying a £7 ticket (£5 reductions) just to take that classic tourist snap of the family straddling the Prime Meridian isn't one of them. After all, the Meridian line is only a bit less than 25,000 miles long, running from north pole to south, so you can straddle it all the way north across Greenwich Park, with Flamsteed House in the background.

Of course, you might want that extra badge of authenticity, to which end there are official plaques set along the line of 0° Longitude in several London boroughs. Our favourite is close to Greenwich Park, on the bank of the Thames near the O2 Arena (Millennium Way, SE10 0BB, 8463 2000, www.theo2.co.uk). It's a rather unusual-looking waymarker, reminiscent of a man-sized totem pole someone forgot to paint in the traditional bright colours, but a photo here will give you a fine watery backdrop.

983-987

Net yourself some pondlife

As children the world over know, there's nothing quite as fascinating as poking around the murky waters of ponds, swooping up the creatures they contain. Even in urban London, you can indulge in this primeval pursuit.

The London Wetland Centre (Queen Elizabeth's Walk, SW13 9WT, 8409 4400, www.wwt.org.uk/london) has the most impressive pond-dipping facilities, with a dedicated area that includes an underwater camera and a virtual pond that ripples as you walk over it. Supervised sessions are held every weekend and during school holidays.

Other dipping venues include the small but delightful Camley Street Natural Park (12 Camley Street, NW1 0PW, 7833 2311, www.wildlondon.org.uk), and the new Look Out nature education centre in Hyde Park (0300 061 2119, www.royalparks.org.uk). Finally, there are occasional school holiday sessions at Tower Hamlets Cemetery Park (Southern Grove, E3 4PX, 07904 186981, www.towerhamletscemetery.org), and Holland Park Ecology Centre (The Stableyard, W8 6LU, 7938 8186, www.rbkc.gov.uk).

988-1012

Scoff a superior roast

Central

Adam & Eve
Sundays bring two roasts to this cracking gastropub – rib of beef with Yorkshire pudding or roast chicken, perhaps, with plates piled high with potatoes and veg.
77A Wells Street, W1T 3QQ (7636 0717, www.geronimo-inns.co.uk).

Dean Street Townhouse
The Soho House group has made elegantly English meals fashionable again, and serves a fine Sunday lunch. Top quality roasts are served as smart two- or three-course set menus.
69-71 Dean Street, W1D 4QJ (7434 1775, www.deanstreettownhouse.com).

Duke of Wellington
Meat and trimmings are of excellent provenance at this smart venue. Enjoy 28-day-aged Longhorn beef with potatoes roasted in duck fat, carrots, savoy cabbage, yorkshire pud and gravy.
94A Crawford Street, W1H 2HQ (7723 2790, www.thedukew1.co.uk).

Hawksmoor Seven Dials
Steak-specialist the Hawksmoor serves one roast: rump of Longhorn, cooked over charcoal for smokiness before being finished in the oven. Bone marrow and onion gravy is the pièce de résistance.
11 Langley Street, WC2H 9JJ (7856 2154, www.thehawksmoor.co.uk).

Hix at the Albemarle
This restaurant of the moment has an extensive and unusual Sunday lunch menu that changes every week. A carving trolley (remember them?) also trundles around the formal dining room.
Browns Hotel, 33 Albemarle Street, W1S 4BP (7518 4004, www.thealbemarlerestaurant.com).

National Dining Rooms
Follow a Sunday stroll through the Gallery with a superb (if pricey) roast at Oliver Peyton's restaurant. Provenance is key: White Park beef from Bickleigh, say, or organic Poll Dorset lamb.
Sainsbury Wing, National Gallery, WC2N 5DN (7747 2525, www.thenationaldiningrooms.co.uk).

Restaurant at St Paul's
Light and airy despite its crypt location, this place adheres strictly to local produce and dishes. Potted brown shrimps might precede roast English beef with potatoes roasted in duck fat.
St Paul's Cathedral, St Paul's Churchyard, EC4M 8AD (7248 2469, www.restaurantatstpauls.co.uk).

North

Bull & Last
This Kentish Town gastropub's Sunday menu is a cut above: beef roasts come with yorkshire puds, roast spuds, parsnips and greens, and rich gravy.
168 Highgate Road, NW5 1QS (7267 3641, www.thebullandlast.co.uk).

Charles Lamb
Bookings aren't taken at this bijou Islington local, so arrive early to assure a table for one of their classic roasts with all the trimmings.
16 Elia Street, N1 8DE (7837 5040, www.thecharleslambpub.com).

Lexington
The Sunday menu at this Islington whisky bar features pork loin with crackling, aged Galloway beef with gravy or ham roasted in root beer.
96-98 Pentonville Road, N1 9JB (7837 5371, www.thelexington.co.uk).

Marquess Tavern
The Marquess delivers a sophisticated but satisfying menu on Sundays. Tuck into a plate of roast Kilravock Farm pork loin with rosemary sweet potatoes, parsnips and apple sauce.
32 Canonbury Street, N1 2TB (7354 2975, www.marquesstavern.co.uk).

York & Albany
The sumptuous Sunday lunch at this pubby hotel restaurant offers a choice of the four popular roast staples – beef, lamb, chicken and pork – with accompaniments both classic and modern.
127-129 Parkway, NW1 7PS (7388 3344, www.gordonramsay.com).

South

Canton Arms
This Stockwell gastropub does an unconventional Sunday lunch, but there's always at least one concession to a roast – slow-cooked venison shank with mash and red wine gravy, for example.
177 South Lambeth Road, SW8 1XP (7582 8710, www.cantonarms.com).

Joanna's
A Crystal Palace stalwart serving roasts to locals for what seems like forever. Beef sirloin is here served with buttered savoy cabbage, yorkshire pudding, broccoli, carrots and roast potatoes.
56 Westow Hill, SE19 1RX (8670 4052, www.joannas.uk.com).

Wallace & Co
Gregg 'the Egg' Wallace's all-day deli-café is a pleasant little place to sit down for lunch. It's a good deal, too; £15 for a roast and dessert.
146 Upper Richmond Road, SW15 2SW (8780 0052, www.wallaceandco.com).

Westbridge Draft House
As well as standard roasts, this craft-ale pub offers large groups the chance to 'Host Your Own Roast', featuring such large sharing dishes as saddle of blackface lamb or whole roast pork belly.
74-76 Battersea Bridge Road, SW11 3AG (7228 6482, www.drafthouse.co.uk).

East

Carpenter's Arms
This convivial pub knows that Sunday lunch shouldn't be limited to roasts, and offers various alternative mains – a rich cassoulet, perhaps.
73 Cheshire Street, E2 6EG (7739 6342, www.carpentersarmsfreehouse.com).

Galvin La Chapelle
This Grade II-listed church hall is a lush setting in which to enjoy a three-course set lunch that usually has a roast option.
St Boltoph's Hall, 35 Spital Square, E1 6DY (7299 0400, www.galvinrestaurants.com).

A Little of What You Fancy
Kingsland Road's latest serves a mix of classic Sunday roasts and the occasional themed meal, such as a Greek roast lunch.
464 Kingsland Road, E8 4AE (7275 0060, www.alittleofwhatyoufancy.info).

Princess of Shoreditch
À la carte offerings at this *Time Out* award winner have a French slant, but Sunday lunch is staunchly British: roasted pork belly, aged Irish sirloin and organic chicken.
76 Paul Street, EC2A 4NE (7729 9270, www.theprincessofshoreditch.com).

West

Cadogan Arms
A countrified boozer with a snug dining room at the back, the Cadogan Arms lays on a traditional Sunday roast, with roast fore-rib of beef or free-range Devonshire Bronze chicken, plus the trimmings.
298 King's Road, SW3 5UG (7352 6500, www.thecadoganarmschelsea.com).

Crabtree
The Sunday lunch menu at this vast riverside boozer features a massive 28-day aged Longhorn côte de boeuf, served with gratin dauphinoise, spinach, and peppercorn and bearnaise sauces.
Rainville Road, W6 9HA (7385 3929, www.the crabtreew6.co.uk).

Jam Tree
This quirky Kensington pub has a global menu, but the roasts stick to the straight and narrow: rib of beef with yorkshire pud, roasted root veg, french beans, broccoli, and spuds roasted in duck fat.
58 Milson Road, W14 0LB (7371 3999, www.thejamtree.com).

Orange Public House & Hotel
Sunday lunch at this light, relaxed dining room consists of your choice of 28-day-aged Castle of Mey beef rib, Kilravock Farm pork rack or free range chicken with bacon and sage stuffing.
37-39 Pimlico Road, SW1W 8NE (7881 9844, www.theorange.co.uk).

Princess Victoria
An impressive people's pub, serving roasted rib of Angus beef with yorkshire puds, horseradish and roast potatoes. Save room for dessert.
217 Uxbridge Road, W12 9DH (8749 5886, www.princessvictoria.co.uk).

1013

Writing under appropriate noms de plume (Egon Toast, Megan Bacon and the prolific Hashley Brown among them), the writers of the London Review of Breakfasts are devoted to finding the finest fry-ups in town. Read their witty reviews at http://londonreviewofbreakfasts.blogspot.com – and don't forget to leave a condiment.

1016 *Go down the drain*

A new display at the London Wetland Centre (Queen Elizabeth's Walk, SW13 9WT, 8409 4400, www.wwt.org.uk/london) walks you through a life-size sewer pipe to show you what happens after you flush the loo or pull the plug. Promising sights and sounds (but happily, no smells), it also explores the environmental impact of chucking nappies, fat and other nasties down the drain.

1017 *Make Time for Tea*

Step back in time on a Sunday afternoon by dropping by Time for Tea. This 1940s-style tea parlour is hosted by Johnny Vercoutre – vintage enthusiast and modern-day dandy about town. Knock back the earl grey and tuck in to freshly baked scones and banana bread while you listen to old school jazz and lose track of time for a while. Opening times vary; check before visiting. **Time for Tea** *110 Shoreditch High Street, E1 6JN (07540 227148, www.timefortea.org.uk).*

1014 *Meet the Handlebar Club*

On the first Friday of the month, tradition dictates that the only large table of the Windsor Castle Pub (27-29 Crawford Place, W1H 4LQ, 7723 4371) is reserved for members of the Handlebar Club (www.handlebarclub.co.uk). Founded in 1947, the Club was formed to bring moustaches from across the globe together for a puff and a pint. To qualify for membership and a natty regulation tie (burgundy, with a fetching tache print), chaps must sport a moustache 'with graspable extremities' – although those with a beard (officially banned under club regulations) or no moustache at all are welcome to attend as a Friend of the Club. Meetings are jovial affairs, with the conversation meandering from whisker lengths to the best moustache waxes.

Crammed with Royal memorabilia, the pub itself is a delight: look out for the snap of the late Queen Mum, pulling herself a pint behind the bar.

1015 *Get an Eyeful of London*

For unrivalled views across the city, head 443 feet (135 metres) skywards in one of the London Eye's glass pods (Jubilee Gardens, SE1 7PB, 0871 781 3000, www.londoneye.com). From the top, if the weather's clear, you can see as far as Windsor Castle, some 25 miles away.

1018 *Get inky on Fleet Street*

Whether you choose to spend a weekend or several weeks over it, a course at the St Bride's Print Workshop will teach you the art of printing the old-fashioned way. Slow paced and mathematical, letter-press is typography at its most physical. Set just off Fleet Street, this place is populated with the ghosts of newspapermen and printers past. The presses are grand old cast iron Victorian affairs, while metal and wooden type comes in huge cases. The capitals are stored in the upper part of the case (hence talk of letters being 'upper-case'), with the lower-case letters, of course, stored below. You'll leave lead-stained and ink-splattered, with your very own handmade posters and cards. **St Bride Foundation** *Bride Lane, Fleet Street, EC4Y 8EQ (7353 4660, www.printworkshop. stbridefoundation.org).*

1019-1025

Become a cider connoisseur...

A band of London publicans are turning their backs on the mass produced, sugar-packed ciders of old, and serving a range of toothsome drinks, sourced from independent UK producers. Round these parts, people can get as passionate about their apples and pears as their real ales.

Builders Arms

Three keg ciders and a perry are on tap at this neat Victorian pub, set on a manicured Kensington backstreet.

1 Kensington Court Place, W8 5BJ (7937 6213, www.thebuildersarmskensington.co.uk)

Bree Louise

Plain, noisy and brightly lit, this is a place for drinkers rather than stylish types. But with 11 real ciders and perries from the cask and box on offer, it's pretty hard to beat.

69 Cobourg Street, NW1 2HH (7681 4930, www.thebreelouise.com)

Chimes

Cider and traditional English grub are the forte at Chimes, served up in a woody, faintly rustic bar. There are usually four draught ciders, along with plenty of bottled offerings.

26 Churton Street, SW1V 2LP (7821 7456, www.chimes-of-pimlico.co.uk)

Green Man

There are usually a dozen ciders on draught in this student pub, including one keg choice and unusual offerings from small cider producers like Hogan's and Thistly Cross.

36 Riding House Street, W1W 7EP (7580 9087, www.thegreenmanw1.co.uk)

Harp

A daily changing menu of real cider and perry, from lesser-known producers around the UK, is on sale in this narrow drinking den. The names are as intoxicating as the brews: who could resist a drop of Devon Moonshine or Two Trees Perry?

47 Chandos Place, WC2N 4HS (7836 0291, www.harpcoventgarden.com)

The Jolly Butchers

This unfussy Stoke Newington venue aims to have three or four interesting draught ciders and perries at any one time: Hereford Dry Cider from Upper House Farm, or perhaps a medium farmhouse perry from Dennis Gwatkin.

204 Stoke Newington High Street, N16 7HD (7249 9471, www.jollybutchers.co.uk).

Southampton Arms

A tiny but lovely little ale and cider house, with a 1940s-style interior and a garden out back. Eight real ciders and perries flow from the taps, all proudly sourced from independent breweries and producers, and there are proper sausage rolls on the bar. It's cash only, so bring some readies.

139 Highgate Road, NW5 1LE (no phone, www.thesouthamptonarms.co.uk).

1026

... And sup a drop at Borough

One of Borough's fixtures, New Forest Cider (01425 403589, www.newforestcider.co.uk) offers succour to weary shoppers from its stand on Rochester Walk. In summer there's medium or dry Snake-Catcher, in winter, hot mulled cider; ask for a taster and staff will be happy to oblige.

Southampton Arms

Curator's top ten

1027-1036

*Meriel Jeater, Curator
of the Medieval Gallery
at the Museum of London*

Woolly mammoth tusk (c200,000 BC)
This almost complete tusk of a woolly mammoth is from Uphall Pit in Ilford, and was donated to the London Museum by the Natural History Museum in 1913.
London Before London Gallery

Brick with Roman graffiti
A graffito has been roughly incised into this ordinary brick while its red clay was still soft: AVSTALIS DIBVS XIII VAGATVR SIB COTIDIM ('Austalis has been wandering off on his own every day for the past 13 days'). The rhyming couplet hints at a worker's irritation with a colleague for not showing up at work.
Roman Gallery

Roman face-cream (AD 150-200)
Such cream is a very rare survival, with the fine condition of its tightly shut lead alloy tin due to the waterlogged nature of the ditch where it was found. The main constituent of the moist white paste is animal fat. It was mixed with starch (produced by adding boiling water to roots or grains) to make the fat whiter and smoother in texture; starch is still used in cosmetics today.
Roman Gallery

Loaded dice (AD 1460-1500)
Gambling with dice was very popular in 16th-century London. These bone dice are all fraudulent: three have the numbers one to three repeated; three only have four, five and six; and X-rays showed all the others had been weighted with drops of mercury. These 'loaded' dice would fall the same way every time. Loaded dice were called 'fulhams' – presumably Fulham was notorious as the haunt of dice-sharpers.
Medieval Gallery

Great Fire model
The Great Fire Experience is the oldest model in the collection. It was delivered in autumn 1914, with a model of a Thames Frost Fair. It was the idea of a benefactor, Mr Joicey, who developed a passion for models of the city. The museum's director, Guy Laking, told Joicey: 'Your idea of the models is too splendid, there is no doubt the British public prefer them to anything'.
War, Plague & Fire Gallery

John Dwight's hand grenade (c1673)
In 1678, John Evelyn wrote in his diary about 'a new sort of soldier called Grenadiers who were dexterous in flinging hand-grenades'. This salt-glaze stoneware grenade would have been filled with gunpowder, sealed with a wooden plug and then lit with a fuse.
Expanding City Gallery

Wellclose prison cell (c1750)
This small prison – off Wellclose Square, near the Tower of London – was below a public house called the Cock

& Neptune. The tavern was connected to a courthouse, for which the pub's landlord acted as gaoler. Beer and spirits were sold freely in the prison which, like other gaols in this period, was run on a commercial basis.
Expanding City Gallery

Lord Mayor's coach (1757)
The coach was designed by Sir Robert Taylor and completed by many different artisans, including carvers, gilders and painters; its allegorical painted panels depict London's commercial activities. Commissioned in 1757, the coach was inaugurated for that year's Lord Mayor's Parade. It remains the property of the Corporation of London, and still leaves the museum for the annual Parade.
City Gallery

Prison bread (1907-1914)
A piece of bread removed as a souvenir from Holloway Prison by a hunger-striking Suffragette. The Suffragettes fought to win votes for women, with their militant action on the streets of London leading to the imprisonment of more than 1,000 women.
People's City Gallery

Alexander McQueen pashmina (2009)
This wool pashmina has fringe edging printed with the Union Jack, but the main decoration is a cut-out from a photo of Queen Elizabeth II taken in 1952 by Dorothy Wilding. A red rose has been added near the Queen's left elbow, as well as a rosette in Union Jack colours with the McQueen logo. The image looks as if it has been slightly scorched.
World City Gallery

Museum of London *150 London Wall, EC2Y 5HN (7001 9844, www.museumof london.org.uk).*

1037
Shop for stationery at Liberty

Notebook fiends and journal junkies rejoiced when Liberty launched its swanky new stationery room. As well as its exquisite Liberty of London notebooks, pencil cases and paper – in the distinctive floral and peacock-feather prints – you can also lay your hands on Vivienne Westwood silk-printed writing pads and the full Moleskine range. For those pen-to-paper moments when only the best will do, there's the gold leather Liberty of London notebook (£45), embossed with the classic Ianthe print. That'll give you something to write home about.
Liberty *Regent Street, W1B 5AH (7734 1234, www.liberty.co.uk).*

1038
Admire the Olympic medals

Between 27 July and 12 August 2012, the Royal Opera House (Covent Garden, WC2E 9DD, 7240 1200, www.roh.org.uk/theolympicjourney) is hosting a free exhibition that will include an example of every Olympic medal since Athens 1896, as well as all the Olympic Torches since the tradition began at Berlin 1936. 'The Olympic Journey: the Story of the Games' will use archive film, audio and artefacts from the Olympic Museum in Lausanne to tell the story of the Olympic Games, from its ancient Athenian roots, through Baron Pierre de Coubertin's revival, right up to the feats of modern-day sporting heroes.

1039 ## Go retro at EW Moore

Escape from Farrow and Ball'd ubiquity with a trip to vintage wallpaper warehouse EW Moore's. This family run business is in the secret little black book of many an interior designer, lured by the range of limited-run vintage wallpapers and wallcoverings from the 1960s to the '80s.
EW Moore *39-43 Plashnet Grove, E6 1AD (8471 9392, www.ewmoore.com).*

1042
See opera for a song

If you thought opera (and its prices) were elitist, give Opera Holland Park (7361 3570, www.operahollandpark.com) a whirl. From early June until mid August, OHP sets up its canopied stage amid the greenery of Holland Park, with a programme that runs from obscure Italian operas to crowd-pleasers such as *Carmen*. Every season, the company releases thousands of cut-price tickets as part of its Inspire scheme, which aims to introduce opera to a wider audience. It gets even better if you have children – or can borrow one – as 1,200 free tickets are set aside for nine to 18-year-olds. (Under-16s must be accompanied by an adult, who also qualifies for a free ticket.) Unsurprisingly, they're soon snapped up; consult the website to find out when you can apply.

1040
Nail the look at WAH

Once the domain of wannabe WAGs and ladies who lunch, nail art is cool again – thanks to WAH Nails. Designs run from studded beauties, animal prints and anchor-adorned Bretton stripes to incredible one-offs (tiny Russian dolls, say, or collaborations with the likes of Marc Jacobs). The Dalston set-up also sells fashion 'zines and limited edition T-shirts; while you're waiting for your nails to set, you can get a double-dip dye at its in-store salon, Bleach.

WAH Nails Dalston *420 Kingsland Road, E8 4AA (7812 9889, wah-nails.com).*

1041
Learn about London's new postcode

Thanks to the London 2012 Olympic and Paralympic Games, London is getting a whole new postcode to cover the Olympic Park: E20. We say 'new', but in fact the EastEnders of Walford bagged it 25 years ago – fictionally. Which is somehow fitting. The Olympic Stadium gets a whole suffix to itself: E20 2ST.

1043-1046
Move in literary circles

Breaking the unwritten law that literary events must be terribly serious, Book Slam (www.bookslam.com) is London's original and best literary club night. The brainchild of Whitbread-winning author Patrick Neate and Everything But the Girl's Ben Watt, this thriving monthly soirée was once described as 'a book event for people who don't go to book events'. An impressive line-up of writers (Zadie Smith, Will Self, Nick Hornby and Louis de Bernières) have appeared, alongside comics, poets and musicians.

In addition to Book Slam, you can catch the literati at Book Club Boutique (www.thebookclubboutique.com), the boozy book club breathing new life into the 'literary salon' in Soho, and Bedtime Stories at 40 Winks (109 Mile End Road, Stepney Green, E1 4UJ, 7790 0259), a story-reading soirée in the flamboyantly decorated home of designer David Carter, where the dress code is pyjamas, nightgowns and 'glamorous boudoir attire'.

Look out, too, for flying visits from Literary Death Match (www.literarydeathmatch.com), a globe-trotting showdown that started life in New York, in which four literary luminaries battle to impress the judging panel and audience.

Join the Romantics at Keats House

If you're fed up with commodified couples' nights on Valentine's Day, celebrate instead by attending a reading at Keats House (Keats Grove, NW3 2RR, 7332 3868, www.keatshouse.cityoflondon.gov.uk). It was here, after all, that Keats fell in love with the girl next door, Fanny Brawne. Bear in mind, though, that we're talking tortured souls as much as hearts and flowers; last year's soirée was entitled 'Love Hurts'. Other poetic events are held at the house year-round.

1048 *See holy remains*

Yards from Marble Arch is an unlikely haven of tranquillity and religious observation. Tyburn Convent was founded in 1901, on the site of the old Tyburn gallows; among those executed here were 105 Catholic martyrs. In the ground-floor chapel, 25 resident nuns maintain a continual silent contemplation, while the basement contains a shrine to the martyrs. Wall-mounted cases contain the relics: fingernails, splinters of bone, bloodstained linen and hanks of hair. A sister is available for guided tours daily at 10.30am, 3.30pm and 5.30pm.
Tyburn Convent *8 Hyde Park Place, W2 2LJ (7723 7262, www.tyburnconvent.org.uk).*

1049

Play hide and seek in Thames Barrier Park

Now you see me, now you don't: with its split levels and high, undulating rows of shrubs and hedges, the Thames Barrier Park (North Woolwich Road, E16 2HP, 7476 3741) makes the perfect venue for hide and seekers of all ages. After your exertions, you can cool off in the dancing fountains or with a superior ice-cream from the café. The prize for winner and losers both is the view to the Thames Barrier and beyond across the river.

Read the Yellow Book

The National Gardens Scheme (www.ngs.org.uk) initiative sees thousands of private gardens opening their gates to the public on selected dates. The proceeds go to charity, and you get to explore some rarely seen horticultural gems: home-made teas or a glass of Pimms may be on the cards too. The scheme is countrywide, but the capital has plenty of gems – from 5 St Regis Close, with its abundant planting and quirky architectural features, to the lovely Garden Barge Square in SE1, with seven floating gardens connected by walkways and bridges. Search for a garden near you on the NGS website, or invest in a copy of the *Yellow Book* directory, published each February.

Thames Barrier Park

Cantelowes

1051-1055
Sample the skate scene

In the past six or seven years, London's classic skateparks have been joined by several landmark additions. Here's a rundown of the best the capital has to offer.

Cantelowes

Backing on to Cantelowes Park on Camden Road, this is a perfect example of the kind of quality concrete public skateparks that are on the rise in London. Built in 2007, it offers a good mix of transition and street obstacles, catering for all abilities.
212 Camden Road, NW1 9HG
(www.cantelowesskatepark.co.uk).

Meanwhile 2

A popular skate spot since the 1970s, Meanwhile 2 is located underneath the Westway, a short walk from Royal Oak tube. The legendary waves remain, while the street section benefited from a 2008 refurbishment that added extra ramps, a hip and grind boxes. Coverage from the gloomy motorway overpass makes this an ideal spot in inclement weather.
Below the Westway, off Harrow Road, W2.

Mile End

The spot of choice for street-skaters in London. Ledges of various height, length and shape keep the more technical-minded occupied, while those favouring transition take it in turns to carve around the deep pool.
Mile End Park, corner of Burdett Road & St Paul's Way, E3 5BH (www.mileendskatepark.co.uk).

Southbank

This space below the Royal Festival Hall remains the most readily identifiable skate spot in London. Today, the bank and stair area is joined by a series of semi-permanent concrete blocks, and Southbank continues to be a place of pilgrimage for any travelling skateboarder.
Belvedere Road, SE1.

Stockwell

Affectionately known as 'Brixton Beach', this 1970s-built, bowl-heavy park encountered a series of problems with poor surfacing. Now, thanks to tireless work from locals, it has been resurfaced with some minor design modifications.
Stockwell Park Road, SW9.

1056-1072 *Get a taste for Maltby Street*

Maltby Street is emphatically not a street market – merely a collection of rented railway arches, where several Borough Market stalwarts had set up storage and production. (The cool, damp vaults provided the ideal conditions for maturing cheese, for a start.) When the traders decided to experiment with opening to the public in late 2010, London's foodies found a new shopping destination. Most traders open 9am-2pm on Saturday; www.maltbystreet.com has updates on who's trading where.

Monmouth Coffee in Arch 34 on Maltby Street marks the caffeine-fuelled starting point of a greedy amble. Outside, you might find Kitty Travers presiding over La Grotta Ices' three-wheeled ice-cream van; stop for a scoop of rhubarb and custard ripple. At no.40, meanwhile, is the Gergovie Wines warehouse, with natural wines to sample, drink in and take away. Pick your way through the rubble of Rope Walk to find (sharing an arch) the Ham & Cheese company and the production site of the Kernel Brewery. A five-minute detour east of here, Kappacasein occupies no.1 Voyager Railway Arches,

dispensing its trademark toasted cheese sandwiches and delicious raclette.

No.55 Stanworth Street houses a number of delights: Fern Verrow's biodynamic vegetables, Aubert & Mascoli's French and Italian artisan wines, Coleman Coffee Roasters' brews, and delicious comté at the Borough Cheese Company. In a further arch is a collection of fine cheeses from Neal's Yard Dairy, while Mons is at arch 59, specialising in cheeses from France and the Alps, plus alpine rock salted butter. On the Druid Street side, Arch 104 is home to a warehouse collective, with top-notch hunks of meat (Jacob's Ladder Farms), Polish cured meats (Topolski) and hot oatcakes with Leicestershire cheese, courtesy of Käse Swiss. The venerable Booth's greengrocers (now Tayshaw Ltd) is at the other end of Druid Street (Arch 60). Between them, in Arch 72, the St John Bakery was a significant arrival, selling oven-hot loaves and the finest custard doughnuts in the city from a humble trestle table.

If you're expecting lots of snacks and jolly stallholders, you'll be disappointed – this is just a row of railway arches in a former industrial quarter. You do, however, get the space and time to find out about provenance directly from producers who really care about sourcing.

1073-1076
Cast off

London's knitting fixation is still going strong. Clicking the needles in public will never again be viewed as a social shame, and hand-knits fit neatly into today's downsized, ethical vibe.

You'll find knitting groups at http://stitchn bitch.org and on Facebook (including Knitty Gritty, which knits tents at festivals, among other activities). For classes, inspiration, supplies and general knitworking, try Fabrications (7 Broadway Market, E8 4PH, 7275 8043, www. fabrications1.co.uk), Loop (15 Camden Passage, N1 8EA, 7288 1160, www.loopknitting.com) or Prick Your Finger (260 Globe Road, E2 0JD, 8981 2560, www.prickyourfinger.com).

We're also very fond of I Knit London (106 Lower Marsh, SE1 7AB, 7261 1338, www.iknit.org.uk), which sells yarns, books and needles. Hosting film nights, meet-ups and classes, it's also licensed: just don't drop your stitches after supping a cider or two.

1077
See the world from a fresh perspective

Dedicated to promoting independent journalism, the Frontline Club hosts an up-to-the-minute programme of debates, talks and exhibitions, offering a fresh take on current events. Its calm confines provide a stark contrast to the hard-hitting documentaries it shows in its Sunday Screenings: Mexico's murderous drug cartels, the links between mobile phone manufacture and illegal mining in the Congo and the war in Afghanistan have all come under on-screen scrutiny. The club also showcases the work of journalists, photographers and documentary-makers who have lost their lives on assignment.
The Frontline Club *13 Norfolk Place, W2 1QJ (7479 8960, www.frontlineclub.com).*

1078
Take aim

Instead of the thwack of leather on willow, Lord's Cricket Ground will hear the whistle of arrows this summer, as it hosts the London 2012 Games Archery competition. If you're inspired by the athletes (or visions of Robin Hood), there are plenty of clubs where you can have a go: www.archerygb.org, is a good starting point. Among them is London Bridge-based 2020 Archery (7515 4944, www.2020archery.co.uk), which offers taster sessions for £20. The man from Sherwood Forest is still remembered in the sport; there's considerable kudos if you get a Robin Hood (splitting an arrow's shaft by firing another arrow into it).

1079
See hard-hitting drama for a tenner

The Royal Court (Sloane Square, SW1W 8AS, 7565 5000, www.royalcourttheatre.com) has always showcased new British talent – from John Osborne's *Look Back in Anger* in 1956 to the numerous playwrights it's nurtured over the past decade: Jez Butterworth, Anya Reiss and Conor McPherson among them. On Mondays, every ticket costs just £10 – available on the day, online and in person. Bargain.

Marawa the Amazing

1084-1087
Sup a pre-market pint

Been out at night and still wide awake? Carry on the excess with a cheeky breakfast pint at one of the city's early-opening pubs. In Smithfields, the beautifully restored Fox & Anchor (115 Charterhouse Street, EC1M 6AA, 7250 1300, www.foxandanchor.com, opens 7am Mon-Fri; 8.30am Sat, Sun) is less spit-and-sawdust than it once was, and offers its own ales alongside a quality fry-up. Meanwhile, the Hope (94 Cowcross Street, EC1M 6BH, 0871 984 1334, opens 6am Mon-Fri) has been serving the market traders for years. The Cock Tavern (East Poultry Avenue, EC1A 9LH, opens 5.30am) offers ales, with or without such breakfast stalwarts as kippers and smoked haddock.

Down in Borough Market, meanwhile, the Market Porter (9 Stoney Street, SE1 9AA, 7407 2495, www.markettaverns.co.uk, opens 6-8.30am Mon-Fri), is firmly on the beer buff's radar for its range of brews.

1080-1083
Hula!

Give hula-hooping a whirl to get your core muscles working hard – and burn around 500 calories an hour. I Love Hula Hooping (www.ilovehulahooping.com) runs hour-long Hoopdance sessions at Islington Arts Factory (2 Parkhurst Road, N7 0SF, 7607 0561, www.islingtonartsfactory.org), while Hoopswirled (www.hoopswhirled.com) offers classes in Woodford and Redbridge. Polestars (7274 4865, www.polestars.net) runs two-hour taster classes and six-week courses, promising a longer, more lithe frame.

Finally, we're big fans of Marawa the Amazing (www.marawatheamazing.com), globe trotting hula girl extraordinaire. The finale of her spectacular live show involves up to 70 spinning hoops; pick up a few tips at one of her regular London workshops, which glory in the name of Marawa's Hoola Schoola. For other classes, visit www.londonhulahoopers.org.uk.

Fox & Anchor

1088-1100

Muck in at a city farm

Belmont Children's Farm
At this leafy city farm, children can join in at feeding time, pet the smaller animals or take tractor and trailer rides; check online for the daily schedule. Animals run from rabbits to reindeer.
The Ridgeway, Mill Hill, NW7 1QT (8959 3308, www.belmontfarm.co.uk).

Crystal Palace Park Farm
Kune pigs, alpacas, goats and Shetland ponies populate the small yard and paddock, but it's the reptile room that utterly fascinates kids.
The Croft, Ledrington Road, SE19 2BS (8778 5572, www.crystalpalaceparkfarm.co.uk).

Deen City Farm
Set on National Trust land, this five-acre farm has an unexpectedly rural feel. Its inhabitants include Shetland sheep, pigs, cows, ducks, chickens, peacocks, alpacas and a huddle of rabbits and guinea pigs.
Morden Park Estate, 39 Windsor Avenue, SW19 2RR (8543 5300, www.deencityfarm.co.uk).

Freightliners City Farm
Among Freightliners' star turns are Olivia and Matilda the dexter cows, Berkshire and British middle white pigs and some huge Giant Flemish rabbits. Cookery lessons, a gardening club and myriad school holiday events add to the appeal.
Paradise Park, Sheringham Road, off Liverpool Road, N7 8PF (7609 0467, www.freightliners farm.org.uk).

Hackney City Farm
Hackney City Farm is thriving, with its pretty golden Guernsey goats, Tamworth pigs and friendly donkey. It's also a community hub, with a veg box scheme, pottery classes, courses (gardening, beekeeping) and a great Italian café.
1A Goldsmiths Row, E2 8QA (7729 6381, www.hackneycityfarm.co.uk).

Hounslow Urban Farm
Now here's something you don't see very often – pig racing. It's held every weekend at this 29-acre urban farm, along with animal handling sessions.
A312 at Faggs Road, Feltham, Middx TW14 0LZ (8831 9658, www.hounslow.info).

Kentish Town City Farm
London's oldest city farm features a frog-filled pond with a dipping platform, mucking out sessions and pony rides for a pound on Saturdays, from March to September.
1 Cressfield Close, off Grafton Road, NW5 4BN (7916 5421, www.ktcityfarm.org.uk).

Lee Valley Park Farms
Not the cheapest of city farms, but you do get two farms for the price of one. Hayes Hill is a traditional farm and rare breeds centre (with play zones and pedal tractors), while Holyfield Hall is its commercial neighbour. In spring, visitors can bottle-feed the new lambs.
Stubbins Hall Lane, Crooked Mile, Waltham Abbey, Essex EN9 2EF (01992 892781, www.leevalley park.org.uk).

Mudchute City Farm
With Canary Wharf's towers as its backdrop, Mudchute is a bucolic escape. Follow the paths through woods and hedgerows, past fields of donkeys, goats, pigs, sheep, cows and llamas. The Mudchute Kitchen's terrific, too.
Pier Street, Isle of Dogs, E14 3HP (7515 5901, www.mudchute.org).

Hackney City Farm

Newham City Farm

Towering over the poultry, sheep, pigs and goats is Blaze the shire horse, who pulls a dray cart that visitors can ride in. There are also smaller, furrier chaps (rabbits, guinea pigs and two ferrets), a house of finches and a barn owl.
Stansfeld Road, E6 5LT (7474 4960, www.newham.com).

Spitalfields City Farm

This compact community farm feels a world away from the encroaching towers of the Square Mile, with a full complement of pigs, sheep and poultry, plus donkeys and a pony.
Buxton Street, off Brick Lane, E1 5AR (7247 8762, www.spitalfieldscityfarm.org).

Surrey Docks Farm

Sheep, goats and chickens wander the farmyard, while pens house organically reared cows, pigs, horses and a donkey. Kids can also learn about food production from the dairy, milking barn, bee room, orchard and veg plots.
South Wharf, Rotherhithe Street, SE16 5ET (7231 1010, www.surreydocksfarm.org.uk).

Vauxhall City Farm

Vauxhall's answer to the countryside is this tiny patch of mud, muck and enthusiasm. Rare breed pigs and cows, alpacas, goats and sheep inhabit a straw-bale animal house, while the ecology garden hosts pond-dipping sessions and mini-beast hunts.
165 Tyers Street, SE11 5HS (7582 4204, www.vauxhallcityfarm.org).

1101 Cheer on Doggett's Coat & Badge Race

Blink and you'll miss it: one of London's most historic and intriguingly titled pieces of pageantry is a river race that covers the 'four miles and seven furlongs' between London and Albert Bridges in under half an hour. Doggett was the actor who established the event in 1715, while the coat (the resplendent red tunic of the Company of Watermen and Lightermen, which organises the race) and badge (large and silver) are the traditional prizes. The event is contested between half a dozen newly qualified Freeman of the Company, each rowing their own modern craft. London Bridge makes a good viewing point for the start of the race, and Battersea Park for the finish.

1102 Eat authentic udon

Udon – a type of thick Japanese noodle – is the speciality at Koya. Using wheat flour imported from Japan, the chefs make the noodles from scratch every day, taking up to five hours. The technique involves kneading the dough with their feet, creating a firm but supple texture. The dashi, or broth, is made fresh from shaved air-dried skipjack tuna, and is incredibly umami-rich.

Noodles are served in four different ways, hot or cold, and there are donburi (rice bowls), small side dishes and sake as well. Go for the Niku udon and savour the thin slivers of beef, tender onions and scallions, or try the Tempura udon, which comes with a huge, lightly-battered prawn. If the flavours are too delicate for your tastes, Kinoko udon with walnut miso and wild mushrooms is more intense.
Koya *49 Frith Street, W1D 4SG (7434 4463, www.koya.co.uk).*

1103 Take a tour of the St Pancras hotel

Sir George Gilbert Scott's piece of 'exuberant Gothic', as Sir John Betjeman called it, originally the Midland Grand, has been magnificently reborn as the St Pancras Renaissance hotel. Tours can be booked by contacting Royden Stock, Hotel Historian and Tour Guide (7841 3540, royden. stock@renaissancehotels.com); they cost £20 per person and include tea, coffee and pastries (daytime) or a glass of sparkling wine (evening).

House of spirits

Stephanie Wolff **is haunted by a very unusual house.**

On the kitchen table at 18 Folgate Street, a simple breakfast lies half-eaten, the bread knife mid-chop; another slice is speared on the toasting fork, in front of the fire's embers. A starched linen bonnet perches haphazardly on the arm of a chair, and a handwritten recipe book lies open in readiness for an afternoon's baking, the ingredients already neatly laid out. In the corner chair, Madge the rat-catching cat is curled up asleep. It's a vision of domesticity with a quietly disquieting edge: a landlocked, east London *Mary Celeste*.

Upstairs, the unmade beds are in disarray, a letter has been left half-written, and a cotton bud lies askew in an oyster shell of face powder. In the dining room, the glasses and detritus strewn on the table testify to an evening of heavy smoking and drinking– but whoever caroused until the early hours is gone now. The clatter of horses' hooves and incessant toll of church bells are the only sounds: outside, though, there are no horses on the streets of Spitalfields, and the bells of Hawksmoor's Christ Church have already pealed the hour. Welcome to the house of Dennis Severs: a unique, intrinsically theatrical space, described by David Hockney as 'one of the world's greatest works of opera'.

A Californian by birth, Dennis was drawn to our little island by the 'English light'. In 1979, he bought the house on Folgate Street – a red-brick Georgian affair on one of one of Spitalfields' imposing Georgian terraces – and set about its gradual transformation. The house wasn't simply a showcase for its owner's 18th-century antique finds, but also an outlet for his artistic leanings. Dennis wrote that he 'worked inside out to create what turned out to be a collection of atmospheres. Moods that harbour the light and the spirit of various ages',

Dennis imagined a family of Huguenot silk weavers, whom he called the Jervises, living in the house alongside him. Peppering the rooms with tangible traces of their presence, he began to create what he described as a 'still-life drama'. In essence, the house became a walk-in, three-dimensional work of art, whose wonderfully rich still life set-ups hark back to the golden age of the Dutch masters. Dennis wanted his audience to feel as if the occupants had just left the room, and to fill in the gaps for themselves; in other words, to complete the puzzle with too few pieces.

It's an imaginative, darkly atmospheric tour de force, with all sorts of playful clues and cross-references woven into its texture. For the kitchen, he took inspiration from the artwork in Beatrix Potter's *The Tailor of Gloucester*, a copy of which lies open on the kitchen table. Upstairs, he based his bedroom on illustrations taken from a catalogue of the work of Daniel Marot, cabinet-maker to King William III.

A closer inspection of the fireplace's blue and white tiles, meanwhile, reveals some unexpectedly familiar figures. Gilbert and George stand side by side on one, while east London historian Raphael Samuel sits between two towering piles of books on another, his wastepaper basket overflowing

with paper. The antique-looking tiles are, in fact, tiny, mischievous vignettes of Spitalfields locals, created in the 1980s by Dennis's partner, the ceramicist Simon Pettet, and inspired by the 17th-century tiling in the kitchen.

When Dennis died in 1999, the future of the house looked uncertain. In fact, it has survived and continued to evolve, thanks to the efforts of two loyal custodians. The house's manager, Mick Pedroli, originally from Holland, came to help manage the house in the spring of 1995. 'Dennis was a brilliant man, but he needed someone to help keep him on track,' he confides. 'I remember

the first time I came to the house, there were massive piles of unanswered letters.' Curator David Milne, meanwhile, was a longstanding friend and visitor to the house for many years, helping to arrange the rooms and host lavish dinner parties ('We would simply leave the remnants of the dinner from the night before, as if it had been the Jervises"). The Spitalfields Trust, which now owns the house, gives Mick and David free reign to their creativity, so long as they uphold Dennis's spirit and legacy.

And uphold it they have. The sheer accumulation of detail and sensation has a powerful effect, from the smell of cloves and orange peel in the bedroom to the dank, mouldy

air of the scullery. The cobwebs clinging to the bed's velvet drapes in the Dickens Room, the light from the windows making shadow play with the peeling wallpaper, the distant chatter of the Jervis family, the tick-tock of the clock and the occasional ringing of the maid's bell all combines to create a vivid, if peculiarly disjointed, sense of time and place. Visitors are left to wander the candle-lit rooms at will and talking isn't allowed, as it breaks the spell.

With the scents, noises and even temperatures carefully manipulated to complete the ambience (the National Trust has sent curators here to learn more about creating atmosphere), it is like being immersed in a waking dream. David's set-ups are extraordinarily meticulous: rather than merely placing a half-written letter on a table, he will sit at the spot and imagine what its writer was doing and thinking as he wrote, then place the feather quill to one side, adjusting the teacup and tea spoon to a logical angle.

It would, however, be wrong to see the house as a museum or a painstaking period reconstruction – and to quibble over historical anomalies, as certain visitors do, is to miss the point. At the other extreme, some take the experience a little too literally. Mick once got into an argument with a lady claiming to be a direct descendant of the Jervis family; refusing to see reason, she was ejected from the premises – with a full refund.

For the imaginative visitor, though, the house can induce a curious reverie and tap into some unexpected emotions: on several occasions, people have emerged in floods of tears. 'Dennis's house makes real connections with people,' explains David. 'It taps into a tangible form of nostalgia.' It's not for everyone, of course – hence the house's motto, *Aut Visum Aut Non!* (You either see it or you don't).

The writer Jeanette Winterson, another Spitalfields local, grasped its essence, writing that 'fashions come and go, but there are permanences, vulnerable but not forgotten, that Dennis sought to communicate'. This seems poignant, since Dennis is no longer around– yet at the same time his energy and spirit grow, the more people discover his extraordinary house.
Stephanie Wolff writes about and photographs curious corners of London in her blog, http://londoninsight.wordpress.com. Dennis Severs' House (18 Folgate Street, E1 6BX, 7247 4013, www.dennissevershouse.co.uk) is open to visitors 6-9pm Mon, noon-4pm Sun.

South of Twickenham and bang midstream in the Thames, Eel Pie Island is connected to the mainland – but only since 1957 – by a narrow, arching footbridge. Around 550 metres long by 140 wide at its midriff, it's covered in a miscellany of quirky low-lying wooden homes, boatyards, studios and trees, and sprigged with houseboats. The fact that so many of the buildings face out to the river for easy boat access, along with the absence of roads, gives it an inside-out architecture that's perfectly in keeping with the independent spirit of its residents. The name derives from the island's trademark food staple, which was supposedly snacked on by Henry VIII when hopping between Hampton Court and the riverside homes of his many mistresses.

Eel Pie has long been a destination for day-tripping revelry, particularly during the 140-year tenure of the grand Eel Pie Hotel and dancehall, which opened in 1830. A party from *Nicholas Nickleby* danced here 'in the open air to the music of locomotive band'. In the 1950s jazz greats topped the bill, succeeded in time by young Mods and rock 'n' rollers. Other regulars who played at the hotel before it closed down in 1967 after attention from the police included the Rolling Stones, David Jones (later Bowie) and the Who; Pete Townshend was so taken by the island that he named his music company after it.

Eel Pie is privately owned and the public usually have access only to the main path. But on two weekends a year, the 25 or so Eel Pie Island Artists (www.eelpieislandartists.co.uk) open their studios to visitors. It's a congenial occasion featuring cups of tea, plates of Cheezy Wotsits and community chat, not to mention the opportunity to buy or commission art, visual and craft-based – some of it pleasantly affordable.

The best way to get to Eel Pie Island is to take the train to Twickenham and turn left into London Road, then Water Lane. That way you'll appreciate how much of an island Eel Pie is, as the chainstores and Rugby pubs of Twickenham cede place to the quirky republic of eeldom.

1106-1122 *Hunt down London's spies*

Begin your mission at Hyde Park Corner tube at around 11am. Sneak out through Exit 1 (Hyde Park) and turn into the park through the stone gateway. Cross the road and veer left down Rotten Row. Eager younger spies might recognise the neighbouring sand track from the horseback chase in the Alex Rider film *Stormbreaker*. At the Serpentine, sit on one of the benches: Len Deighton's working-class spy, Harry Palmer, had a clandestine meeting here in *The Ipcress File*.

As a boy, Deighton is said to have witnessed a German agent's dramatic arrest in a nearby tea room, so be discreet when you set off again. You're going to take a surreptitious walk beside the lake as far as the road, cross over and turn left down Exhibition Road towards South Kensington. In the 1930s, an official handbook for communist spies recommended this area as an ideal base; you can't help but admire their style. On your right, as you cross Kensington Gore, is the Royal Geographical Society, which has a long pedigree when it comes to espionage. It was a front for 19th-century spying in the era of the 'Great Game', when RGS explorers informed their superiors about imperial Russian activities in Central Asia.

South down Exhibition Road, also on your right, Imperial College counts among its alumni the enigmatic Sidney Reilly. Known as the 'Ace of Spies', he's thought to have been the real-life inspiration for James Bond. At the Science Museum, Alex Rider fans can relive his parachute heroics in the Making the Modern World gallery, while, just before the crossroads, the Natural History Museum saw service as a demonstration room for disguised radios, secret inks and even exploding cowpats during World War II.

Skulk left around the V&A Museum and, a bit further along, creep into Brompton Oratory. Cold War KGB agents used the war memorial to the right of the entrance as a *dubok* (dead letter box), depositing secret microfilms behind the columns for later collection. But keep that confidential – the Oratory isn't proud of having played an unwitting part in the history of international espionage.

Escape across the road and head right, then follow Thurloe Place left as it forks into Exhibition Road. Go left to the corner near

Westminster CCTV Control Centre

South Kensington tube and fortify yourself with lunch at atmospheric Gessler at Daquise (20 Thurloe Street, 7589 6117, http://gesslerlondon.com). Founded by a Polish fighter pilot in 1947, it was a favourite hangout of East European agents. Past diners include Oleg Gordievsky (the highest-ranking KGB double agent, 'exfiltrated' to this country in the mid 1980s) and three of the 'Cambridge Five'. In the 1960s, a young showgirl called Christine Keeler found herself regularly lunching here with the Soviet Embassy's Senior Naval Attaché. She was clearly a huge fan of *pierogi*, since she has always denied passing on or receiving classified information from her other lover: John Profumo, Secretary of State for War.

After lunch, duck through tube's arcaded entrance and head left down Pelham Street (which turns into Sloane Avenue). When you hit the King's Road, head right, then take the second right. At 9 Bywater Street, the blue house is the fictional home of John le Carré's 'small and podgy' spy, George Smiley.

Back on the King's Road, you'll find Wellington Square almost opposite. Ian Fleming never provided an exact address, but Bond experts think no.30 is most likely the 'comfortable flat in the plane-tree'd square' which 007 called home. Keep going until Oakley Street, and turn down it to your left.

Just before the river, dip right into Cheyne Walk. Amble past Cheyne Walk Brasserie (no.50, 7376 8787) – George Smiley's local – and have a snoop at Ian Fleming's post-war home in the red-brick Carlyle Mansions. *Casino Royale*, intended as 'the spy novel to end all spy novels', was planned in flat no.24, although the text itself was written at

Fleming's Jamaican home. In his teens and twenties, Fleming lived ten minutes further on, at Turner's House (no.119).

Join the river and double back past Albert Bridge and the Royal Hospital Chelsea (7881 5200, www.chelsea-pensioners.org.uk), used as a dead letter box by 'Cambridge Five' spy Guy Burgess. The alcoholic Burgess, code-named 'Little Girl', was a flamboyant figure – in exile in Moscow, he continued to get suits delivered from his Savile Row tailor.

It's now time for you to do some quick reconnaissance: you're looking for the bus stop. Turn left off Chelsea Embankment up Chelsea Bridge Road and, outside the Lister Hospital, hop on a no.360 bus (Elephant & Castle). Sit on the left.

In Bond's day, the Secret Intelligence Service was just that: secret. Now, both MI6 and MI5 openly operate from imposing Thameside HQ. Once the bus is on Vauxhall Bridge sneak a peek through the glaring green glass of MI6's £240m home, Vauxhall Cross, believed to extend five storeys below ground on the south bank. As you shadow the river, you'll also spy the long yellow roofs of Thames House on the far side. This is the home of MI5, sometimes known by its rather impressive postal address, 'Box 500'.

In another five minutes, disembark at the Imperial War Museum. The first floor has a permanent Secret War gallery, devoted to British espionage. Here you'll find concealed bugs, shirt collars impregnated with invisible ink and a German Enigma code machine.

From the museum, take a diagonal through the park on your left, cross Kennington Road and catch the no.59 bus (King's Cross) for the five-minute journey to Waterloo Bridge. Jump off beside the National Theatre. Be careful: in 1978, Bulgarian dissident and BBC journalist Georgi Markov was stabbed with a poison umbrella as he waited here.

If the coast is clear, duck into the subway behind you, skirting the IMAX and proceeding towards Waterloo station. Once you're on the main concourse, try to blend in with the crowd as you scout out the CCTV surveillance cameras that tracked another doomed hack in *The Bourne Ultimatum*. If you manage to spot more than 30 cameras, you've proved your worth: mission accomplished!

1123
Share the pleasure of pedalling

Operating from Bushy Park in southwest London since 1995, Companion Cycling (07961 344545, www.companioncycling.org.uk) pairs people who can't cycle alone with volunteer co-cyclists. Offering side-by-side recumbents, tandems and two-seater trikes, along with a rickshaw for those with restricted mobility, it caters for a huge range of users. Anyone 'from nine months to 90' with a need for the service is welcome to sign up for a spin, with members' special needs running from learning difficulties and visual impairments to mobility problems. 'After not being able to walk any distance for a long time, it was like being let out of prison,' declared one 80-year-old user. Volunteers are always welcome at the weekend sessions, and you're given an induction before your first foray.

1124-1126
Indulge in some public pampering

Dispel visions of cockroaches and cracked tiles: London has some beautifully revamped public Turkish baths, offering steam rooms, saunas, and a range of treatments at democratic prices.

The grandaddy of them all is the historic Porchester Spa (Porchester Centre, Queensway, W2 5HS, 7792 3980). Its capacious Grade II-listed marble and green-tiled relaxation room is an art deco delight. To one side is the swimming pool, while down a sweeping staircase lies a warren of hot rooms, steam rooms and a sauna – plus the skin-tingling, icy cold plunge pool. The mood is inclusive, and the café even serves bacon sarnies. In similar white-tiled mode, Bethnal Green's Spa London (York Hall Leisure Centre, Old Ford Road, E2 9PJ, 8709 5845) is slightly less atmospheric but offers considerably fancier facilities, such as an ice fountain, aroma steam room and a wider range of treatments. In spring 2012, we're also looking forward to the reopening of Ironmonger Row Baths (Ironmonger Row, EC1V 3AF, www. aquaterra.org/ironmonger-row-baths), another early 20th century hot-room-and-steam institution, set in Grade II-listed premises.

Primrose Hill

1127-1152

Enjoy all London's protected views

'Earth hath not anything to show more fair', was William Wordsworth's verdict on the view from Westminster Bridge, while Ray Davies of the Kinks was inspired by a Waterloo sunset. In 2010, the Mayor recognised the importance to the capital of 26 of its classic vistas, listed below, by protecting their sightlines from development.

This may have been the most comprehensive legislation of its kind, but it wasn't the first: the view of St Paul's Cathedral from King Henry VIII's Mound in Richmond Park, created in 1710, is the only one in England to have been protected by an Act of Parliament, in 1902. It remains an awe-inspiring sight: tall trees and hedges seem to frame a tiny dome floating mystically on the horizon a good ten miles away. To get to the mound, enter Pembroke Lodge and turn right.

Panoramas

Alexandra Palace; Parliament Hill; Kenwood; Primrose Hill; Greenwich Park; Blackheath Point.

Linear views

The Mall to Buckingham Palace; Westminster Pier to St Paul's Cathedral; King Henry VIII's Mound, Richmond, to St Paul's Cathedral.

River Prospects

Tower Bridge; London Bridge; Southwark Bridge; Millennium Bridge and Thames side at Tate Modern; Blackfriars Bridge; Waterloo Bridge; the South Bank; Golden Jubilee/Hungerford footbridges; Westminster Bridge; Lambeth Bridge; Victoria Embankment between Waterloo and Westminster Bridges; Jubilee Gardens and Thames side in front of County Hall; Albert Embankment between Westminster and Lambeth Bridges along the Thames path near St Thomas' Hospital.

Townscape Views

Bridge over the Serpentine to Westminster; Island Gardens, Isle of Dogs, to Royal Naval College; the Queen's Walk to Tower of London; St James's Park to Horse Guards Road.

1153 *Climb aboard a Floating Cinema*

Occupying a customised narrowboat, the Floating Cinema (www.floatingcinema.info) hosts free on-board film screenings, canal tours, talks and workshops, as well as larger scale outdoor movie nights, held by the water's edge.

1154 *Stop for tea with the cyclists...*

Epping Forest: ancient royal hunting grounds, gorgeous woods, an abundance of fungi and atmospheric winding paths. What more could you want? How about a couple of the best east London caffs this side of Ian Beale? No phone, no loos and no seats (bar some fence posts); in fact, nothing much other than a green shed, brilliant bread pudding (70p) and cups of tea. This is a de-facto clubhouse for the mountainbike fraternity (and some roadies); at weekends you can barely fight your way to the hatch for bikies and their wheels.
Carl's Tea Hut *near Epping Forest Visitor Centre, Nursery Road, IG10 4AE.*

1155 *... Or the bikers*

If leather's more your thing, visit the similarly basic tea hut at the corner of Cross Roads and Fairmead Road, just off the A104 at the Robin Hood roundabout (IG10 4AA). We say basic, but it does serve up an awesome bacon buttie. If you visit at the weekend, odds are you'll find it swamped by bikers: this is a regular club rallying point and ride stop-off.

1156 *Attend Horseman's Sunday*

This charming ceremony takes place every September, at the Church of St John's Hyde Park (Hyde Park Crescent, W2 2QD, 7262 1732, www.stjohns-hydepark.com). It all began in 1968, when a local stables, threatened with closure, held an outdoor service to protest. Since then, it's become an equine institution: at noon, after morning service, the vicar rides out to bless and present rosettes to a procession of horses and riders.

1157 *Join the pizza purists*

Although it now has a bigger outpost on Chiswick High Road, we're still attached to Franco Manca's rough and ready original incarnation in Brixton Market. The sourdough is left to rise for 20 hours before being baked in the wood fired oven, and the ingredients are mainly organic. Don't expect an elaborate menu or fancy presentation: instead, there are six simple pizzas (ricotta and pork, say), all under £7, washed down by a glass of house red or white at ramshackle communal tables.
Franco Manca *4 Market Row, Electric Lane, SW9 8LD (7738 3021, www.francomanca.co.uk).*

1158-1161

Get a prime view of the Olympic Park

Almost in touching distance of the Olympic Stadium is a vivid yellow-green collection of recycled metal shipping containers. The View Tube (www.theviewtube.co.uk) has been carefully positioned on a ridge, a short walk from Pudding Mill Lane DLR, to provide the best possible vantage on the Olympic Park. While devouring scrambled eggs in the excellent Container Café within, you can see the Stadium to the left, Zaha Hadid's low-slung Aquatics Centre to the right, and between them the distant Velodrome and Basketball Arena. Boards show the park's layout and explain how it was all built.

For a high-rise take on the Olympic Park, try the Olympic Park Viewing Gallery (Holden Point, Waddington Road, E15 1QN, 3373 0421, www. opvg.co.uk). This meeting room was created on the 22nd floor of a residential tower block, and can be booked by members of the public from 2-3pm on the fourth Friday of each month, for a modest sum (minimum booking five people).

If eating is important while you're peeking, there is a posh alternative and a cheap one on Fish Island, a pleasant walk to the north of the View Tube. Forman's Restaurant (Stour Road, E3 2PA, 8525 2365, www.formans.co.uk/restaurant) offers a truly local speciality in plain view of the Olympic Park: London-cure smoked salmon, made in the East End since 1905. Next door, the Counter (Stour Space, 7 Roach Road, E3 2PA, 07834 275920 mobile, www.thecountercafe.co.uk) is a café in an arts space, run by the same cheerful bunch as the Container Café. Its two floors offer views of the Stadium across the Lee Navigation that are barely bettered even from Forman's.

1162 *Take the plunge*

Interested in scuba diving, but not sure if you'd enjoy it? A two-hour taster session with Big Squid (7627 0700, www.bigsquid.co.uk), held in Dulwich or Battersea, should help to make up your mind – and, at £25, is a darn sight cheaper than commiting to a pricey long haul trip.

View Tube

1163

Worship an Arts & Crafts icon

Just off Sloane Square, Grade I-listed Holy Trinity church is crammed with artistic treasures – so much so that Sir John Betjeman declared it to be the 'Cathedral of the Arts & Crafts movement'. Its architect, John Dando Sedding, was a founding figure of the movement, and enlisted the help of a host of his talented cohorts, including Henry Hugh Armstead, John Tweed and Frederick Pomeroy. Its crowning glory is the enormous East Window (designed by Edward Burne-Jones and manufactured by Morris & Co), whose jewel-like panes depict prophets, saints and apostles. During the war, the window miraculously survived a series of air raid attacks – including a direct hit in May 1941, which destroyed the church's roof.
Holy Trinity *Sloane Street, SW1X 9BZ (7730 7270, www.holytrinitysloanesquare.co.uk).*

1164

Go to the dogs at Battersea

It's a little known fact that London's iconic sanctuary for lost and abandoned pets is open to casual visitors, as well as would-be adopters. Established in 1860, Battersea houses around 280 dogs and 80 cats at any one time; visiting hours are 1-4pm on weekdays, and 10.30am-4pm at weekends. Alternatively, attend the 'Annual Reunion', held each September in Battersea Park. It brings together some of the families that have rehomed pets from the centre and features a fancy dress competition (for the dogs, of course). **Battersea Dogs & Cats Home** *4 Battersea Park Road, SW8 4AA (7622 3626, www.battersea.org.uk).*

1165

Befriend Arnold Circus

At the centre of the red brick, Grade II-listed Boundary Estate, Arnold Circus is a historic bandstand and gardens – and a unique part of the East End's heritage. Rescued from disrepair by a group of locals in 2004, it's now a spruced-up resource for all, hosting picnics, brass bands and even an annual Carrom championship. Become a friend of Arnold Circus (http://foac.org.uk), and help continue the good work.

1166

Snoop around the Petrie

The Petrie Museum of Egyptian Archaeology (University College London, Malet Place, WC1E 6BT, 7679 2884, www.petrie.ucl.ac.uk) is a little-known delight. It's crammed with dim cases (the museum supplies wind-up torches to help you see into the dusty corners) full of Egyptological minutiae. Among 80,000 assorted artefacts (pottery shards, combs, a rat trap, cubit rods, jewellery, cosmetics jars, a duck-shaped jug), the most seductive item on display is a 4,000-year-old dress – a saucy beaded net affair, thought to have been worn by an ancient Egyptian dancer.

1167

Ride the new Routemaster…

For many Londoners, the classic red double-decker bus – the open-backed, hop-on hop-off Routemaster, with its peaked-cap conductor and cheery ding-ding bell – was an irreplacable loss when it was taken out of service in 2005, after five decades of dutiful service. Mayor Boris Johnson is hoping to cash in on the nostalgia by launching a new, eco-friendly Routemaster (technically called 'The New Bus for London'). The new bus is certainly impressive, with fuel-efficiency technology that includes recharging the battery with energy generated by braking and, yes, a new take on the open rear platform. The first five prototypes will be on the roads from spring 2012.

1168-1169

… Or hop on one of the originals

You can still ride in an old Routemaster on one of two 'heritage routes'. Beautifully refurbished buses from the 1960-64 fleet run on routes 9 (from Aldwych via the Strand, Trafalgar Square and Piccadilly Circus and to the Royal Albert Hall) and 15 (from Trafalgar Square to Tower Hill, with glimpses of the Strand, Fleet Street and St Paul's Cathedral). Head to stops B or S in the south-west corner of Trafalgar Square for a central jumping-on point; fares match ordinary buses, but you must buy a ticket before boarding.

1170

Learn a language for a song

One of London's best-kept secrets: respected language school International House runs evening classes taught by teachers in training. It costs a bargain £25 for a course of eight to ten lessons, of beginner or intermediate French, Spanish, Italian or German. We've found them to be well supervised and a great way to learn. **International House London** *16 Stukeley Street, WC2B 5LQ (7611 2400, www.ihlondon.com).*

1171

Take to the ice at the Tower...
Londoners have always relished ice-skating in the great outdoors – not least in the 17th century, when the Thames regularly froze over. Locals made the most of it, as writer John Evelyn observed, not only with sleds and 'sliding with skates', but bull-baiting, horse and coach races and puppet plays, among other pursuits (he also noted the 'tippling' that went on). Milder winters may have put paid to such revelry on the river, but you can seek consolation with a skate around the Tower of London (8241 9818, www.toweroflondonicerink.com). Every winter, a section of the moat at this London landmark becomes an outdoor rink – with mulled wine and mince pies to keep out the chill.

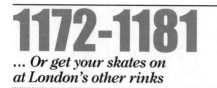

1172-1181

... Or get your skates on at London's other rinks

Alexandra Palace
After a £2.3 million refurbishment, Alexandra Palace Ice Rink is back on sparkling form. There are courses for all ages; nervous novices can also book one-on-one lessons with a private coach.
Alexandra Palace Way, N22 7AY (8365 4386, www.alexandrapalace.com).

Broadgate Ice Arena
This City rink is open from mid November to late January. Although compact, it's often less crowded than the capital's other outdoor rinks. Unusually, it operates a no-bookings policy – great if you're not one for forward planning.
Broadgate Circle, EC2A 2BQ (7505 4100, www.broadgateice.co.uk).

Canary Wharf Ice Rink
See if you can out-skate the City slickers at this seasonally opening rink. The vertiginous towers of Canary Wharf loom over the ice; at night, when they're lit up, it's particularly atmospheric.
Canada Square Park, E14 5FW (0844 847 1556, www.canarywharficerink.com).

Hampton Court Palace
With Henry VIII's impressive old pad as its backdrop, this 900-metre-square rink has space for 250 skaters. Wheelchairs are welcome on the ice, except during the last session of the day.
East Molesey, Surrey KT8 9AU (8241 9818, www.hamptoncourticerink.com).

Lee Valley Ice Centre
Disco nights are a big hit at this modern (and comparatively warm) indoor ice centre. Lessons are also offered, and the rink rarely feels too crowded.
Lea Bridge Road, E10 7QL (8533 3154, www.leevalleypark.org.uk).

Michael Sobell Leisure Centre
This small ice rink hosts well-attended after-school sessions and ice-skating courses. The are fast-paced, fun ice hockey sessions for over-sixes too.
Hornsey Road, N7 7NY (7609 2166, www.aquaterra.org).

Natural History Museum
Set in front of the museum, between trees strung with twinkling fairylights, this 1,000-metre-square winter ice rink has a magical feel.
Cromwell Road, SW7 5BD (7942 5725, www.nhmskating.com).

Queens
Beginners are well looked after at this indoor ice rink, which also holds disco nights on Fridays and Saturdays. Belgian waffles in the café are a big hit with kids.
17 Queensway, W2 4QP (7229 0172, www.queensiceandbowl.co.uk).

Somerset House
The magnificent courtyard at Somerset House is probably London's most iconic temporary rink, iced over from late November to late January.
Strand, WC2R 1LA (7845 4600, www.somersethouse.org.uk).

Streatham Ice Arena
The arena offers the combined attractions of an ice rink and karting track. Streatham has had a rink since 1931, but concerns over its future rumble on; for details, see www.sisag.org.uk.
386 Streatham High Road, SW16 6HT (8769 7771, www.streathamicearena.com).

1182

Survive some deadly plantlife

Plants have been trying to kill us, not cure us – or so says the controversial Royal College of Physicians Garden Fellow Dr Henry Oakley. His tour of the RCP's Medicinal Garden, on the first Wednesday of the month from February to October, will lead you through 1,000 medicinal (or historically medicinal) plants such as star anise (from which Tamiflu is derived), *teucrium marum* (a feline aphrodisiac) and blue liverwort (a 17th-century liver 'tonic' that is in fact toxic to that organ). It's a fascinating eye-opener to the uses, dangers, history and folklore of plants.
Royal College of Physicians *11 St Andrews Place, NW1 4LE (7935 1174, http://old.rcplondon.ac.uk).*

A few of my favourite things

1183-1192

Ade Adepitan,
TV presenter & Paralympian

East London today is very different to the East London I grew up in. I particularly like the Whitechapel Gallery (77-82 Whitechapel High Street, E1 7QX, 7522 7878, www.whitechapel gallery.org); they converted an old public library into a bright new space for art, while retaining its original features. There are people who visit it now who still remember it back when it was a functioning library.

The 2012 Olympic and Paralympic Games (www.london2012.com) being held in East London is like a dream come true for me. The Olympic Village is on the site of where I trained as a kid. I played Paralympic Basketball in Sydney in 2000 and Athens in 2004, so I can't believe I've retired and it has come here.

Dans Le Noir (30-31 Clerkenwell Green, EC1R 0DU, 7253 1100, www.danslenoir.com), a restaurant where you eat in the dark, is great fun. I found it quite scary at first because I get claustrophobic: it's so dark you can't see your own hand. It's weird trying to get food into your mouth without dropping it, and topping up your wine glass. You can't always work out what the food is, even though you do taste it more. You're given a choice of menu – meat, vegetarian or a surprise menu – and they tell you afterward what you've eaten. I chose the surprise menu and ate shark.

I really like the Telegraph pub (Telegraph Road, SW15 3TU, 8788 2011, www.the telegraphputney.co.uk). It's an old place with a proper log fire in the winter. I'm not a big drinker, but when I do have a tipple I have a soft spot for the cider they serve. The pub is on Putney Heath, and in summer you can sit out on the benches under the trees.

I do a lot of training by riding through Putney Heath (SW15 3TU) to Wimbledon Common (SW19 5NR, 8788 7655, www. wpcc.org.uk). It's very leafy, and popular with horseriders; there are a couple of stables round here. I have a hand bike that's three-wheeled and low to the ground, and operated by using both hands moving forward at the same time.

I often go to the Theatre Royal Stratford East (Gerry Raffles Square, E15 1BN, 8534 0310, www.stratfordeast.com), and really enjoy their productions. Last year I saw *Reasons To Be Cheerful*, a musical built around Ian Dury's music: most of the cast was disabled, which was really cool.

Growing up in east London, we went to Queen's Market (Green Street, E13 9AZ, 8475 8971, www.friendsofqueensmarket. org.uk) for pie, mash and liquor. The pie and mash stall closed, but there are still traditional greengrocers and butchers that have been there for four generations, next to newer stallholders from all over the world: West Africa, Mauritius, Pakistan. You find locally grown strawberries next to cassava from Nigeria and preserved lemons from Algeria.

My friends and I used to go to the boating lake in Valentines Park (Cranbrook Road, Essex IG2 6EA, 8708 8100, www.redbridge. gov.uk) in Ilford. We would hire the boats and try and throw each other into the water. It used to be £1 a go.

When Victoria Park (Old Ford Road, E3 5DS) had open-air cinema screens we'd try to sneak in – now it has the Lovebox festival (www. lovebox.net) which is so much fun. I try to go every year, and have great memories of seeing Groove Armada and Norman Jay there. Back in the day, I was a big drum 'n' bass fan. The places I used to go to aren't around anymore, though – Paradise Club in Islington, Roller Express in Edmonton and Camden Dingwalls. My mates try to get me to go to Fabric, but I'm not up for all-nighters anymore. That's why Lovebox is perfect. It's during the day, the sun's shining, and you get that festival vibe – plus a good night's sleep in your own bed.

The gardens at Kenwood House (Hampstead Lane, NW3 7JR, 8348 1286, www.english-heritage.org.uk) are gorgeous. They hold concerts there in summer; the audience sit on the hill by the lake, while the artists perform on a floating stage in the middle. The House is better known for its café, but it has a really nice art gallery too.

1000s of things to do...

1193 *Rethink science at the Dana Centre*

Think science and scientists are dull, irrelevant and best confined to labs? Think again. An evening spent at the Science Museum's Dana Centre (165 Queen's Gate, SW7 5HD, 7942 4040, www.danacentre.org.uk), an adult-only venue exploring issues in contemporary science through dialogue, performance and art, should be enough to convince you otherwise. Every night the creative minds here roll out something different, from haute couture catwalk shows and video gaming cabaret nights to stand-up comedy. Come with an open mind, be prepared to participate, and enjoy a drink or two at the café-bar.

1194

See Napoleon in the nude

On the north side of Hyde Park stands Apsley House – gifted to the first Duke of Wellington after his victory at the Battle of Waterloo, and one of the finest Georgian residences in London. At the foot of the stairs stands an unexpected reminder of the Iron Duke's vanquished foe: an 11-foot statue of Napoleon, stark naked but for the smallest of fig leaves. The museum's other treasures – including paintings by Velazquez and Rubens and an ordinarily astonishing collection of silver and porcelain – pale by comparison.
Apsley House *149 Piccadilly, W1J 7NT (7499 5676, www.english-heritage.org.uk).*

1195-1198

Contemplate a Japanese garden

On the roof of the Brunei Gallery at the School of Oriental and African Studies (Thornhaugh Street, Russell Square, WC1H 0XG, 7898 4046, www.soas.ac.uk) is a small pocket of peace and tranquillity – a Japanese garden, accessible when the gallery is open. With minimal planting, its effect lies in its geometric aesthetic and subtle contrasts of colour and texture: the chequerboard squares of gravel and lemon thyme, say, or the 'river'

of silver grey granite chippings, bridged by slabs of basaltic rock.

The Japanese Landscape at Kew Gardens (Kew Road, Surrey TW9 3AB, 8332 5655, www.kew.org) features gardens of Peace (a traditional tea garden), Harmony (inspired by Japan's mountainous areas) and Activity (raked gravel and rocks represent the flow of water). All three are entered via the Chokushi-Mon (Gateway of the Imperial Messenger) – an intricately-carved replica of a 16th-century gateway that stands in Kyoto.

In Holland Park (Ilchester Place, W8 6LU, www.rbkc.gov.uk), the Kyoto Garden is perhaps London's loveliest Japanese garden, with its tumbling waterfall, serene koi carp pool and variegated foliage – at its best in autumn. Alternatively, head down to Peckham Rye Park (Peckham Rye, SE22 0LR, 7525 2000, www.southwark.gov.uk), whose Japanese garden is a little-known gem. Opened in 1908 and restored in 2004, it features a series of streams and ponds, and has an appealingly wild, untamed feel.

Kyoto Garden

1199-1211
Rummage for vinyl

Alan's Records
Run by the affable Alan Dobrin, this East
Finchley record shop is a laid-back place to buy
some tunes. From post punk to psychedelia,
its stock is joyously eclectic; customers are
welcome to give potential purchases a spin on
the listening decks. Opening times can be erratic.
218 High Road, N2 9AY (8883 0234,
www.alansrecords.com).

BM Soho
Junglist Nicky Blackmarket's vinyl-only store
has kids queuing to bag his latest promos.
Expect nothing other than upfront club music:
the ground floor stocks house, minimal and
techno, while the basement remains London's
most reliable dispenser of new and pre-release
drum 'n' bass, dubstep, bassline and UK garage.
25 D'Arblay Street, W1F 8EJ (7437 0478,
www.bm-soho.com).

Flashback
Boxes of bargain basement 12-inches stand
by Flashback's front door, luring customers in.
The basement is vinyl only: a vast jazz collection
jostles for space alongside soul, hip hop and an
astonishing array of library sounds (regularly
plundered by producers looking for samples).
50 Essex Road, N1 8LR (7354 9356,
www.flashback.co.uk).

Haggle
Famed for its plain-speaking owner, Haggle is
a delightfully old-school operation. Stuffed with
precariously-piled records and closely packed
boxes, it has something to suit every budget.
114-116 Essex Road, N1 8LX (7704 3101,
www.hagglevinyl.com).

Harold Moores Records
Harold Moores isn't your stereotypical classical
music store: young, open-minded staff and an
expansive stock of new and second-hand music
and independent labels all broaden its appeal.
The basement is dedicated to second-hand
classical vinyl, and there's plenty to appeal
to amateur enthusiasts as well as aficionados.
2 Great Marlborough Street, W1F 7HQ
(7437 1576, www.hmrecords.co.uk).

Honest Jon's
This legendary record shop's owner had the
foresight to lend former hired hand James Lavelle
£1,000 to set up Mo' Wax records in the early
1990s. Prints of old blaxploitation posters crowd
the walls – a sign that jazz, soul, revival reggae
and global sounds remain the house specialities.
278 Portobello Road, W10 5TE (8969 9822,
www.honestjons.com).

Intoxica!
Big on character and classic records, this vinyl-
only store is kitted out with bamboo wall cladding
and glowering tribal masks. Shelves are stacked
with everything from reggae, funk and '60s beat
to exotica and easy listening; there's also a good
range of alternative and new wave from the
1970s to today, and a great soundtrack selection.
Head to the basement for soul, blues and jazz.
231 Portobello Road, W11 1LT (7229 8010,
www.intoxica.co.uk).

Phonica
More organised than most, Phonica's orderly
racks of records are thumbed by a clued-up
crowd. Its selections tend towards the deeper,
edgier side of club music, taking in French
electro, minimal techno, dubstep and nu-disco:
it also has its own record label.
51 Poland Street, W1F 7LZ (7025 6070,
www.phonicarecords.co.uk).

Reckless Records

This second-hand record store sells everything from rare rock vinyl to classic drum 'n' bass, punk and reggae, and eagle eyes can unearth some real gems. If you're considering flogging your collection, Reckless will buy most kinds of music for cash or exchange.
30 Berwick Street, W1F 8RH (7437 4271, www.reckless.co.uk).

Rough Trade West

Since it opened here in 1983, the Rough Trade shop has been a beacon for independent-minded music lovers. Scuffed around the edges, its walls plastered with posters, album covers and sleeves, this place is a shrine to vinyl: look out for in-store exclusive, limited-edition releases.
130 Talbot Road, W11 1JA (7229 8541, www.roughtrade.com).

Sister Ray

Sister Ray remains a mecca for Berwick Street's beat obsessives, with its customer turntables and impressively broad stock. Much of the music is on vinyl (over 20,000 plates and counting), and the shop's dedication to back-cataloguing genres like drum 'n' bass, gothic and industrial, hip hop and rock puts most megastores to shame.
34-35 Berwick Street, W1F 8RP (7734 3297, www.sisterray.co.uk).

Second Layer Records

Not far from Highgate tube, this lesser-known record store is well worth seeking out. The owners enthusiasms are many and varied: power-electronics, DIY underground, free-folk, avant-rock, krautrock and 'generally music that defies categorisation'.
323 Archway Road, N6 5AA (07878 051726 mobile, www.secondlayer.co.uk).

Sounds of the Universe

This Soho store's affiliation with reissue kings Soul Jazz records means its remit is broad: on the ground floor, grime and dubstep 12-inches jostle for space alongside new wave cosmic disco, electro-indie re-rubs, Nigerian compilations and electronic madness. A good number of listening posts offer insights into a diverse mix of new releases. The second-hand vinyl basement offers soul, jazz, Brazilian and alt-rock.
7 Broadwick Street, W1F 0DA (7439 2923, www.soundsoftheuniverse.com).

1212 *Make headlines*

The Newspaper Club (7183 2812, www.newspaperclub.com) is sheer genius: a small-scale, bespoke newspaper printing service, run by an East London studio. Designs (sent in as PDFs, or created using the online layout tool) go to press every Tuesday and Thursday at 2pm: less than a week later, you get your papers. For digital printing, prices start at £14 for a single copy; for traditional printing, the minumum order is 300 copies (from £465). Customers' publications have ranged from wedding day special editions to school newspapers, while several enterprising artists have had their portfolios printed up.

1213 *Hear a new take on Hitchcock*

As part of the London 2012 Cultural Olympiad in summer 2012, the BFI will be screening some of Alfred Hitchcock's early, rarely-seen silent films. The one-off events will be accompanied by specially commissioned orchestral scores by leading contemporary musicians: pick of the bunch is *The Lodger: A Story of the London Fog* (1926), set to the music of Nitin Sawhney. If you miss out on tickets, don't despair: BFI Southbank is also planning a major Hitchcock autumn retrospective. For the latest updates, visit www.bfi.org.uk.

1214 *Become a puppet master*

The cutting-edge Complicite theatre company use them, and they helped the wondrous *War Horse* scoop six Tonys on Broadway: puppets are no longer just for kids. To see some masters at work, visit London's Little Angel Theatre (14 Dagmar Passage, N1 2DN, 7226 1787, www.littleangel theatre.com) – a small-scale delight, tucked away in a former temperance hall on a cobbled Islington alley. Next door to the tiny foyer and auditorium, with its rows of rough wooden pews, is the workshop where the puppets are created; if you fancy having a go, there are puppet making and performing courses for adults and children.

1215-1224

Enjoy a classic cocktail...

American Bar

The American Bar in the Savoy is England's oldest surviving cocktail bar. It opened in the hotel in 1893 and has been in its current spot since 1904. The drinks list pays homage to bartenders past: our top tipple is the sweet Martini variant that Ada 'Coley' Coleman mixed for actor Sir Charles Hawtrey. On tasting the confection of gin, Italian (sweet rather than dry) vermouth and Fernet Branca, Hawtrey exclaimed; 'By Jove, that's the real hanky-panky!' – and so it has been known ever since.

The Savoy *Strand, WC2R 0EU (7836 4343, www.fairmont.com/savoy).*

Bar at the Dorchester

To head further back in time, try a Martinez in the Dorchester'sground-floor bar – presided over by Giuliano Morandin for almost three decades. Check out his expertise with this forerunner of both the Martini and Manhattan, that mixes gin ('Old Tom', a 17th-century recipe revived for the hotel), sweet-bitter Italian vermouth and bitters.

The Dorchester *Park Lane, W1K 1QA (7317 6501, www.thedorchester.com).*

Coburg Bar

Pretty much every type of mixed drink will be impeccably delivered at the Connaught's cosily contemporary bar, but why not try one of the rarer varieties? Perhaps a quick Fix, which adds sugar, lemon juice, egg white and fresh fruit to your spirit of choice.

The Connaught *Carlos Place, W1K 2AL (7499 7070, www.the-connaught.co.uk).*

Dukes Bar

After a classic bar, it's time for London's best rendition of *the* classic cocktail. Dukes brings ceremony and real panache to the making of a Martini – concocted at your table, from a smart wheeled trolley. Drops of dry vermouth are flicked from a flask into your iced glass, which is then filled with the finest gin (or, if you must, vodka) and finished with a sliver of Sicilian lemon.

35 St James's Place, SW1A 1NY (7491 4840, www.dukeshotel.com).

Hawksmoor Seven Dials

The world of cocktails might be dominated by the US, but Britain has made its own classic contributions. One such, that the Victorians adored but which has fallen almost entirely out of favour, is the Cobbler. Hawksmoor's Covent Garden outpost serves a superb Sherry Cobbler, made with manzanilla, lemon, sugar and fruit.

11 Langley Street, WC2H 9JJ (7856 2154, www.thehawksmoor.co.uk).

Lonsdale

Among many cocktails invented by British drinks supremo Dick Bradsell (the Snood Murdekin, the Wibble), the Bramble is perhaps the most enduring. Sample this mix of gin, crème de mûre, lemon juice and sugar syrup here, at one of the many London bars Bradsell established. They'll make you a Wibble too, or, if you're hungover, one of Harry Craddock's Corpse Revivers.

48 Lonsdale Road, W11 2DE (7727 4080, www.thelonsdale.co.uk).

Mark's Bar

Having revived classic cocktails at the first Hawksmoor, Nick Strangeway has now taken on the basement at Hix. Among the 'Early British Libations', we concur with George IV in extolling the virtues of the Punch à la Regent, a heady brew combining sherry, rum and brandy with curaçao, pineapple syrup and lemon sherbet.

Hix *66-70 Brewer Street, W1F 9UP (7292 3518, www.marksbar.co.uk).*

Portobello Star

At this long, thin, converted Notting Hill pub, Jake Burger makes a classic Manhattan. The secret is the authentic bitters, recreated according to an early 20th-century recipe. A rare, but not inexpensive, treat.

171 Portobello Road, W11 2DY (7229 8016).

Spuntino

While we're talking ancient cocktails, try a sazerac at this hip little Soho eaterie. Spuntino not only follows the classic recipe – glass washed with absinthe, then add rye whiskey, sugar, Peychaud's bitters and a lemon peel garnish – but serves the drink in a bashed metal teacup for extra speakeasy authenticity.
61 Rupert Street, W1D 7PW (no phone, http://spuntino.co.uk).

Trailer Happiness

The tiki craze brought kitsch, ukeleles and a fantasy of Polynesian excess to drinking in 1950s America. Notting Hill's Trailer Happiness mainlines that exotica vibe – come here for a Vic's Mai Tai (rum and orange curaçao shaken with orgeat, grenadine and lime juice), just how 'Trader Vic' Bergeron used to make 'em.
177 Portobello Road, W11 2DY (7065 6821, http://trailerhappiness.com).

1225-1230

... Or savour the concoctions of the new experimentalists

Callooh Callay

One concoction really stands out at this Lewis Carroll-inspired bar: the massive Mad Hatter tiki punch. Designed to share, it's served in a gramophone-shaped punchbowl.
65 Rivington Street, EC2A 3AY (7739 4781, www.calloohcallaybar.com).

Experimental Cocktail Club

Experimental Cocktail Club

Hidden behind an unmarked door, the ECC provides enough twists for even the most jaded of palates. A less bitter twist on the Negroni, using lavender-infused gin and Suze bitters, makes for an approachable aperitif: the Havana (with cigar-infused bourbon) and Rag Time (Rittenhouse 100 Rye, Peychaud's bitters, Aperol and absinthe) are more potent.
13A Gerrard Street, W1D 5PS (7434 3559, www.chinatownecc.com).

Purl

This eclectically-decorated speakeasy pulls out all the stops with Mr Hyde's Fixer Upper. It arrives in a silver wine cooler, smoking with liquid nitrogen. Reach inside to take out your wax-sealed elixir bottle.
51 Blandford Street, W1U 7HX (7935 0835, www.purl-london.com).

69 Colebrooke Row

Tony Conigliaro's tiny bar produces superb cocktails, developed in a laboratory in the attic. In summer, quaff a La Rose ('English rose garden aromatics topped with champagne'); in autumn, perhaps a Somerset cider brandy sour, complete with a miniature, hay-scented 'bobbing apple'.
69 Colebrooke Row, N1 8AA (07540 528593 mobile, www.69colebrookerow.com).

Whistling Shop

Ryan Chetiyawardana's concise cocktail list revives Victorian recipes with modern techniques: vacuum stills to extract botanicals from gin; liqueurs steeped in herbs and spices; and tonics, syrups, sodas and bitters induced from, among other things, salt and pepper or chlorophyll. We recommend the Panacea, a whisky cocktail infused with sage dust, honey and lavender shrub.
63 Worship Street, EC2A 2DU (7247 0015, www.whistlingshop.com).

Zetter Townhouse

Decorated by Russell Sage to look like the parlour of an eccentric aunt, this cosy hotel bar serves some terrific cocktails. The most elaborate is the Flintlock – a combination of gin, gunpowder tea tincture, sugar, Fernet Branca and dandelion and burdock bitters, served with a little hand-held explosion. Less flashy but every bit as clever, the Master at Arms mixes dark Myers's rum, an evaporation of port and own-made grenadine.
49-50 St John's Square, EC1V 4JJ (7324 4545, www.thezettertownhouse.com).

Market forces

Once almost forgotten, Granville Arcade has found a new lease of life. But what's brought about the change? Katie Dailey investigates.

It seems incredible in a metropolis so over-crowded, and with property at such a premium, that there should be so many retail spaces in abandoned disrepair. In Brixton, up until 2009, Granville Arcade was one of them.

It opened in 1937, with a smart art deco façade that proclaimed it 'London's Largest Emporium'. Under a glazed roof, its bright, airy avenues teemed with grocers and all manner of specialist retailers. In the 1960s, it became a Caribbean market, and a flagship outlet for the fruits and vegetables newly available from the West Indies. For a while, it thrived – but as Brixton's main market expanded, and its principal artery, Electric Avenue, became the capital's destination for Caribbean produce, business began to dip. By the mid 1990s many of the arcade's units were unoccupied, and its handsome old avenues were falling into a dilapidated state.

In 2009, Lambeth Council and LAP, the building's owners, called in Spacemakers, an agency specialising in the regeneration of challenging urban spaces. Its founder, Dougald Hine, visited the arcade. 'I remember feeling what a great space it was – but also how sad it was to see parts of it almost deserted. At the

side furthest away from Atlantic Road, you just saw one empty shop after another.'

Spacemakers embraced the challenge, launching a competition whereby local entrepreneurs, food suppliers, artists and creatives could apply for a unit; the best bids would be rewarded with a free three-month lease. Locals embraced the idea from the start: when the arcade was opened up for an evening so that prospective tenants could have a look and a drink, they arrived in their hundreds.

Spacemakers then awarded the best ideas a place on site and renamed the arcade Brixton Village, in line with its eclectic, locally minded new contents – from bijoux bakeries and vintage boutiques to international eateries and fledgling fashion labels.

What started as a pop-up endeavour soon gained a firmer foothold, much to Hine's delight. 'I don't think we ever anticipated how dramatic the transformation would be,' he admits. 'To see it go from being the dead end of Brixton town centre to a place that was full of life and energy was extraordinary.'

After three months, while no longer free, the rents remained affordable, and many of the market's original applicants – from old-fashioned

confectioners Sweet Tooth (unit 66) to the French-owned Leftovers vintage emporium (unit 71) – were able to keep their homes in the arcade. They've been joined by newcomers like Emy, who runs interiors shop Brixi in unit 7. A Brixton local, originally looking for shop premises in Stoke Newington, she applied for a space in the arcade as soon as she saw the redevelopment. 'The community aspect of the place is amazing,' she enthuses. 'We all make each other tea and host events together. It's still Brixton – it smells of jerk chicken and weed – but it has really changed and stepped up a gear. It's all about variety: there's a new gelaterie, but my neighbour is a healer who offers card reading, and there are some great Jamaican grocery shops.'

Two years on, and Brixton Village is open all week, drawing a cosmopolitan cross-section of visitors. Head there around lunchtime, and you'll be treated to a voyage round the world in 80 paces. Bookended by cheap and cheerful cafés from Venezuela and Jamaica, where you

can eat your fill for a fiver, international food vendors representing every continent on the globe pepper the arcade's avenues. The clientele are a reassuringly international bunch; when we visited, there were plenty of noisy Colombians chattering outside Santa Fereño and enjoying the extremely cheap *arepas* and *empanadas*. Likewise, Thai families were crammed into Kaosarn for a taste of home – although they had to compete for seats with culinary trend-chasers, drawn by a flurry of favourable broadsheet reviews.

Didas (unit 52) is a grocer's selling Jamaican goods, and sits in the more Caribbean corner of the market, where you can find breadfruit, coconuts and custard-fruit. Pull up a chair outside Etta's Seafood Kitchen (unit 85) for a plate of seafood (around £6 a main), courtesy of the charismatic Etta Burrell and her daughter Sheryl. This place has been part of the market since it re-opened: Etta happened to be in the old arcade on the morning before submissions were due, and was invited by Spacemakers to apply for a place. 'They asked me for a business plan. I said – "What's a business plan?!" But I won a double unit all the same.' She remembers the old arcade as a desolate affair. 'A lot of units were empty. It was a sad state. They [Spacemakers] didn't help us do anything to the units, it was all our own work. But by giving us the opportunity to use the space, we could do whatever we wanted. No one really came here before. Now, at 10pm, I can't get rid of anyone!' As with most of the arcade's eateries, the food here is simple and reasonably priced – don't expect dainty china, and be warned that at busy times (most lunches), the windows steam up and you can barely hear yourself eat above the good-humoured din.

For the unashamed bourgeoisie, there are numerous places to break artisan bread. Quirky bakery and café Breads Etcetera (unit 88) supplies a Dualit toaster on every table so you can toast your own (excellent) home-baked bread. For students and arabica lovers, Federation Coffee (unit 46) is an artsy, Kiwi-run café serving superior cakes and coffee among mismatched tables and pictures. One of the most enduringly popular restaurants is Cornercopia (unit 65). Firmly focused on local, market-sourced ingredients, it is closed on Mondays and Tuesdays – a time reserved for producing the pickles and pies that line the deli counter.

All of this may ring a few bells for those Londoners who remember the chaotic variety and noise of Spitalfields Sunday Market before it was redeveloped in 2005. The comparison also rings true for the arcade's independent, idiosyncratic retail offerings; look out for Margot Waggoner's Leftovers, with its stash of Marseille lace and vintage sailor dresses. A few doors up, Binkie and Tabitha's flotsam and jetsam shop Circus (unit 70) juxtaposes retro glassware and '60s vases with an assortment of Socialist literature.

By night, the arcade is represented by some of its residents at regular Thursday and Saturday 'lates'. Soundtracked with live music, these open house events run from workshops and poetry evenings to pop-up supper clubs. Cyndi from United 80 (unit 80), a shop that combines music with African clothes and hand-made leather bags, recently invited Felix of Basement Jaxx down to DJ, drawing huge crowds. 'Brixton's always been a musical place. That night was exactly what Brixton is about,' she says. 'Some locals don't come here anymore: you hear the word gentrification. But gentrification is about property prices, not people. They should come.'

In late 2010 Spacemakers decided that their work here was done, and moved on to a similar venture in West Norwood. 'Our role is to be a catalyst, to help bring people together and get things happening,' says Hine. 'We were originally invited to do a three-month project at the arcade, which was extended and extended again. When it reached a year, it was the right time to step back; we didn't want to build ourselves into the long-term fabric of the arcade. Instead, we're working with people in places from West Norwood to Penrith, sharing what we've learned in Brixton, and exploring new ways of coming together to make spaces that people want to spend time in.'

Brixton Village *Granville Arcade, Atlantic Road, SW9 8PS (7274 2990, http://spacemakers. org.uk/brixton).*

1232-1235
Four market eats

Casa Sibilla (unit 67)
A tiny but accomplished restaurant and deli, whose goods include jars of preserved lemons and chunky tomato ragu. It's open for lunch, and three evenings a week.

Cornercopia (unit 65)
Modern British and European food made from local ingredients (including wines from Kent and Essex) served in one of the arcade's best settings. The menu changes weekly but expect the likes of pork terrine with piccalilli or golden beetroot and sheep's cheese tart.

Etta's Seafood Kitchen (unit 85)
Noisy, cheap and fun. Dishes come with a long serving of chatter and laughter from the indomitable Etta.

Kaosarn (unit 2)
Cheap but very authentic family-run Thai place that lets you bring your own booze. Conventional curries and satays are accompanied by exotic sweet and sour salads. Few dishes cost more than £6.50.

1236

Get your hands on the FA Cup...

The white twin towers that once symbolised English football are just a memory to football fans now, but a tour of the new Wembley Stadium (0844 800 2755, www.wembleystadium.com/tours; £15, free-£8 reductions) is still a great afternoon out. Under Norman Foster's landmark arch, you'll be taken into the changing rooms, the press room, down the Players' Tunnel and even up the Trophy Winners' steps to seize an FA Cup. Not *the* FA Cup – it's a perfect replica – but you'd have to have a wooden heart not to find it thrilling to stand in the footsteps of your sporting heroes.

1237-1243

... Then gawp at further football memorabilia

A stroll around the stands, a photo-op in the home dressing-room, a trot out of the tunnel and on to the hallowed turf: that's what to expect at a football stadium tour at any of the London clubs. But only at Chelsea's Stamford Bridge (Fulham Road, SW6 1HS, 0871 984 1955, www.chelseafc.com) do you learn how a dog bite led to the foundation of the club; and only at Fulham's Craven Cottage (Stevenage Road, SW6 6HH,

7384 4777, www.fulhamfc.com) will you experience the Victorian grandeur of master football architect Archibald Leitch's last surviving London stand. And, for an extra £5, you can be introduced to what must be the most bizarre statue in London: Fulham chairman Mohamed Al Fayed's tribute to the pop singer Michael Jackson.

At West Ham (Upton Park Stadium, Green Street, E13 9AZ , 0871 222 2700, www.whufc.com), you get to drop into the manager's office and hear about how Bobby Moore, Martin Peters and Geoff Hurst won the World Cup. At Arsenal (Emirates Stadium, Ashburton Grove, N7 7AF, 7619 5000, www.arsenal.com) you can stare deep into Michael Thomas's boots, one of which scored the last-minute goal at Anfield in 1989, and won the League Championship. Spurs (White Hart Lane Stadium, 748 High Road, N17 0AP, 0844 844 0102, www.tottenhamhotspur.com) offers the opportunity to sit in Harry Redknapp's hotseat in the dugout, while only in the half-term holidays will you make it on to one of the more sporadic tours of Charlton's Valley (Floyd Road, SE7 8BL, 8333 4000, www.cafc.co.uk).

As an alternative, get along to Brentford FC (Braemar Road, Middx TW8 0NT, 0845 345 6442, www.brentfordfc.co.uk) for a different kind of stadium tour. Griffin Park is the only football ground in the world to have a public house on all four corners. The New Inn, the Griffin, the Royal Oak and the Princess Royal (now taken over by the club) offer a handy pre- or post-match pub crawl for fans appreciative of an historical feature... not to mention a pint or four.

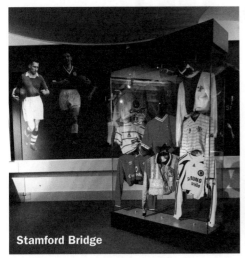

Stamford Bridge

Kensal Green Cemetery

1244-1250 *Dally with the dead*

Things that go around London: the M25, the Circle Line – and a ring of seven Victorian cemeteries, built to alleviate the very real problem of an overload of urban dead, caused by the city's rapid expansion. Most have now ceased to receive incumbents, but remain open to visitors.

Tending towards the decrepit, the 'Magnificent Seven' have become peaceful woodland oases with a romantic atmosphere of ivy-covered neglect. They make natural wildlife havens and some are managed as nature reserves, with all kinds of attendant activity, from tree walks to pond-dipping. Highgate Cemetery is probably the most famous, with Christina Rossetti and Karl Marx among its august residents, and grandiose funerary architecture that includes an Egyptian

Avenue of Pharaonic tombs. Note that entry to the West Cemetery is by guided tour only.

Abney Park Cemetery *Stoke Newington High Street, N16 0LH (7275 7557, www.abney-park.org.uk).*
Brompton Cemetery *210 Old Brompton Road, SW5 0BS (7352 1201, www.royalparks.org.uk).*
Highgate Cemetery *Swains Lane, N6 6PJ (8340 1834, www.highgate-cemetery.org).*
Kensal Green Cemetery *Harrow Road, W10 4RA (8969 0152, www.kensalgreencemetery.com).*
Nunhead Cemetery *Linden Grove, SE26 5PH (7732 9535 www.southwark.gov.uk).*
Tower Hamlets Cemetery Park *Southern Grove, E3 4PX (www.towerhamletscemetery.org).*
West Norwood Cemetery *Norwood Road, SE27 9JU (7296 7999, www.lambeth.gov.uk).*

1251

Watch vintage gas guzzlers...

The London to Brighton Veteran Car Run (www.veterancarrun.com) first ran in 1896, to celebrate the new speed limit of 14 miles an hour, and the fact that 'horseless carriages' no longer needed to be preceded by a man waving a red flag. It's still going strong. On a November Saturday, around 100 pre-1905 automobiles and dapperly dressed motorists process down Regent Street in a 'Concours d'Elegance'. It's free to watch, and a splendid sight. You can also see them setting off the following day, leaving in the early morning from Serpentine Road in Hyde Park.

1252

... Or clean, green machines

On Saturday, the route is driven in reverse by 'electric, hybrid or low-emission internal combustion engine passenger cars' competing in the Future Car Challenge (www.futurecar challenge.com). The winner isn't the first past the post, but the lowest energy user.

1253-1258

Take over the big screen

Whether you're after a lavish screening of your favourite film with 200 of your closest friends, or an intimate viewing of an old family holiday, venues across the capital can oblige.

Seating 25, the cosy, timber-clad basement at the Garrison (99-101 Bermondsey Street, SE1 3XB, 7367 6351, www.thegarrison.co.uk) is available for private hire (£100-£150, depending on the night; £80 for an afternoon at weekends). There's a five by four foot screen, plus inviting banquettes and armchairs on which to sprawl. The swanky One Aldwych (1 Aldwych, WC2B 4BZ, 7300 0700, www.onealdwych.com) is another 30-seater, with seat upholstered in Italian leather, Dolby Digital surround sound and free popcorn. Prices start at £150 per hour; alternatively, book

a deal that includes a glass of champagne and three-course dinner (from £55 per person).

Another upmarket option is the Movie Mogul package offered at the Soho Hotel, Charlotte Street Hotel and Covent Garden Hotel (7287 4434, www.firmdalehotels.com), involving a three-course dinner or a champagne and canapé reception, for £55 a head, exclusive of film rights (minumum ten people). There's even a kids' version, at £30 per child (minimum 20).

Set in the old Constitutional Club in Kensal Rise, the Lexi (194B Chamberlayne Road, NW10 3JU, 0871 704 2069, www.thelexicinema.co.uk) is an 80-seater beauty. There's digital projection, and arty light-bulb installation overhead, and a cracking bar area. Private hire costs from £165 per hour.

The Roxy Bar & Screen (128-132 Borough High Street, SE1 1LB, 7407 4057, www.roxybar andscreen.com) is a more capacious option, with a maximum capacity of 220 and a four-metre screen. The battered leather sofas and sweeping red curtains are cosily atmospheric: prices start at £100 per hour. Equally roomy is the art deco Phoenix Cinema (52 High Road, N2 9PJ, 8444 6789, www.phoenixcinema.co.uk), which holds 255 people and charges £200 to £1,000 an hour. Romantics take note: it was once hired for an audience of two to watch *Gone With the Wind*.

London to Brighton Veteran Car Run

1259-1266

Dine at a supper club

The Pale Blue Door

London has a profusion of supper clubs, run by anyone from amateur enthusiasts to moonlighting chefs. Most involve wining and dining with an amiable bunch of strangers (usually no more than the average flat can fit), generally on communal tables. Menus run from comfort food to blow-out feasts; you usually need to bring a bottle.

You'll have to book well in advance for most of our picks, usually via email. We'd recommend signing up to their mailing lists – it's the fastest way to get in the loop, and in the running for a coveted place at the table. Prices are subject to change, so check before booking.

The Clove Club

The trio of young, ambitious chefs behind this Dalston supper club (http://thecloveclub.com) have worked in some of London's best kitchens. Menus are delightfully inventive, but grounded in careful flavour combinations: buttermilk fried chicken in pine salt, say, or smoked trout tartare with cod roe, brown bread and pickled cucumber.

Fernandez & Leluu

Well-established in the supper club circuit, Uyen Luu (www.fernandezandleluu.co.uk) cooks up a seven-course feast every week in her East London flat, for £35. Spanish and Vietnamese influences often feature – and Luu makes a heavenly beef pho.

Lex Eat

The duo behind this Hackney-based supper club (www.lexeat.co.uk) currently charge just £20 per head for a a three-course feast. It's also delightfully intimate, with room for a maximum of 12 guests around the table.

The Pale Blue Door

Tony Hornecker's idiosyncratic east London supper club (http://tonyhornecker.wordpress.com) is a visual feast: step through the blue door and into a warehouse-turned-wonderland, with candlelit cabaret and cross-dressing waiters. The menu, by contrast, is simple and seasonal, often culminating in a classic British pud.

Rambling Restaurant

The Rambling Restaurant (www.rambling restaurant.com) lives up to its name, making regular forays outside its Camden headquarters; last year, it ran a pop-up café from the back of a decommissioned ambulance at the Urban Physic Garden in Borough. Past supper clubs have run from singles' dinners to uproarious Burns Night celebrations, with haggis in pride of place.

Saltoun Supper Club

This bijou, Brixton-based operation (www. eatwithyoureyes.net) is headed by food stylist Arno Maasdorp, so the presentation is exquisite. Happily, so's the food: four expertly executed dishes (seared scallop with salted caramel, gnocchi with cauliflower and truffle oil), followed by petits fours. It currently costs £35 per head.

The Secret Larder

Run by brother and sister team James and Mary Ramsden, this not-so-secret north London supper club (www.jamesramsden.com/the-secret-larder) takes place every fortnight. Themed three-course dinners are terrific value at £30 a pop – but with just 20 covers, you'll need to book well ahead.

The Underground Restaurant

Food blogger-turned cookbook author Kerstin Rodgers, aka MsMarmiteLover (http://marmite lover.blogspot.com) hosts one of London's best-known supper clubs at her Kilburn abode. She and her team change the menu each time – there has even been a Marmite-themed soirée.

1267
Go on an art safari

Belgium-based street artist Roa's finely detailed, monochrome depictions of birds and animals can be found in cities across the world – with a concentration in east London. The crane that looms large over Hanbury Street is a beauty, while the council's plans to paint over the much-loved Hackney Road hare met with furious opposition. Elsewhere, you'll find a beaver, an ostrich, a squirrel and more, all on a giant scale. The city's street art is, of course, ever changing; consult the regularly updated map of Roa's sites on the Londonist's blog (http://londonist.com).

1268
Jump to it

Launched in spring 2011 as one of the London 2012 Inspire projects, the Jump London initiative hopes to train 500 new parkour coaches by the time the Games roll round. Invented in France in the 1980s, parkour (also known as freerunning) involves bounding over bollards, vaulting over barriers and ricocheting off walls: in essence, using your body to navigate a series of obstacles, at often impressive speeds. For details of classes, visit www.parkourgenerations.com.

1269
See Sundance come to London

Founded by Robert Redford and best known for its annual festival in Utah, the Sundance Institute is launching a mini London offshoot in 2012, showcasing the best independent American cinema. A series of film screenings, music events and panel discussions will take place at the O2 Arena between April 26 and 29 2012; visit www.sundance-london.com for details.

1270
Harvest lavender at Carshalton

Carshalton was once the lavender capital of the world – a tradition kept alive at the three-acre, community-run Carshalton Lavender Field (Stanley Road Allotments, Oaks Way, Carshalton Beeches, Surrey SM5 4NQ, 07948 174907, www.carshaltonlavender.org). Everyone's welcome at the annual harvest weekend in July, when you can pick your own fragrant flowers (£1 for a small bunch or from £6 a bucket). Face painting and a barbecue add to the festive feel.

1271 *Cheer on London's alternative marathon*

Less po-faced than the Oxbridge boat race and much more colourful, the Great River Race (www.greatriverrace.co.uk) follows a 21-mile course along the Thames. Over 300 crews turn up each year from around the globe, crewing all manner of boats; past entrants have included a Viking longboat, a Chinese dragonboat and traditional Irish curraghs. The race runs from Millwall Dock to the riverside below Ham House in Richmond, with thousands lining the banks.

1272
See the city as it used to be

The Museum of London's nifty Streetmuseum map app (www.museumoflondon.org.uk/ Resources/app/you-are-here-app/index.html) is stuffed with interesting images of London's past, from the devastation of the Blitz to the arrest of Emmeline Pankhurst in May 1914 by the gates of Buckingham Palace. Browse the map at leisure or let your phone alert you to featured locations as you wander, then hold the captured image up against the present-day reality to peer through a window in time. Available, free, for iPhone and Android.

Great River Race

1273 *Journey to the South Pole*

'Heart of the Great Alone' at the Queen's Gallery commemorates the 100th anniversary of Captain Scott's fateful journey to the South Pole. Stunning photos from Scott's *Terra Nova* expedition of 1910-13 and the 1914-16 foray undertaken by Ernest Shackleton depict ice-locked ships, towering glaciers and Shackleton's bearded, famished crew. Another, poignantly, depicts a dinner held to celebrate Scott's 43rd birthday – which was to be his last. Celebrating the extraordinary achievements of both men, the show runs from 21 October 2011 to 15 April 2012.
Queen's Gallery *Buckingham Palace, SW1A 1AA (7766 7301, www.royalcollection.org.uk).*

1274 *Put your hands together for Oxjam*

With more than 40,000 musicians playing at over 3,000 events nationwide since its inception in 2006, Oxjam (www.oxfam.org.uk/oxjam) now officially boasts the biggest line-up of any festival in the nation. The scale of its success is thanks to its community dynamic: as a month-long, nationwide event, Oxjam is actually comprised of a series of micro-festivals run by individuals or groups across the country. Hot Chip, Editors and Basement Jaxx are among the big names who have played intimate gigs to help launch proceedings, though the festival remains a grassroots operation at heart; visit the website for details of how to organise your own event.

1275 *Drive a train (or go along for the ride)*

It's the capital's cheapest train journey: £1 return, from the Herne Hill gate of Brockwell Park, SE24 (www.brockwellpark.com) to the lido – some 220 metres away. But then it may well also be the capital's smallest train, with a gauge of 7.25 inches. Battery-operated and steam driven miniature trains ply the route – all accurate scale models. They run from 11am to 4pm on summer Sundays, and are staffed and driven by volunteers. Which could mean you.

The Athenaeum Hotel

1276-1280

See a living wall...

Tranforming barren walls into densely planted patches of biodiversity, living walls are springing up in cities across the globe. The trend was pioneered by Parisian designer Patrick Blanc. Two of his walls can be seen in London, at the Driver (2-4 Wharfdale Road, N1 9RY, 7278 8827, www.driverlondon.co.uk) in King's Cross, and at Mayfair's Athenaeum Hotel (116 Piccadilly, W1J 7BJ, 7499 3464, www.athenaeumhotel.com). The Athenaeum's was the tallest when built, but the beautiful courtyard wall at the Mint Hotel (7 Pepys Street, EC3N 4AF, 7709 1000, www.minthotel.com) has recently outstripped it, at 11 storeys high. View it and the nearby Tower of London from the Skylounge rooftop bar. In Shepherd's Bush, the green wall at Westfield Shopping Centre (Ariel Way, W12 7SL, 3371 2300, http://uk.westfield.com/london) is low-rise but dense with ferns, sedums and woodland wildflowers, with a curving bench along its base. The prettiest living wall in town, though, remains the three-storey beauty at Anthropologie (158 Regent Street, W1B 5SW, 7529 9800, www. anthropologie.eu), covering an internal wall of the store in vertical, verdant greenery.

1281-1283

... Or a green roof

Green roofs – made of plant mats, turf or biodiverse plantings – are also increasingly popular for green, aesthetic and practical reasons. As well as filtering pollutants and providing a valuable habitat for wildlife, they help to reduce urban temperatures and provide insulation in winter. Look out over Canary Wharf when you fly from City Airport and you'll see several, including one on top of the skyscraper at One Churchill Place. More visible from ground level are those found on the Komodo Dragon House at London Zoo (Regent's Park, NW1 4RY, 7722 3333, www. zsl.org) and the sloping roof of the Cue Centre at the Horniman Museum (100 London Road, SE23 3PQ, 8699 1872, www.horniman.ac.uk) – a glorious tangle of meadow grass, moss and wildflowers.

1284-1292

Play pétanque

The French game of pétanque couldn't be simpler. The aim is to throw each metal boule as close as possible to the golfball-sized jack (properly called the cochonnet). The player or team whose boule is nearest at the end of the frame wins a point, and the first team to win 13 points wins the game. You can play singly, or in teams of two or three; for more on the rules, visit www.petanque.org. The Balls Brothers wine bar chain runs a free pétanque pitch in the middle of Hay's Galleria shopping arcade, with bookings taken throughout the summer; see www.ballsbrothers.co.uk for details. Down in Kennington, the lovely Georgian square by the Prince of Wales pub (Cleaver Square, SE11 4EA, 7735 9916) is another boules hotspot; there's also a pitch in Queen's Park, NW6, near the Chevening Road entrance (8969 5661).

If you develop a taste for the game, consider joining a club. The London Pétanque Club (www.londonpetanque.co.uk) organises events for other clubs and individual members to take part in, and meets up monthly in various locations. London's biggest club, the Harrow Pétanque Club (www.harrowpetanque.co.uk), gathers twice a week at the Old Lyonian Sport & Social Club, with members aged ten to 80. All ages are also welcome at Croydon Pétanque Club (07400 455055), which has around 50 members. At Epping Horizons Pétanque Club (www.ehpetanque.supanet.com), beginners are offered free tuition. Kingston (07939 104626) also has its own club, based in the Alexander Tavern on Park Road, while the Parliament Hill Pétanque Club (07880 948105) battles it out on the pitches on Hampstead Heath.

1293-1296

Collect athletic street names

Some of Great Britain's most famous Olympic athletes are commemorated in the following street names. To celebrate London 2012, how about visiting all four – on foot? The circuit is about the length of a marathon.

Bev Callender Close, SW8 3DF
Daley Thompson Way, SW8 3DA
Akabusi Close, CR0 6YL
Ovett Close, SE19 3RX

1297-1298

Experience life as a cabby

How does it feel to be behind the wheel of a licensed London Hackney Carriage? Find out by perusing All in a Day's Work (http://london cabby.blogspot.com) or The Cabbies Capital (http://thecabbiescapital.co.uk). Both blogs are loaded with Knowlegeable wisdom; Day's Work explores London curios, transport politics and how much celebrity customers tip while Cabbies Capital offers nuggets of esoterica and a handy Cabbie Phrasebook.

Museum of Everything

1299 *Sing with the pros*

The BBC Singers (www.bbc.co.uk/orchestras/singers) are the UK's only professional chamber choir. A few times a year, rehearsals are opened to public participation: it's fascinating to see how they work, and a privilege to be conducted by the charismatic David Hill. The venue is generally Maida Vale Studios, worth a visit in its own right for its architectural interest, and the echoes left by the artists who have recorded there, including Jimi Hendrix, David Bowie and The Beatles.

1300 *Explore the Museum of Everything*

Behind a nondescript-looking door, on a leafy street in Primrose Hill, lies this gloriously eccentric enterprise. A showcase for 'the odd, the spectacular and the extraordinary', the museum stages assorted temporary shows of outsider art and curiosities. Its exhibition of artist Peter Blake's extraordinary collections was a classic, featuring kitsch Victorian taxidermy tableaux (boxing ferrets, hard-drinking rats and card-playing squirrels), photographs of fairground freakshows and cosmic embroideries of buxom beauties, stitched by an ex-serviceman who was taught to sew after being injured in World War II. If you like the sound of that, sign up to the mailing list at www.museumofeverything.com.

1301 *Follow in Dr Johnson's footsteps*

Preserved in an atmospheric little square off Fleet Street is the four-storey Georgian residence of Dr Samuel Johnson – poet, literary critic, and author of the *Dictionary of the English Language*. Turn up outside at 3pm on the first Wednesday of the month to take part in the Dr Johnson Walk (£5, no booking required). One route explores the crooked alleyways and antiquated courts around Fleet Street, while the other is a tour of the City; both end back at the house, and take place whatever the weather. Before wending on your way, soak in more local history with a pint at Ye Olde Cheshire Cheese (145 Fleet Street, EC4A 2BU, 7353 6170). Dr Johnson is said to have been a regular at this wood-panelled 17th-century pub; you'll find his portrait in pride of place in the Chop Room.

Dr Johnson's House *17 Gough Square, off Fleet Street, EC4A 3DE (7353 3745, www.drjohnsons house.org).*

1302-1314 *Prance about Theatreland*

Start at Leicester Square tube station. Dive straight for Exit 1, head upstairs and turn left down the main road. Ignore St Martin's Court and instead take the next left, pedestrianised Cecil Court. At the far end is David Drummond at Pleasures of Past Times (no.11, 7836 1142). This eccentric shop has terse advice to mobile phone users stuck to the window, and old playbills, books and theatre programmes within. Switch off your phone and have a quick riffle through the Victoriana.

Turn right past Freed of London (94 St Martin's Lane, WC2N 4AT, 7240 0432, www.freedoflondon.com), supplier of shoes to the Royal Ballet. Further down St Martin's Lane, you can see the bauble atop the Coliseum (WC2N 4ES, 0871 911 0200, www.eno.org) home to the English National Opera (ENO). Head past it to St Martin-in-the-Fields and into the National Portrait Gallery opposite (St Martin's Place, WC2H 0HE, 7306 0055, www.npg.org.uk) for pictures of Shakespeare, David Garrick and Sir Ian McKellen.

Retrace your steps to May's Court. Behind you is the late Victorian red-on-white façade of the Duke of York's Theatre (St Martin's Lane, WC2N 4BG, 0871 297 5454); back in 1893, this saw the English première of Ibsen's *The Master Builder*. At the far end of May's Court, you might see vans loading scenery from the Coliseum's back door or hear the warm-up warblings of a soprano.

Turn left up Bedfordbury as far as the bookshop, right, then left down the hill. The first opening on your left is Inigo Court, leading to a delicious cemetery garden in front of a rather plain red-brick church. Designed by master architect Inigo Jones to be 'the handsomest barn in England' (his patron didn't want to spend much money on it), this is the Actors' Church, St Paul's Covent Garden (Bedford Street, WC2E 9ED, 7836 5221, www.actorschurch.org). In the airy interior, celebrity-hunters pay homage at memorials to Charlie Chaplin, Vivien Leigh and Noël Coward, but we prefer the oddities: Boris Karloff, Pantopuck the Puppetman and Edna Best 'The Constant Nymph'.

From the front door, follow the path round the church to the left, past a fountain that turns into an open scallop shell, poised as if for Botticelli's *Venus*. Through the gate, you're in Covent Garden piazza. The grand portico is where George Bernard Shaw's *Pygmalion* begins.

Cut right through the market and you come out with the back entrance to the Royal Opera House (Covent Garden, WC2E 9DD, 7240 1200, www.roh.org.uk) on your left. It was founded in 1732 by John Rich on the profits of his production of John Gay's Beggar's Opera. The current eight-floor edifice is only about 150 years old – and the third on the site after predecessors were destroyed by fires and riots. Exit via the main entrance on to Bow Street and turn right, then do a chicane left to the Theatre Royal Drury Lane (Catherine Street, WC2B 5JF, 0844 412 4660, www.theatre-royal.com). This oddly blocky but imposing theatre, which faces on to Catherine Street, has a rambunctious history, including assassination attempts on both George II and, decades later, his grandson George III. There's also a ghost, but only in the circle, so you're safe to nip in and try for same-day tickets.

Left out of the Theatre Royal's foyer you can see the Novello (Aldwych, WC2B 4LD, 0844 482 5170, www.delfontmackintosh. co.uk). Opposite is the Duchess (Catherine Street, WC2B 5LA, 0844 482 9672, www.nimaxtheatres.com) and, to your right as you hit the Strand, the Lyceum (21 Wellington Street, WC2E 7RQ, 7420 8100, http://lyceum-theatre.co.uk). This is only a taster of the density of playhouses that has led to this area of the West End being called 'Theatreland'.

Cross the Strand and head on to Waterloo Bridge. To your left are St Paul's, the Gherkin, the Shard and the grey, brutalist National Theatre (South Bank, SE1 9PX, 7452 3000, www.nationaltheatre.org.uk). The big concrete box nearest the bridge is the massive flytower that enables stagehands to whisk scenery on and off stage. Descend the stairs and you can queue for day-tickets (from 9.30am) or (from 90 minutes before a show) maybe get your hands on stand-by seats.

1315 *Try whoopie pie*

It's not a pie at all, but a cross between a cake and biscuit: two discs of flavoured sponge, sandwiching a generous buttercream filling. Whoopie pie may be an American delicacy, but sweet-toothed Londoners can sample the real deal. As the author of *The Whoopie Pie Book* and the former pastry chef at California's Chez Panisse, Claire Ptak has impeccable credentials. She makes the pies – along with London's prettiest cupcakes, and a variety of other bakes – at her Hackney café-bakery Violet (47 Wilton Way, E8 3ED, 7275 8360, www.violetcakes.com), and also runs a stall at Broadway Market.

1316 *Stroll London by gaslight*

Although most of London's street lights now use electric bulbs, there are still hundreds of gas-powered lamps dotted around the capital. You'll find them at the Tower of London, outside Buckingham Palace, and along the Mall and Pall Mall, among other locations. Casting a softer glow than their modern-day counterparts, they're in operation from dusk until dawn.

1317 *Learn about London at Bishopsgate Institute*

Founded in 1895, the historic Bishopsgate Institute aims to make education and culture open to all Londoners. Its talks and debates often take the capital as their theme, and explore it in learned but accessible detail: 'London in Peril', 'Forgotten London Writers' and 'Can We Really Trust the City of London?' are among past topics. The events are often held in the beautiful wood-panelled library, lined with leather-bound books. This place has moved with the times, though: you can also download podcasts.
Bishopsgate Institute *230 Bishopsgate, EC2M 4QH (7392 9200, www.bishopsgate.org.uk).*

1318-1321

Grow your own...

The rise of organic food and growing trend for self-sufficiency means that allotments are much in demand – and getting your hands on a plot can require luck, perseverance and a lengthy stint on a waiting list. For a list of local sites, visit www. london.gov.uk/allotments. While you're waiting for that elusive plot to come up, check Landshare (www.landshare.net) – a national organisation that connects would-be veg growers with people who have space they're prepared to share; last time we were looked, there were modest patches in Clerkenwell, Tooting and elsewhere.

Another way to get back to the land is through the Capital Growth scheme. Its aim is to create 2,012 community food-growing spaces for London by the end of 2012, offering support and training to volunteer-run projects. Londoners have embraced the idea wholeheartedly: by July 2011 green shoots were already sprouting in well over 1,000 disused patches of land. If you'd like to get involved, www.capitalgrowth.org details ways to volunteer at sites across the capital.

Two Royal Parks have also got in on the act, with neatly tended allotments planted in Kensington Gardens and Regent's Park. For details of opening hours, family fun days and 'ask the experts' sessions, see www.royalparks. org.uk/about/allotments.cfm.

1322

... Or tend some heritage veg

Sign up to the Heritage Seed Library (£20 per year), and you can chose six seeds from the library's annual catalogue of rare and heirloom vegetable varieties. In doing so, you'll help to safeguard the future of such gems as Hasshill's Champion Scarlet runner beans, or Carruther's Purple Podded peas.

1323 *Meet the Queen*

To mark the Queen's Diamond Jubilee, the National Portrait Gallery is bringing together 60 of the most remarkable images – from press pictures to works by contemporary artists – of Elizabeth II in 'The Queen: Art and Image' (17 May-21 October 2012). Artists and photographers include Cecil Beaton, Andy Warhol, Lucian Freud, Pietro Annigoni and Gerhard Richter, and works will be accompanied by archival material – from film footage to postage stamps.
National Portrait Gallery *St Martin's Place, WC2H 0HE (7306 0055, www.npg.org.uk).*

1324

See a painting come to life

The National Gallery (7747 2885, www. nationalgallery.org.uk) and the Royal Opera House (7304 4000, www.roh.org.uk) are pooling their considerable artistic resources for the London 2012 Festival to create a new work called *Metamorphosis: Titian 2012* (14-20 July). Seven choreographers will collaborate to produce three new works, inspired by three of Titian's paintings on display in the National – the dramatic *Diana & Actaeon, The Death of Actaeon* and *Diana & Callisto*. If you can't get tickets to a performance, you'll still be able to catch it on the BP Summer Big Screens, for free. For the latest on the London 2012 Festival line-up, visit www.london2012. com/festival.

1325-1326

Ponder Babbage's brain

Born in London in 1791, artifical intelligence pioneer Charles Babbage was a man far ahead of his time: although it was never completed, his gigantic, steam-powered Analytical Machine was a pioneering precursor of the computer. When he died, Babbage donated his exceptional brain to science. You'll find one half in a jar at the Hunterian Museum (Royal College of Surgeons, 35-43 Lincoln's Inn Fields, WC2A 3PE, 7869 6560, www.rcseng.ac.uk/museums), the other at the Science Museum (Exhibition Road, SW7 2DD, 7942 4000, www.sciencemuseum. org.uk); the latter also has a 1980s re-creation of Babbage's seven-foot-high 'Difference Engine No.2' – which was never actually constructed during the mathmatician's lifetime.

1327-1329

Buy groceries in Chinatown...

Liven up your weekly shop with a visit to one of Chinatown's excellent Asian supermarkets – crammed with comestibles you won't find at Sainsbury's. We start at SeeWoo (18-20 Lisle Street, WC2H 7BE, 7439 8325, www.see woo.com), notable for its well-stocked freezers: here, you'll find cleaned baby octopus, raw squid tentacles, black tiger prawns and boneless roast duck. For a quick-fix supper, buy a pack of pork and kimchi dumplings. Next to the cashiers is a smörgåsbord of dried goods, from honeysuckle flower to Chinese bacon (air-cured pork belly, infused with star anise and spices) and snacks; pick up a pack of sweet, freeze-dried durian chips, or seasoned roasted seaweed.

New Loon Fung (42-44 Gerrard Street, W1D 5QG, 7437 7332, www.loonfung.com) caters more to the Mainland Chinese crowd. It's one of the only Asian supermarkets in this part of town to have a butcher's counter, selling tripe, pigs' hearts, lung and chicken feet alongside more standard cuts. Myriad fresh fruit and vegetables are displayed inside and outside the shop, while seafood includes carp, bream and razor clam. Hunt out the fried round gluten puffs, which are delicious stuffed with meat, stir-fried with vegetables or roasted with soy sauce.

New Loon Moon (9 Gerrard Street, W1D 5PP, 7734 3887, www.newloonmoon.com) claims to import over 4,500 products from all over Asia, and has three floors stuffed with Chinese, Japanese, Korean, Thai, Malaysian, Indonesian, Filipino and even Burmese food. Look out for the impressive array of Thai sauces on the lower ground floor: kaeng kua, masman, panang, hunglay, yellow, green and red curry pastes. Upstairs, you'll find chocolate candy that looks like multi-coloured pebbles, seedless liquorice olives (an acquired taste) and various dried Chinese herbs. Buy a packet of dried pears and boil them with honey, red dates and white fungus if you have a cough, or throw some Chinese angelica root into a pot with ginseng and goji berries to boost immunity.

1330-1340

... Then investigate the city's other global specialists

Al-Abbas

Al-Abbas is one of our favourite Middle Eastern stores in west London. The range of grains and pulses is astonishing, and includes hard-to-find freekeh and moth beans. Teetotallers can enjoy exotic cordials of tamarind and mint; the crates of fresh falafel by the till are hard to resist, too.
258-262 Uxbridge Road, W12 7JA (8740 1932).

Giacobazzi's

You'll find products from all over Italy at this Hampstead Heath deli: helpful labels explain the difference between, say, the various types of pecorino, or Sicilian and Puglian quince pastes. The filled pastas and desserts are made on site.
150 Fleet Road, NW3 2QX (7267 7222, www.giacobazzis.co.uk).

Green Valley

The meze counter at this Middle Eastern food hall offers myriad possibilities for quick, after-work suppers, while fresh produce includes squat, round Lebanese pears, aubergines, guava, young coconuts and fresh juices. For dessert, investigate the eye-catching display of baklava.
36-37 Upper Berkeley Street, W1H 5QF (7402 7385).

I Camisa & Son

This Italian deli is a Soho stalwart, opened in 1929. It's well worth a visit, if only for its fresh pasta and sauces; the pesto is particularly good. There's a tempting array of cheeses (pecorino, gorgonzola – both sweet and piccante – ricotta, parmesan, mozzarella) and charcuterie, along with olives, risotto rices, cakes, biscuits and more.
61 Old Compton Street, W1D 6HS (7437 7610).

Japan Centre

Sweet, creamy edamame gateau? You'll find at the bakery here, along with cakes flavoured with red beans and sesame. Elsewhere are organic herbs, takeaway sushi, myriad types of tofu, rice, snack foods and Fuji apples, as well as a mind-blowing (and occasionally roof-of-mouth-blowing) range of sauces, seasonings and pickles.
14-16 Regent Street, SW1Y 4PH (3405 1151, www.japancentre.com).

Lina Stores

This iconic Italian deli has been in business for over half a century; Jane Grigson used to buy spaghetti in blue wax paper here years before celebrity chefs coasted the streets on scooters. The deli counter is full of cured meats, salamis, olives, cheeses and fresh pastas.
18 Brewer Street, W1F 0SH (7437 6482, www.linastores.co.uk).

Lisboa

Among the groceries at this friendly Portuguese deli are tins of sweet potato and guava paste, beans, pastas and the essential strong coffee. You'll also find white anchovies in vinegar, pasteis de bacalhau (salt cod fritters), pasteis de nata (custard tarts) and some terrific sausages and cured meats (merguez, chorizo, morcilla).
54 Golborne Road, W10 5NR (8969 1586).

Olga Stores

This unpretentious Italian deli has everything from canned tomatoes to whole fresh foie gras, as well as the customary salamis, pasta, oils and wines. It's also a welcome source of creamy burrata cheese, and buttery fuerte avocados.
30 Penton Street, N1 9PS (7837 5467).

Persepolis

Sally Butcher's colourful Iranian corner shop is a great place to stock up on the likes of fresh Persian dates, saffron, sumak, dried limes, verjus, herbs and spices.
28-30 Peckham High Street, SE15 5DT (7639 8007, www.foratasteofpersia.co.uk).

R García & Sons

Established in 1958, R García is one of London's largest Spanish grocer-delis. Tins of smoked paprika, marcona almonds, olive oils, sherry vinegar and slabs of turron line the shelves, while cheeses include manchego, mahon, cabralles and tetilla. The meat counter is a joy to peruse.
246-250 Portobello Road, W11 1LL (7221 6119, www.garciacafe.co.uk).

Turkish Food Centre

This popular supermarket has a superb range of fresh fruit and veg flown in from Greece, Cyprus and Turkey. An in-house bakery rolls out baklava, breads and moreish pastries. There are fresh meats and poultry, savouries and sweets and an enormous range of groceries.
89 Ridley Road, E8 2NH (7254 6754, www.tfcsupermarkets.com).

1341-1348

Tune in to an orchestral overload

One of the most ambitious events in the London 2012 Festival will be Music Nation on 3-4 March – a huge weekend of concerts, staged across the country. A total of 65,000 free and paid-for tickets will be available, and 25,000 participants are expected to get involved via tutorials, workshops and as part of a massive youth orchestra.

Activity is especially intense in London. The Barbican (Silk Street, EC2Y 8DS, 7638 4141, www.barbican.org.uk) will be one of the busiest venues, with the annual multi-arts Barbican Weekender, a grime-classical collaboration called Urban Classic, the Guildhall School Opera's take on Britten's *A Midsummer Night's Dream,* and the BBC Symphony performing the UK première of Rufus Wainwright's setting of five Shakespeare sonnets. There will also be Simon Dybbroe Møller's art-film take on classical musicians in the Curve. Just north of the Barbican, the London Symphony Orchestra will play via a live link with their counterparts in Beijing from LSO St Luke's (161 Old Street, EC1V 9NG, 7490 3939, www.lso.co.uk).

The Southbank Centre (Belvedere Road, SE1 8XX, 7960 4200, www.southbankcentre.co.uk) will also be busy: the Budapest Festival Orchestra plays Brahms, Lalo and Rimsky-Korsakov; the Orchestra of the Age of Enlightenment stages a concert for under-fives, an open rehearsal, a programme of Bach and a relaxed late-night gig; while young classical musicians will be getting stuck in to Heiner Goebbels' *Surrogate Cities.*

Elsewhere, the Roundhouse (Chalk Farm Road, NW1 8EH, 7424 9991, www.roundhouse.org.uk) hosts two days of choral music, the Academy of St Martin-in-the-Fields will celebrate Brahms at Kings Place (90 York Way, N1 9AG, 7520 1490, www.kingsplace.co.uk) and Cadogan Hall (5 Sloane Terrace, SW1X 9DQ, 7730 4500, www.cadoganhall.com) stages a concert with the City of London Sinfonia that will also incorporate photos, diary entries and letters from Scott's explorations in the Antarctic.

Croydon's Fairfield Halls (Park Lane, Surrey CR9 1DG, 8688 9291, www.fairfield.co.uk), celebrating its 50th anniversary in 2012, will be joining in with a concert from the resident London Mozart Players and local schoolchildren.

However, we're most looking forward to *What the River Sings,* performed by the Grand Union Orchestra (www.grandunion.org.uk), Water City Festival Orchestra (www.watercityfestival.org.uk) and the East London World Choir, somewhere close to the Thames Barrier.

1349

Waltz around the Broadwalk Ballroom

Each summer, Dance Al Fresco (07970 599445 mobile, www.dancealfresco.org) organises a series of outdoor dance events in Regent's Park. A polished parquet dance floor is laid along one of the leafy avenues of the park's Outer Circle, then the dancers descend. There's ballroom and Latin American dancing on Saturday, and sultry Argentine tango on Sunday. The afternoon kicks off with a beginners' class at 1pm, before everyone takes to the floor from 2pm until 6pm. Tickets are a tenner and include a lesson from event organiser Kele Baker, a consultant on BBC TV's *Strictly Come Dancing,* with proceeds going to the Royal Parks Foundation.

1350

Support the (self-) printed word

The self-publishing movement has grown in leaps and bounds over the past few years, spurred on by the accessibility of desktop publishing programmes and as a reaction to the digitalisation of the written word. Formed by a group of London-based artists, the International Alternative Press Festival, held in early summer, consists of a two-day Press Fair where artists exhibit their self-published zines, comics, art books, radical literature and poetry – as well as talks, a reading area, a 'zine swap' and assorted arty workshops.

The International Alternative Press Festival
Conway Hall, Red Lion Square, WC1R 4RL
(www.alternativepress.org.uk/festival.html).

Some sights are worth a crick in the neck: here are nine of our favourites.

Floral Street bridge

High above the throng of shoppers and tourists, an extraordinary bridge spans Floral Street. Sadly, the twisting, concertina-like walkway is restricted to staff and dancers of the Royal Ballet, affording an aerial shortcut from the rehearsal rooms to the stage.

Royal Opera House *Floral Street, WC2E 9DD (7304 4000, www.roh.org.uk).*

The spire of St George's

Built by Nicholas Hawksmoor in 1731, this Baroque church is topped off by a pyramid-inspired spire. Lions and unicorns cling to the corners of its base, while George I stands on top, clad in a Roman toga.

St George's Bloomsbury *Bloomsbury Way, WC1A 2HR (7242 1979, www.stgeorges bloomsbury.org.uk).*

The Monument

Built to commemorate the Great Fire of London, the Monument was also designed to function as a telescope – a plan that vibrations from passing traffic put paid to. But you can still look up though the core of the spiral staircase and glimpse the gilded urn atop.

Monument *Monument Street, EC3R 8AH (7626 2717, www.themonument.info).*

The Painted Hall

Sir James Thornhill was paid three pounds per square yard to paint the trompe l'oeil ceiling of the Old Royal Naval College's dining hall – a vast, awe-inspiring masterpiece that took 19 years to complete. Yeoman guides give free 15-minute talks, exploring its dense symbolism.

Old Royal Naval College *2 Cutty Sark Gardens, SE10 9LW (8269 4747, www.oldroyalnavalcollege.org).*

Floral Street bridge

Royal Exchange

The current Royal Exchange is the third stock exchange on this site since Sir Thomas Gresham came up with the idea in 1565. Look closely at the weathervane, and you'll see an incongruous gilt grasshopper at the top – a tribute to Gresham, on whose family crest the skittish critter featured.

Royal Exchange *Bank, EC3V 3LR (www.theroyalexchange.com).*

The Royal Standard

When Her Majesty is in residence, the Royal Standard flutters over Buckingham Palace; when she's away, the Union Flag flies in its stead.

Buckingham Palace *The Mall, SW1A 1AA (7766 7300, www.royal.gov.uk).*

The Time Ball

Looking like a speared maraschino cherry, the Time Ball is a bright red sphere set on a spike above Flamsteed House. See it rise, then – at 1pm – fall, as it has done since 1833, when it signalled the time to ships on the Thames.

Royal Observatory Greenwich *Blackheath Avenue, SE10 8XJ (8312 6565, www.nmm.ac.uk/rog).*

Village Underground

Perched on a roof above Great Eastern Street is a most unlikely apparition: a pair of graffitied old tube train carriages. They now provide affordable, aerial studio space for artists.

Village Underground *54 Holywell Lane, EC2A 3PQ (7422 7505, www.villageunderground.co.uk).*

Winged Figure

Clinging to the side of John Lewis' flagship store on Oxford Street is sculptor Barbara Hepworth's dramatic *Winged Figure*, commissioned by the department store in the 1960s.

John Lewis *300 Oxford Street, W1A 1EX (7629 7711, www.johnlewis.com).*

1360-1369

*Ben Roberts, Curator of
the European Bronze Age,
British Museum*

Swimming reindeer
(France, 11000 BC)

This is the oldest art
in the British Museum.
Carved during the last
Ice Age – 13,000 years
ago – from the tusk of
a mammoth, it depicts
a male and female
reindeer swimming
one behind one the
other. Hunter-gatherer

communities relied on reindeer to survive
the long harsh winters, using them for food,
clothing, tools and weapons. Since this object
has no practical function, in our modern world
it would be considered to be 'art'.
Room 2: The Changing Museum

Standard of Ur (Iraq, 2600-2400 BC)

Ur was one of the earliest cities in the world.
When it was excavated by Leonard Woolley in
the 1920s, he found the spectacular burial of
a queen and her female attendants, dressed
in gold ornaments. There were sumptuous
headdresses, a lyre of gold and lapis lazuli,
the world's earliest known board game – and
this mysterious mosaic of shell, red limestone
and lapis lazuli. One side depicts the
king humiliating
his enemies,
while the other
shows him
banqueting.
*Room 56:
Mesopotamia
6000-1500 BC*

Head of
Augustus
(Sudan,
25-27 BC)

The calm,
distant gaze

of inset eyes of glass and stone must have
given the original statue of Emperor Augustus
an air of quiet, assured strength. Thought to
have been erected in Alexandria, Egypt, it
would have been a continuous reminder of
the all-embracing power of Rome – yet the
statue's head was found in Sudan. It had
been taken during a series of raids into
Roman Egypt led by the fierce, one-eyed
Queen Candace. The head was buried where
its captors would walk over it on entering
a temple, apparently in a deliberate act
of desecration.
Room 70: Roman Empire

Double-headed serpent
(Mexico, 15th-16th century AD)

Made of about 2,000 tiny pieces of turquoise
on a curved wooden frame, this Aztec serpent
has snouts and gums done in a grisly red
shell, and huge fangs picked out in white
shell. Aztec ruler Moctezuma II conducted
great rites of human sacrifice wearing a
turquoise diadem, turquoise nose-plug and
a loin-cloth with turquoise beads. When
Moctezuma met the conquistadors, he
is reported to have presented them with
gifts including 'a serpent wand inlaid
with turquoise'. It might have been this
very serpent.
Room 27: Mexico

Rosetta Stone (Egypt, c196 BC)

The Rosetta Stone is famous as a valuable
key in the decipherment of hieroglyphs,
but few people know what is written on
it. It is a decree that affirms the royal cult
of the 13-year-old Ptolemy V on the first
anniversary of his coronation. It also gives
the priests a number of very attractive tax
breaks. They were critical in keeping the
Egyptian
masses on
the side of
the ruling
Greek
Ptolemies.
The stone is
expressed in
hieroglyphic
(suitable for
a priestly
decree),
demotic
(the native
script used

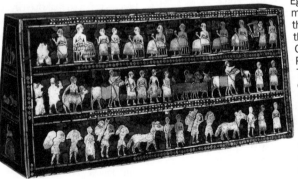

for daily purposes) and Greek (the language of the administration).
Room 4: Egyptian Sculpture

Parthenon sculptures
(Greece, 447-432 BC)
The Parthenon was a temple dedicated to the goddess Athena Parthenos, meaning Athena the Virgin. It was built on the Acropolis – a rocky citadel at the heart of the city. Its central hall housed a colossal statue of the goddess herself, made of gold and ivory. The sculptures present an Athenian universe made up of gods, heroes and mortals, woven together in complex scenes drawn from myth and daily life.
Room 18: Greece: Parthenon

Mold Gold Cape
(Wales, 1900-1600 BC)
Workmen quarrying for stone in 1833 in a field named Bryn yr Ellyllon (the Fairies' or Goblins' Hill) found a superb ceremonial gold cape in an ancient burial mound. It is one of the finest examples of prehistoric sheet-gold working, and unique in form and design. It was laboriously beaten out of a single ingot of gold about the size of a golf ball, then embellished with intense decoration of ribs and bosses to mimic multiple strings of beads amid folds of cloth.
Room 51: Europe & Middle East 10,000-800 BC

Hoa Hakananai'a
(Easter Island, c 1000 AD)
This statue – his name translates as 'hidden friend' – was almost certainly made to house an ancestral spirit. Originally, he stood on a special platform on the coast of Rapa Nui (Easter Island), with giant stone companions, all of them keeping watch over the island with their backs to the sea. When *HMS Topaze* arrived in 1868, only a few hundred people were left on the island. The chiefs presented Hoa Hakananai'a to the ship's officers. We don't know why they wanted him to leave the island, but he now stands facing south towards Rapa Nui, over 8,500 miles away.
Room 24: Living & Dying

Lewis Chessmen (Scotland, 1150-1200 AD)
Chess was invented in India at some point after AD 500, spreading through the Middle East and into Europe over the next two centuries. In every place, the chess pieces were changed to reflect the society that played the game. The Lewis Chessmen were probably made in Norway in the 12th century from walrus tusks and whale teeth. Their faces and clothes reflect their origins in medieval courts of northern Europe. They were found in the vicinity of Uig on the Isle of Lewis in the early 19th century.
Room 40: Medieval Europe

Kilwa pot sherds (Tanzania, AD 1000-1500)
Broken bits of pot are virtually indestructible. These were found at the bottom of a low crumbling cliff by a beachcomber – pale green fragments of porcelain made in China and blue pieces with black patterns from Iraq or Syria, surviving there for up to 900 years. Today Kilwa Kisiwani is a quiet Tanzanian island with a few small fishing villages, but the pottery tells us that by 1200 it was one of many rich and thriving East African port cities that constituted a vast Indian Ocean trade network. As foreign merchants mixed with the African community, Arabic and Persian words were absorbed into the local Bantu language to create a new lingua franca – Swahili.
Room 25: Africa
British Museum *Great Russell Street, WC1B 3DG (7323 8299, www.britishmuseum.org).*

1370-1380

Share some classic tapas...

Dehesa

Angels & Gypsies

The menu at this low-key but stylish eaterie intersperses Spanish classics (jamón croquetas, padrón peppers) with more unusual dishes (Devon snails with chilli and passata) and local ingredients (Neal's Yard cheeses).
29-33 Camberwell Church Street, SE5 8TR (7703 5984, www.churchstreethotel.com).

Barrafina

This Soho tapas bar may be somewhat cramped, but the food makes up for it. Nab a stool at the counter and watch the waiter-cooks at work. It's first-rate stuff: tortillas, cooked in high-lipped frying pans, are often checked by two or three staff to ensure they're suitably moist and spongy.
54 Frith Street, W1D 4SL (7813 8016, www.barrafina.co.uk).

Barrica

With its chequerboard tiled floor, Spanish posters and hanging ham, this small, busy restaurant has the feel of a smart taverna. The trad-with-a-twist food comes in proper tapas-sized portions, rather than the larger *raciones* you often get in England.
62 Goodge Street, W1T 4NE (7436 9448, www.barrica.co.uk).

Dehesa

Dehesa's ham and cheese selection is noteworthy and its tapas exceptional, raising the bar with dishes such as saffron-cured sea trout with spiced aubergine, quail eggs and beetroot dressing, or squid with grilled chorizo salad.
25 Ganton Street, W1F 9BP (7494 4170, www.dehesa.co.uk).

Fino

A smartly dressed clientele fills this sleek basement, which offers a modern take on classic Spanish dishes – *morcilla ibérica* with quail eggs, say, or seared tuna on a piquillo pepper salad. There's also a great wine and sherry list.
33 Charlotte Street, entrance on Rathbone Street, W1T 1RR (7813 8010, www.finorestaurant.com).

Ibérica Food & Culture

A tapas bar, a deli with a walk-in cheese and wine room and a mini-art gallery: this place has a little bit of everything. The menu includes a broad selection of small plates: alongside authentic Asturian *fabada* you'll find plenty of flair in dishes such as mussels with sea urchin vinaigrette or chorizo 'lollypops' with pear alioli.
195 Great Portland Street, W1W 5PS (7636 8650, www.ibericalondon.com).

Lola Rojo

Lola Rojo's sophisticated sense of nueva cocina (new-wave Spanish cooking) is evident in dishes such as roast peppers with home-made tuna pickle or spinach and goat's cheese rice. For afters, sample the signature white chocolate soup with thyme toffee and mango ice-cream.
78 Northcote Road, SW11 6QL (7350 2262, www.lolarojo.net).

Mar i Terra

This unpretentious restaurant attracts a steady stream of diners to its bright, inviting dining room and walled garden. The rustic menu offers a tempting selection of standards (chorizo cooked in cider, stuffed baby squid, Asturian bean stew with morcilla), all reliably good.
14 Gambia Street, SE1 0XH (7928 7628, www.mariterra.co.uk).

Morito

While the menu at Sam and Sam Clark's pared-down tapas venture looks beyond Spain for its inspiration, it includes a handful of beautifully made classics: silky jamón croquetas, say, or chicharrones de Cadiz (cubes of juicy pork belly, seasoned with lemon, salt and cumin).
32 Exmouth Market, EC1R 4QL (7278 7007).

Tapas Brindisa

Top-quality ingredients assembled into eminently tempting tapas are Brindisa's hallmark: a cup of

green pea soup with manchego, say, or black rice with squid and aïoli. The set-up is equally simple, with a bar area at one end and a close-packed, concrete-floored dining room at the other.
18-20 Southwark Street, SE1 1TJ (7357 8880, www.brindisa.com).

Tendido Cero
Tendido Cero offers a menu of modern, artfully presented tapas, such as cod confited in olive oil or mini 'hamburgers' of sardine, tomato, padrón pepper and aïoli. Gazpacho or rabbit and manzanilla olive terrine are fabulous cold snacks.
174 Old Brompton Road, SW5 0BA (7370 3685, www.cambiodetercio.co.uk).

1381-1388

... Or go global

The inherent appeal of sharing small portions has not gone unnoticed by London's leading restaurateurs, and tapas-inspired 'small plates' have become something of a trend. One of the pioneers was Ottolenghi (287 Upper Street, N1 2TZ, 7288 1454, www.ottolenghi.co.uk), whose meze-style menu is perfect for sharing: deep-fried courgette flowers with herby ricotta stuffing and a drizzle of date syrup encapsulates the kitchen's seasonality, skill and flair.

New Zealander Peter Gordon's Kopapa (32-34 Monmouth Street, WC2H 9HA, 7240 6076, www.kopapa.co.uk) is another fine example, serving small portions of complex and inventive fusion food: juniper-cured beef with thyme oil and gin-and-tonic tapioca was on the menu recently.

French food also works well served this way. Terroirs (5 William IV Street, WC2N 4DW, 7036 0660, www.terroirswinebar.com) offers superlative wine-matching and snacking possibilities, with a menu that runs from no-nonsense French charcuterie and cheese to simple small plates (potted shrimps on toast, globe artichoke with vinaigrette). More polished (and pricey) is La Petite Maison (53-54 Brooks Mews, W1K 4EG, 7495 4774, www.lpmlondon. co.uk), whose sharing dishes provide exquisite tasters of its accomplished Provençal-meets-Mediterranean cuisine.

Some restaurants offer dishes in both small and large portions, amenable to sharing on both. These include international experimentalist Caravan (11-13 Exmouth Market, EC1R 4QD, 7833 8115, http://caravanonexmouth.co.uk), whose Sichuan salt and pepper pork has to be a large plate to avoid an undignified scrum, and celebrated Italian Bocca di Lupo (12 Archer Street, W1D 7BB, 7734 2223, www.boccadilupo.com), where options range from dainty crostini and risottos to more daring meaty dishes, such as fried tripe with lemon, chilli, mint and pecorino.

An Italian take on tapas has also proved a hit at Polpo (41 Beak Street, W1F 9SB, 7734 4479, www.polpo.co.uk), whose small, flavour-packed dishes are notable for their simplicity and intensity: laced with gremolata, the cuttlefish and ink risotto is a standout.

For something more unusual, book a table at Dinings (22 Harcourt Street, W1H 4HH, 7723 0666), which serves sushi and Japanese tapas. The ceviche-like preparations of fish are exceptional, while seafood-stuffed 'tar tar' chips (small, taco-like crisps) are playful morsels, big on flavour.

Bocca di Lupo

Drink
in the past

*Derek Hammond **quaffs a pint in London's secret pub.***

'This is London's most hidden pub,' says barman John Wright, with just a hint of insane pride. 'We had a gentleman in the other week who said he'd worked around the corner on Hatton Garden for six years and never found the place.'

That's something you can have some sympathy with, especially if you ever come seeking out a discreet sherbet in this quaint old corner of Cambridgeshire that's tucked away in the heart of the City of London.

When you pass the security barrier and guardpost into Ely Place from Charterhouse Street, there's no longer a top-hatted, frock-coated beadle to point out that you're technically no longer in London. You also have to be sharp-eyed to spot Ye Olde Mitre's sandwich board at the end of an anonymous alley. (The approach is easier from Hatton Garden, where a turquoise mitre on a lamp post shows you where to look: the alley is between numbers 8 and 9.)

A short way up from Ely Place, the black brick alley widens out a yard or two, opens up to the sky, and reveals a tiny pub with a frontage of oak and leaded windows. The date on the sign says

1546, but this version of the Mitre was actually built around 1772, soon after the demolition of the nearby Palace of the Bishops of Ely – the origin of all the geographical and historical anomalies in these parts.

Built in 1291, St Etheldreda's Church – aka Ely Chapel – is the oldest Catholic church in England and the only surviving part of Ely Palace. With 58 acres of orchards, vineyards and strawberry fields, plus fountains, ponds and terraced lawns stretching down towards the Thames, the Palace was the London residence of a long line of Ely Bishops, and a seat of great power. The Bishop of Ely and his strawberries feature in Shakespeare's *Richard III*, while Ely Palace itself provides the setting for John of Gaunt's 'This scepter'd isle' speech in *Richard II*. In 1531, a five-day feast was attended by Henry VIII and Catherine of Aragon, the Lord Mayor of London, sundry foreign ambassadors, barons and aldermen: between them, they put away '24 great beefs, the carcase of an ox, 100 fat muttons, 91 pigs, 34 porks, 37 dozen pigeons, 340 larks' and the King's contribution of 13 dozen swans.

The original Mitre Tavern was built for servants at the Palace, 13 years into the reign of Elizabeth I. In 1576 she commandeered a gatehouse and a portion of the Palace grounds for her court favourite Sir Christopher Hatton, and regularly came visiting. After stints as a prison and a Civil War hospital, the Palace reverted to the Crown in Georgian times and was demolished – although the reconstructed pub had built into its front wall a stone mitre from a palace gatepost and a cherry tree, which once marked the boundary separating the ground gifted to Hatton and the Bishop's remaining diocese.

The tree is still here, preserved behind glass in a corner of the cosy panelled front bar – in fact, according to Wright, it was throwing out leafy branches and blossom up until the end of last century, when structural subsidence led to the decapitation of the tree once used as a maypole by Good Queen Bess. John Wright first found his way to the Mitre Tavern back in 1953, but it wasn't until the '70s that he got a job here pulling pints. In those days the pub closed at 10pm along with the gates of Ely Place, and the drinks licence was still issued in Cambridgeshire rather than London. That's about all that's changed since: certainly not the stained-glass mitre or the toy-size furniture in the crooked little front bar, nor the settles, skylight and 'Ye Closet' micro-snug in the back. The Mitre still only opens one weekend per year, but now it corresponds with the Great British Beer Festival at Olympia in August, rather than St Etheldreda's annual charity Strawberry Fayre in June.

Ely Place remains quite literally a law unto itself, and long may it continue. 'Many times we've had robbers run in here from Hatton Garden,' Wright recalls fondly. 'They know the City police don't have the right to follow them. It's still the same today: the police just have to seal all the exits and ring the Cambridgeshire force, then wait around till they jump in their cars and get down here.'

Ye Olde Mitre *1 Ely Court, Ely Place, EC1N 6SJ (7405 4751, www.fullers.co.uk).*

1390-1395

Find your favourite London bench...

Some seats are special simply by dint of their location – not least the otherwise unremarkable wooden bench at the top of Parliament Hill. Taking in the city skyline in one glorious swoop, it has one of the finest views in London. As a result, it's notched up a couple of film appearances – notably in the creepy closing scene of *Notes on a Scandal* (2006).

For something a little grander, stroll along the Victoria Embankment. Here, you can take in the river view from a series of magnificent benches, supported by busty sphinxes or kneeling camels, in tribute to nearby Cleopatra's Needle.

Those of a minimalist bent will prefer the modern, sculptural-looking bench at the West Smithfield Rotunda, at the centre of the Smithfield Rotunda Garden (EC1A). Designed by two

In loving memory of
Patrick Laurance
24.12.1919 - 11.01.2008
Who liked to support people

architecture students and carved from six tonnes of Portland stone, its multi-level perches allow for both solitary seats and companionable huddles.

Far less capacious is the Allies bench, on the corner where Old and New Bond Street meet. Here, bronze statues of Roosevelt and Churchill can be found enjoying a good chinwag. Both gentlemen being on the portly side, there's not a great deal of room between them – though Arnold Schwarzenegger managed to squeeze in for a photo op a few years back.

A more spacious favourite of ours is Kirsty MacColl's memorial bench in Soho Square, a place immortalised in her song of the same name. The lyrics ('One day I'll be waiting there/No empty bench in Soho Square') are engraved on a brass plaque on the handsome three-seater. At Poets' Corner in Richmond Park, meanwhile, you can plug your headphones in to Ian Dury's solar-powered bench and listen to *Hit Me with Your Rhythm Stick* as you survey the park.

West Smithfield Rotunda

1396

... Or discover the stories behind the brass plaques

Writer Stephen Emm's investigations into the commemorative inscriptions on benches around town ran in *Time Out* magazine for over a year. The tales are collected at www.benchpoetry. blogspot.com, and make for a touching tribute to all sorts of Londoners; there's the odd famous name, but it's the stories of ordinary folk that really touch a chord.

1397

See Lady Godiva ride again

According to Anglo-Saxon legend, Lady Godiva rode naked through the streets of Coventry in protest at her grasping husband's taxation of his tenants. Her ladyship is to ride again in 2012 (fully clothed, this time), in the form of a ten-metre-high marionette that will travel from Coventry to London as part of the Cultural Olympiad. A collaboration between West Midlands engineers, industrial workers, craftspeople and performers, this 'moving piece of public art' will start of in Coventry on 28 July (the day after the Olympic Opening Ceremony in the capital), then set off down the A5 to London the following day. Riding atop a structure called the 'Cyclopedia', powered by rotating teams of 33 cyclists, she will arrive on 5 August for a celebration in Walthamstow.

1398

Spot a King's Cross kingfisher

A flash of brilliant blue and orange and it's gone: seeing a kingfisher is always a natural high, and particularly so in the grimy heart of London. Camley Street Natural Park trails the Regent's Canal among the railyards and redevelopments in the hinterland of King's Cross and St Pancras International stations. A special kingfisher bank was recently installed, to encourage breeding (the birds nest at the end of tunnels up to a metre long that they excavate by flying into earth walls at speed, their sharp bills extended). Ask at the visitor centre for the best vantage point. Breeding season is typically March to July, and spurs much fish-catching activity.

Camley Street Natural Park *12 Camley Street, N1C 4PW (7833 2311, www.wildlondon.org.uk).*

1399-1420

Explore the East London Line

The East London Overground line, with its distinctive architectural style, opened in 2010 as a much-needed north–south conduit. Eastsiders on both banks of the river are discovering that once-hard-to-access parts of town are now in their own backyard. Here's a station-by-station tour of some points of interest along the route.

Highbury & Islington
Set in a fine townhouse on Canonbury Square, the little-known Estorick Collection of Modern Italian Art (no.39A, N1 2AN, 7704 9522, www.estorickcollection.com) is home to a remarkable collection of Futurist art, along with pieces by Modigliani and de Chirico.

Canonbury
Unfeted, London's oldest terraced houses are found at nearby Newington Green, numbers 52-55. Look carefully and you'll see the date: 1658. The Green is also home to some appealing shops, and a pleasant little Italian deli, Trattoria Sapori (Alliance House, nos.44-45, N16 9QH, 7704 0744, www.trattoriasapori.co.uk), famed for its generous slabs of home-made cake.

Dalston Junction
A cultural cluster here includes Café Oto (Print House, 18-22 Ashwin Street, E8 3DL, 7923 1231, www.cafeoto.co.uk), a key venue for left-field music of all genres. During the day, it operates as a relaxed, airy café.

Haggerston
Access the Regent's Canal from here and stop for Italian *cicchetti*-style bar snacks at the waterfront Towpath Café (between Whitmore Bridge & Kingsland Road Bridge, N1 5SB, no phone).

Hoxton
The 18th-century almshouses of the Geffrye Museum (136 Kingsland Road, E2 8EA, 7739 9893, www.geffrye-museum.org.uk) now house a series of recreated period rooms, showcasing the history of domestic interiors. There's a great café and garden too.

Shoreditch High Street
The Terence Conran-designed Boundary Project (2-4 Boundary Street, E2 7DD, 7729 1051,

www.theboundary.co.uk) contains a boutique hotel, a rooftop bar and restaurant (Boundary) and a ground-floor deli and café (Albion).

Whitechapel
Powerhouse modern art exhibits are brilliantly curated at the Grade II-listed Whitechapel Gallery (77-82 Whitechapel High Street, E1 7QX, 7522 7888, www.whitechapelgallery.org).

Shadwell
Visit Shadwell Basin (3-4 Shadwell Pierhead, Glamis Road, E1W 3TD, 7481 4210, www.shadwell-basin.org.uk) to watch watersports – or learn to participate yourself, in sailing, kayaking and canoeing. They'll have you out on the Thames in no time.

Wapping
The long and narrow bar of the Grade II-listed Town of Ramsgate (62 Wapping High Street, E1W 2PN, 7481 8000) leads you out to a tiny Thames-side terrace.

Rotherhithe
The East London Line crosses the Thames in the Brunel-designed Thames Tunnel, a marvel of its day (its construction began in 1825). Learn more at the Brunel Museum (Railway Avenue, SE16 4LF, 7231 3840, www.brunel-museum.org.uk).

Canada Water
You don't have to travel far here: our pick is the adjoining Jubilee Line station, a curvaceous symphony of metal and glass.

Surrey Quays

The railway affords the non-car owner access to the sprawling Surrey Quays shopping complex, with chainstores, cinemas and bowling lanes. The real find here is the only London outpost of French sports megastore Decathlon (Surrey Quays Road, SE16 2XU, 7394 2000, www.decathlon.co.uk).

New Cross

Grab an own-made muffin and organic coffee at the funky Deptford Project Café (121-123 Deptford High Street, SE8 4NS, thedeptfordproject.com), housed in an brightly painted old train carriage. There's a weekend market and events too.

New Cross Gate

If you're tired of gastro-fication, the antidote is the Montague Arms (289 Queens Road, SE14 2PA, 7639 4923), an enjoyably bonkers pub with zebra heads and Casiotone entertainment, plus gigs of a (truly) alternative nature.

Brockley

The Jack Studio Theatre (410 Brockley Road, SE4 2DH, 8291 1206, www.brockleyjack.co.uk) is a handsome 50-seat cinema-cum-theatre, adjoining a foodie pub.

Honor Oak Park

The views are fabulous in all directions from One Tree Hill Park (SE23, www.onetreehill.org.uk), stretching from Canary Wharf to the Surrey countryside. It's a two-acre nature reserve based around a patch of ancient woodland, with a hilltop beacon and other historic curios.

Forest Hill

An engaging anthropological museum, set in 16 acres of landscaped gardens, the Horniman (100 London Road, SE23 3PQ, 8699 1872, www.horniman.ac.uk) is stuffed with curiosities, from mummies and musical instruments to a Haitian voodoo shrine.

Sydenham

Exemplary local bookstore the Kirkdale Bookshop (272 Kirkdale, SE26 4RS, 8778 4701, www.kirkdalebookshop.com) has great new and second-hand selections, a gallery, storytelling for children and an stimulating events programme.

Crystal Palace/Penge West

These two stations are gateways to Crystal Palace Park, a treasured green space with playgrounds, a farm, a sports centre and some restored Victorian dinosaur sculptures. Crystal Palace Museum (Anerley Hill, SE19 2BA, 8676 0700, www.crystalpalacemuseum.org.uk) commemorates the Great Exhibition of 1851; the 'Crystal Palace' that housed the exhibition in Hyde Park was moved here, but later razed in a fire.

Anerley

One of the area's nicest pubs is right next to the station: the Anerley Arms (2 Risdale Road, SE20 8AG, 8659 5552). It's a Sam Smiths joint, with wood fittings, Croydon canal memorabilia and outside seating.

Norwood Junction

South Norwood Lake & Country Park (Albert Road, SE25, 8656 5947, www.croydon.gov.uk) is a 125-acre green space with wild flower meadows, lakeside walks, a pitch and putt course, a playground and sailing.

West Croydon

Croydon's imposing former town hall is now a cultural complex with a cinema, art galleries, library, café and the Museum of Croydon (Katherine Street, CR9 1ET, 8253 1022, www.museumofcroydon.com).

Horniman

1421 *Joust with brollies in Bedford Square*

Hosted by the tweed-wearing gents behind *The Chap* magazine, the Chap Olympiad is 'a celebration of athletic ineptitude and immaculate trouser creases', held each July in leafy Bedford Square. Dapperly-clad contestants compete for gold, silver and bronze cravats in events such as the Moving Hat Stand (competitors attempt to throw their hats on to a hat stand as the opposing team manoeuvres it out of reach) and Umbrella Jousting, in which bicycles and brollies stand in for horses and lances. Other entertainment includes music, Martinis and dancing. For ticket information, visit www.thechap.net.

1422 *Enter the Great Spitalfields Pancake Race*

Each Shrove Tuesday, in celebration of Pancake Day, the Great Spitalfields Pancake Race (7375 0441, www.alternativearts.co.uk) sees fancy dress-clad teams of four dashing along Dray Walk, flipping pancakes as they go. It's all in aid of the London Air Ambulance charity; if you want to take part, register in advance and bring your own pan (pancakes are provided). There's an engraved frying pan for the winner, and prizes for the best dressed team, so come imaginatively attired.

1423-1425 *Tackle a (film) marathon*

The BFI IMAX (1 Charlie Chaplin Walk, SE1 8XR, 7199 6000) regularly runs all-nighter screenings. They're generally devoted to box office-busting epics like *Harry Potter* or *Lord of the Rings*; look out, too, for gory Halloween specials. The Prince Charles (7 Leicester Place, WC2H 7BY, 7494 3654, www.princecharles cinema.com) also has a soft spot for an epic, once hosting a three-day marathon that screened 121 episodes of the TV series *Lost* back-to-back; what's more, fans queued overnight to make sure they got a seat.

It's also worth checking out the programme of the London International Festival of Science Fiction & Fantastic Film (www.sci-fi-london.com). Movie marathons invariably feature on its line-up, and are pleasingly playful in theme: in 2011, a 'Royal Wedding' all-nighter involved screenings of *Bride of Frankenstein* and *I Married a Witch*.

1426

Tune into your pyschic side...

The Atlantis Bookshop (49A Museum Street, WC1A 1LY, 7405 2120, www.theatlantis bookshop.com) is an occult bookshop of some renown, selling new and second-hand titles on everything from fairies and werewolves to dowsing and divination. People interested in the subject, but unsure of where to begin, are invited to drop by the Psychic Café, held on the fourth Wednesday of the month at the Devereux Arms (20 Devereux Court, WC2R 3JJ, 7583 4562). Admission is £5, and previous themes have included past lives, hands-on healing, divination and 'psychic fun'.

1427

... Or dabble in the occult

Those with a more serious interest are welcome at the Wednesday-night Moot With No Name, also held at the Devereux Arms. A moot is a gathering of pagans, and those who attend these themed talks include occultists and magicians (and once, the bookshop's co-owner Geraldine Beskin tells us, a vampire). Subjects under often lively discussion are esoteric and intense; they have included neuromagic, sexuality and sacred sites, the magician's mind and ancient Egypt.

1428

Buy a vintage pen from a vintage shop

Even in this computerised age, buying a pen remains a pleasurable ritual at Penfriend. Set in Burlington Arcade and Bush House, its two shops are traditional emporia, where respectful assistants hover behind wooden cabinets that contain hundreds of fountain pens, ballpoints and propelling pencils. Classic new brands are carried, but it's hard to resist the beautiful vintage versions (from around £75, fully restored). Choose a pen, watch as it's carefully filled, try it out on thick white paper and cherish the moment when your fingers first clutch the model that perfectly suits your handwriting.
Penfriend *Bush House Arcade, Bush House, Strand, WC2B 4PE (7836 9809); 34 Burlington Arcade, Piccadilly, W1J 0QA (7499 6337, www.penfriend.co.uk).*

1429-1430

Attend a cheese tasting

There's plenty of scope to hone your cheese appreciation skills at Neal's Yard Dairy. Tutored tastings (£50-£60) are held at the Borough Market shop (6 Park Street, SE1 9AB, 7500 7662, www.nealsyarddairyshop.co.uk), and are devoted to different themes: beer and cheese, perhaps, or the controversial 'England vs France' taste-off.

Tastings are also offered at the Marylebone (2-6 Moxon Street, W1U 4EW, 7935 0341) and Highbury (30 Highbury Park, N5 2AA, 7359 7440, www.lafromagerie.co.uk) outposts of the excellent La Fromagerie. Events are often seasonally themed: summer sheep's and goat's cheeses (£30), say, paired with an enjoyable assortment of wines, and new season Vignola cherries. If you'd prefer to conduct your own investigations, the tiny on-site café at Moxon Street offers a fragrant array of cheese plates, with five perfectly ripe cheeses on each, and suggested wines to match.

La Fromagerie

1431-1446

Tune in to London's festival scene

Festival season starts in late spring, with a couple of 'microfestivals' offering something between a pub crawl and a music festival. April's two-day Camden Crawl (www.thecamdencrawl. com) is the original, presenting a mix of hip indie acts, with a few nods to the area's Britpop-era heyday: headliners for 2011 included Graham Coxon and Saint Etienne. Also in April is the fortnight-long La Línea (www.comono.co.uk). London's biggest contemporary Latin music festival, it takes in everything from Argentinian electronica to classical Spanish guitar, and often stages big events at the Barbican.

In late May, the focus shifts to Shoreditch and the one-day Stag & Dagger shindig (www.stag anddagger.com), co-produced by the well-connected Adventures in the Beetroot Field crew. At £15 for a wristband, it's a good opportunuity to catch up on some rising musical talents.

As the weather improves, outdoor events take over. June's Get Loaded in the Park (http://get loadedinthepark.com) is one of the first big rock/pop festivals of the season (The Cribs and Razorlight headlined in 2011). It's held on Clapham Common – also the venue for Jamie Oliver's Big Feastival (www.jamieoliver.com/the bigfeastival) in early July, providing three days of music, food, arts, crafts and storytelling. Next up, over the August bank holiday, it's the turn of South West Four (www.southwestfour.com), which focuses on electronic music.

As well as one-off mega gigs, Hyde Park hosts heritage-rock weekender Hard Rock Calling (www.hardrockcalling.co.uk) and the Wireless Festival (www.wirelessfestival.co.uk) in late June/early July. Top of the latter's line-up in the past couple of years have been big electronic acts such as LCD Soundsystem and Aphex win, as well as pop legends Pulp.

Over in east London, since 2007, Shoreditch Park has been the venue for July's 1-2-3-4 Shoreditch Festival (www.the1234shoreditch. com), featuring emerging new acts and groundbreaking artists, many of whom cut their teeth in the local area. Nearby Victoria Park is another key festival venue, traditionally playing host to several big summer music events. The line-up includes June's dance-music-oriented LED Festival (www.ledfestival.net), the lively Lovebox Weekender (www.lovebox.net) – the hedonist's festival of choice – and the rocktastic High Voltage Festival (www.highvoltagefestival. com). August brings another three events: the left-field Field Day (www.fielddayfestivals.com); the under-18s-only Underage Festival (www. underagefestivals.com); and the new, family-friendly Apple Cart Festival (www.theapplecart festival.com), offering chilled tunes (Badly Drawn Boy, Saint Etienne), comedians, cabaret and a village fête area. With Vicky Park one of four official Festival Live Sites for the London 2012 Olympic Games, however, it remains to be seen whether dates will shift, or if these festivals will need to find temporary new homes in 2012.

One festival venue that won't be changing anytime soon is the venerable Somerset House (www.somersethouse.org.uk/music). In mid July, the Summer Series at Somerset House brings an array of big-name acts to its stately fountain court for roughly ten days of open-air shows; in 2011, acts ran from Lamb to Imelda May, so it's nothing if not varied.

Later that month, the Greenwich Summer Sessions (www.greenwichsummersessions.co.uk) follow a similar formula, taking place at the equally atmospheric Old Royal Naval College. Past performers have included big-name old-timers (Status Quo, The Pogues), as well as comparative newcomers such as Mark Ronson.

1447-1449

Discover Dickens

2012 sees the 200th anniversary of the birth of Charles Dickens. Alongside a new Dickens monument in Southwark, a host of celebrations are planned, among them a major exhibition, 'Dickens and London', at the Museum of London (9 December 2011-10 June 2012) and a three-month Dickens-inspired film retrospective (from January 2012) at the BFI Southbank. We're also looking forward to the collaboration between the always-innovative Punchdrunk theatre company (www.punchdrunk.org.uk) and Hackney's Arcola Theatre, involving an immersive exhibition set in an east London greengrocer's. For more on the projects, see www.dickens2012.org.

1450-1455

Scale new heights

Climbing is great for your balance, strength, flexibility and social life (climbers are a friendly bunch), and London has plenty of indoor walls. Call the venues below for details of induction sessions and longer courses.

The dominant venue is the Castle: 450 routes and 95 lines on hugely varied terrains, in a turret-topped Victorian water pumping station. But Westway Climbing Centre competes on all counts. Only slightly smaller, it has a higher wall (14.5m) and a dramatic setting beneath the Westway.

Opened in the 1980s and housed in an old pipe engineering works, Mile End Climbing Wall retains a community feel, and offers a great first-time climb deal for £12 all in. Swiss Cottage Climbing Wall, meanwhile, has a 14m lead wall and over 60 routes, and is big on kids' activities.

The Reach is south London's largest climbing wall. It's not enormous but is designed to be challenging at various levels, and is very friendly. Another alternative is the Arch. Set in a railway arch near London Bridge station, it was recently expanded to include a traverse area and a challenging tunnel section.

The Arch *6 Bermondsey Street, SE1 2ER (7407 0999, http://archclimbingwall.com).*
The Castle *Green Lanes, N4 2HA (8211 7000, www.castle-climbing.co.uk).*
Mile End Climbing Wall *Haverfield Road, E3 5BE (8980 0289, www.mileendwall.org.uk).*
The Reach *Unit 6, Mellish Estate, Harrington Way, SE18 5NU (8855 9598, www.thereach. org.uk).*
Swiss Cottage Climbing Wall *Swiss Cottage Leisure Centre, Adelaide Road, NW3 3NF (7974 2012, www.climblondon.co.uk).*
Westway Climbing Centre *1 Crowthorne Road, W10 6RP (3432 5215, www.westway sportscentre.org.uk).*

The Castle

1456

Join the fast track

The London Roller Girls (www.londonrollergirls.com) founded Europe's first roller derby league in 2006, and are still going strong (and fast). Roller derby involves four defensive players trying to stop an attacking 'jammer' from circling the track, and is fast, physical and strategic. There are six teams, with names like Ultraviolet Femmes and Suffra Jets, playing in halls around the city; spectators are welcome and so are budding recruits – tryout dates are posted on the website.

1457-1462

Embrace the rockabilly scene

There's more to the rockabilly scene than a few tubs of Brylcreem and a cartoonish quiff. In fact, it's one of London's most interesting after-dark domains. Its all-swinging, immaculately coiffed fraternity spans a diverse range of cats, from Teddy Boys to hillbillies and psychobillies (the punker version), who go boozing, dancing and romancing in venues ranging from late-night back-alley boozers to chic, wallpapered lounges. In addition to rockabilly's signature sounds (black rhythm 'n' blues, western swing, honky tonk and hillbilly), nights often take in a performance element, from burlesque to hula hooping.

Events tend to move around, but look out for the following organisers: Rock-A-Billy Rebels (on Facebook), Lady Luck (www.ladyluckclub.co.uk), which runs a weekly club at Slim Jim's Liquor Store in Islington, the Virginia Creeper Club (see *Time Out* magazine for listings) and Hillbilly Hop (www.hillbillyhop.com).

The scene is fluid and creative, and the look ever evolving, but it's the original rockers that inspire the new generation. You'll find many up at the Ace Café (North Circular Road, NW10 7UD, 8961 1000, www.ace-cafe-london.com). The trailer-like diner looks as if it has been airlifted out of the Californian desert and plonked on the North Circular. Here, rockabillies exercise their other passion: motors. Every evening there's a different tribe parked up front admiring one another's engines, from hot rods and rat rods to classic bike nights.

You've got the venues, got the wheels: all you need is the threads. Any vintage shop will oblige, but the doyenne of the women's look is Vivien of Holloway (294 Holloway Road, N7 6NJ, 7609 8754, www.vivienofholloway.com), with its circle-skirt dresses, halternecks and sassy '50s styles.

1463 *Play in a gamelan*

Often thought to be a single instrument, a gamelan is, in fact, a whole percussion ensemble, from Indonesia. The delicate sound it produces, based on five-note scales, is lovely. LSO St Luke's (161 Old Street, EC1V 9NG, 7490 3939, http://lso.co.uk) has a full set of instruments from Bali, with bronze keys and magnificently carved frames. Its Community Gamelan Group welcomes new members; the first session is free, and no musical experience is necessary.

1464-1476

Visit London's original waxworks

Down in the vaulted, 11th-century undercroft of Westminster Abbey is its museum – home to a series of extraordinary, life-size effigies of kings, queens, and powerful public figures. Some were dressed in clothing from the subject's personal wardrobe, and over the centuries the depictions became ever-more sophisticated; while earlier models were carved from wood, the hands and heads of those made from the mid 17th-century onwards were cast in wax, lending them an eerily lifelike feel. The mannequin of Lord Nelson was so realistic that Lady Hamilton is said to have swooned at its feet.

The first effigies were made and used for funeral processions, but turned out to have a fringe financial benefit for the Abbey. Crowds flocked to see the figures, which were displayed in sentry boxes in a room of their own, and an admission fee was charged. This income became so valuable that the Nelson model was made specifically to counter the interest in St Paul's Cathedral generated by Nelson's burial there.

The cathedral authorities stopped the practice shortly afterwards, when the rise of Madame Tussaud's brought inappropriate associations of the carnivalesque to wax reproductions.

Not that there wasn't already a sense of theatre. The effigy of Frances Stewart, a great Restoration beauty, is dressed in her Coronation finery in a somewhat bombastic tableau, while Catherine, Duchess of Buckingham, is poignantly exhibited with her sons, Robert and Edmund, who died aged three and 19 respectively.

Queen Elizabeth I, modelled in 1760, suffered the post-mortem embarrassment of having her corset discovered during recent conservation work; it's now displayed separately. But King Charles II still wears the robes of the Order of the Garter, albeit somewhat wearily, 300 years on. Other wax effigies on display include King William III and Queen Mary II, Queen Anne, James I, Edward III, and William Pitt the Elder, Earl of Chatham.

Westminster Abbey Museum *20 Dean's Yard, SW1P 1PA (7222 5152, www.westminster-abbey.org).*

1477

Become a guerilla gardener

At its most basic level, guerilla gardening can be as simple as blowing a dandelion clock or shaking out a seed pod. Alternatively, you can join forces with like-minded souls to beautify neglected public spaces with targeted (if unsanctioned) horticultural interventions. All sorts of green-fingered forays are recorded on www.guerilla gardening.org, many of them in London. As well as offering tips, techniques and details of proposed planting missions, the site tells you how to make clay 'seed bombs' that will make wastelands explode with life.

1478

Watch your MP at work

The public are welcome to watch the proceedings of the Houses of Commons and Lords from their respective public galleries. Just turn up a little in advance of the debate you want to hear (consult http://services.parliament.uk/calendar for a list of upcoming Bills) to allow for queueing and security checks. UK residents can ask their MP for a ticket to one of the world's most dramatic examples of democracy in action: Prime Minister's Question Time, on Wednesdays at noon.

1479

Scale the ice in Covent Garden

The largest of Southampton Street's mountain sports shops, Ellis Brigham also houses London's only ice-climbing wall. The eight-metre high wall is in a refrigerator, starting in the basement and rising through the ground floor, where there are viewing windows. Two people can climb at any one time (£50 per person per hour, £25-£35 if you have your own kit and don't need instruction). Book at least a day ahead for weekdays, and around six weeks in advance for weekends.

Ellis Brigham *3-11 Southampton Street, WC2E 7HA (7395 1010, www.vertical-chill.com).*

1480-1496

Join London's blogosphere

London is home to a lively and informative community of bloggers, giving a voice to everything from historical esoterica to current culture, underground and mainstream. Below is our pick of the best. (Mentioned elsewhere in this book, you'll also find the wonderful London Review of Breakfasts, and the Pigeon Blog.)

A Little Bird
www.a-littlebird.com
A carefully curated run-down on the hottest shops, exhibitions, pop-up projects and more, chosen by two style journalists.

Dave Hill's London Blog
www.guardian.co.uk/uk/davehillblog
Scrutinising London politics.

Dos Hermanos
www.doshermanos.co.uk
Opinionated, entertaining reviews of London's restaurants, written by the food-obsessed Majumdar brothers.

Going Underground
www.london-underground.blogspot.com
News, trivia and irreverent comment on the tube.

The Great Wen
http://greatwenlondon.wordpress.com
From London's worst statues to weird museum exhibits, Peter Watts has an eye for the unusual.

Hookedblog
www.hookedblog.co.uk
Street art in the capital.

Jane's London
www.janeslondon.com
The fading artifacts of old London: ghost signs, coal holes and more.

London Cyclist
http://www.londoncyclist.co.uk
The inside track on cycling in the city.

London-in-Sight
http://londoninsight.wordpress.com
London's quirkier corners and characters, seen through the lens of photographer Stephanie Wolff.

London 2012 Blog
http://www.london2012.com/blog
The official London 2012 Olympic and Paralympic Games blog.

London Shopfronts
www.londonshopfronts.com
Curiously addictive for typography fans, this blog is a photographic paean to shopfronts.

Spitalfields Life
www.spitalfieldslife.com
Offbeat articles on the East End past and present.

Style Bubble
http://stylebubble.typepad.com
A personal take on fashion, written by the über-stylish, London-based Susie Bubble – who has a keen eye for the city's most intriguing shops.

The Style Scout
www.stylescout.blogspot.com
A roving photographer documents the best-dressed on London's streets.

Time Out London – Now. Here. This.
www.now-here-this.timeout.com
Our very own blog. The ultimate guide to eating and drinking, clubbing, fashion, the arts and more in London.

Tired of London, Tired of Life
www.tiredoflondontiredoflife.com
Not sure what to do in the city? TOLTOL's daily posts provide varied suggestions.

West End Whingers
www.westendwhingers.wordpress.com
Entertaining, irreverent reviews of current West End productions.

1497

Have a Craftacular Christmas

BUST magazine's Christmas Craftacular events (www.bust.com/craftacular/about-london.html) provide imaginative – and carefully selected – makers and designers with the chance to sell their wares. Cutting-edge knitwear, jewellery, handbags, cards, silk-screened prints and more are on sale – at Bethnal Green's York Hall for the past few years – and there are crafting activities and DJs. Other smaller versions of the Craftacular are held around London throughout the year.

1498-1500

Seek out a bargain beauty salon

Beautiful Nails Studio

This little nail bar sorts out your nails with little ceremony and only moderate cost attached (£15 gets you a good manicure). The sole glossy thing about the place is the nails, but that means staff are happy to get stuck in with the tools of the trade to file off dead skin; our tester left after a pedicure with feet seemingly half a size smaller. We're not the only ones to have discovered it: often the queue is out the door, so it's worth booking.
28 Tottenham Street, W1T 4RH (7580 5922, www.thebeautifulnailstudio.co.uk).

Cucumba

This express Soho salon specialises in fast, no-frills beauty treatments. Choose between 'Topups', 'Quickfixes' and 'Pitstops'– and pay about £23 for a duo like an eyebrow shape and nail job, which will take about 17 minutes. The top-up ten-minute treatments (massage, manicure or pedicure) are a steal at £9.50.
12 Poland Street, W1F 8QB (7734 2020, www.cucumba.co.uk).

Esthetique

For the cheapest beauty treatments in town, make for the student-run Esthetique salon at the London School of Beauty & Make-up. Here, supervised students will beautify you for a fraction of the normal cost; an hour-long French manicure will set you back £12, for instance, while a 90-minute aromatherapy massage costs just £28. Treatments are carried out under the eye of a note-taking tutor.
48 Margaret Street, W1W 8SE (7580 0355, www.lond-est.com/student_salon).

1501

Step into a Little Shop of Horrors

Peek through the windows at this Hackney curiosity shop and you'll see a world in which velvet-cloaked Victorians might reside. Entering the shop, which is also the spiritual home of the esoterically minded Last Tuesday Society, reveals a *wunderkammer* of skulls, dolls, taxidermic specimens and oddities. Lectures and events are also held – from literary talks to 'an erotic magic lantern show', held to mark St Valentine's day .
Viktor Wynd Fine Art & Little Shop of Horrors
11 Mare Street, E8 4RP (7998 3617, www.the lasttuesdaysociety.org).

1502

Guerrilla gardener and blogger Steve Wheen (aka the Pothole Gardener) is a man on a mission: to beautify the unsightly potholes that dot the city's streets. Planted in the craters, his gardens are small-scale – though transitory – things of beauty. As well as making passers-by smile, the idea is to draw attention to the dire state of the capital's streets, and the menace they pose to cyclists. For photographs of Steve's latest forays, visit http://thepotholegardener.com.

Wimbledon car boot

1503-1511

Snaffle a boot-sale bargain...

Battersea

Not the cheapest around, but with bargains of the high-end and vintage variety for late risers – the Sunday sale opens at noon – what's not to love?
Battersea Park School, Battersea Park Road, SW11 5AP. Open 11.30am-5pm Sun.

Capital Car Boot Sale

Faye Marriott's chichi car boot attracts a youthful crowd. Not everything's a designer find (though we've heard rumours of Mulberry and Isabel Marant), but with over 100 sellers on good days, you're bound to find a pre-loved to love.
Pimlico Academy (Chichester Street entrance), SW1V 3AT (www.capitalcarboot.com). Open 12.30-4pm Sun.

Holloway

With the odd fashion gem, funky bric-a-brac and a good spread of second-hand DVDs, this car boot sale is worth a rummage. Prices are very reasonable – we picked up a pair of tan Chelsea boots for £8.
Holloway Road, opposite Odeon Cinema, N7 6LJ. Open 8am-4pm Sat; 10am-2.30pm Sun.

Nags Head

The Nags Head sells everything from decorative Victorian knife sets and stamp collections to (mostly) working toasters, DVDs and remote controls. A no-frills, rough-around-the-edges retail experience; arrive early for the bargains.
22 Seven Sisters Road, N7 6AG (7607 3527, www.nagsheadmarket.co.uk). Open 7.30am-3.30pm daily.

Princess May

The bright young things of Stokie and Dalston gather here to rummage among the junk (half a bottle of foot lotion? plate hangers?), clothes and costume jewellery. In summer, you can punctuate bargain-hunting with bangers off the barbecue.
Princess May School, Princess May Road, N16 8DF (thelondoncarbootco.co.uk). Open 9am-3pm Sat; 9am-2pm Sun.

Shepperton

Shepperton's all about cheap and cheerful; you'd be hard put to find a car boot in London with a friendlier atmosphere. With its knowledgeable, attentive stall holders, it's a great starter-sale for car boot newbies, as well as seasoned booters willing to travel for their second-hand bargains.
New Road, Shepperton, Surrey TW17 0QQ (www.sheppertoncarboot.co.uk). Open 8.30am-late afternoon Sat.

St Augustine's

Like any car boot sale worth its second-hand salt, it packs all kinds of bric-a-brac, from old tins to TVs. If you want to poke around the goods before 11am, you'll need to pay a £3 'early bird' fee.
St Augustine's School, Kilburn Park Road, NW6 5SN (www.thelondoncarbootco.com). Open 10.30am-3pm Sat.

St Mary's

A mecca for would-be interior designers and DIY lovers: think quirky home furnishings, retro light fittings, vintage vinyls and textiles. Run by the same company as St Augustine's, it also charges bargain-hunters for early entry.
St Mary's Church of England Primary School, Quex Road, NW6 4PG (www.thelondoncarbootco. com). Open 10am-3pm Sat.

Wimbledon

Still one of London's best boot sales, selling everything from vintage and jewellery to books, furniture and toys. With over 2,000 stalls to browse, bring a big bag and expect to fill it.
Wimbledon Stadium, Plough Lane, SW17 0BL. Open 10.30am-2pm Wed; 6.30am-1.30pm Sat; 7am-1.30pm Sun.

1512

... Or attend the Art Car Boot

Now in its eighth year, Brick Lane's Art Car Boot Fair (www.artcarbootfair.com) has become a playful highlight of London's art calendar, taking place on a Sunday in June. In past years, the likes of Peter Blake, Damien Hirst and Tracey Emin have rolled up to sell their wares – ranging from exclusive prints to more eccentric items, such as the signed hens' eggs sold by artist Gavin Turk at the 2011 event.

1513-1517
Get your tresses trimmed for less

To get a haircut on the cheap, volunteer as a hairdressing model. Trainees' work is checked by a qualified supervisor, though that does mean it takes time – generally two to three hours for a cut. All the salons listed here need models on a regular basis, but you have to call ahead.

At the Toni & Guy Training Academy (71-75 New Oxford Street, WC1A 1DG, 7836 0606, www.toniandguy.com), cuts cost a fiver and are closely supervised, highlights £25.

Vidal Sassoon Creative Academy (48 Brook Street, W1K 4HB, 7399 6901, www.sassoon.com) is equally well established, offering weekday appointments between 10am and 2pm. Cuts cost £12 (£5 for students), highlights £30, and there's a maximum 12 to one student-teacher ratio.

Brooks & Brooks (Sicilian Avenue, WC1A 2QH, 7405 8111, www.brooksandbrooks.co.uk) is a multi-award-winning salon in Bloomsbury (three times London Hairdresser of the Year, for starters). On Mondays and Tuesdays you can get a restyle for free; cuts are by trainees, but fully supervised by the best in the business.

Soho's Fish Hairdressing (30 D'Arblay Street, W1F 8ER, 7494 2398, www.fishsoho.com) offers cut-price Monday morning appointments as in-house training for salon juniors. There's close supervision from stylists, and some flexibility over styles. Cuts are from £5, colour from £15.

Finally, the Aveda Academy (174 High Holborn, WC1V 7AA, 7759 7355, www.aveda.co.uk) holds a host of colour and cutting workshops and classes, and frequently requires models.

1518
Ski Richmond Park

When London has a deep snowfall, residents head for the high ground with skis, snowboards and sledges. Greenwich Park and Parliament Hill are popular, but that means the 'slopes' are crowded and soon turn to mush. Richmond Park (Richmond, Surrey TW10 5HS, 8948 3209, www.royalparks.gov.uk) gets busy too, but it offers a much larger area, varied terrain and good car access and parking.

1519-1525
Travel smart with transport apps

The smartphone is a gift for navigating London's public transport system. Complex journeys can be planned in seconds, taking any current closures and delays into account, and you can add all kinds of bells and whistles to your commute.

First, getting from A to B. Tube Map provides a route planner and live status updates for all underground lines, while the London BusMapper plots the most convenient bus routes from your location to your destination on an interactive map. London Journey planner uses live data from TfL to offer routes using all means of public transport. And UK Train Times, though pricier than the others, is indispensible for rail commuters.

And now the fun stuff. Tube Alarm is an alarm clock, but one that finds out, while you sleep, whether there are any delays on the lines you plan to use, and wakes you up early if so. Tube Exits tells you where to stand on the platform in order to be perfectly aligned for your exit, and so beat the crowds. Finally, augmented reality helps Nearest Tube to superimpose tube lines and stations on your view of the real world via your phone's camera. Surreal, man.

1526
Join the mudlarks

In Victorian times, mudlarks eeked out a meagre existence from reselling lumps of coal, iron rivets and other flotsam found on the Thames' muddy foreshore: as Henry Mayhew recorded in his *London Labour & London Poor*, they were often children ('For the most part they are ragged, and in a very filthy state, and are a peculiar class').

Nowadays, it's a different story, as mudlarking has become the preserve of metal detecting enthusiasts and amateur archaelogists. Although you need a permit to mudlark on the river, you can go on an introductory foray with Steve 'Mud God' Brooker, from the Thames & Field Metal Detecting Society (8310 8817, www.thamesandfield.co.uk), who will guide you along the foreshore. You might unearth anything from Roman coins and 18th-century clay pipes to clay Diwali lamps. Just don't forget your gumboots.

A few of my favourite things

1527-1533

Susie Lau
Fashion blogger

I'm a big fan of Black Gull Books (121 High Road, N2 8AG, 8444 4717) in East Finchley. It's a second-hand bookstore that stocks every book imaginable – including a great selection of art and fashion titles, all at decent prices. You see things you'd never find in a mainsteam bookshop, and books that have been out of print for years. My best buy? A '70s copy of *Cheap Chic*, with chapters by Diana Vreeland.

LN-CC (18 Shacklewell Lane, E8 2EZ, 3174 0736, www.ln-cc.com) is a bit like Dover Street Market, but more off the beaten track. It's open by appointment, which makes it feel extra-special, and the premises are amazing. You walk in through a forest of twigs, then an octagonal wooden tunnel that feels very Clockwork Orange: it was built by a set designer, Gary Card. The clothes are displayed in shelves that look like Tetris blocks, and there are different rooms to explore. It's high-end – Margiela, Ann Demeulemeester, JW Anderson and some great Japanese labels like Toga – but also stocks things like books and records.
There are some fabulous magazines, books and old knitting patterns at the Pattern Market (no phone, Kingsland Road, E8 4DG), which is down by the canal on Kingsland Road. It's like a well-curated charity shop, with clothes and furniture, and is perfect for a rummage – without the crowds of somewhere like Spitalfields.

The croissants are terrific at Le Péché Mignon (6 Ronalds Road, N5 1XH, 7607 1826, www.lepechemignon.co.uk), and baked fresh every morning. I took a Parisian friend here, and even she was impressed. The back garden is lovely in summer, and the breakfast sandwiches are delicious. I'm a bit particular about eggs – the yolk has to be runny, and cooked just so – and they always get it right.

I go to Pelicans & Parrots (40 Stoke Newington Road, N16 7XJ, 3215 2083, www.pelicansandparrots.com) for vintage clothes, antiques and contemporary homeware. It's part of a burgeoning row of shops in Dalston, and is run by a couple with a great eye for clothes – they had some fantastic 1940s men's workwear last time I went in.

I never get tired of walking around the V&A (Cromwell Road, SW7 2RL, 7942 2000, www.vam.ac.uk); it feels as if you could never, ever see all of it. I particularly love the 18th-century furniture and ceramics departments, and the Arts & Crafts collections, but there's always more to discover. Some bits of are really hard to find, but getting lost in obscure corners and stairwells is all part of the fun. The exhibitions are amazing too; I try to go on Mondays, to avoid the crowds.

The Merchant Archive (320 Kilburn Lane, W9 3EF, 8969 6470, www.merchantarchive. com) is set in an old Lipton's General Store, with some of the original tiling. The selection of vintage is stunning, with lots of Victorian, Edwardian and 1920s pieces. I found the dress I wore to the British Fashion Awards here – a beautifully simple 1960s shift, embroidered with pearls.

1534 *Be transplanted to the tropics at Kew*

There is a corner of Kew Gardens that is forever not England. A sturdy brick building conceals a dazzling interior of intensely detailed oil paintings, depicting the flora and fauna of the Americas, India, South Africa and Australasia – anywhere but Europe. Hung frame-to-frame and floor-to-ceiling, this cornucopia of pictures is the work of one individual – the Victorian adventurer and amateur botanist Marianne North, who, at the age of 40, set off around the world, in search of botanical wonders.

Marianne North Gallery *The Royal Botanic Gardens, Kew, Richmond, Surrey TW9 3AB (8332 5655, www.kew.org).*

1535-1552

Dine alfresco

Amphitheatre Terrace

A bit of a secret, this one: the terrace at the Royal Opera House, overlooking Covent Garden, is open to the public most days (call to check), and only surrendered to ticket holders come the evening. The food is quintessentially British: chilled pea soup, say, with poached salmon to follow.
Royal Opera House, Bow Street, WC2E 9DD (7212 9254, www.roh.org.uk).

Boundary Rooftop

The Conran-backed Boundary Project has a fine rooftop bar and restaurant, with panoramic views of London. The simple, summery menu is based around grills (lobster, rib-eye steak), and goods from the deli downstairs. Sunscreen is supplied on bright afternoons; in the evening, heaters and thick wool blankets keep diners warm.
2-4 Boundary Street, E2 7DD (7729 1051, www.theboundary.co.uk).

Brew House

If you can get to Hampstead Heath early, head to the Brew House for a terrific cooked breakfast, then potter around the terraces with your tray until you find the right combination of parasol shade and sunshine above Kenwood House's sweeping lawn. Lunches are of the superior canteen variety. And did we mention the cakes?
Kenwood House, Hampstead Lane, NW3 7JR (8341 5384, www.companyofcooks.com).

Clerkenwell Kitchen

Clerkenwell Kitchen no longer accepts bookings for its six outdoor tables, so you'll have to turn up and take your chances. Surrounded by office buildings, the quiet courtyard is a lovely spot to enjoy seasonal, organic fare.
27-31 Clerkenwell Close, EC1R 0AT (7101 9959, www.theclerkenwellkitchen.co.uk).

Coq d'Argent

If panoramic views are high on your wish list, you can't go far wrong with the Coq d'Argent: St Paul's, the Gherkin and the Shard are all in plain sight from its rooftop terrace, and on a clear day you can see all the way to Crystal Palace. The food is all about top-end City sophistication, but there's a good-value set lunch.
1 Poultry, EC2R 8EJ (7395 5000, www.coqdargent.co.uk).

Engineer

The sun-trap courtyard at this Primrose Hill gastropub is an inviting prospect, with tables shaded by canopies or moveable brollies, a pergola at one end, and heaters for chilly evenings. The food is equally polished, though prices reflect the smart locale.
65 Gloucester Avenue, NW1 8JH (7722 0950, www.the-engineer.com).

Gallery Mess

You win indoors and out at the Saatchi Gallery's brasserie, either surrounded by modern art or enjoying the capacious, buzzy patio. The food is classy café: salmon ceviche with guacamole and chilli, perhaps, or quinoa and chicken salad.
Saatchi Gallery, Duke of York's HQ, King's Road, SW3 4LY (7730 8135, www.saatchi-gallery.co.uk).

Greek Affair

This relaxed little bistro has a sweet first-floor terrace, with parasols, heaters and plants. The menu is a celebration of Greek meze, from dips and stuffed peppers to grilled octopus.
1 Hillgate Street, W8 7SP (7792 5226, www.greekaffair.co.uk).

Petersham Nurseries Café

Marco Polo

With 100-odd tables spread across a pair of riverfront decks, this is a great place to watch the Thames flow by. The kitchen sticks to Italian classics, and has a real flair for desserts.
6-7 Riverside Quarter, Eastfields Avenue, SW18 1LP (8874 7007, www.marcopolo.uk.net).

Modern Pantry

Anna Hansen's Clerkenwell restaurant has 13 alfresco tables on St John's Square. It's at a decent remove from the traffic of Clerkenwell Road, but close enough to people-watch. The globetrotting menu is well suited to summer days – Hansen's signature sugar-cured prawn omelette speaks eloquently of South-east Asian sunshine.
47-48 St John's Square, EC1V 4JJ (7250 0833, www.themodernpantry.co.uk).

Narrow

Gordon Ramsay's Narrow makes the most of its river setting, with a bright conservatory and outdoor seating area overlooking the wharves of Rotherhithe on the far bank. The handful of alfresco tables can't be booked, so turn up early for well-executed takes on pub grub.
44 Narrow Street, E14 8DQ (7592 7950, www.gordonramsay.com/thenarrow).

Paradise By Way of Kensal Green

The yard of this gastropub has been converted into a 30-cover 'garden', with wooden tables, heaters, and access to the surprisingly good cooking (potted ham hock, salmon with crab and brioche crust), but we think the no-bookings rooftop is more special. Serving only a bar menu and weekend roasts, it has a handful of tables, parasols and palms, and an ivy-clad trellis.
19 Kilburn Lane, W10 4AE (8969 0098, www.theparadise.co.uk).

Petersham Nurseries Café

Few London dining rooms can compete with this magical glasshouse, alive with palm trees and scented jasmine. Mismatched tables are ornamented with pots of sage and lavender, while Skye Gyngell's food is beautiful to behold. After lunch, you can potter around the nurseries outside, then walk across the fields to Richmond. Reserve well ahead.
Church Lane, off Petersham Road, Surrey TW10 7AG (8605 3627, www.petershamnurseries.com).

Princess Victoria

We like this gastropub a great deal, but were tempted to keep secret its lovely herb garden in a walled courtyard. If you don't mind the smoke from cigars purchased on the premises, the food is very good. Also impressive are the drinks – more than 300 bins of wine, with over 30 by the glass.
217 Uxbridge Road, W12 9DH. (8749 5886, www.princessvictoria.co.uk).

Rochelle Canteen

Where once there were school bike sheds, now you'll find the unassuming but excellent Rochelle Canteen. The portable outdoor tables have been replaced by permanent versions, seating around 20 diners. Seasonal treats on the daily menu might run from lamb chop with violet artichokes and anchovy to gooseberry eton mess.
Rochelle School, Arnold Circus, E2 7ES (7729 5677, www.arnoldandhenderson.com).

Sardo Canale

Sardo Canale doesn't take bookings for the eight tables in its canalside garden, set beneath the boughs of a 150-year-old Sardinian olive tree. On a warm night, arrive between 6pm and 7.30pm to have any chance of nabbing a spot. Specialities include spaghetti with bottarga (dried grey mullet roe), and there's an exemplary Sardinian wine list.
42 Gloucester Avenue, NW1 8JD (7722 2800, www.sardocanale.com).

The Terrace

There are ten alfresco tables at the Terrace, a discreet, single-storey eaterie that's set amid the greenery of Lincoln's Inn Fields. It's open weekdays only, so it's the legal fraternity that makes the most of chef Patrick Williams' cooking – an accomplished blend of Modern British and Caribbean influences.
Lincoln's Inn Fields, WC2A 3LJ (7430 1234, www.theterrace.info).

Victoria

On the edge of Richmond Park, the Victoria is headed by TV chef Paul Merrett. In the garden, an impressive grill is fired up in good weather, but there are always summery options on the regular menu (charred lamb, red onion and pomegranate salad, perhaps).
10 West Temple Sheen, SW14 7RT (8876 4238, www.thevictoria.net).

1553 *Shop in a box*

Occupying a long-abandoned railway goods yard in Shoreditch, Boxpark, opening in autumn 2011, is an ambitious twist on the pop-up shop. Running on a five-year lease, it comprises over 50 disused shipping containers, stripped and refitted to create a complex of 'box shops'. The organisers hope to attract a mix of local creative brands and established urban labels (Original Penguin and Lacoste have already signed up).

Boxpark *Corner of Shoreditch High Street & Bethnal Green Road, E1 6JJ (8133 0182, www.boxpark.co.uk).*

1554

Swop headphones with a stranger

A Note Well Speed Listening bash (www.the notewell.com) is a bit like speed dating – except that it's about sharing songs rather than romance. Pre-load an mp3 player with six songs on a given theme, then swap playlists with strangers and talk them through your choices. You should come away with some new bands to listen to – and perhaps some new friends.

1555

Invest in a masterpiece at the National Gallery

Don't have a few million quid spare to buy yourself the Van Gogh you so enjoyed seeing at the National Gallery? No problem: pop into the gallery shop to have your own copy printed out on demand while you wait (15 to 30 minutes). There are 2,500 paintings on the system, with Van Gogh's *Sunflowers* jostling with Turner's *The Fighting Temeraire* for top spot in the popularity stakes. Prints and unstretched canvasses are available on the spot; if you want them framed or stretched, order in the shop or online for home delivery. Prices start at £15.

National Gallery *Trafalgar Square, WC2 5DN (7747 2870, www.nationalgallery.org.uk).*

1556-1560 *Go in search of old London Bridge*

Our search for the remains of old London Bridge begins in the porch of St Magnus the Martyr (Lower Thames Street, EC3R 6DN, www.st magnusmartyr.org.uk). The church used to stand on the sloping approach to the 19-arch medieval bridge, which was sited 60 metres downriver from its modern counterpart. It's hard to imagine this quiet churchyard, now hemmed in by office blocks, as the busiest riverside thoroughfare in all the city, but the wonderful 20-foot model of the bridge inside the church evokes the scene.

In the churchyard lies a historic clutter of half-ton stones from the first arch of Old London Bridge. Unmistakeably ancient, they were unearthed in 1920 during the construction of Adelaide House. To complete St Magnus's set is a granite coping stone from the Rennie bridge of 1831, salted here by God's will while its brethren made the trip to Lake Havasu City, Nevada, where the recreated bridge stands to this day.

Towards the end of its life, in 1762, the medieval bridge's seven storeys of teetering shops and houses were cleared to allow the passage of traffic – and its 14 quarter-spherical 'refuge booths' for pedestrians were sold off. Over the river in Borough, one survives in the grounds of Guy's Hospital – now peopled by convalescents rather than footpads and prostitutes. Another relic from the clearance is to be found a couple of roads south on Newcomen Street: the plaster royal coat-of-arms which was added to the bridge tollgate in 1728 adorns the front of the King's Arms pub (no.65, SE1 1YT, 7407 1132).

Two more of the 18th-century pedestrian alcoves survive in Hackney's Victoria Park (Victoria Park Road, E9 7BT, 7364 2494) and a fourth remains in the Courtlands estate, off Sheen Road in Richmond. A survivor from the gardens of a mansion demolished in the 1930s, it stands only a mile from Kew Gardens (Kew, Richmond, Surrey TW9 3AB, 8332 5655, www.kew.org) where, at the edge of the lake, there's another clutch of stones from Rennie's London Bridge of 1831.

1561

Celebrate the Barbican Centre's 30th birthday

Under its saw-toothed, concrete residential towers, the Barbican (Silk Street, EC2Y 8DS, 7638 8891, www.barbican.org.uk) is Europe's largest multi-arts centre. Its angular, Brutalist architecture has attracted plenty of opprobrium since it opened in 1982 – but up close, the Barbican is a much more friendly place. The austerity of the architecture is softened by water features – a rectangular lake with fountains, and several square duck ponds – and there's a steamy Conservatory (open noon-4pm Sundays and bank holidays) that's full of tropical plants, exotic fish and twittering birds.

Learn to love the Barbican by taking one of the regular, 90-minute architectural tours of the complex (www.barbican.org.uk/education) – which will also help you navigate its famously confusing layout.

Of course, the main reason to visit is for the arts themselves. Highlights for the Barbican's birthday year include a Bauhaus exhibition and several projects for the London 2012 Festival (Cate Blanchett in *Gross und Klein*, Philip Glass's *Einstein on the Beach*, a season of Pina Bausch's contemporary dance and a collaboration between African singer Rokia Traoré and novelist Toni Morrison among them). Even better, there are free foyer events themed to complement the performances in the main halls.

1562-1569

Try a real kebab

Know where to look in London and you can eat some of the finest kebabs this side of Istanbul.

Abu Zaad
Try kebab bil tahina – a traditional dish of spicy lamb topped with yoghurt and tahina – at this homely Syrian restaurant.
29 Uxbridge Road, W12 8LH (8749 5107, www.abuzaad.co.uk).

Kebab Kid
This little takeaway is a cut above the rest, with proper shawarmas (chicken or lamb).
90 New Kings Road, SW6 4LU (7731 0427).

Mangal Ocakbasi
Shish (marinated lamb chunks), beyti (spicy minced lamb) and pirzola (lamb chops) are all exemplary at this Turkish trailblazer.
10 Arcola Street, E8 2DJ (7275 8981, www.mangal1.com).

19 Numara Bos Cirrik I
One of Dalston's best Turkish restaurants: top marks for its spicy minced kebabs and skewered chunks of meat with garlicky tomato sauce.
34 Stoke Newington Road, N16 7XJ (7249 0400).

Patogh
An Iranian café offering wonderful flatbreads with minced lamb or chicken wrapped around skewers, then chargrilled.
8 Crawford Place, W1H 5NE (7262 4015).

Ranoush Juice
The original branch of this Lebanese café chain is a great pitstop for either of the two formidable shawarmas (chicken and lamb).
43 Edgware Road, W2 2JR (7723 5929).

Tayyabs
Hugely popular Pakistani canteen, with queues for beautifully cooked seekh and shami kebabs.
83-89 Fieldgate Street, E1 1JU (7247 9543, www.tayyabs.co.uk).

Zengi
Middle Eastern staples are done well at the Whitechapel eaterie; we rate the the spicy lamb kebabs with bread from the wood-fired oven.
44 Commercial Street, E1 6LT (7426 0700).

Back on track

Herne Hill Velodrome is a slice of sporting history – but it needs your support. Elizabeth Winding pays a visit.

Hidden behind a neat terrace on a leafy Dulwich street lies one of the capital's long-forgotten sporting treasures. Its narrow entrance shoehorned between two semis, Herne Hill Velodrome is easily missed – and was, until recently, in danger of being forgotten altogether. Follow the trickle of cyclists turning in here, though, and you'll discover Dulwich's best-kept secret: a vast outdoor track, encircled by magnificent trees.

Built in 1891, Herne Hill is the sole survivor of the Victorian velodromes that once peppered the capital, including sites at Putney, Paddington, Kensal Rise and Catford. In its heyday, weekend meets were thronged: in 1926, 13,000 people attended the annual Good Friday event.

Bill Rowney first rode the track at Herne Hill in 1946. Today – a spry 80 – he is one of track's stalwart volunteers; back then, he was a keen as mustard 14-year-old, legs a whirr of speed. He still remembers the 'sea of bicycles' and crowds of spectators, three deep around the track. 'Once, I flew off the track, went over the fence – which was only about a foot high, back then – and ended up in the crowd. There were so many people, they caught me; I never even hit the ground.'

Two years later, Bill was among the crowds that packed the stands for the 1948 Olympic Games, roaring their approval as Reg Harris took silver in the Sprint (pipped to the post, alas, by the Italian Mario Ghella), and Tommy Godwin pedalled his way to two bronze medals.

Today it's a different story. The stands, like the dilapidated grand pavilion, are structurally unsafe and cordoned off; instead, spectators watch training sessions and races from temporary tiers of sun-bleached plastic seats, while the cyclists get changed in portacabins. Amid the peeling paint, encroaching weeds and flaking concrete are reminders of the track's glory days, like the empty flagpoles that flank the overgrown entrance gates.

'You can just feel the history,' says Hillary Peachey, a driving force behind the campaign to save the track. 'This place has been here for over 100 years, and is the last London venue still in use from the 1948 Games. There's a real sadness when you look at the site; it's wrong for it to be sitting here in this state.'

Run-down it may be, but the track is still full of life. On a sunny Saturday morning, riders pedal by in sociable clusters. Snippets of conversation drift over the barrier ('My bits have gone numb!' ... 'Single file please, we're coming over the top'); beyond the track's perimeter, a group of six-year-olds are learning to cycle one-handed. Once the intermediates have come off the track, a line of beginners will line up along the barrier, waiting for the induction to start at noon. It's open to all, and brilliantly inclusive; anyone over eight can turn up and have a go, with fixed-gear bikes and helmets provided.

The sessions are led by members of the Vélo Londres club, who have been running the site on a voluntary basis since 2005 – supervising meets, instructing wobbly novices, running the kids' cyclo cross and school holiday club, and maintaining the track. It's an epic amount of work. 'It's amazing,' says Hillary. 'These people have kept it going for years: cleaning the toilets, cutting the grass, clearing the weeds, running the sessions... they've done an incredible job.'

In the tiny café, Jan and George are perhaps the longest-serving volunteers, turning up every Saturday and Sunday morning (plus competition days) to dispense tea, slabs of cake and bacon sandwiches from a cramped portacabin. How long have they been coming for? 'Twenty-five years?' hazards Jan. 'Since forever,' confirms George. Neither has ever cycled the track.

In 2010, Hillary was asked to launch a fundraising campaign to resurface the velodrome's crumbling track. Like many locals, she'd been oblivious to its existence for years, until her son started cycling there – first on the kids' mountainbiking trails, then on the main track. 'He'd never been good at ball sports, but he completely took to cycling,' she says. 'It's been amazing for him; three years on, he's still down there every week.'

It seemed to strike a chord with all sorts of other people, too. That October, at Save Herne Hill Velodrome's first public meeting, 700 people showed up. 'We couldn't fit them all into the Dulwich College Great Hall,' recalls Hillary. 'It was an incredible turnout.'

The campaign swiftly gathered momentum, amassing some high-profile supporters along the way. Lord Coe's father used to train at the track, as did fashion designer Paul Smith's dad.

Olympic gold medallist Bradley Wiggins, who started cycling at Herne Hill, was quick to lend his support, while Kate Hoey and Tessa Jowell threw their political weight behind the campaign. In February 2011 there was a breakthrough, when a new 15-year-lease was agreed with the site's landlords. With this secured, the track's much-needed resurfacing could finally go ahead, funded by British Cycling.

The plan now is to reinvent the velodrome as a place for local people as well as the cycling community, broadening access to the facilities. Funding allowing, one idea is to run a new family-friendly cycling track around the edge of the ten-acre site, and there's talk of a new café overlooking the track. 'Getting the lease was incredible, but it was only the first step,' says Hillary. 'Now, the hard work needs to begin.'

It's hoped that this place will act as a training ground for a new generation of cyclists, and a feeder for the state-of-the-art new London 2012 Velodrome at Stratford. It's not an impossible dream. The current National Points Race Track Champion, Corinne Hall, trained here, and people still remember Bradley Wiggins training here as a child. 'I've known Bradley since he was eight, coming in for a bit of bread pudding,' says Jan, pouring another cup of tea in the café. 'My son-in-law still brags that he beat Bradley Wiggins – though it wasn't recently, I can tell you.'

Herne Hill Velodrome

Burbage Road, SE24 9HE (www.hernehill velodrome.com). Induction sessions currently take place on Saturdays, at noon; for details, check the website. To join the campaign to save the velodrome, visit www.savethevelodrome.com, or sign up on Facebook or Twitter.

On your bike: track cycling for beginners

As velodromes go, Herne Hill is relatively forgiving for novice riders. The shorter the track, the steeper the banking needs to be; Herne Hill, being a generous 450 metres long, has a relatively mild maximum gradient of 30 degrees.

Nonetheless, it looks pretty daunting once you're lined up at the top edge of the track, holding tight to the rail that runs around the barrier. Right now, though, my main worry is stopping. We're on fixed gear bikes, which don't have brakes: instead, you pedal at a slower rate, gradually coming to a halt – though as I've never ridden one before, I'm going to have to take that on trust. What's worse is that my feet are strapped into the pedals; if I come a cropper, I won't be able to break the fall, but will slam straight into the track.

Happily, there's not much time to contemplate my own mortality. After an introduction to track safety and techniques, we're off – a straggling line of novices, wobbling away from the barrier one by one.

Hopelessly slow as are, it's adrenaline-pumping stuff – particularly when we progress to half-lap changes, taking it in turns to lead the pack. Reassuringly, an instructor rides alongside, bellowing kindly exortations and advice – mostly trying to persuade us to ride a little closer to the rider in front, and keep a tight formation. Being out in front feels like flying, though taking the brunt of the wind is hard work; by the time the session ends, my lungs and legs are burning.

As our confidence grows, we move up to the steeper sections of the track. It's on the curving, 180-degree bends that the gradients are steepest – and at first, it seems impossible that the thin tyres will cling to the track and the bike stay upright. It does, of course, and I swoop around the bend, on a heart-pounding wave of exhilaration. Was I terrified? Completely. But will I be back to ride the track again? Absolutely.

1571-1583

Investigate Arcadia, ancient and modern

Built in 1819 by Lord Cavendish, to provide 'industrious females' with employment, and to stop people throwing oyster shells into the garden of Burlington House, Burlington Arcade (Piccadilly, W1, www.burlington-arcade.co.uk) is the city's grandest shopping arcade. Decorum is guarded by the ever-present Beadles, who to this day prevent shoppers from whistling, running, and 'making merry loudly'; you've been warned.

Step into Ladurée's golden grotto (nos.71-72, 7491 9155, www.laduree.fr) for a dainty macaron before idling past the arcade's sparkling row of jewellers. The strands of pearls in Milleperle (nos.60-61, 7499 3535, www.milleperle.co.uk) catch the eye, as does the antique jewellery in Matthew Foster (no.25, 7629 4977, www.matthew-foster.co.uk). Luxury goods abound in the form of watches from David Duggan (no.63, 7491 1675, www.daviddugganwatches.co.uk), pens from Pen Friend (no.34, 7499 6337, www.penfriend.co.uk) and custom-made gloves from Sermoneta Gloves (no.51, 7491 9009, www.sermonetagloves.com). Make sure you step into the quintessentially English fragrance house, Penhaligon's (nos.16-17, 7629 1416, www.penhaligons.com). Burlington Arcade also houses a proper shoe-shine boy, working with waxes and creams for just £3.50.

Across town there's a very different feel in Portobello Green Arcade (281 Portobello Road, W10, www.portobellodesigners.com) – a showcase for new and established designers, minutes away from the markets of Portobello Road. Loved by Jerry Hall, Zarvis London (no.4, 8968 5435, www.zarvis.com) is a pampering shop with a difference – all the ingredients for its products are derived from plants grown in England. Also check out Preen (no.5, 8968 1542, www.preen.eu), the hip, minimalist fashion label for women and men, and which counts Kate Moss and Chloë Sevigny among its followers.

Accessorise your look with some fabulous jewellery from Sarah Bunting (no.22, 8968 2253), who specialises in silver, platinum and gold contemporary jewellery, inspired by organic forms. Then make like a pre-war pin-up and slip into something slinky at What Katie Did (no.26, 0845 430 8943, www.whatkatiedid.com), which makes beautiful, vintage-style lingerie.

Gents in search of sharp tailoring should make a beeline for Adam of London (no.11, 8960 6944, www.adamoflondon.com), selling 1960s-inspired ready-to-wear suits, shirts and ties. Finally, childrenswear shop Sasti (no.6, 8960 1125, www.sasti.co.uk) is one of *Time Out*'s favourite children's boutiques, with an affordable range of colourful, stylish togs.

1584-1597

Find the city's secret galleries

Housed in 'alternative' spaces that range from church crypts to old car salesrooms – even a pub toilet – London's lesser-known galleries are well worth scouting out.

Agency Gallery

Concentrating on innovation and emerging artists, Agency plays host to pop-up events as well as curated shows. Performance, sound art and electronic media are particular interests.
66 Evelyn Street, SE8 5DD (8692 0734, www.theagencygallery.co.uk).

Arch 402 Gallery

Set in a railway arch by Hoxton Overground station, this place provide a spacious forum for multidisciplinary projects, with writers and art critics often involved in the curating process.
402 Cremer Street, E2 8HD (7043 2027, www.arch402.com).

Auto Italia South East

Now occupying an old car salesroom (it previously occupied a former VW garage on Glengall Road), Auto Italia is run by a group of young artists, hosting performance art, music nights, lectures, studios, exhibitions and symposia. The lively Peckham art scene is a stone's throw away.
434-452 Old Kent Road, SE1 5AG (www.autoitaliasoutheast.org).

Between Bridges

Wolfgang Tillmans's Between Bridges is an example of a mega-successful artist funding a non-profit venue. The gallery occupies little more than the entrance hall and stairwell of an anonymous Bethnal Green building (Tillmans's studio is on the first floor); shows run from hip US collectives to obscure German typographers.
223 Cambridge Heath Road, E2 0EL (www.betweenbridges.net).

Cabinet Gallery

Cabinet has been a fixture on the scene for 20 years, moving from Brixton and Farringdon to its current spot on Old Street. Despite being a favourite of heavyweight curators, it's so secret that it doesn't even tell *Time Out* about its exhibitions. It's soon to be moving to new premises in Vauxhall.

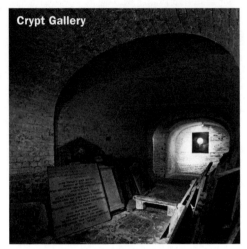

Crypt Gallery

Apartment 6, 49-59 Old Street, EC1V 9HX (7251 6114, www.cabinet.uk.com).

Charlie Smith

Hidden away above the Reliance pub, this gallery's exhibitions aim to challenge, provoke and seduce – beauty, death and sexuality are common themes.
336 Old Street, EC1V 9DR (7739 4055, www.charliesmithlondon.com).

Crypt Gallery

Since 2002, the arches and alcoves of the crypt beneath St Pancras Church have hosted contemporary art exhibitions and events, from large-scale sound installations to an alternative Christmas grotto. If you get the feeling that you're not alone down there, you're right – the space still houses the remains of its 557 original occupants, interred here in the early 19th century.
St Pancras Church, Euston Road, NW1 2BA (7388 1461, www.cryptgallery.org.uk).

Danielle Arnaud

Danielle Arnaud has hosted thought-provoking exhibitions in her Georgian townhouse in Kennington – an area largely unburdened by art-world attention – since the mid 1990s. Wandering round the elegant, furnished rooms makes looking at art a more relaxing affair than the usual white cube experience.
123 Kennington Road, SE11 6SF (7735 8292, www.daniellearnaud.com).

Model Gardeners

Based in a purpose-built garden shed in Stoke Newington, the Model Gardeners gallery opened in May 2010. Starting life as a workshop/ studio, it now exhibits around five annual shows, mainly by British artists such as Liam Scully and Joseph Hallam. *74 Brighton Road, N16 8EG (no phone, www.modelgardeners.com).*

Old Police Station
This abandoned cop shop in deepest Deptford provides DIY spaces for artists to show and make art, from the original tiled cells (complete with latrines) to the shipping containers in the courtyard that now house artists' studios. *114-116 Amersham Vale, SE14 6LG (07981 681842 mobile, www.theoldpolicestation.org).*

Pertwee Anderson & Gold
This discreet Soho newcomer has demonstrated a flair for forward-thinking exhibitions since opening in spring 2011. Well worth seeking out. *15 Bateman Street, W1D 3AQ (7734 9283, www.pertweeandersongold.com).*

Tank Gallery
The art world is no stranger to strong drink, so a gallery attached to a pub is the perfect pairing. In an old carriage house at the back of the Ladywell Tavern, Tank hosts a wide range of events, where you're as likely to find a poetry reading by performers in animal masks as see art on the walls. *The Ladywell Tavern, 80 Ladywell Road, SE13 7HS (07866 984727 mobile, www.tanklondon.co.uk).*

White Cubicle Toilet Gallery
Located in a toilet, upstairs from the hedonistic George & Dragon pub, the wittily-named White Cubicle aims to provide an antidote to London's commercial art galleries. Working with no staff or budget, the programme is nevertheless international in scope, with past exhibitions by the the likes of Costa Rican Federico Herrero and North American Steven Gontarski. *George & Dragon, 2 Hackney Road, E2 7NS (7012 1100, www.whitecubicle.org).*

Zero 10
Ex-White Cube staffer Johann Bournot originally ran Zero 10 in his own home. Now, it's moved to the reception of the Assembly Rooms, better known as a film editing and screening centre. The space is far more intimate than the standard white-walled gallery, and Bournot cherry-picks some terrific new talents. *8 Silver Place, W1F 0JU (07800 796314 mobile, www.zero10gallery.com).*

1598-1602
Sing your heart out

Bloomsbury Lanes
Two no-frills, retro-style rooms overlook the bowling lanes. There's an abundance of tunes to choose from and plenty of time to belt 'em out, with minimum time slots set at two hours. *Basement, Tavistock Hotel, Bedford Way, WC1H 9EU (7183 1979, www.bloomsburybowling.com).*

Hip Hop Karaoke at the Social
If you've ever fancied yourself as a Missy, Eminem or Snoop, then this regular night is your chance to act out your rap fantasies. Free beer and prizes to be won for all who have a go. *5 Little Portland Street, W1W 7JD (7636 4992, www.thesocial.com).*

Karaoke Box
Regulars avow Karaoke Box is the best of the bunch, thanks to its value for money, friendliness and – vitally – reliable mics. *18 Frith Street, W1D 4RQ (7494 3878, www.karaokebox.co.uk).*

Lucky Voice
Kitsch pink lighting and dimly lit private rooms make Lucky Voice the swishest karaoke joint in town. Some rooms have wigs and other props. *52 Poland Street, W1F 7NQ (7439 3660, www.luckyvoice.co.uk).*

Shanghai
The two large karaoke rooms at this pie and mash shop turned Chinese restaurant are packed with enthusiastic private parties. *41 Kingsland Road, E8 2JS (7254 2878, www.shanghaidalston.co.uk).*

1603 *Buy London's freshest flour*

The stone-ground flour made by Brockwell Bake (http://brockwell-bake.org.uk) is never on the shelf for longer than a week, which means that the oils and enzymes it contains are in perfect condition for making and flavouring bread. Three biodynamic farms in Sussex and Kent contribute a mix of grains that result in a light brown colour and medium strength. Look out for the flour on stalls at Druid Street and Kennington Farmers' markets, buy a bag from Brixton Wholefoods (59 Atlantic Road, SW9 8PU, 7737 2210, www.brixtonwholefoods.com) or order larger quantities direct on 7733 3879.

1604
See eight concerts in a day

Over four days in September, King's Place (90 York Way, N1 9AG, 7520 1490, www.kingsplace.co.uk) hosts 100 performances, running consecutive 45-minute concerts all day long in four performance spaces. With each session priced at £4.50, you can string together a whole festival's worth of events in day: we reckon you could fit eight in, if you include foyer jazz curated by the Spitz while you refuel at the café. Taking in music and the spoken word, the bill is as eclectic as it is imaginative: in 2011, events included '45 years of jazz in 45 minutes', a tuba picnic and traditional Indian dance.

1605 *Sample food in the raw at Saf*

The provision of vegan, mostly raw food is Saf's raison d'être, and the concept is carried off in style. Its reworkings of the classics are endlessly inventive: a 'fettuccine' of wafer-thin ribbons of salsify rather than pasta, perhaps, or a lasagne featuring macadamia 'ricotta', made with pressed nuts. The botanics-infused cocktails are terrific, too: worthy this place may be, but it's certainly not dull.
Saf *152-154 Curtain Road, EC2A 3AT (7613 0007, www.safrestaurant.co.uk).*

1606 *Be a voyager*

The story of Britain's relationship with the sea is told at a stunning gallery in the new Sammy Ofer Wing at the National Maritime Museum. Opened in July 2011, the gallery acts as an introduction to the museum, and contains a dramatic audiovisual installation by the Light Surgeons.
National Maritime Museum *Romney Road, SE10 9NF (8858 4422, www.nmm.ac.uk).*

1607
Pay tribute to a clowning great...

On the first Sunday in February, clowns from all over the country descend on Dalston's Holy Trinity Church (Beechwood Road, E8 3DY, 7254 5062), in full motley and slap. They're here to attend the annual service held in remembrance of Joseph Grimaldi (1778-1837). London-born Grimaldi was a pioneer of modern clowning, popularising the use of white face paint and exaggerated physical theatre. The public are welcome to attend the service, but turn up early as pews fill fast.

1608
... Then dance on his grave

Grimaldi was buried next to his friend and mentor Thomas Dibden at St James's chapel, Islington. The chapel was demolished, but the graves were preserved in what is now Joseph Grimaldi Park. There the great comedian rested in peace. (Or so we hope – he was known to harbour a terrible fear of being buried alive.) At least, he did until 2010, when a piece of innovative public art was installed directly on top of his grave, and that of Dibden. It's a coffin-shaped stamp-to-play musical piece by Henry Krokatsis. The bronze tiles are tuned to the notes of one of Grimaldi's signature numbers, a tragi-comic hymn to gin called 'Hot Codlins'. Hit the right tiles, and you'll find yourself dancing on Grimaldi's grave.
Joseph Grimaldi Park *corner of Pentonville Road and Rodney Street, N1 9PE (www.islington.gov.uk).*

1609-1616

Take a twilight tour

Perhaps our favourite twilight tour is at Sir John Soane's Museum (13 Lincoln's Inn Fields, WC2A 3BP, 7405 2107, www.soane.org), on the first Tuesday of the month. One of Britain's most innovative architects, Soane used his home as a testing ground for his ideas on light and space, and crammed it full of art and antiquities. On his death in 1837 the house become a museum, kept 'as nearly as circumstances will admit' to its appearance during his lifetime. It's hugely atmospheric by candlelight, as death masks, Egyptian statues and bronzes loom out of the gloaming; it also helps you appreciate Soane's light-enhancing devices, such as the convex mirrors in the domed ceiling of his breakfast room. No advance bookings are taken, and numbers are limited: as a result, queues form along the pavement well before it opens at 6pm.

No less fascinating are the Monday evening candlelit tours of Dennis Severs' House (18 Folgate Street, E1 6BX, 7247 4013, www.dennis severshouse.co.uk). This intricate re-creation is as much art as history, set up as if its occupants might return at any moment. The low light conspires with your imagination to make it seem real.

For an even more theatrical experience, look out for occasional 'twilight encounters' at 18 Stafford Terrace (W8, 7602 3316, www.rbkc.gov.uk), the former home of Victorian *Punch* cartoonist Linley Sambourne. Led by costumed actors, the tours explore the scandalous side of life in the house, so be prepared for a few surprises.

Things are more sedate at Dr Johnson's House (17 Gough Square, EC4A 3DE, 7353 3745, www. drjohnsonshouse.org), which has run curator-led twilight tours as part of the Museums at Night event – so dark that you can't help but wonder how Johnson managed to put together his *Dictionary of the English Language.*

Considerably grander but equally murky is Apsley House (Hyde Park Corner, W1J 7NT, 7499 5676, www.english-heritage.org.uk), once home to the Duke of Wellington. Check the website for details of upcoming twilight tours, which generally take place in winter. With the heavy curtains drawn and chandeliers dimly lit, it's wonderfully atmospheric.

So, too, is Strawberry Hill (268 Waldegrave Road, Twickenham, Middx TW1 4ST, 8744 1241, www.strawberryhillhouse.org.uk), Horace Walpole's theatrical, neo-gothic pile. Visiting after dark enhances the effect considerably – as does the glass of prosecco with which the tours begin.

Walpole must have envied the natural gothic splendour of the Tower of London (Tower Hill, EC3N 4AB, 0844 482 7777, www.hrp.org.uk). The Beefeater-led evening tours here are awe-inspiring from the moment you realise that the great gates have been locked behind you – and, in the half light, the stories of those who died here take on an eerie new resonance.

Spookier still are the after-hours ghost tours of Hampton Court Palace (East Molesey, Surrey KT8 9AU, 0844 482 7777, www.hrp.org.uk), which take you round sites where staff and visitors claim to have seen spectres. Crossing the Haunted Gallery in the darkness is nerve-jangling – especially if you chose to go it alone.

Sir John Soane's Museum

1617-1627
Learn a brand new skill

Beekeeping
Urban beekeeping has become something of a trend – even Fortnum & Mason has a hive on its roof. The London Beekeepers Association's (www.lbka.org.uk) runs introductory courses in the Roots and Shoots community garden in Kennington (from £30); check online for details.

Bookbinding
If you're inspired by the beautiful bookbinding papers and silks at Shepherds Falkiners (76 Southampton Row, WC1B 4AR, 7831 1151, http://store.falkiners.com), consider enrolling on a one- or two-day bookbinding course (£110-£160).

Breadmaking
Learn to bake artisan breads at E5 bakehouse (Arch 395, Mentmore Terrace, E8 3PH, 07548 300244, www.e5bakehouse.com). You'll find out to how make and nourish a sourdough 'mother', and bake several different types of loaf.

Butchery
The esteemable Ginger Pig (8-10 Moxon Street, W1U 4EW, 7935 7788, www.thegingerpig.co.uk) runs regular butchery classes (£135), tackling pork, lamb or beef, and culminating in dinner around the butcher's block.

Chocolate-making
Attend a masterclass with London's hottest chocolatier, Paul A Young, at his Soho flagship (143 Wardour Street, W1F 8WA, 7437 0011 www.paulayoung.co.uk). Mail info@paula young.co.uk for advance dates.

Coffee-brewing
Tapped & Packed (114 Tottenham Court Road, W1T 5AH, 7580 2163, www.tappedandpacked. co.uk) are masters of coffee-making. Staff run evening classes to introduce you to the aeropress and V60 filter, along with coffee tastings.

Cupcake-icing
Swirls of icing can disguise a multitude of sins. Learn how to pipe like the professionals with Cookie Girl (3565 3414, www.cookiegirl.co.uk), who counts Will Young and Sienna Miller among her regulars. Two-hour masterclasses cost £55, including eight cupcakes and all materials.

Fish skills
Learn a battery of fish preparation and cookery skills from the pros at Billingsgate Seafood Training School (30 Billingsgate Market, Trafalgar Way, E14 5ST, 7517 3548, www. seafoodtraining.org). Your day starts at 6.15am, includes a tour of the market, and ends with a lunch you've helped to cook.

Magicianship
Sign up for the beginners' course (£135) at Davenports Magic (7 Charing Cross Underground Arcade, WC2N 4HZ, 7836 0408, www.davenportsmagic.co.uk) to discover the secrets behind the art of illusion.

Screen-printing
Unleash your artistic side at Print Club London (Unit 3, Millers Avenue, E8 2DS, 07837 185927, www.printclublondon.com) with a six-hour paper screen-printing workshop (£45).

Ukulele-strumming
Duke of Uke (88 Cheshire Street, E2 6EH, 7247 7924, www.dukeofuke.co.uk) runs ten-week evening courses in ukulele-playing, for beginners and intermediates (from £195 per person). One-off sessions cost from £25 per hour.

1628

Consume crayfish, Swedish style...

In Sweden, the end of summer means crayfish season, and a host of *kräftskiva* (crayfish parties), with lanterns strung on the tables and buckets of crustaceans to consume. Here in London, a special seasonal menu is laid on at Madsen (20 Old Brompton Road, SW7 3DL, 7225 2772, www.madsenrestaurant.com). Available to groups of four and above, the spread includes herring, new potatoes, Västerbotten cheese with berry compôte and, in pride of place, the dill-marinated crayfish. The traditional way to tackle the crayfish is to suck out the juices, then shell it: a shot or two of akvavit should conquer any inhibitions.

1629-1631

... Or get a taste for Nordic snacks

Just off Oxford Street, Scandinavian Kitchen (61 Great Titchfield Street, W1W 7PP, 7580 7161, www.scandikitchen.co.uk) offers a smorgasbord of delights, from *smørrebrød* (open-topped rye or sourdough sandwiches) to tasty Danish hotdogs, known as *rod pølse*. It also provides homesick Scandies with specialist grocery items – among them the brown, sweet Norwegian cheese called *brunost* (an acquired taste that some people never acquire) and Salt Sild – curiously addictive, fish-shaped salted licorice.

Alternatively, head to the Nordic Bakery on Golden Square (no.14a, W1F 9JG, 3230 1077, www.nordicbakery.com) for dark rye sandwiches and fragrant cinnamon buns. Filled with subtly spiced potato- or rice, its Karelian pies are a steal at £1.60 – say yes to the egg butter spread.

There's also a simple cafeteria at the Finnish Church in London (33 Albion Street, SE16 7HZ, 7237 4668, www.finnishchurch.org.uk) – not to mention a well-stocked shop selling groceries and newspapers, and a proper Finnish sauna, with separate sessions for men and women.

1632 *Play horseball*

Sometimes described as a combination of rugby and basketball – played on galloping horses – horseball is not for the fainthearted. Opposing teams score points by netting a ball through a high hoop, while scooping up the ball from the ground involves dropping the reins and leaning backwards towards the ground, feet firmly in the stirrups. If you're already at ease in the saddle and fancy some high-adrenalin horseplay, contact Lee Valley Riding Centre, which has its own team and runs regular training sessions.

Lee Valley Riding Centre *71 Lee Bridge Road, E10 7QL (8556 2629, www.leevalleypark.org.uk).*

1638 Shop at SHOWstudio

Photographer Nick Knight's SHOWstudio has pumped out avant-garde, ultra-creative fashion shoots, films, articles and oddities since 2000. Its Mayfair space hosts regular exhibitions, and also sells intriguing artworks and fashion props: past gems have run from one-off haute couture Chanel headpieces, made from paper, to prints by the likes of Corinne Day or Guy Bourdin. It's fascinating stuff, even if you can't afford to buy. **SHOWstudio** *1-9 Bruton Place, W1J 6LT (7399 4299, www.showstudio.com).*

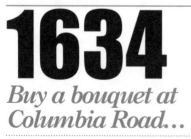

1634

Buy a bouquet at Columbia Road...

Of a Sunday morning (from 8am until around 2pm), there's no lovelier place to be than this East End flower market (www.columbiaroad. info). Columbia Road becomes a sea of blooms, lined with hothouse beauties, buckets of roses and bargain bedding plants. Savvy locals turn up at the close of play: as the stallholders start packing up, you can score some real bargains.

1635-1638

... Or from the city's finest florists

For old-fashioned charm, Scarlet & Violet (76 Chamberlayne Road, NW10 3JJ, 8969 9446, www. scarletandviolet.com) is hard to beat. Peonies, holyhocks and other old-fashioned blooms are artfully arrayed in enamel jugs, glass jars and even milk bottles in the Kensal Green shop; staff will make you up a small bouquet from £15.

Down in Hither Green, a similarly quirky, homespun feel pervades the wonderfully-named You Don't Bring Me Flowers (15 Staplehurst Road, SE13 5ND, 8297 2333, www.youdontbring meflowers.co.uk). It's also a café, so you can ponder the flowers with a slice of cake in hand.

If you're after a statement bouquet, try Rebel Rebel (5 Broadway Market, E8 4PH, 7254 4487, www.rebelrebel.co.uk). Seasonal English flowers are the focus, from fragrant Lincolnshire stocks to narcissi from the Isles of Scilly. Artful presentation is a forte – not least the trademark tulips, artfully arranged in a vintage handbag.

For event flowers, meanwhile, you're in safe hands with Robbie Honey (7720 3777, www. robbiehoney.com), whose counts Dior and the V&A among his clients. Alternatively, bouquets start at £45. Honey's trademark is elegant simplicity, generally with just one variety of flower: a ribbon-tied bunch of summer stocks, perhaps, or elegant cluster of long-stemmed roses.

1639-1644

BYOB

Not 'Bring Your Own Bottle' but '*Buy* Your Own Bottle' – a new pricing slant taken by venues that double as wine shops and bar/restaurants. Choose your wine from the shelves, buy it at retail price, then pay a corkage fee to consume it *in situ*.

Bedales

Browse a terrific array of wines in the shop, then pull the cork and get stuck in, with a platter of meat, cheese or antipasti.

5 Bedale Street, SE1 9AL (7403 8853, www.bedaleswines.com). Corkage £8.

Green & Blue

This shabby-chic wine shop and bar stocks around 150 wines. There's a small but enticing bar food menu, or for a £3 'chippage' charge you can bring your own grub.

36-38 Lordship Lane, SE22 8HJ (8693 9250, www.greenandbluewines.com). Corkage £7.

Negozio Classica

A small selection of wines is available by the glass at this Italian deli-eaterie and wine shop, but you can also scour the shelves and choose your own bottle to take home or drink in.

283 Westbourne Grove, W11 2QA (7034 0005, www.negozioclassica.co.uk). Corkage £8.50.

1707 Wine Bar

1707 Wine Bar

Buying and supping wines from Fortnum's cellar is a very civilised affair. The restaurant itself is deliciously chic, while snacks are based on fresh, seasonal produce from the famous food hall.

Lower Ground Floor, Fortnum & Mason, 181 Piccadilly, W1J 9FA (7734 8040, www.fortnum andmason.com). Corkage £10.

Planet of the Grapes

Over 450 wines are available at this unfussy wine merchant's, where you can pre-book older bottles for decanting before you arrive. Platters and pies accompany.

9-10 Bulls Head Passage, Leadenhall Market, EC3V 1LU (7929 7224, www. planetofthegrapes.co.uk). Corkage £10.

Wine Library

In its atmospheric vaulted cellars, the Wine Library offers a great range of retail wines, plus an impressive buffet lunch.

43 Trinity Square, EC3N 4DJ (7481 0415, www.winelibrary.co.uk). Corkage £7.25.

1645

Kayak at dawn

For an unusually peaceful perspective on the city, sign up for a sunrise kayaking tour of Regent's Ca nal, organised by Thames River Adventures (0845 453 2002, www.thames riveradventures.co.uk). You may have to meet the group at Primrose Hill Bridge at an unearthly hour (4am in summer, 7am in winter), but the serene slice of city life more than makes up it; aside from the odd jogger or dog walker, you'll hardly see a soul.

1646

Fix your street

Spotted a street light on the blink, or a loose paving slab? Fix My Street (www.fixmystreet. com) passes your postings about neighbourhood nuisances to the relevant authority, then tracks the outcome. Which, encouragingly, is that lots of problems end up getting fixed.

1647-1652

Admire an almshouse

London's almshouses, an early form of social housing, track the city's history in brick and mortar. Many were connected to particular trades; a list drawn up in 1867 included, 'For Bootmakers, Mortlake; Pawnbrokers, Forest-gate; Booksellers, King's Langley; Aged Pilgrims, Edgware-road; Butchers, Walham-green; Bookbinders, Ball's-pond; Printers, Wood-green; Tailors (journeymen), Haverstock-hill; and Poulterers and Fishmongers, Southgate.'

The guilds and benefactors that founded them represent 300 years of private-sector power, from the shipshape little terraces at Trinity Green (Mile End Road, E1), founded by one Captain Henry Mudd, for '28 decay'd Masters & Comanders of Ships, or ye widows of such' in 1695, to the 1988 extension of Weavers' House in Wanstead (78-82 New Wanstead, E11 2SZ, www.weavers.org.uk).

Victorian almshouses were often built on what was then the edge of the country; Penge has a whole cluster, notably the Royal Watermen's Almshouse of 1840-41 (Watermen's Square, SE20 7EL). Earlier examples, though, were often plum in central London; some, such as St Giles-in-the-Fields Almshouses on Macklin Street, WC2, remain in social use, though many were lost to property development.

Almshouses are always an evocative sight, but to enjoy more than just a view of the exterior, visit the Grade I-listed almshouses of the Ironmongers Company. Built in 1714, the neat row of houses now accommodates the Geffrye Museum (136 Kingsland Road, E2 8EA, 7739 9893, www.geffrye-museum.org.uk). It comprises a series of re-creations of domestic English interiors from 1600 to the present day (including rooms from the original almshouse), along with some lovely period gardens.

In Burgess Park, you can also have a cup of tea in the almshouses in Chumleigh Garden, built in 1921 for the splendidly named Friendly Female Society. One wing is now occupied by a café (Albany Road, SE5 0RJ, 7252 6556); while there aren't many original features to see inside, the terrace is pleasant on a sunny day. Afterwards, you can stroll the park's Islamic, Oriental and Mediterranean gardens.

1653

Listen to the city

Created by a dedicated audiophile, the London Sound Survey (www.soundsurvey.org.uk) makes sound recordings of everyday life in London – from a beggar playing a penny whistle to blackbirds in Telegraph Hill, or ticket touts outside Wembley – and presents them as playback files on this website. The site also gathers historical accounts of what the city sounded like in past eras, from novels, diaries and autobiographies: a 1950s account of 'charwomen's banter on a bus' from ER Braithwaite's *To Sir With Love*, say, or an excerpt from wartime diarist Winifred Vere Hodgson, describing 'doodle-bug' flying bombs.

1654 Dedicate a tree

Trees for Cities (www.treesforcities.org) is a national network dedicated to cherishing Britain's 34 native species and fostering their planting and protection within urban areas. Support its work by dedicating a new tree to a friend, family member or loved one. For £175, a plaque with an inscription of your choice will be erected on the supporting stake, and you will receive a photo and a map giving the exact location.

1655

Get creative at Drink Shop Do

Set in a Victorian bathhouse near King's Cross Station, this friendly café runs all sorts of arty activities. Many are free, including the popular play with clay sessions; others (headdress-making, ice-cream sundae-assembling) are a fiver. If you like the quirky decor, you can take a bit of it home; almost everything's for sale, from the tables and tea sets to the art on the walls.

Drink Shop Do *9 Caledonian Road, N1 9DX (3343 9138, www.drinkshopdo.com).*

Ronnie Scott's

1656-1665 *Dine at a jazz bar*

Fancy a side order of jazz or soul with your dinner? Try one of the following.

Blues Kitchen
Soul food, blues music and a lengthy selection of bourbons, ryes and Tennessee whiskeys.
111-113 Camden High Street, NW1 7JN (7387 5277, www.theblueskitchen.com).

Dover Street
Three bars, a dancefloor, bands playing funk, soul and swing, and French/Med food until 2am.
8-10 Dover Street, W1S 4LQ (7629 9813, www.doverstreet.co.uk).

Green Note
Organic and vegetarian dishes and tapas served to the sound of folk, blues, Americana and jazz.
106 Parkway, NW1 7AN (7485 9899, www.greennote.co.uk).

Jazz After Dark
This unpretentious spot is a hit with the young afterwork crowd, mixing blues, funk, jazz and soul.
9 Greek Street, W1D 4DQ (7734 0545, www.jazzafterdark.co.uk).

Jazz Café
The music, like the menu, is international, ranging from Cuban sosa to New Orleans jazz.
5-7 Parkway, NW1 7PG (7485 6834, www.jazzcafelive.com).

Pizza Express Jazz Club
This laid-back basement club has a tradition of staging fresh talent, along with more established musicians.
10 Dean Street, W1D 3RW (0845 602 7017, www.pizzaexpresslive.com).

Le Quecum Bar
A wine bar specialising in gypsy jazz and serving French bistro food. Bring your own instrument for the Gypsy Swing Jam on Tuesdays.
42-44 Battersea High Street, SW11 3HX (7787 2227, www.quecumbar.co.uk).

Ronnie Scott's
Opened in 1959, and one of the most respected jazz venues in the world. Everyone who's anyone has played here.
47 Frith Street, W1D 4HT (7439 0747, www.ronniescotts.co.uk).

606 Club
A long-running jazz club, with music every night and a relaxed bistro menu.
90 Lots Road, SW10 0QD (7352 5953, www.606club.co.uk).

Wellesley
Due to open in late 2012, this luxe hotel will include a 1920s-style dinner-and-jazz room.
11 Knightsbridge, SW1X 7QS (http://thewellesley.co.uk).

Museum of London

1666-1680

Sample some after-hours culture

Imagine a museum free of children, that can be explored with a glass of wine in hand. Over the last few years, Lates events (www.lates.org) have enabled visitors to do just that, becoming a monthly fixture at 15 of London's finest museums and galleries. The programmes – which are often themed to tie in with the current blockbuster exhibition – generally combine DJs or live music, talks, a pay bar and reduced ticket prices. The V&A Friday Lates, held on the last Friday of the month, are perhaps the most dynamic: in 2011, themes included Afropolitan (an exploration of contemporary African culture) and I Do (a celebration of the royal wedding that involved a karaoke wedding band, advice on vintage styling, a gold-plated cake and make-your-own bunting).

Barbican *Silk Street, EC2Y 8DS (7638 8891, www.barbican.org.uk).*
British Library *96 Euston Road, NW1 2DB (7412 7676, www.bl.uk).*
British Museum *Great Russell Street, WC1B 3DG (7323 8299, www.britishmuseum.org).*
Design Museum *(Shad Thames, SE1 2YD (7403 6933, www.designmuseum.org).*

ICA *The Mall, SW1Y 5AH (7930 0493, www.ica.org.uk).*
Museum in Docklands *No.1 Warehouse, Hertsmere Road, E14 4AL (7001 9844, www.museumindocklands.org.uk).*
Museum of London *150 London Wall, EC2Y 5HN (7001 9844, www.museumof london.org.uk).*
The National Gallery *Trafalgar Square, WC2N 5DN (7747 2885, www.nationalgallery.org.uk).*
National Portrait Gallery *Saint Martin's Place, WC2H 0HE (7306 0055, www.npg.org.uk).*
Royal Academy of Arts *Burlington House, Piccadilly, W1J 0BD (7300 8000, www.royal academy.org.uk).*
Southbank Centre *Belvedere Road, SE1 8XX (7960 4200, www.southbankcentre.co.uk).*
Tate Britain *Millbank, SW1P 4RG (7887 8888, www.tate.org.uk/britain).*
Tate Modern *Bankside, SE1 9TG (7887 8752, www.tate.org.uk/modern).*
V&A *Cromwell Road, SW7 2RL (7942 2000, www.vam.ac.uk).*
Whitechapel Gallery *77-82 Whitechapel High Street, E1 7QX (7522 7888, www.whitechapel gallery.org).*

1681-1684

Get threaded for less...

One of the advantages of being in a city that's a cocktail of different cultures is the chance to dip into a rich heritage of tried and tested beauty techniques – often very cheaply. Threading is a hair removal method whereby the therapist twists a length of thread around stray hairs, whipping your eyebrows into shape at lightening speed. It can be pricey at high end places, but is often just as accomplished in the little front room salons across Whitechapel and East Ham.

Apsara Herbal
The staff are no conversationalists, but this authentic Asian beauty parlour has threading from £6.
249 Whitechapel Road, E1 1DB (7377 2004, www.apsaraherbal.co.uk).

Sheer Bliss
This reasonably priced Turkish salon offers threading as well as a full range of waxing and hair treatments, from £3.50.
2-4 Kingsland Road, E8 2JP (7254 5605).

Essence Beauty
The further you go from the centre of London, the cheaper threading gets. At Essence in Harrow, unruly eyebrows can be tamed for £3.
32 Eastcote Lane, Middx HA2 8BP (07717 793912).

Salma's Hair and Beauty
Salma's offers a great – and enduringly popular – threading service on the cheap.
179A High Street North, E6 1JB (8472 2532, www.salmassalon.co.uk).

1685

... Or splash out on a threading legend

With over 25 years' experience – and an infallible eye for which arch will best suit your face shape – Kamini Vaghela is regarded as an eyebrow alchemist in the industry (from £55 a session).
14-16 Lancer Square, off Kensington Church Street, W8 4EP (7937 2411, www.kaminibeauty.com).

1686

Get inside some brilliant minds

The idea behind 5 x 15 (www.5x15stories.com) is sheer genius. Five influential thinkers stand up to deliver 'true stories of passion, obsession and adventure', with two rules: no scripts, and no going over 15 minutes. Past speakers have included Brian Eno on nuclear disarmament, AS Byatt on myth, and art critic Martin Gayford on posing for a portrait by the late Lucian Freud.

1687

Taste Stokie smoked salmon

Norwegian Ole-Martin Hansen produces London's tastiest smoked salmon in his small-scale Stoke Newington smokehouse. Cold-smoked with juniper and beech wood, according to Ole's great-grandfather's recipe, the salmon – which never touches plastic – comes from sustainable sources in Scotland and is prepared 48 hours after it has been fished. Buy it direct from the smokehouse, or Ole's stall at Broadway Market in Hackney.
Hansen & Lydersen Ltd *3-5 Shelford Place, N16 9HS (07411 693712, www.hansen-lydersen.com).*

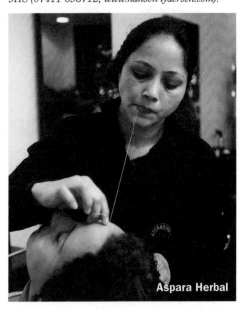

Aspara Herbal

Anthropologie

1688-1696

Get with the concept

Offering a quirky, immersive retail experience, concept stores are big news in London. Most stock a beguiling mix of fashion and homeware, with one-off and vintage pieces sometimes thrown in for good measure: even if you can't afford to buy, they're an excellent source of style inspiration.

123 Boutique

This avant-garde emporium opened in 2010, in an imposing Grade II-listed warehouse. The Dover Street Market of the East End isn't packed with big brands, though: instead, it specialises in 'upcycled' clothing. Accessories and books are arranged on antique fixtures and fittings, while the second floor houses 123's self-titled sustainable fashion label.
123 Bethnal Green Road, E2 7DG (7729 8050).

123 Boutique

Anthropologie

Anthropologie hit London in its style solar plexus when it opened its vast King's Road branch – not least thanks to its soothing in-store waterfall and lush tropical foliage. The stock is of a feminine bent, taking in vintage-inspired homeware as well as fashion and accessories.
131-141 King's Road, SW3 4PW (7349 3110, www.anthropologie.co.uk).

Bermondsey 167

Former Burberry designer Michael McGrath has poured his heart into this intriguing store. Its own-label (M2cG) menswear is a big draw, as is the furniture, homeware and jewellery, sourced from artists and artisans around the world.
167 Bermondsey Street, SE1 3UW (7407 3137, www.bermondsey167.com).

Beyond the Valley

This concept boutique is a showcase for creations by talented young designers, and its own clothing label. Alongside boundary-pushing fashion and footwear, its offerings run from swirling wallpaper to witty oven gloves.
2 Newburgh Street, W1F 7RD (7437 7338, www.beyondthevalley.com).

Couverture & the Garbstore

Couverture stocks clothes, accessories and jewellery, children's items, homeware, furniture and the odd vintage knick-knack. Garbstore, downstairs, sells Ian Paley's vintage-inspired menswear label and hip international brands.
188 Kensington Park Road, W11 2ES (7229 2178, www.couvertureandthegarbstore.com).

Darkroom

Darkroom adds further credence to Lamb's Conduit Street's claim to being one of London's most intriguing shopping destinations. The shop is quite literally dark (the walls and lampshades are black), creating a blank canvas for the unisex fashion, accessories and interiors pieces on sale.
52 Lamb's Conduit Street, WC1N 3LL (7831 7244, www.darkroomlondon.com).

Dover Street Market

Comme des Garçons designer Rei Kawakubo's six-storey space combines the edgy energy of London's markets with rarefied labels and serious style cachet. Its list of labels is a who's who of fashion's great and good, and there's a chic top-floor café to boot.
17-18 Dover Street, W1S 4LT (7518 0680, www.doverstreetmarket.com).

Shop at Bluebird

John and Belle Robinson (the founders of Jigsaw) offer a mixed portfolio of designer clothing, shoes, accessories, hard-to-find skincare, books, music (both CDs and vinyl) and the odd piece of furniture, plus a spa. Launched in 2005, this is one of the capital's concept-store pioneers.
350 King's Road, SW3 5UU (7351 3873, www.theshopatbluebird.com).

Wolf & Badger

Set on W11's millionaires' mile, Wolf & Badger was started by bag designer Zoe Knight (who has created arm candy for Chloë and Jimmy Choo) and her gallery-owner husband Samir Ceric. It comprises an impressive collective of emerging and independent designers, each renting a portion of the slick retail space.
46 Ledbury Road, W11 2AB (7229 5698, www.wolfandbadger.com).

1697-1722

Eat the alphabet (for peanuts)

You can sample a planet's worth of world-class food in London, for not much more than the price of a single Michelin meal.

A is for Austrian

Get open sandwiches on rye, strudels and sausages of every stripe at Kipferl (20 Camden Passage, N1 8ED, 7704 1555, www.kipferl.co.uk) – along with its namesake vanilla biscuits.

B is for báhn mi

Báhn mi is Franco-Vietnamese street food – a baguette, stuffed with all manner of fillings, from sardines to barbecued pork, plus daikon radishes, coriander, pickled carrots and more. Broadway Market-based Bánhmì 11 (07765 982146 mobile, www.banhmi11.com) makes a terrific rendition.

C is for chaat

'Chaat' means snack, and that's what a meal at Chaat (36 Redchurch Street, E2 7DP, 7739 9595, www.chaatlondon.co.uk) begins with: lamb patties, vegetable samosas and more. Spicy comfort food follows, in the homely surrounds of this bang-on Bangladeshi kitchen.

D is for dim sum

Within weeks of its opening a few years back, savvy Chinese students and Primrose Hill locals were filling the tables at Yum Cha (27-28 Chalk Farm Road, NW1 8AG, 7482 2228), enjoying the stellar dim sum prepared by its Hong Kong chefs.

E is for Eritrean

Brixton café Asmara (386 Coldharbour Lane, SW9 8LF, 7737 4144) executes two of Eritrea's major contributions to world cuisine to perfection: spongy, pancake-like injera bread and excellent coffee, ceremonially served with warm popcorn.

F is for French

Good French cuisine doesn't have to empty your wallet, even in the centre of town. Family-run Savoir Faire (42 New Oxford Street, WC1A 1EP, 7436 0707, www.savoir.co.uk) delivers two courses for £11 at lunch, £19 at dinner.

G is for gastropub

The first and the best: the Eagle (159 Farringdon Road, EC1R 3AL, 7837 1353) still serves up big, bold flavours from its behind-the-bar kitchen, at prices that put its imitators to shame.

H is for haggis

Grazing (19-21 Great Tower Street, EC3R 5AR, 7283 2932, www.grazingfood.com) is the only café we know where you can pick up a haggis and fried egg sandwich on the way to work; it'll be the best meal you'll have all day.

I is for Iranian

Mahdi (217 King Street, W6 9JT, 8563 7007) serves gargantuan portions of lovingly prepared Iranian food, from succulent lamb kebabs to flavoursome stews.

J is for Jewish

Best value at the impeccable Dizengoff's (118 Golder's Green Road, NW11 8HB, 8458 7003) are the side dishes – including chopped liver and fluffy-centered falafel.

K is for kimchee

This addictive fermented cabbage dish is served as part of the great-value set lunch at Jindalle (6 Panton Street, SW1Y 4DL, 7930 8881), along with miso soup and a choice of starters and mains – including barbecue dishes prepared at your table.

L is for Lebanese

You can get very decent meze dishes, such as pomegranate-dotted baba ganoush, at Fresco (25 Westbourne Grove, W2 4UA, 7221 2355), but it earns its place here as much for its great range of fruit and veg juice – freshly pressed, of course.

M is for Mongolian hotpot

Meals at Little Lamb (72 Shaftesbury Avenue, W1D 6NA, 7287 8078) are based around an enormous metal pot filled with a chilli or herb broth into which the party dip meat, fish and veg (we like the squid and lamb best). Lots of fun.

N is for Nigerian

The simply decorated 805 Bar Restaurant (805 Old Kent Road, SE15 1NX, 7639 0808, www.805restaurant.com) offers southern Nigerian staples: egusi stews, grilled tilapia, and sides such as moyin moyin (steamed bean pudding).

Chaat

O is for ocakbasi

In Turkey – and Dalston – an ocakbasi is a restaurant with an open grill. 19 Numara Bos Cirrik (34 Stoke Newington Road, N16 7XJ, 7249 0400) is an expert practitioner, turning out tender, flavoursome meats; free salads include the legendary pomegranate-dressed grilled onion.

P is for pho

The canteen-like Song Que (134 Kingsland Road, E2 8DY, 7613 3222, http://songque.co.uk) sets the benchmark for Vietnamese cooking in London. Its beef pho – a spice-rich broth, served with fresh herbs – is hard to beat.

Q is for quattro formaggi

For traditional pizzas on well-made, firm but elastic bases, cooked in a wood-fired oven, go to Santoré (59-61 Exmouth Market, EC1R 4QL, 7812 1488).

R is for Russian

You can't beat a bowl of borscht after a walk across Primrose Hill on a chilly Sunday afternoon: Trojka (101 Regent's Park Road, NW1 8UR, 7483 3765, www.trojka.co.uk) fills the need admirably.

S is for set menus

The three-course set menus at Arbutus (63-64 Frith Street, W1D 3JW, 7734 4545, www.arbutus restaurant.co.uk) are terrific value, at £16.95 for lunch, £18.95 pre- and post-theatre. You get the same Mod Euro cooking and sleek environment as à la carte diners, at a fraction of the price.

T is for tacos

For Mexican street food try Taqueria (139-143 Westbourne Grove, W11 2RS, 7229 4734, www. taqueria.co.uk), with its real-deal tortilla-making machine from Guadalajara.

U is for upscale

If you want a taste of food from a rated (but not over-exploited) name in lovely surroundings, check out Ottolenghi (287 Upper Street, N1 2TZ, 7288 1454, www.ottolenghi.co.uk). Go for a cake or light deli lunch to keep the cost down.

V is for vegetarian

At Tibits (12-14 Heddon Street, W1B 4DA, 7758 4110, www.tibits.co.uk), you help yourself from the central buffet and pay by weight. That's the only gimmick: the food is organic and delicious.

W is for while-you-wait

For a takeaway that's demonstrably prepared fresh, visit Wok to Walk (4 Brewer Street, W1F 0SB, 7287 8464, www.woktowalk.com). You choose a base, a main ingredient and a sauce and then watch as they're stir-fried in front of you.

X is for 'Eggs'

Breakfast is buzzy at the Rivington Bar & Grill (28-30 Rivington Street, EC2A 3DZ, 7729 7053, www.rivingtongrill.co.uk). The dedicated egg section on the menu includes a noteworthy fried duck egg with black pudding.

Y is for Yorkshire pudding

Not the cheapest choice, but the Sunday-lunch Yorkshires at the Bull & Last (168 Highgate Road, NW5 1QS, 7267 3641, www.thebulland last.co.uk) are sublime.

Z is for zen-like

Bento Café (9 Parkway, NW1 7PG, 7482 3990) has a Zen-like feel to its layout, but the mixed crowd that packs it out counterbalances the calm. Sushi is hand-rolled behind a central counter.

Curator's top ten

1723-1732

Katy Tarbard, Adult Learning Officer at the National Gallery

View from the Portico Entrance
Just standing looking out from the front of the National Gallery is exciting. You often arrive at the gallery after shuffling along subway passages looking at your feet, so it's a treat to be able to pause for a moment at the top of the Portico steps to watch the crowds and take in the London skyline.

John Rossi *Relief of a Camel and Horse*
Few people who enter the gallery by the Portico Entrance notice that they pass under a camel. When the gallery was built, architect William Wilkins needed to cut costs and ended up recycling pieces of sculpture intended for John Nash's triumphal gateway, Marble Arch. Nash's arch commemorates the successes of Nelson and Wellington, and Rossi's camel and horse statues symbolised Asia and Europe.

Boris Anrep *Mosaics* (1928-52)
When you're in the gallery, it's always worth looking at the ceilings and floors. The colourful mosaics decorating the staircase landings at the main entrance were designed by the Russian artist Boris Anrep, who was inspired by the pavement artists he saw in Trafalgar Square. They depict 'The Labours & Pleasures of Life' (look out for the football and Christmas pudding) and 'The Modern Virtues', represented by well-known public figures of the day – Winston Churchill is shown as 'Defiance', in front of the White Cliffs of Dover.

The 'Barry' Rooms (1876)
Rooms 32-40 are some of the most beautiful in the gallery, and staff still refer to them by the name of their architect: EM Barry. In Room 36, look up at the light-filled dome and you'll see it is surrounded by sculptural busts of great artists, including Titian, Michelangelo, Raphael, Rembrandt and Turner. The rooms are fondly remembered as the location for the Myra Hess wartime concerts – a beacon of cultural light and hope through the hard years of World War II.

Sassetta *The Wolf of Gubbio* (1437-44)
This small work (one of seven panels from the back of a large altarpiece) always raises a smile. It depicts a miracle from the life of St Francis. The face of the wolf looks so sweet, but behind him are the gruesome remains of some townspeople. Francis has managed to tame the wolf and agree to a peace pact, as long as the creature is fed at public expense. These unusual business partners are shaking on the deal, but the faces of the lady-folk peeking over the tower suggest they aren't buying into it.

The Wilton Diptych (c1395-9)
This little folding 14th-century altarpiece was made for the private devotion of a king: Richard II. It was designed to be carried around by him; the outside wings are more damaged than the painting inside, showing it was well used. On the inside, Richard is shown being presented by three saints to the Virgin and Child and a company of 11 angels. It is such a beautiful, carefully made thing, with such tiny details. If you look closely you can see a small orb on top of the banner being passed between Christ and King Richard. Look closer and, in the orb, you can see a tiny representation of England – a green island with a white castle.

Jan van Eyck *The Arnolfini Portrait* (1434)
If the gallery housed this painting alone, it could still occupy visitors every day of the year. It must have taken van Eyck a great deal of time to have constructed the painting in so much detail: a convex mirror (above which he has signed 'Van Eyck was here') reflects every inch of the room, except, oddly, the dog at the couple's feet. There are many theories as to what the painting

means – are they getting married? is she expecting? – but the couple don't give up their secrets easily, and remain all the more intriguing and human for that.

JMW Turner *The Fighting Temeraire* (1839)
Top in a 2005 poll to find the nation's favourite painting, this artwork was also particularly beloved by Turner, who called it 'My Darling'. The *Temeraire* played a distinguished role in Nelson's victory at the Battle of Trafalgar in 1805. This painting depicts the last voyage of the once-great warship. Turner evokes the moment of transition with a glorious sunset strung out over a mauve sky in which the light of the moon can just be seen. The old warship's masts, and anything else that could be reused, had already been removed before she was towed upstream to be broken up, but Turner painted them in, giving the ship dignity.

Monet *The Beach at Trouville* (1870)
Monet painted this sketch of his wife and a friend while on holiday at this fashionable Normandy resort. The painting is reminiscent of our own family snapshots. Working in the open air, with loose, rapidly applied brushstrokes that capture the luminosity and breezy atmosphere of the place, Monet caught more than just an impression on the canvas. The sea breeze animating the flag and scudding clouds also blew grains of sand and shell from the beach on to Monet's palette that can still be seen trapped in the paint surface.

Vincent van Gogh *Sunflowers* (1888)
When we think of van Gogh, we often remember his deteriorating mental health, his failure to sell his paintings and his tricky love life. However, when you see the vibrant yellow hues of this painting, a different van Gogh comes to the fore. Van Gogh painted the sunflower canvases in happy anticipation of a visit by Gauguin to his yellow house in Arles. Your eyes can trace van Gogh's hand movements as he stippled the seeds of the flower heads and used the wooden end of his brush to scratch out the green sepals of the lower left sunflower.

National Gallery *Trafalgar Square, WC2N 5DN* *(7747 2885, www.nationalgallery.org.uk).*

1733-1735

Sneak a preview of the three top venues for the London 2012 Games

Just like the athletes due to perform in them, the venues hosting the London 2012 Olympic and Paralympic Games will need a trial run to ensure they're absolutely ready. Although most of this fine-tuning goes on behind closed doors, the London Prepares series (www.londonprepares series.com) of ticketed test events gives the public a chance to take a close-up look at some of the Olympic Park venues well in advance of the Games themselves.

If your prime motivation is to admire the structures rather than the sport, the hot tickets are for the Track Cycling (17-19 Feb) in the gorgeous Velodrome; for the Diving (20-26 Feb), Synchronised Swimming (18-22 Apr 2012) and Water Polo (3-6 May) under the swooping roof of Zaha Hadid's Aquatics Centre; and, in the Olympic Stadium itself, the Athletics (4-7 May) and Paralympic Athletics (8 May).

The Hockey (Hockey Centre, 2-6 May) and Wheelchair Tennis (Eton Manor, 3-6 May) also take place in the Olympic Park – you'll be able to see the Hockey Centre's blue pitches introduced for the 2012 Games to improve visibility for players and spectators alike.

To score a seat for these events (or other test events in venues outside the Olympic Park), visit www.ticketmaster.co.uk/london preparesseries.

1736

Attend the Hackney Weekend

Radio 1's Hackney Weekend 2012 looks set to be a key event in the London 2012 Festival (http://festival.london2012.com). This free (but ticketed) musical extravaganza will be held on 23-24 June on Hackney Marshes, just upriver from the Olympic Park. Some 100,000 people are expected to watch more than 80 British and global musicians on six stages. Leona Lewis and Plan B, who grew up respectively in the Host Boroughs of Hackney and Newham, are already confirmed.

1737-1752

Go bespoke

Biondi

This luxury bikini boutique also offers a great bespoke service (from £300). Staff work from existing shapes and materials, tweaked to a perfect fit before your eyes.
55B Old Church Street, SW3 5BS (7349 1111, www.biondicouture.com).

Buttress & Snatch

'Handmade in Hackney by honest hard-working girls' is the company motto; fully bespoke bikinis and lingerie cost from £350 and take up to four weeks to make. Note that it's appointment only.
(7502 3139, www.buttressandsnatch.co.uk).

Celia Birtwell

This famed textile designer offers bespoke wallpaper and furnishing fabrics in a range of current and archive designs. Colours can be matched to specific paints, and fabrics can be anything from chiffon to velvet.
71 Westbourne Park Road, W2 5QH (7221 0877, www.celiabirtwell.com).

Chris Kerr

Having trained alongside his father, legendary Soho suit-maker Eddie Kerr, Chris offers sharp bespoke suits, shirts and ties in a friendly, unostentatious shop. With two-piece suits starting at £1,350, and shirts from £150, it's an affordable way to indulge in real tailoring.
31 Berwick Street, W1F 8RJ (7437 3727, www.chriskerr.com).

Condor Cycles

At this family-run shop, in business since 1948, road bikes can be built to order. You'll be propped on a fitting jig and measured for the correct frame size, with staff adding appropriate parts according to the buyer's budget.
46-53 Gray's Inn Road WC1X 8PP (7269 6820, www.condorcycles.com).

Ede & Ravenscroft

A bespoke shirt from Ede & Ravenscroft (from £225) makes a stylish gift. Your chosen length of material is boxed up for the recipient, who then visits the shop to be measured up and to choose his collar and cuffs.
8 Burlington Gardens, W1X 1LG (7734 5450, www.edeandravenscroft.co.uk).

Gieves & Hawkes

With four centuries of bespoke supremacy under its belt, Gieves & Hawkes offers made-to-measure suits from £1,000. Handmade bespoke is the premier service, costing from £3,800. It's a long procedure, but the quality is superb.
1 Savile Row, W1S 3JR (7434 2001, www.gievesandhawkes.com).

John Lobb

Giving his name to one of the best shoemakers in the world, Mr Lobb was cobbler to King Edward VII. At £2,600 plus VAT, these made-to-measure shoes might cost nigh-on a king's ransom, but will be the finest footwear you'll ever buy.
9 St James's Street, SW1A 1EF (7930 3664, www.johnlobbltd.co.uk).

Liberty's

Monograms are a subtle (and inexpensive) way to go bespoke. In Liberty's stationery department, notebooks and diaries can be personalised with the recipient's initials, for £5 per letter.
Great Marlborough Street, W1B 5AH (7734 1234, www.liberty.co.uk).

Miller Harris

Paris-trained perfume supremo Lyn Harris can mastermind the creation of your personal fragrance using the world's finest ingredients. From consulation to lab work to final patent, the

Celia Birtwell

process takes several months. It costs around £8,000; even so, there's a substantial waiting list.
14 Needham Road, W11 2RP (7221 1545, www.millerharris.com/bespoke).

Mr Start

Made-to-measure suits at this Rivington Street boutique cost from £595. The laid-back atmosphere and friendly staff will soon put novice suit-buyers at their ease.
40 Rivington Street, EC2A 3BN (7729 6272, www.start-london.com).

N'Damus

Fancy a sky-blue satchel or a bright yellow tote? Then head to bag designer Nneka Onyenakala's tiny store in Brixton Market. Prices for the customised service are a steal: from £50 to £250 for a bag, depending on size.
Unit 80, Brixton Village, Coldharbour Lane, SW9 8PS (07812 782770 mobile, www.ndamus.com).

Opera Opera

Established in 1978, this family-run business exudes a real sense of pride in its craftsmanship. Bespoke glasses, made at the company's factory, cost from £375; sunglasses are also offered.
98 Long Acre, WC2E 9NR (7836 9246, www.operaopera.net).

Rigby & Peller

For lingerie that fits to perfection, consider investing in the made-to-measure service offered by Rigby & Peller. Prices start from £305 for a bra, depending on style and materials.
2 Hans Road, SW3 1RX (0845 076 5545, www.rigbyandpeller.com).

Smythson

Printed on finely milled paper, using an engraved copper die, Smythson's bespoke letter-writing paper comes with tissue-lined envelopes. It costs from £239 for 100 letterheads and envelopes.
40 New Bond Street, W1S 2DE (7629 8558, www.smythson.com).

Terry de Havilland

This shoemaker extraordinaire began making his gorgeous wedge heels and platform shoes back in the '60s. Bespoke show-stoppers can be created in two to three weeks, costing from £450-£850; Kate Moss recently purchased a pair. By appointment.
336 Kingsland Road, E8 4DA (7254 4445, www.tdhcouture.com).

1753
See some Victorian smut

The home of *Punch* cartoonist Linley Sambourne, 18 Stafford Terrace (W8 7BH, 7602 3316, www.rbkc.gov.uk) is a perfectly preserved, William Morris-papered slice of Victorian, middle-class life. All is suitably decorous – until you get to the bathroom, where some of Sambourne's saucy photographs are displayed. He claimed the photographs of young ladies in a state of undress were studies for his cartoons, but – as you can see from the dispay – his subjects are fully clothed in the finished drawings.

1754
Spot Hitchcock at Leytonstone tube...

Film fanatics will love this one: see how many of the 17 mosaics lining the entrance corridors to the tube station you can identify. Created by the Greenwich Mural Workshop, they commemorate Alfred Hitchcock's birth in east London a century ago. See if you can spot the Hitch portraits and cameos among scenes from such classics as *Psycho*, *Vertigo* and *North by Northwest*. Fans should also check out the London Locations Walk (http://sandrashevey.tripod.com/hitchcock.walks), which explores various locales in the great director's London-based films.

1755
... Or come face to (giant) face

Gainsborough Studios (1 Poole Street, N1 5EA) is home to an enormous homage to Hitchcock: a 25-metre high sculpture of the great director's head, unveiled in 2010. Anthony Donaldson's *Master of Suspense* is made from weathered steel, and surrounded by silver birch trees. It's not entirely flattering, but it is extremely striking. Several of Hitch's early films, including *The Lady Vanishes*, were made at the canalside studios – now business and residential units.

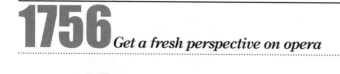

1756 *Get a fresh perspective on opera*

Opera unplugged

Opera in a pub? Jenny Landreth *enjoys Puccini with a pint.*

A woman is standing on a table in the pub – a glamorous young woman, in a little black dress, singing opera. The audience gather around the action and stand in the middle of it, watching her and subtly scoping one another out (who, exactly, is *in* the cast here?) as other singers emerge from the crowd and from behind the bar. People who've come to the pub for a quiet drink try – and fail – to carry on with their conversations. The table is in front of the pub window, and as she belts it out (probably not an operatic term) a man in a foldable sun hat – a tourist, no doubt – walks past on Islington's main drag. He looks through the window with a baffled expression. Is this a pub? Is this opera? Is this normal, for London?

The answers to those questions are yes, yes, and maybe. The King's Head is unquestionably a pub – famous as the first pub theatre in London, and, given that it has survived when many haven't, one of the more successful ones. And that *was* opera he heard: now billed as 'London's little opera house', the pub is home to the Olivier award-winning OperaUpClose, a company committed to 'redefining the boundaries of opera'. The final answer is maybe. While fringe opera isn't quite normal yet, OperaUpClose are

committed to making it so – and in any case, London is great at redefining the boundaries of what constitutes 'normal'.

It's an idea, at this point, to set your gaze firmly forward and ignore the clamour of operatic clichés vying for your attention, clichés that provide a handy tick-list of all the things OperaUpClose are not. What they are is more important, and that is, put baldly, a fringe opera company, working mostly in intimate spaces like the King's Head – a traditional pub that feels a bit lost in time (spot the old publicity photos of a young Hugh Grant on the wall), in the way any pub that's not a converted bank does. The theatre space at the back is small and dark with cheap bench seats; you get the feeling that the ceilings once dripped with a combination of beer and sweat.

The company directors, Adam Spreadbury-Mayer and Robin Norton-Hale, reference London's theatrical landscape for their fringe opera concept, likening the dynamic to that of fringe and mainstream theatre: each complements the other, and they are perfectly able to coexist. They are clear that OperaUpClose is an addition to the city's operatic offering, not a replacement.

The statistics show that their aim of bringing new audiences to opera is working. A survey during one sell-out run revealed that just over half of the audience had never been to an opera before. That's an impressive achievement, opening the form to people who may have felt distanced by its connotations of privilege and inaccessibility. OperaUpClose is becoming a dynamic antidote to the frustration, as patron Jonathan Miller put it, of 'casting pearls before pearls'.

How are they doing it? The big innovation, says Robin Norton-Hale, who adapted and directed their award-winning *La Bohème*, is 'to perform opera in English where you can actually understand what they're saying'. What they produce are versions, not translations, which can stay true to the heightened emotions of the stories, but in a realistic way. The librettos are vernacular yet poetic. And while contemporising something can highlight the mismatch between, say, the new reality of modern Dalston references and the almost-ridiculously over-the-top 'love at first sight' and 'she has betrayed me, kill her' storylines, they mine that mismatch cleverly; they wink in its general direction, but not mockingly, clearly holding the original material in high regard. Basically, it's childishly funny to hear a tenor singing 'Piss off, piss off' in full operatic throttle – and they know it. The process is, says Spreadbury-Mayer, one of 'demystifying opera', and he professes himself 'baffled that no one has done it before'.

You might argue that even demystified, opera is always going to be a bit posh. The music is huge and twiddly, and so are the stories – dramas of gods and men, of high metaphor and implausible action. But when you make the language and

setting accessible (call it singing and stories), it opens the door right up. In the production of *La Bohème*, the cast are students, so the set is studenty: a tatty sofa, a cheap string of fairy lights, roll-ups on the table.

Celebrated playwright Mark Ravenhill, the Associate Director of OperaUpClose, is behind its current production, *The Coronation of Poppea*. This time, the minimal staging consists of a modern sun-lounger and a sunken metallic water trough (yes, you will get wet if you sit in the front row and no, plastic ponchos are not provided; this isn't Alton Towers' log flume). In accordance with the stripped-back staging, the music, too, is pared: not just a small version of a big orchestra, but a thoughtful reworking. While you do lose the swell of lush strings, and time-consuming choral commentary, what you gain is worth it: being up-close to performers, singing and playing right in your face.

Sounds a bit full on? It is. Not to mention engaging, exciting and compelling; the level of intimacy it engenders, both with the story and its performers, is entirely different to the distanced, expensive, proscenium arch staging of London's big opera houses. You're not a far-off observer trying not to clap at the wrong bits, you're plunged into the thick of it.

Spreadbury-Mayer has ambitious plans for the future – not only to stage new versions of existing operas, but to commission at least one new opera a year. 'The future of opera is much brighter if there are numerous access points for everyone,' he says – and we'll raise our glass to that.

OperaUpClose at the King's Head Theatre *115 Upper Street, N1 1QN (7478 0160, www.kingsheadtheatre.com).*

1757-1758

Sip a tot of gin...

Held every second Monday of the month at the Graphic Bar (4 Golden Square, W1F 9HT, 7287 9241, www.graphicbar.com), the Juniper Society celebrates gin, in its many and varied distillations. Events showcase gins from all over the world – but to sample a proper London gin, order a Sipsmith, brewed in a Hammersmith micro-distillery.

Meanwhile, for the best dry – that is, gin-rather than vodka-based – martini in town, we recommend a visit to Duke's (St James's Place, SW1A 1NY, 7491 4840, www.dukeshotel.com) – erstwhile haunt of Ian Fleming, and said to be the inspiration behind Bond's favourite tipple.

1759-1766

... Then drink in a gin palace

With its ornate mirrors, polished wooden partitions and acres of etched glass, the 19th-century gin palace was a 'perfectly dazzling sight', according to Charles Dickens. Only a handful still exist, but they're worth seeking out.

In Maida Vale, the Prince Alfred (5a Formosa Street, W9 1EE, 7286 3287, www.theprincealfred. com) is possibly the best of the lot, with its beautiful old tiling, exquisitely curved glass frontage, series of wood-panelled snugs and fabulously ornate half-moon bar.

Built in 1872, the Princess Louise (208-209 High Holborn, WC1V 7BW, 7405 8816) is another fine example, with ornate woodwork, sumptuous tiling and a high, stucco ceiling. In Soho, the Argyll Arms (18 Argyll Street, W1F 7TP, 7734 6117) boasts Victorian etched mirrors and mahogany screens. The original layout is intact too, with a corridor leading to the large back saloon past three small snug bars. For more knockout Victoriana, head for the Albert (52 Victoria Street, SW1H 0NP, 7222 5577) – a fabulous confection of hand-cut glass, carved dark wood and old gaslight fittings.

Dating from 1869, the Viaduct Tavern (126 Newgate Street, EC1A 7AA, 7600 1863, www.fullers.co.uk) stands just across the road from the Old Bailey – and has cells for prisoners down in the basement. Up in north London, meanwhile, is the Island Queen (87 Noel Road, N1 8HD, 7354 8741, www.theislandqueenislington. co.uk). A gleaming vision of wood and etched glass, it celebrates nautical glory with a wave-damaged wooden figurehead, palm leaves and prints of ships; a vast island bar presides over the lofty room.

South of the river, the best example is probably the cathedral-like Duke of Devonshire (39 Balham High Road, SW12 9AN, 8673 1363, www.dukeof devonshirebalham.com) with its ornate, hall-of-mirrors interior.

Finally, for a 21st-century take on the gin palace, head for the Worship Street Whistling Shop (63 Worship Street, EC2A 2DU, 7247 0015, www.whistlingshop.com). Opened in 2011, this Dickensian-inspired drinking den features gas lamps, cosy wood panelling and staff in period clobber. There are 12 different gins and genevers, plus an array of outré, gin-based cocktails – not least the unusual, olive oil-spiked house gin fizz.

Princess Louise

1767-1773

Meet London's beauty gurus

Margaret Dabbs

Chiropodist Margaret Dabbs fuses foot health and beauty, offering everything from massages to her signature 'medical pedicures' (from £120).
Margaret Dabbs Foot Spa *7 New Cavendish Street, W1G 8UU (7487 5510, www.margaretdabbs.co.uk).*

Natasha Devedlaka

Natasha Devedlaka has over ten years' make-up experience in fashion, advertising, TV and beauty. Book a private lesson (£150 for two hours) to benefit from her expertise.
2 People's Hall, 2 Olaf Street, W11 4BE (07899 831552 mobile, www.hairandmakeupdept.com).

Vaishaly Patel

Vaishaly Patel has been tending to the visages of the rich and famous for years. Her signature facial (from £250), using her range of natural, organic products, has won high-profile devotees.
Vaishaly Clinic *51 Paddington Street, W1U 4HR (7224 6088, www.vaishaly.com).*

James Read

As the UK expert on sun-free tanning, James Read (www.thetantalist.com) is much in demand at the Sanderson's Agua spa; prices start at £45.
Agua *Sanderson Hotel, 50 Berners Street, W1T 3NG (7300 1414, www.sandersonlondon.com).*

Otylia Roberts

Credited with bringing the Brazilian to London a decade ago, and famous for her hot (as opposed to strip) waxing technique, Otylia Roberts has a legion of dedicated followers. Appointments with Otylia cost £25 for a basic bikini wax and £52 for a Brazilian.
Otylia Roberts Beauty Centre *23 George Street, W1U 3QA (7486 5537, www.otyliaroberts.co.uk).*

Sophy Robson

Nail artist to the stars Sophy Robson's fantastical creations (prices from £22) are available at her nail bar in Hari's hair salon, on the King's Road.
Sophy Robson Nail Salon *Hari's Salon, King's Road, SW3 2DY (7349 8722, www.sophyrobson.com).*

Johnnie Sapong

Johnnie Sapong has built up a cult following in the two decades he's been styling hair. When he's not cutting the barnets of famous clients, he can be found at his studio above Fitzrovia's Lazarides Gallery. There's only one hairstylig station, so you're guaranteed the great man's individual attention.
The Studio *11 Rathbone Place, W1T 1HR (0844 412 7620, www.johnniesapong.com).*

1774

Look for Eine's alphabet

East London graffiti writer Eine (aka Ben Flynn) has become of the UK's most celebrated street artists – not least since the Camerons presented Barrack Obama with one of his paintings in 2010. His trademark is bold, gigantic individual letters and words – choice examples of which can be found on walls and shop shutters around Brick Lane, Redchurch Street, Broadway Market and Holywell Lane. 'Alphabet Street' is his best-known piece – a row of shop shutters on Middlesex Street in Spitalfields, spray-painted with the entire alphabet. Visit at night to see the work in its fully glory. For more on his latest projects, see www.einesigns.co.uk.

1775-1787

Have dinner à deux

Andrew Edmunds
Whether you're in the bistro-like ground floor or mirror-lined basement, this unassuming townhouse restaurant in the heart of Soho has a deliciously intimate feel.
46 Lexington Street, W1F 0LW (7437 5708).

Angelus
A slice of Paris – from its thickly accented staff to its art nouveau decor – serving polished, contemporary dishes and ravishing desserts.
4 Bathurst Street, W2 2SD (7402 0083, www.angelusrestaurant.co.uk).

Assaggi
A discreet affair, serving Mediterranean Italian dishes in a modestly proportioned – but lively – room, with spectacular flower arrangements.
1st Floor, 39 Chepstow Place, W2 4TS (7792 5501).

The Bingham
This boutique hotel's dining rooms are dauntingly opulent, with their dusty gold tones, heavy curtains and gilt-topped chandeliers. If it's all a little too much, opt for a table on the heated riverside terrace.
61-63 Petersham Road, Richmond, Surrey TW10 6UT (8940 0902, www.thebingham.co.uk).

Hakkasan

Bob Bob Ricard
A glamorous, if slightly surreal 1930s-style dining room provides the backdrop for the decadent Slavic-Russian menu. And did we mention the 'press for champagne' buzzer?
1 Upper James Street, W1F 9DF (3145 1000, www.bobbobricard.com).

Le Café Anglais
A stylish, grand-but-modern brasserie that feels as though its been here forever – which adds to its romantic appeal. There's also a new oyster bar.
8 Porchester Gardens, W2 4DB (7221 1415, www.lecafeanglais.co.uk).

Clos Maggiore
Clos Maggiore transports you to a picturesque corner of Provence, with an elegant boxwood-lined dining room that leads into a courtyard filled with (fake) blossoms and fairy lights. Just don't expect to be the only couple here.
33 King Street, WC2E 8JD (7379 9696, www.closmaggiore.com).

Hakkasan
With its dimly-lit oriental opulence – courtesy of interiors maestro Christian Liagre – Hakkasan might seem a little over the top for everyday dining – but for a special date it still hits the spot. The high-end, modern Chinese food is superb.
8 Hanway Place, W1T 1HD (7927 7000, www.hakkasan.com).

Locanda Locatelli
The sultry interior of beige leather booths, etched glass screens and low lighting works best of an evening. Food-wise, this place is a temple to Italian fine dining: gnocchi with goat's cheese and black truffle, perhaps, or roast monkfish with walnut and caper sauce .
8 Seymour Street, W1H 7JZ (7935 9088, www.locandalocatelli.com).

Odette's
This Primrose Hill stalwart has cosy alcoves in the bar, a pretty walled garden, and soft lighting in the restaurant, plus some classy Mod Euro food courtesy of chef Bryn Williams.
130 Regent's Park Road, NW1 8XL (7586 8569. www.odettesprimrosehill.com).

Pasha
For voluptuous glamour, Pasha's Arabian Nights decor (not to mention the belly dancing girls) is incomparable. The North African dishes are reliable, though service can be patchy.

1 Gloucester Road, SW7 4PP (7589 7969, www.pasha-restaurant.co.uk).

St Pancras Grand
There's something irresistibly romantic about even the most mundane train station and St Pancras, gateway to the continent, is the daddy of them all. The Grand brasserie is a great place for a brief – or otherwise – encounter.
Upper Concourse, St Pancras International, Euston Road, NW1 2PQ (7870 9900, www.searcys.co.uk).

Les Trois Garçons
With its baroque chandeliers, bejewelled stuffed animals and accomplished French cuisine (a shared chateaubriand is a popular main) Les Trois Garçons can always be relied upon for a decadent evening out.
1 Club Row, E1 6JX (7613 1924, www.lestroisgarcons.com).

1788-1795

... Or enjoy eating alone

Arbutus
Dine at the bar in style and enjoy a carafe of wine for one with exquisite British dishes. The set lunch is a good-value treat.
63-64 Frith Street, Soho, W1D 3JW (7734 4545, www.arbutusrestaurant.co.uk).

L'Atelier de Joël Robuchon
Sit at the counter by the open kitchen to see the culinary fireworks, and sample some exquisitely-presented tasting dishes – a less formal take on haute cuisine.
13-15 West Street WC2H 9NE (7010 8600, www.joel-robuchon.com).

Benito's Hat
Perch on a stool, munch on a generously-filled burritos and watch the world go by outside.
56 Goodge Street, W1T 4NB (7637 3732, www.benitos-hat.com).

Busaba Eathai
The window seats at Busaba are great for watching Soho streetlife. There's a friendly vibe, and large shared tables mean that lone diners don't stand out.
106-110 Wardour Street, W1F 0TR (7255 8686, www.busaba.com).

Canton Arms
Solo dining comfort has a lot to do with the staff; at this gastropub, they put you at your ease early and keep you there. The food's great, and you can belly up to the well-kept bar.
177 South Lambeth Road SW8 1XP (7582 8710, www.cantonarms.com).

Great Queen Street
No bookings are taken here, and singles can often slip on to one of the bar stools – the best seats in the house. Staff look after you brilliantly, and you can watch all the action, be it bartending or cooking in the open kitchen.
32 Great Queen Street WC2B 5AA (7242 0622).

Kulu Kulu
Pull up a seat facing the conveyor-belt at this long-established sushi joint. Not only will you not feel self-conscious, but you can take your pick of the good-value sushi.
51-53 Shelton Street, WC2H 9HE (7240 5687).

J Sheekey
Fish-restaurant cousin to the Ivy, Sheekey has the feeling of a members' club, including its accommodating attitude to singles. Pretend to read a book while you secretly people-watch.
28-34 St Martin's Court, WC2N 4AL (7240 2565, www.j-sheekey.co.uk).

Great Queen Street

1796

Take in a vertiginous view at St Paul's...

As one of the London skyline's most recognisable landmarks, it's no wonder that the view from the Golden Gallery atop the dome of St Paul's Cathedral is second to none. Those that climb the 528 steps to the Gallery, some 280 feet above the City of London, can see London stretched out before them, from the river and Tate Modern in the south to the City in the east. But that's not all: the small peephole at the top of the stairs leading up to the Golden Gallery, affords a dizzying view into the Cathedral below.

St Paul's Cathedral *Ludgate Hill, EC4M 8AD (7236 4128, www.stpauls.co.uk).*

1797

... Or cheat and take the lift at Westminster Cathedral

Often overlooked due to its proximity to the more famous Westminster Abbey, Westminster Cathedral is almost as spectacular, with its Byzantine-style architecture banded in red and white stone. Crane your neck upwards and you will be able to see the top of the 273-foot bell tower that affords some of the best views of London, to all points of the compass. Access to the viewing platform is by lift only, and tickets can be purchased from the gift shop.

Westminster Cathedral *42 Francis Street, SW1P 1QW (7798 9055, www.westminster cathedral.org.uk).*

1798-1803

Find a folly

As a natural home for well-bankrolled egotists, London has its fair share of follies. The term was first used in the early 18th century, when Sir John Vanbrugh introduced the concept of rearranging landscapes to please the human eye; follies were meant to enhance a view, and any other use was incidental. The neo-classical Queen's Temple in Kensington Gardens (W2 2UH, 7298 2100, www.royalparks.org.uk) was built in 1734-35 by William Kent specifically to be seen across the Round Pond from Kensington Palace; its role as a summerhouse was secondary.

Although Horace Walpole lived at Strawberry Hill (268 Waldegrave Road, Twickenham, Middx TW1 4ST, 8744 1241, www.strawberryhillhouse. org.uk), thus giving it a useful purpose, it is undoubtedly a folly. Over four decades, Walpole transformed an ordinary house into a neo-Gothic castle, complete with sham battlements; its lavish ornamentation (some of it papier-mâché) was, and remains, deliciously over the top. Even in Walpole's lifetime, it became a tourist attraction, though only four visitors were admitted per day ('between the hours of Twelve and Three before Dinner', according to the official rules), and children were barred; recently restored, it's now open to visitors of all ages.

Walpole, in a bout of hypocritical Nimbyism, made loud complaint about a tower rising in the Royal Gardens at nearby Kew (Kew Road, Richmond, Surrey TW9 3AB, 8332 5655, www. kew.org). 'In a fortnight,' he told a friend, 'you will be able to see it in Yorkshire.' He was referring to the still-standing, 163-feet-high Pagoda – a ten-storey edifice, designed, by Sir William Chambers (of Somerset House fame), specifically *not* to blend into the background.

The neat, well-kept Pagoda is at odds with the tumbledown folly of popular imagination, which is better represented by the romantic, ruined castle found in the heart of Sydenham Hill's ancient woodlands, now a wildlife reserve (www.wildlondon.org.uk).

The three-towered, triangular Severndroog Castle on Shooters Hill (Castle Wood, SE18 3RT), built by Lady James in 1784 as a memorial to her husband, is also in a woodland setting, but kept in good condition with help from volunteers. Join them, or sponsor a brick, at www.severndroog castle.org.uk.

Folly-building died out with the wealthy land-owning classes, so it is refreshing to see a modern example, and in the public domain. One side of Barking Town Square is given over to a striking 23-foot-high red-brick wall (concealing a supermarket) whose campanile, niches and bricked-up doors and windows are firmly in the folly tradition. Its conceit is that it 'recreates a fragment of the imaginary lost past of Barking', as envisioned by local community groups, and it works beautifully.

Severndroog Castle

1804

Learn the rules of the road

It's not widely known, but most London boroughs offer heavily subsidised or free cycle training to adults who live, work or study in the borough, in addition to in-school cycle training for children. What's on offer varies: in Hackney, for example, anyone over 11 is entitled to two hours' free training. Find out what you're eligible for by calling your local training officer; for a full list, see www.tfl.gov.uk/cycletraining.

1805-1813

Enjoy the grassroots game

From television and newspaper coverage, you would be forgiven for assuming no football is played in London that doesn't involve £100,000-a-week prima donnas pleading for soft penalties. But head down the leagues and there are live games to be watched for £10 or less, offering a heady mix of tradition, pride and passion.

Bromley FC
Record attendance at the Lilywhites' Hayes Lane ground is 10,798 for a game against Nigeria in 1950. Crowds are rather smaller these days for matches in the Blue Square Conference South, but the club's website does offer BFCtv: full video match highlights.
The Stadium, Hayes Lane, Beckenham, Kent BR2 9EF (8460 5291, www.bromleyfootballclub.co.uk).

Carshalton Athletic FC
Surrey's oldest club (founded in 1903) and one of the county's most active in terms of community football development, the Robins are on a mission 'to become the most friendly football club in the league pyramid'. The team's not bad either, comfortably placed mid-table in the Premier Division of the Ryman League.
War Memorial Sports Ground, Colston Avenue, Carshalton, Surrey SM5 2PW (8642 8658, www.carshaltonathletic.co.uk).

Clapton FC
Five times winners of the FA Amateur Cup, the Tons were the first English team to play in Europe, beating a Belgian XI in Antwerp in 1892. The team still plays at the Old Spotted Dog Ground in Forest Gate, but finished bottom of the modest Essex Senior League in 2010/11.
The Old Spotted Dog Ground, Upton Lane, E7 9NP.

Corinthian-Casuals FC
The Corinthians were founded in 1882 (merging with Casuals FC in 1939) as a reaction against the professionalism that was sweeping through football. They had no home ground, training was outlawed and the team eschewed penalties, refusing to take the spot kick if awarded one and removing their goalkeeper if they conceded. Yet the team inflicted Manchester United's record defeat and twice fielded the entire England side. Social change brought an end to the club's sporting superiority, but Corinthian-Casuals battle on – still as amateurs – in Division 1 South of the Ryman League, still wearing their spectacular chocolate and pink halved shirts. The greatest ever amateur football club.
King George's Field, Hook Rise South, Tolworth, Kent KT6 7NA (8397 3368, www.corinthian-casuals.com).

Dulwich Hamlet FC
Pink and navy striped shirts. Giants of the amateur game between the two World Wars. One of the great football addresses: Champion Hill Stadium, Dog Kennel Hill, SE22. What's not to like? When the Hamlet are playing away (they're in the Ryman League Division 1 South), you can watch tenants Fisher Athletic tussling in the higher-grade Blue Square Conference South.
Champion Hill Stadium, Dog Kennel Hill, SE22 8BD (07956 554590, www.dulwichhamletfc.co.uk).

Enfield Town FC
Until 1999, Enfield were one of England's top amateur clubs, close to gaining admission to the Football League. Then they sold their stadium and began a series of catastrophic groundshares, which alienated fans and led to the formation of fan-owned Enfield Town FC. The Towners have recently moved to the Queen Elizabeth Stadium and are making solid progress in Ryman League Division 1 North.
The Queen Elizabeth Stadium, Donkey Lane, Enfield, Middx EN1 3PL (www.etfc.co.uk).

Hampton & Richmond FC
Steptoe & Son scriptwriter Alan Simpson is club president and has a stand named after him at the tree-fringed Beveree Stadium in the heart of Hampton village, while Vince Cable MP is the club patron. Former West Ham hero Alan Devonshire led the club for nearly a decade, securing its position in the Blue Square Conference South, before leaving at the end of the 2010/11 season. His team is still saddled with one of the game's worst nicknames: the Beavers.
Beveree Stadium, Beaver Close, Hampton, Middx TW12 2BT (8979 2456, www.hamptonfc.net).

Hoddesdon Town FC
Inaugural winners of the FA Vase back in 1975, the Lilywhites (yet another club with the nickname) play in the Spartan South Midlands League, despite being only 25 minutes from

Liverpool Street. Former Tottenham Hotspur legend Ossie Ardiles is the club patron.
The Stewart Edwards Stadium, Lowfield, Park View, Hoddesdon, Herts EN11 8PX (01992 463133, www.hoddesdontownfc.co.uk)

AFC Hornchurch
The Urchins emerged from the ruins of Hornchurch FC, who went bankrupt in 2004/05. The reconstituted club holds its own in the Premier Division of the Ryman League, under more cautious financial management.
The Stadium, Bridge Avenue, Upminster, Essex RM14 2LX (01708 220080, www. afchornchurch.com).

1814 Spot parakeets in London's parks

Their introduction may be shrouded in myth (some say Jimi Hendrix released the first flock on Carnaby Street in the 1960s), but it's a fact that emerald-green parakeets can now be spotted in parks and gardens all over the capital, with a particular concentration in south-west London. That these noisy birds originate from the Himalayas explains how they have survived the cold English winters. They've positively thrived, in fact, with population estimates around the 20,000 mark. The best spots to see them are Richmond Park, Kew Gardens and the suburbs on the London-Surrey border; Hampstead Heath and Hyde Park also harbour a fair number.

1815-1817
See three ecclesiastical oddities

The Agapemonite Church
Standing by Clapton Common, the Agapemonite Church (Rookwood Road, N16 6SS) was erected in 1895 by the Brides of Christ, a flock of wealthy females devoted to their self-declared immortal Messiah, Henry James Prince. Angelic cows, horses and lions are among the wealth of colossal, off-kilter statuary still adorning the spire. When Prince died in 1899, much to his congregation's surprise, a second charlatan, the Rev John Hugh Smyth-Pigott, stepped into his immortal shoes, and attempted to walk on water on Clapton Pond. More successfully, he thrice impregnated one of his 'disciples', and was thereafter defrocked.

St Ethelreda's
The first Roman Catholic church in London, and a survivor of the Great Fire, St Etheldreda's (14 Ely Place, EC1N 6RY, 7405 1061, www.stetheldreda. com) is one of only two buildings in London dating from Edward I's reign. Originally built by the Bishop of Ely in 1290, the adjoining Palace and surrounding land were officially part of Cambridgeshire until the 1970s. St Etheldreda herself was an East Anglian princess, and part of her hand is kept in a jewel cask beside the high altar; she's commemorated on 3 February, with a ritual Blessing of the Throats.

St Sepulchre-without-Newgate
St Sepulchre-without-Newgate (Giltspur Street, EC1A 9DE, www.st-sepulchre.org.uk) is well-known as 'the National Musicians' Church' – but also has grisly associations with Newgate Prison, which stood opposite. The church bellman would take an underground passage to the prison to ring the dreaded Execution Bell outside the cells of the condemned; the bell is now displayed under glass in the church. Other historic oddities include the watchtower in the churchyard, built to deter bodysnatchers from stealing fresh cadavers, and the handsome drinking fountain with two chained metal cups, set into the railings – a Victorian charity's attempt to discourage drinkers from patronising the pub across the road.

1818-1819
Meet the pearlies

One autumn day in central London, you might spot a shimmering crowd, decked out in pearl-festooned whistle and flutes (that's suits to non-Cockney folk). For this is the season when the two rival societies of Pearly Kings and Queens hold their harvest festivals, which double as conventions. You can also catch representatives of the Cockney royals year-round, at charitable and civic events such as the Lord Mayor's Show, the New Year's Day Parade: check their respective websites for scheduled appearances.

Original London Pearly Kings & Queens' Festival
St Martin-in-the-Fields, Trafalgar Square (www.thepearlies.com). First Sunday of October.
London Pearly Kings & Queens Society's Harvest Festival *St Paul's Church, Bedford Street, WC2E 9ED (www.pearlysociety.co.uk).*

1820
Walk in a Winter Garden

Cheer yourself up on a dark cold December day by visiting the Winter Garden in Battersea Park (Albert Bridge Road, SW11 4NJ, 8871 7530, www.batterseapark.org). Adjacent to the Sun Gate in the south-west corner of the park and opened in March 2011, it's the creation of Dan Pearson, award-winning garden designer and the *Guardian*'s horticultural guru. It's at its best from November to March, with colour coming from berries, leaves and branches rather than showy blossoms. At the centre of the one-and-a-half-acre site is a cluster of Persian ironwood trees, their python-patterned trunks splaying in all directions. Elsewhere are white birches, orange and rust-coloured witch hazel and autumn-flowering pink camellias, while fragrance comes from sweet-smelling sarcococca, wintersweet, honeysuckle and viburnums.

1821
Bag a right royal souvenir

Lucky invitees to garden parties or honours ceremonies at Buckingham Palace are seldom so overwhelmed by the occasion that they forget to pocket a napkin or other royal keepsake. Now, visitors to Her Majesty's home during its summer public opening can snaffle their own souvenir: a café has recently opened, and the paper cups are a pretty blue-green, clearly marked with the Palace crest. Oh, and they can also enjoy a fascinating behind-the-scenes glimpse of the State Rooms, used to entertain dignitaries and guests of state, and walk through part of the beautiful gardens. **Buckingham Palace & Royal Mews** *The Mall, SW1A 1AA (7766 7300, www.royalcollection.org.uk).*

1822
Hang out with the literati

It may not be on quite the same scale as Hay-on-Wye, but Hampstead and Highgate's annual literary festival (www.hamhighlitfest.com) is a lot closer to home. Over 60 lively talks, debates, interviews, workshops and tours are scheduled over three days in September. Themes and contributors are an esoteric mix: previous events have featured everyone from Alan Hollinghurst and Peter Snow to Barbara Taylor Bradford.

1823
Get up with the lark

Each May, International Dawn Chorus Day (www.idcd.info) celebrates the beauty of birdsong. To take part in an event, you'll need to get up before dawn – but it's an unforgettable experience. Both the WWT London Wetland Centre (www.wwt.org.uk/visit-us/london) and London Wildlife Trust (www.wildlondon.org.uk) organise guided walks before daybreak, the latter through the lovely Sydenham Hill Wood; visit the IDCD website for details of other events.

1824
Pay your respects to Marx

Karl Marx's tomb, topped with a large bust of the impressively-bearded thinker, is a highlight of Highgate Cemetery – and if you're visiting in early May, you might happen upon the annual Marx Oration. Organised by the Communist Party of Britain and Marx Memorial Library, it commemorates the anniversary of Marx's birth on May 5. Marxists from all over the world gather to lay wreaths and listen to the guest speaker, before proceedings conclude with a rousing rendition of 'The Internationale'. **Highgate Cemetery** *Swains Lane, N6 6PJ (8340 1834, www.highgate-cemetery.org).*

1825
Follow the Street Kitchen

Grab a gourmet takeaway lunch from the Street Kitchen, a sleek Airstream trailer that pops up at various locales around central London. Chefs Jun Tanaka (of fine dining restaurant Pearl) and Mark Jankel are behind the operation, so standards are high. The menu changes daily, according to what's in season, with ingredients sourced entirely from the UK; summer dishes might include grilled mackerel with potatoes, watercress and horseradish dressing, followed by eton mess and rhubarb compôte. Check www.streetkitchen.co.uk for the latest location.

1826-1831

See a floating...

... Art gallery

Housed in a fleet of historic Thames barges, the Couper Collection includes major installation works by Max Couper, temporary exhibitions and a gallery of work by young Londoners.
Riverside Walk, between Albert & Battersea Bridges, SW11 4AN (7738 1935, www.coupercollection. org.uk).

... Bookshop

We can't give you an exact location, because it plies the London length of Regent's Canal – but Twitter can. *Word on the Water* is a Dutch barge, recently refitted as a second-hand bookshop; it also has a rooftop stage for readings and gigs. *@wordonthewater.*

... Boutique hotel

Thought houseboats had to be all craftsy and cluttered? Not so. *On the Water*, a hotel and venue-for-hire, is surprisingly spacious and beautifully kitted out. It offers overnighters all hi-tech mod cons, plus a home-baked breakfast delivered to the door.
Cumberland Basin, Prince Albert Road, NW1 7SS (7586 6666, www.beonthewater.co.uk).

... Church

Moored on West India Quay near the Museum of Docklands, St Peter's Barge is London's only floating church. It's of an evangelical Anglican persuasion and caters for its office-bound clientele with lunch-hour Bible readings.
West India Quay, Hertsmere Road, E14 4AL (www.stpetersbarge.org).

... Garden

Downing's Road Moorings is a community of houseboats and other craft moored on the Thames that's created its own 'garden square' on the decks of several large boats. Visit on Open Garden Squares weekend (www.open squares.org) or peer over the sea wall to scope out the luxuriant vegetation.
Off Bermondsey Wall West, opposite Mill Street, SE1.

... Festival

For the nine days of the Shoreditch Festival, the mile or so of Regent's Canal between Shoreditch Park and Broadway Market becomes a ribbon of festivity. There are all manner of floating attractions, plus walks, workshops, three music stages, food vendors and arts events.
Regent's Canal, N1 & E8 (7033 8520, www.shoreditchfestival.org.uk).

1832-1838

Appreciate some Modernist masterpieces

For a taste of Modernist London, start with the Isokon building in Lawn Road, Hampstead (NW3 2XD). Designed by architect Wells Coates in the early 1930s, this linear, concrete block of flats was awarded Grade I status in 1974; former resident Agatha Christie described it as looking like a 'giant liner, which ought to have had a couple of funnels'. Follow this with the more intimate 2 Willow Road (NW3 1TH, 01494 755570, www.nationaltrust.org.uk) in Hampstead. It was designed by Ernö Goldfinger as his family home; inside, his collection of 20th-century art includes pieces by Bridget Riley and Max Ernst.

In nearby Highgate is the stunningly sited, Berthold Lubetkin-designed Highpoint residential complex (http://highpointn6.com) – a beacon for architecture aficionadoes. You can see two more of Lubetkin's works in Islington: the Grade I-listed Finsbury Health Centre (17 Pine Street, EC1R 0LP) and his Spa Green Estate (between Rosebery Avenue and St John Street); both can easily be admired from the street. Perhaps his best-known masterpiece, though, is the Penguin Pool at London Zoo (Regent's Park, 7722 3333, www.zsl.org/london-zoo); although the penguins have moved to more naturalistic surrounds, it remains a design icon.

Finally, in Crouch End, what was Hornsey Town Hall (The Broadway, N8 9JJ, www.hornsey-town-hall.org.uk) is a fine example of municipal Modernism, designed by architect Reginald Uren.

For more edifices from the last century – and the chance to see inside some landmark buildings – see the Twentieth Century Society (www.c20 society.org.uk) and Open House London (www. londonopenhouse.org).

1839 *Partake of a midnight feast*

Occupying the car park behind Old Street and Rivington Street, Red Market (288-299 Old Street, EC2, www.redmarketlondon.com) is inspired by the late-night street markets of South-east Asia. Its stalls sell an eclectic range of eats, from Swedish meatballs to pulled pork. With music and art events thrown into the mix, it's a welcome alternative to a post-pub kebab. It's open every Friday and Saturday, from noon until midnight.

1840

Step aboard the Gingerline

A Siberian feast with trapeze artists and dancing girls? A Victorian banquet at the Brunel Museum? These are just two of the dinner events Gingerline (www.gingerline.co.uk) has organised. Its soirées take place in clandestine spaces near an East London Line station, whose location is revealed an hour before kick-off. Expect the unexpected: all you can be sure of is that a sumptuous three-course dinner will definitely be involved.

1841

Take control of Tower Bridge The two bascules of Tower Bridge are raised up to 1,000 times a year to allow boats on the Thames to pass below. Now, an annual competition run by the City of London Corporation is giving one lucky entrant the chance to take the helm and control the parting of the bridge. Supervised by the bridge's operating team, the winner will deliver a series of tannoy announcements before using a joystick and button sequence to unlock, raise, lower and lock the iconic structure. Check www.towerbridge.org.uk for updates on this year's competition.

Working for the Tidal Thames

Xstrata Treetop Walkway

1842-1848

Look down

Bermondsey Abbey

When developers – and their diggers – moved into Bermondsey Square, SE1, a few years ago, they uncovered the foundations of a Benedictine Abbey dating back to the eighth century. You can see some of the foundations underneath the glass floor at the Del'Aziz restaurant, on the north-east corner of the square.

Del'Aziz *11 Bermondsey Square, SE1 3UN (7407 2991, www.delaziz.co.uk).*

British Museum

Inscribed into the floor of the British Museum's Great Court – which was refurbished for the millennium – is a fitting quotation from Alfred, Lord Tennyson: 'And let thy feet, millennia hence, be set in the midst of knowledge.'

British Museum *Great Russell Street, WC1B 3DG (7323 8299, www.britishmuseum.org).*

Centre of London plaque

Charing Cross is generally considered the centre of London, and is the point from which all measurements to the city are taken. Head to the south side of Trafalgar Square, near the statue of King Charles I, for the site of the original cross – erected here in 1290 by Edward I in memory of his beloved Queen Eleanor.

National Gallery

The first piece of art you'll see at the National Gallery – other than the building itself – is below you. As you enter through the Portico entrance, a 1930s mosaic, *The Awakening of the Muses*, greets you. It's the work of Bloomsbury Group artist Boris Anrep – and many of the robustly quotidian models were Bloomsbury friends of Anrep's.

National Gallery *Trafalgar Square WC2N 5DN (7747 2885, www.nationalgallery.org.uk).*

Skateboard graveyard

When you next walk over Hungerford Bridge, spare a thought for all the skateboarders who have lost loved ones nearby. On the downstream side of the bridge, the pier nearest the famous skateboarding area underneath Queen Elizabeth Hall is littered with irreparably damaged boards; for details of the site, visit http://hungerford bridge.pbworks.com.

Tower Bridge

Tower Bridge's exhibition space is located on the structure's upper levels, some 43 metres above the Thames. When shows are held here, visitors can access the lofty upper walkway, looking down on the huge Victorian steam engines that powered the bridge until 1976. Alternatively, book a guided tour for the full lowdown on this engineering marvel.

Tower Bridge Exhibition *Tower Bridge Road, SE1 2UP (7403 3761, www.towerbridge.org.uk).*

Xstrata Treetop Walkway

Kew Gardens' Xstrata Treetop Walkway actually starts underground, as an exploration of tree roots, but soon morphs into an 18-metre-high, 200-metre-long walkway. From here, you can look down at the crowns of lime, sweet chestnut and oak trees – as well as the trees' resident birds.

Royal Botanic Gardens *Kew, Richmond, Surrey TW9 3AB (8332 5655, www.kew.org).*

1849

Get the hottest tickets in town

Culmination of the Cultural Olympiad – £83m of artistic activity right across the country – the London 2012 Festival is the umbrella for more than 1,000 events, across all the arts, that will be happening in the capital from 21 June to 9 September 2012. We've scattered confirmed highlights of the Festival through this book, among them Radio 1's Hackney Weekend pop festival, contemporary dance at the Barbican, and Rivers of Music, the grand finale. Watch out for work under development, including a new opera from Blur frontman Damon Albarn and cartoonist Jamie Hewlett and art commissions from Olafur Eliasson and Martin Creed. Tickets go on sale as this book hits the shelves in October 2011; check http://festival.london2012.com for the latest details.

1850-1854

Mix it up

If your experience of mixing drinks is limited to combining vodka with Coke, consider signing up for a cocktail-mixing course. Twice a month, 69 Colebrooke Row (69 Colebrooke Row, N1 8AA, 07540 528593, www.69colebrookerow.com) offers a chance to learn about selected styles of drinks from a master bartender (£40).

Nightjar

Colebrooke Row

At the sleek Fifth Floor bar in Harvey Nichols (109-125 Knightsbridge, SW1X 7RJ, 7235 5250, www.harveynichols.com), mixology classes (£60) are taught by the head barman; participants are given a stomach-lining breakfast before being guided through the cocktails of the day, then rewarded with a two-course lunch in the Fifth Floor restaurant next door.

Groups of four to ten people can also arrange two-hour cocktail classes (£40) at Soho members' club Milk & Honey (61 Poland Street, W1F 7NU, 7065 6840, www.mlkhny.com), learning how to make (and drink) six styles of cocktail, while the Prohibition-themed Nightjar (129 City Rd, EC1V 1JB, 7253 4101, www.bar nightjar.com) offers groups the run of a private bar, canapés and a progression through four eras of cocktails, with eight drinks to try (£70).

At the panoramic Skylon bar at the Royal Festival Hall (Belvedere Road, SE1 8XX, 7654 7800, www.skylon-restaurant.co.uk), meanwhile, mixologist Zoran Peric hosts masterclasses on the first Monday of every month. The classes are free to attend – you only pay for what you drink.

1855

Get a curry in a hurry, for lunch...

Just because the take-out lunch tray from Rasa Express is ridiculously cheap doesn't mean it isn't also delicious – we'd happily pay more than the £4 it costs (£3.50 for vegetarian). For that, you get three side curries, rice, a chapati or dosa and a dessert. It's currently open weekdays only, from noon to 3pm.

Rasa Express *5 Rathbone Street, W1T 1NQ (7637 0222, www.rasarestaurants.com).*

1856... Or dinner

The folk running the canteen at the Indian YMCA know what their clientele want: good food, fast and cheap. And that's exactly what they get: two bowls of freshly made curry, a generous heap of pilau rice and a chapati, all for a fiver.

The Indian YMCA *41 Fitzroy Square, W1T 6AQ (7387 0411, www.indianymca.org).*

The Loft Project

1857
Sample Sadler's Wells

Are you a fan of dance, but not of the ticket prices? Or perhaps you're not inclined to blow money on an art form you know nothing about? Fear not. Once a year, internationally renowned dance venue Sadler's Wells holds a special 'Sampled' weekend, following the success of the inaugural event in 2007. The idea is to give audiences the chance to check out a variety of different dance styles – in bite-size chunks, and all in the space of one evening. Pretty much everything is covered, from hip hop to Argentinian tango. Tickets are a tenner, or £5 standing.

Sadler's Wells *Rosebery Avenue, EC1R 4TN (0844 412 4300, www.sadlerswells.com).*

1858
Eat like a king at the Loft Project

Originally a supper club and test kitchen for Viajantes' Michelin-starred head chef, Nuno Mendes, the Loft Project has become a platform for young chefs from around the world to showcase their skills. Expect impeccable fine dining (on Thursday, Friday and Saturday evenings) from some world-class talents: Samuel Miller of Copenhagen's Noma, say, or Modern Brazilian rising stars Rogério Maldonado and Ivo Galvao. At £120 per head, it's not cheap – but with a maximum 16 guests around the table, and at least eight courses, it's worth breaking the bank for. Note that it's bring your own wine.

The Loft Project *Unit 2A Quebec Wharf, 315 Kingsland Road, E8 4DJ (www.theloftproject.co.uk).*

1859-1962

Gawp at scandalous sculptures

The British have always had a rather hard time with classical statues, thanks to those difficult bumpy bits, which are often somewhat smoothed over, Ken and Barbie style.

London's first statue to appear complete with genitals was Achilles, at the east end of Hyde Park. Cast from a captured French cannon, it was commissioned as a tribute to the Duke of Wellington from 'the women of England', in 1822. A modesty-preserving fig leaf appeared not long afterwards, following public outcry, but is clearly not integral; indeed, it has been chipped off a couple of times.

The statue Anteros (or Eros, as common usage has it) on top of the fountain at Piccadilly Circus, erected in 1893, is often described as naked – but in fact a fluttering loincloth leaves at least something to the imagination.

By the early 20th century, Victorian mores were receding. Jacob Epstein included penises on the figures comprising his sculpture 'Ages of Man', on what was then the HQ of the British Medical Association at 429 Strand, WC2R 0JR (now the Zimbabwean embassy). They caused a fuss, but survived until 1937 when one allegedly fell on a passer-by; the rest were removed.

Commissions for the headquarters of the Underground Group (now Transport for London) at 55 Broadway, SW1H 0BD, above St James's tube station, also got a few knickers in a twist, and not just for their dramatic Modernism. Henry Moore's reclining figure, 'West Wind', was bump-free; but Jacob Epstein's anatomically correct 'Day and Night' enraged conservative opinion to the point that the head of the Underground was forced to resign over what had become a scandal. In the end, Epstein agreed to remove an inch and a half from the penis of one of the figures, and the controversy died down.

1863-1866

Spend the night at a museum

Check in advance what ages the event is suitable for, and whether parents can (or must) come too.

British Museum

The legendary sleepovers here (£32) are only open to Young Friends of the British Museum and their friends. Themes vary, but usually allow for a bit of spookiness, storytelling and navigation by torch.
Great Russell Street, WC1B 3DG (7323 8195, www.britishmuseum.org).

Golden Hinde

Sleepovers aboard the *Golden Hinde* (£39.95), a replica of Drake's ship moored on the Thames, offer a 'voyage' in search of hidden treasures, and end with the company bedding down below decks among the cannons.
St Mary Overie Dock, Clink Street, SE1 9DG (7403 0123, http://goldenhinde.com).

Natural History Museum

For children in the grip of the dinosaur bug, a sleepover in the Natural History Museum's impressive central hall (£46), watched over by the 150-million-year-old Diplodocus, couldn't be more exciting.
Cromwell Road, SW7 5BD (7942 5792, www.nhm.ac.uk).

Science Museum

Activities at Science Night sleepovers (£45) are based around a different theme each month: hands-on workshops and an IMAX film are always included, though.
Exhibition Road, SW7 2DD (0870 870 4868, www.sciencemuseum.org.uk).

Shop this street

1867-1874

Traditional bookshops: Cecil Court, WC2

Bookended by rumbling Charing Cross Road and St Martin's Lane, this picturesque pedestrian cut-through is known for its line-up of antiquarian book, map and print dealers. But tranquil Cecil Court (www.cecilcourt.co.uk) was once a leader in a brasher form of entertainment. The nascent film industry set up shop here in the late 19th century, when it became known as Flicker Alley; some of the earliest moving pictures shown in this country would have been projected on the walls of its townhouses.

Until fairly recently, there was a steel door within Greening Burland (no.27, 7836 0999), a specialist in mystery, crime and science fiction – a reminder that early nitrate film was flammable and needed to be kept in isolation. Today, its only movie connections are in the form of inspiration as a period location: the passage is reputed to have been the model for Diagon Alley in the Harry Potter franchise, and Renée Zellweger's Beatrix Potter sees her first edition of *Peter Rabbit* in a Cecil Court shopfront in the film *Miss Potter*.

Antique map and book specialist Tim Bryars (no.8, 7836 1901, www.paralos.co.uk), the secretary of the Cecil Court Association, has researched the alley's history, and the antique maps he sells emphasise the absence of development in the area at the time the alley was laid out in the 1670s. The street deserves a mention in the annals of British crime history; its 18th-century residents regularly engaged in highway robbery, forgery and arson, and in 1735 Elizabeth Calloway set fire to her brandy shop for the insurance. The fire destroyed 15 houses in neighbouring St Martin's Court and caused the death of William Hogarth's mother. In more recent times, the street was the site of the 1961 murder of antiques shop assistant Elsie May Batten – the first crime to be solved with the use of Identikit, then a novel import from America.

Although there were booksellers here by the early 20th century – the Foyle brothers opened at no.14 in 1904, before relocating to their current flagship premises – it wasn't until the 1920s that they moved in en masse. Mystical and spiritual specialist Watkins (nos.19-21, 7836 2182, www.watkins books.com) is the oldest store, in situ since 1904. But the longest serving individual resident is David Drummond of Pleasures of Past Times at no.11 (7836 1142), who set up shop here more than 40 years ago. Drummond was dubbed 'the last of the eccentric booksellers' by Simon Callow, and calls himself 'the doyen of the Court'. He caters to a thespian crowd, selling tatty but valuable playbills, magic books and assorted theatrical ephemera.

Other sellers have different specialisms. Travis & Emery (no.17, 7240 2129, www. travis-and-emery.com) stocks new and old books on music, plus opera programmes, photographs and playbills, while Marchpane (7836 8661, www.marchpane.com), at no.16, focuses on children's literature, with an emphasis on Lewis Carroll. The latter also boasts its own Dalek.

Because each Cecil Court shop is unique, they don't seem to tread on one another's toes. For instance, Tindley & Chapman at no.4 (7240 2161) and Goldsboro at nos.23-25 (7497 9230, www.goldsborobooks.com) both specialise in first editions, but the former concentrates on second-hand items, while the latter operates an impressive signed-copy book club.

Atmospheric at any time of year, Cecil Court is particularly quaint around Christmas, when it generally throws a Christmas Fair.

1875-1900

Shop an A-Z of specialists

A is for art supplies

With its stoppered glass jars of pigments and 19th-century shop fittings, L Cornelissen & Son (105 Great Russell Street, WC1B 3RY, 7636 1045, www.cornelissen.com) harks back to another era. Shop here and you'll be following in the footsteps of Dante Gabriel Rossetti and Damien Hirst.

B is for buttons

Button Queen (76 Marylebone Lane, W1U 2PR, 7935 1505, www.thebuttonqueen.co.uk) has a dizzying array of buttons, antique and modern, from humble toggles to jet and glass beauties.

C is comics

At Bloomsbury store Gosh! (1 Berwick Street, W1F 0DR, 7636 1011, www.goshlondon.com), half the basement is taken up with comics, while the other holds a fine stash of manga.

D is for dogs

Spoil your mutt with a luxurious hand-made collar from Holly & Lil (103 Bermondsey Street, SE1 3XB, 3287 3024, www.hollyandlil.co.uk). Leads, beds, bowls and treats are also sold at this supremely posh pet shop.

E is for electronics

The Covent Garden Apple Store (1 The Piazza, WC2E 8HA, 7447 1400, www.apple.com) is the ultimate in geek chic, and currently the world's largest Apple outpost (though soon to be pipped by New York).

F is for fixed wheel

Tokyo Fixed (4 Peter Street, W1F 0AD, 7734 1885, www.tokyofixedgear.com) stocks all things fixed wheel; high-end brands include Nari Furi and CCP.

G is for games

As well as the usual suspects (Ludo, Monopoly, dominoes), Compendia (10 Greenwich Market, SE10 9HZ, 8293 6616, www.compendia.co.uk) carries more obscure games such as mancala – an African game often compared to chess.

H is for herbs

If you're trying to track down more unusual herbs, try the Spice Shop (1 Blenheim Crescent, W11 2EE, 7221 4448, www.thespiceshop.co.uk), whose extensive stock includes zesty Australian lemon myrtle and fragrant Greek throubi.

L Cornelissen & Son

I is for Italian

Visit delicatessen Gazzano's (167 Farringdon Road, EC1R 3AS, 7837 1586) for one of the most comprehensive ranges of Italian food and drink in London: hoards of pasta, fine Italian cheeses and cold meats, and an excellent selection of wines, grappas and proseccos.

J is for jeans

Devoted exclusively to denim, Trilogy (33 Duke of York Square, SW3 4LY, 7730 6515, www.trilogystores.co.uk) promises a perfect fit every time. Premium and cult brands run from Nudie to J-Brand.

K is for kitchenalia

Summerill & Bishop (100 Portland Road, W11 4LQ, 7221 4566, www.summerillandbishop.com) is filled with all manner of covetable kitchen- and homeware, from old-fashioned measuring cups to wooden 'dolly' clothes-pegs.

L is for labels

Founded by the owner's great-grandfather, Gardeners (149 Commercial Street, E1 6BJ) is a tiny treasure trove of labels, tags, paper bags and shopkeeping paraphernalia. Visit while you can – a threatened rent rise may close the shop.

M is for magic

International Magic (89 Clerkenwell Road, EC1R 5BX, 7405 7324, www.internationalmagic.com) is an Aladdin's Cave for aspiring and professional magicians. Invest in an animated banknote, a dodgy deck of cards or even a vanishing cabinet.

N is for nails

WAH Nails (420 Kingsland Road, E8 4AA, 7812 9889, http://wah-nails.com) is a small nail bar that's had a big impact on the London fashion scene. The deft nail technicians can rattle off a photo-real animal print on a nail in a matter of minutes. A basic design such as stripes, zebra or Chanel-style tips will set you back about £15.

O is for Olympic Games

Browse the London 2012 shop (Unit 2A, St Pancras International, Pancras Road, NW1 2QP, 7837 8558, http://shop.london2012.com) for everything from pin badges and mascot toys to Stella McCartney-designed sportswear. For a full list of dedicated shops, see the website.

Button Queen

P is for perfume

The perfumes at Le Labo (28A Devonshire Street, W1G 6PS, 3441 1535, www.lelabo fragrances.com) are freshly mixed at point of sale. Everything smells amazing, from the delicate, musky Ambrette 9 to the 'power bomb' Ciste 18.

Q is for quilts

Over 1,000 bolts of fabrics and panels, together with all the gadgets, books and stencils a quilter could need, can be found at Creative Quilting (32 Bridge Road, East Molesey, Surrey KT8 9HA, 8941 7075, http://creativequilting.co.uk).

R is for roses

Roses of every size and hue fill La Maison des Roses (48 Webbs Road, SW11 6SF, 7228 5700, www.maison-des-roses.com), imparting a heady scent. As well as bouquets and nosegays, there are scented candles, soaps and bath oils.

S is for shop fittings

D&A Binder (101 Holloway Road, N7 8LT, 7609 6300, www.dandabinder.co.uk) is where old shop fittings come to rest, before being snapped up for modern homes. Pieces might include 1940s chrome and glass display cabinets, heavy wooden cash tills and old hospital trolleys.

T is for tea
Tim d'Offey lives for tea: he spent a decade travelling to far-flung estates across Asia before opening the diminutive Postcard Teas (9 Dering Street, W1S 1AG, 7629 3654, www.postcardteas.com). Black, green and white teas come from high-quality estates in India, China, Japan and Sri Lanka.

U is for umbrellas
From wooden-handled heavyweights to dainty sun parasols, James Smith & Sons (53 New Oxford Street, WC1A 1BL, 7836 4731, www.james-smith.co.uk) is famed for its superior umbrellas. Opened in 1830, the shop is perfectly preserved.

V is for vinyl
One of London's most idiosyncratically decorated shops, vinyl-only Intoxica! (231 Portobello Road, W11 1LT, 7229 8010, www.intoxica.co.uk) is a browser's paradise.

W is for waistcoats
Nigerian hand-woven aso oke cloth and Savile Row craftsmanship are married to handsome effect at the African Waistcoat Company (33 Islington Green, N1 8DU, 7704 9698, www.africanwaistcoatcompany.com).

X is for x-rated
With its sumptuous interior, objet d'art dildos and peep-show changing rooms, the South Kensington Coco de Mer store (108 Draycott Avenue, SW3 3AE, 7584 7615, www.coco-de-mer.com) is deliciously decadent.

Y is for yacht chandlers
Behind a trim pale blue frontage, Arthur Beale (194 Shaftesbury Avenue, WC2H 8JP, 7836 9034) dispenses rope, lifejackets, ship's bells and other maritime must-haves. An unexpected treat in landlocked Covent Garden.

Z is for zebra-print
Describing itself as 'the biggest couture fabric store in England', Joel & Son (75-83 Church Street, NW8 8EU, 7724 6895, www.joelandson fabrics.com) can supply anything from animal prints to taffetta.

Wapping Project Screenings

1901-1908 *Get fresh air at the flicks*

There's no need to endure stuffy cinemas as the weather heats up; London has some terrific alfresco film seasons and summer-only venues (check websites for dates and prices). And for the latest one-off events, see www.timeout.com.

Cinema under the Stars
For four evenings in late August, movies are screened among the trees at Syon House (Syon Park, Brentford, Middx TW8 8JF, 8560 0882, www.syonpark.co.uk). Bring a picnic.

Drive-In Movie Experience
On North Weald Airfield in Essex, this drive-in (www.driveinmoviesuk.co.uk) is a fair distance from central London, but accessible from the M11 and M25. Simply turn up in your car, tune your radio to the site's frequency and enjoy movies the American way.

Free Film Festivals
This enterprising community project (www.free filmfestivals.org) puts on free outdoor screenings in interesting public spaces in south east London: *Battleship Potemkin* on the roof of Peckham multistorey car park, say, or a pedal-powered screening of *Belleville Rendez-vouz* at Herne Hill Velodrome.

More London Free Festival: Film
A sunken outdoor amphitheatre by City Hall, the Scoop hosts a series of free film events in summer (www.morelondon.com). Late-summer screenings benefit from earlier starting times

(it's dark enough from around 7.30pm), but you'll need to wrap up. The 2011 schedule included *The King's Speech* and *True Grit*.

The Nomad
The brainchild of Sally Wilton, owner of the Lexi Cinema, and George Wood, manager of Screen on the Green, Nomad (www.whereisthenomad.com) is a huge, easily-transportable inflatable screen. In 2011, Wilton and Wood ran screenings in the Royal Parks, with a programme that ran from *The African Queen* to *ET*.

Rooftop Film Club
In summer, the rooftop garden at the Queen of Hoxton (1-5 Curtain Road, EC2A 3JX, 7422 0958, www.rooftopfilmclub.com) hosts screenings of around five films a week. Everyone is issued with a pair of wireless headphones, and you can sip a beer or order some food while you watch.

Summer Screen at Somerset House
These screenings take place in the neo-classical courtyard of Somerset House (The Strand, WC2R 1LA, 7845 4600, www.somersethouse.org.uk/film); little wonder that tickets sell out way in advance. Bring a picnic and plenty of cushions.

Wapping Project Screenings
The gallery-cum-restaurant Wapping Project (Wapping Hydraulic Power Station, Wapping Wall, E1W 3ST, 7680 2080, www.thewapping project.com) runs a summer season of barbecues and film screenings in its courtyard garden.

Chef's table

Ever wondered where the city's top chefs go for dinner?
Euan Ferguson **finds out.**

'Who shaves the barber?' posited the British philosopher Bertrand Russell. He was making a point about logical paradoxes rather than researching his next male grooming appointment, but apply the same method of thought to dining out and you come to the important question: who feeds the chef?

They're all human – even Gordon Ramsay – and when they're not commanding brigades in some of London's finest restaurants, they have to eat. Follow the experts to some of these places and you'll be in good company.

John Torode is well known in Britain for his work on *MasterChef*, and also runs two London restaurants and bars, the Luxe and Smith's of Smithfield. 'My favourite restaurant is the River Café,' he says. 'I think it's an extraordinary institution. The food changes depending on what's in season: whenever you walk in the door, you know you're going to eat very good food.'

And after a day in the kitchen, Torode says he's taken by the tapas approach to dining. 'When you work in the sort of environment we do, you don't want heavy meals. You want to go somewhere and eat something very tasty, but not

very much of it. I love Barrafina and Bocca di Lupo. The sort of places where you can go late at night, get a lovely glass of wine – perfect. I'm certainly not going out for seven-course degustation menus.'

Jason Atherton agrees. Once head chef of Gordon Ramsay's Maze, he now runs his own Pollen Street Social in Mayfair, serving diners an upmarket procession of small plates. 'If I have a night off or finish service early enough, I'd go to Opera Tavern for pinchos or Barrafina in Soho, where I always have the pan con tomates with chipirones.'

Let's stay in Soho, the epicurean epicentre of London, with Mark Hix. He knows the area better than most – his eponymous restaurant in Brewer Street is a buzzing and robustly British distillation of all that's great about the area. He rates Japanese udon specialist Koya – and after dark, the lights of Chinatown beckon. 'I go to a place that used to be called Crispy Duck, but is now called Hung's,' he says. 'It's straighforward but good-quality Chinese. I often go to Viet Grill too, in the East End. I always have the mixed grill. These places

Barafina

aren't flashy, they're easy; there's none
of the hassle of going to a big, fancy West
End restaurant.'

Hix's own place is mentioned as a must-try by
Thomasina Miers, executive chef and co-founder
of the Wahaca chain of restaurants and writer on
Mexican cooking. She recommends his Welsh
rarebit, and in keeping with the 'grazing and
sharing' trend, a visit to nearby Spuntino for
deep-fried olives and sliders. 'It only has 26
covers, and serves delicious New York-style
food. It's perfect for an early supper or late lunch:
the atmosphere is great and so are the cocktails.

'I also love the laid-back cooking at Hereford
Road, the luxury of the River Café and the great,
seasonal food at Corrigan's. Closer to home, the
Mall Tavern is a firm favourite. Jesse Dunford
Wood cooks the best type of comfort food. His
brawn is to die for and his chicken kiev the
stuff of legend.'

It's the lucky Londoner who doesn't have
to travel far to a favourite restaurant, and
Marcus Wareing, chef patron of his eponymous
restaurant in the Berkeley hotel and 'British
brasserie' the Gilbert Scott in the St Pancras
Hotel, counts himself among them. 'I love Chez
Bruce – I can walk there, it's got a Michelin star
but is very relaxed, and the quality of food is

always high. Also local is Trinity in Clapham –
Adam Byatt's food is superb, and I think it
represents excellent value for money.

'A real treat for me is the deli and takeaway
Elizabeth King – expensive but tempting, and
it sells that amazing Pain Poilâne bread.'

Yotam Ottolenghi's London restaurant/
takeaways are acclaimed for their sleek design
and fresh, inventive, Mediterranean-influenced
cooking, and this year he opened a more
ambitious operation, Nopi, in Soho. But he's
another chef who prefers the down-to-earth over
the starry when eating out. 'One place I really
like going to is Mangal Ocakbasi, a Turkish
place in Dalston. I love the grilled lamb chops
and the mixed salad with tomato and cucumber.

'Another one, along similiar lines, is Abu Zaad
on Uxbridge Road – one of my favourite places.
Wonderful atmosphere – blaring television with
Arab broadcasting and music. The food is cheap
and delicious: kebabs and salads and meze.

'I also like a lot a Japanese grill called Tosa,
in Hammersmith. It's small, consistent, not
pretentious in any way. I have the grilled pork
loin with shiso – like little lollipops. Grilled quail
eggs on a skewer, too, dipped in an aromatic salt,
and the amazing seaweed salad in a sesame
paste dressing.'

Tosa

there it's a joy. And it's not too bad waiting with a bottle of manzana.'

For a more traditional repast Henderson heads to the genuine institution that is Sweetings, in the City – 'It's only open for lunch, but what a lunch!' – although would prefer to let diners arrive at their own culinary choices wherever they visit. 'I'm not one to recommend what people should eat: just go and enjoy the food!'

Abu Zaad *29 Uxbridge Road, W12 8LH (8749 5107, www.abuzaad.co.uk).*
Barrafina *54 Frith Street, W1D 4SL (7813 8016, www.barrafina.co.uk).*
Bocca di Lupo *12 Archer Street, W1D 7BB (7734 2223, www.boccadilupo.com).*
Chez Bruce *2 Bellevue Road, SW17 7EG (8672 0114, www.chezbruce.co.uk).*
Ciao Bella *86-90 Lamb's Conduit Street, WC1N 3LZ (7242 4119, www.ciaobellarestaurant.co.uk).*
Corrigan's Mayfair *28 Upper Grosvenor Street, W1K 7EH (7499 9943, www.corrigansmayfair.com).*
Elizabeth King *34 New King's Road, SW6 4ST (7736 2826, www.elizabethking.com).*
La Famiglia *7 Langton Street, The World's End, SW10 0JL (7351 0761, www.lafamiglia.co.uk).*
Hereford Road *3 Hereford Road, W2 4AB (7727 1144, www.herefordroad.org).*
Hix *66-70 Brewer Street, W1F 9UP (7292 3518, www.hixsoho.co.uk).*
Hung's *27 Wardour Street, W1D 6PR (7287 6578).*
Koya *49 Frith Street, W1D 4SG (7434 4463, www.koya.co.uk).*
Mall Tavern *71-73 Palace Gardens Terrace, W8 4RU (7229 3374, www.themalltavern.com).*
Mangal Ocakbasi *10 Arcola Street, E8 2DJ (7275 8981, www.mangal1.com).*
New World *1 Gerrard Place, W1D 5PA (7434 2508).*
Opera Tavern *23 Catherine Street, WC2B 5JS (7836 3680, www.operatavern.co.uk).*
The River Café *Thames Wharf, Rainville Road, W6 9HA (7836 4200, www.rivercafe.co.uk).*
Royal China *13 Queensway, W2 4QJ (7221 2535, www.royalchinagroup.co.uk).*
Spuntino *61 Rupert Street, W1D 7PW (no phone, www.spuntino.co.uk).*
Sweetings *39 Queen Victoria Street, EC4N 4SF (7248 3062).*
Tosa *332 King Street, W6 0RR (8748 0002, www.tosauk.com).*
Trinity *4 The Polygon, SW4 0JG (7622 1199, www.trinityrestaurant.co.uk).*
Viet Grill *58 Kingsland Road, E2 8DP (7739 6686, www.vietnamesekitchen.co.uk/vietgrill).*

Antonio Carluccio also enjoys a more modest experience when he's not in the kitchen. He's had a distinguished career in hospitality – establishing the now nationwide Carluccio's Caffè chain, fronting many TV shows and writing books on Italian cooking. 'These days I prefer cooking for friends and family, I really don't go out so much. But when I do, I love La Famiglia, in Chelsea: I've been going there for 30 years. It's Tuscan, and the menu always changes with what's best at that time.' But for something different, he visits New World in Chinatown: 'for the dumplings and chicken feet'.

A chef you couldn't imagine shying away from the more esoteric parts of an animal is Fergus Henderson, who champions a nose-to-tail eating philosophy in his three St John restaurants in London. He enjoys Chinese too, particularly dim sum at Royal China: 'It's like short chapters that keep you reading, and keeps you eating all afternoon.

'I can also recommend Ciao Bella: it has splendid lasagne, you can sit outside (very good for us smokers) and they're always happy with kids. An excellent place.' Barrafina, which seems to be a real chefs' favourite, is on his list too: 'Choose your timing carefully as getting a seat at the bar can be quite a wait,' he says. 'Worth it though, as when you get

1932
Discover the Royal Menagerie

These days, it's best known for its ravens – but the Tower of London once housed a far more extensive menagerie.

The monarchy has kept an extravagant collection of animals at the Tower for over 600 years (until the early 19th century), to use as high-status gifts and for the amusement of the royal household and its guests.

The new Royal Beasts exhibition traces their long-forgotten stories, from the first lions and elephants from North Africa to exotic captives from the gradually opening-up New World. It shows you, through wall panels and the latest electronic technology, how they lived, what they smelled like and what happened when they escaped. You'll learn about the polar bear that fished in the Thames and the leopard that stole umbrellas, along with the history of the Brick Tower, newly opened to the public, in which the exhibition is situated. There aren't any actual animals, of course, but the grounds contain life-size sculptures of some of the royal beasts.

Tower of London *Tower Hill, EC3N 4AB (0844 482 7777, www.hrp.org.uk).*

1933-1940
Become a patron of the arts

You don't have to be stinking rich to be a patron of the arts. Getting involved in the life of a venue, ensemble or festival whose work you enjoy can be very rewarding – not just in terms of the benefits it entitles you to, but for the philanthropic pleasure of supporting something worthwhile.

Naturally, rewards are on a sliding scale depending on how much you donate. At the low end (where you might be called a 'friend' rather than patron), they typically include newsletters, priority booking and perhaps a discount at the bar. As the stakes rise, privileges might stretch to a members' bar, reserved seating, invitations to special events and attendance at rehearsals.

Worthwhile venues and events to consider supporting at the most accessible (read: cheapest) level include esteemed chamber music venue Wigmore Hall (7935 2141, www.wigmore-hall. org.uk) and the dynamic Spitalfields Festival (7377 1362, www.spitalfieldsfestival.org.uk), with membership for both starting at £35.

If you're able to cough up a little bit more, Headliner membership of Camden's Roundhouse (7424 9991, www.roundhouse.org.uk) costs £150 a year. You get ticket booking privileges and access to the rather nice members' bar. For annual fees of £250 and up, the Old Vic Club (7928 2651, www.oldvictheatre.com) offers access to sold-out shows, press nights and opportunities to meet the casts and creative team.

Dance aficionados, meanwhile, could consider supporting Sadler's Wells (7863 8134, www.sadlerswells.com). For the £600 Opening Night membership, you get two-for-one tickets, access to rehearsals, and opening night-invites.

The National Theatre (7452 3000, www. nationaltheatre.org.uk) offers a huge range of supporters' packages, with annual patronage for between £1,250 and £4,999 – although 'young patrons' (aged 21 to 45) pay from just £75 per year. And at the top end of the scale, if you donate £1,000 to £5,000, you can join the English National Opera's 'Opera Circle' (7836 0111, www. eno.org) and socialise with the stars at special galas, or become a patron of the London Symphony Orchestra (7588 1116, www.lso.co.uk), for an annual fee of between £1,000 and £10,000.

1941-1943

Pick up a picnic hamper...

Take the hard work out of picnicking with an Afternoon Tea hamper from Bea's of Bloomsbury (44 Theobald's Road, WC1X 8NW, 7242 8330, www.beasofbloomsbury.com). Scones with clotted cream and preserves, Valrhona brownies and macaroons are among the spoils, beautifully presented in an old-fashioned wicker hamper (£15 per person, plus £5 hamper hire charge).

For a more savoury-heavy spread, try famed deli Melrose & Morgan (42 Gloucester Avenue, NW1 8JD, 7722 0011, www.melroseandmorgan.com). Its ready-assembled picnic for two (£39.95) is a splendid feast. Highlights might include ham hock terrine, own-made pear piccalilli, chive and potato salad, and pepper and curd cheese tart: for afters, there's Pimms and cucumber jellies.

Foodie favourite the Bull & Last (168 Highgate Road, NW5 1QS, 7267 3641, www.thebulland last.co.uk), meanwhile, is perfectly situated for picking up a hamper to take to nearby Hampstead Heath. Its basic hampers (£28 for two people) contain all you need for a classic English spread (scotch eggs, sausage rolls, superior quiche, ham hock terrine, cheese and oatcakes), plus real lemonade and a handy map of the Heath.

Hampstead Heath

1944-1955

... Then find a prime spot

Alexandra Park

Ally Pally (Alexandra Park Road, N22 7UJ, www.alexandrapalace.com) is ideal for a Saturday picnic – the sweeping views over the capital are fantastic, and Alexandra Palace Farmers' Market offers plenty of grub. Load up on cheeses, pies and olives, then head for the hills. It's terrific for kids too: waterfowl and deer are among the resident wildlife.

Battersea Park

Once marshland – and a notorious duelling spot – the 200 acres of greenery at Battersea Park (Battersea Park Road, SW11 4JP, www. batterseapark.org) are far more salubrious these days. Spread your rug at the Peace Pagoda, or, on hot days, under the trees on the south side.

Fulham Palace Gardens

To sip your chablis on the shady lawn of a formal garden, head to the Thames-side Fulham Palace (Bishops Avenue, SW6 6EA, www. fulhampalace.org). The palace and its gardens – once a country retreat for the medieval bishops of London – are a well-kept local picnicking secret. Its 12 acres take in woodland, an orchard and a wisteria-draped pergola.

Ham House Gardens

Ensconce yourself on the lawns of Ham House (Ham Street, Ham, Richmond, Surrey TW10 7RS, www.nationaltrust.org.uk), whose 17th-century grounds incorporate formal box and yew parterres as well as a so-called wilderness of hornbeam. There's a small entrance fee.

Hampstead Heath

Hampstead Heath (www.hampsteadheath.net) is full of great picnic spots and stunning views, but we favour the slope above Highgate Pond. Here, you can hide out in the long grass and gaze across to the City and Canary Wharf.

Holland Park

With plenty of secluded corners, Holland Park (Ilchester Place, W8 6LU, www.rbkc.gov.uk) is

great for romantic picnics. Head for the peaceful Kyoto Garden, perhaps, or the lawn beyond the beech enclosure.

Horniman Museum
The 16-acre gardens at the Horniman Museum (100 London Road, SE23 3PQ, www.horniman. ac.uk) are undergoing a £2.3 million revamp, due for completion in spring 2012. There are plenty of choice spots for picnickers, from the rose garden to the sunny, sloping lawns.

Regent's Park
For picnic perfection, stroll to the northern reaches of Regent's Park (www.royalparks. org.uk) and spread your picnic rug near the blossoms and scents of the Rose Garden.

Springfield Park
Hackney's Springfield Park (E5 9EF, www. hackney.gov.uk) is a good spot for a picnic with a view: nibble cucumber sandwiches while looking out over the River Lea, with its narrowboat marina, and the Hackney Marshes beyond.

Thames Barrier Park
The Thames Barrier Park (7476 3741, www. thamesbarrierpark.org.uk) is a triumph of contemporary landscape gardening. Picnic in the midst of 22 acres of lawns, trees and surreal yew and maygreen topiary, overlooking the mighty silver shells of the Thames Barrier.

Waterlow Park
The lawns of Waterlow Park (Swains Lane, N6 6PL, www.waterlowpark.org.uk) offer exhilarating views over London. Sweeping down the steep face of Highgate Hill and criss-crossed with little pathways, the park is dotted with mature trees, lush greenery and secluded, spring-fed ponds.

Victoria Park
This expansive green space is perfect for a quiet picnic; the impressive stone alcoves, saved from the parapets of Old London Bridge, offer shade from the sun. There's plenty to keep you occupied after lunch: playgrounds, wildlife enclosures, tennis courts and bowling greens.

1956-1959

Shop at a sample sale

To keep track of upcoming sales, check the Shopping & Style section of *Time Out London* magazine.

Chelsea Old Town Hall

Children's sales are a particular forte at Chelsea Town Hall, featuring top-end brands such as Caramel and Little Paul & Joe. Orla Kiely and Gina are among the labels that run sample sales for grown-ups here.
King's Road, SW3 5EE.

The Music Room

Cult brands such as Margaret Howell, Chloë and Rupert Sanderson hold sample sales at Mayfair's Music Room. Check the website regularly to ensure you don't miss out.
26 South Molton Lane, W1K 5AB (7629 8199, www.themusicroom.co.uk).

Old Truman Brewery

Designer Sales UK (www.designersales.co.uk) runs five sales a year at the Old Truman Brewery, just off Brick Lane. Items by Vivienne Westwood, Martin Margiela and Yves Saint Laurent are often among the clobber. The Secret Sample Sale (www.secretsamplesale.co.uk) and London Accessory Sale (www.londonaccessory sale.co.uk) also hold events here. Sign up to their online mailing lists for details of dates.
91 Brick Lane, E1 6QL (www.trumanbrewery.com).

The Toy Factory

Ann Louise Roswald, Queene & Belle and Musa have been known to hold sample sales at this Islington space.
11-13 Corsham Street, N1 6DP (7250 1583).

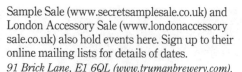

1960

Stay up late at the zoo

For the past couple of summers (August in 2010, June and July in 2011), London Zoo has organised Friday late-night openings for adults only. Attractions have included a Champagne Teepee, the Penguin Beach Bar, international street food, samba music on the picnic lawns, improvised comedy in the aquarium, and a popular 'silent disco' (so as not to scare the animals).
London Zoo *Outer Circle, Regent's Park, NW1 4RY (7722 3333, www.zsl.org).*

1961

Appreciate decorative excess

Much of Eltham Palace, the lavish home of the super-wealthy Stephen and Virginia Courthauld in the 1930s and 1940s, is an art deco showpiece, but there are a couple of areas where self-indulgence perhaps got the better of good taste. First, Ginny's bathroom, a symphony of onyx, gold and marble complete with lion's mouth tap; and second – less excusably – the quarters of their pet ring-tailed lemur, Mah-Jongg. The lemur had free range of the house – but in case he craved some privacy, was provided with spacious, centrally heated quarters of his own, decorated with bamboo wallpaper to ensure he felt at home.

Eltham Palace *Court Yard, SE9 5QE (8294 2548, www.english-heritage.org.uk).*

1962-1965

Discover an unusual grave

Numerous writers are buried in Westminster Abbey (20 Dean's Yard, SW1P 3PA, 7222 5152, www.westminster-abbey.org), but Elizabethan dramatist and poet Ben Jonson is the only one to be interred standing up – supposedly because, despite his fame, he was too poor to afford a standard-sized burial plot. A small grey stone marks the spot in the northern aisle of the nave.

Southwark Cathedral (London Bridge, SE1 9DA, 7367 6700, http://cathedral.southwark.anglican.org) lays claim to a Native American chieftain, Mahomet Weyonomon, who died of smallpox in 1735 while on his way to petition George II about the loss of his Mohegan tribal lands. Buried in an unmarked grave, he was finally given an official send-off in 2006, when the Queen unveiled a memorial (a carved pink granite boulder from Connecticut) in the churchyard.

Architect Sir John Soane had the foresight to design his own mausoleum, located in the graveyard of St Pancras Old Church (Pancras Road, NW1 1UL, 7287 4193), just north of St Pancras station. Surrounded by a balustrade, the four-columned structure with a curved top

Sir Richard Burton

may seem familiar – it provided inspiration for Sir Giles Gilbert Scott, designer of the classic red London phone box.

Best of all is the mausoleum of Sir Richard Burton. Not the tempestuous Welsh actor, but the celebrated Victorian explorer; he traversed the globe from Arabia to Africa, but ended his days near the railway line in Mortlake. His tomb, located behind St Mary Magdalen's church (61 Worple Way, SW14 8PR, 8876 1326, www.stmarymags.org.uk), is in the shape of an Arabian tent, complete with ersatz canvas folds; you can peer through a small window at the back to see the dusty and neglected interior, containing the coffins of Burton and his wife.

1966

Party on a rooftop

Hip rooftop bars are a phenomenon more associated with New York than London – so the Dalston Roof Park is something of a pioneer. The community vegetable garden/live music space above the beautiful Print House building – a stone's throw from Café Oto and the new Arcola Theatre – has been a welcome source of leftfield tunes, rooftop views and cult film screenings for the past couple of summers. Sink a cold beer on the astroturf lawn, surrounded by strawberry plants, green beans and a relaxed crowd; the punters may be an arty bunch, but the vibe is inclusive – and membership free.

Dalston Roof Park *Print House, 18 Ashwin Street, E8 3DL (7275 0825, www.bootstrapcompany.co.uk).*

1967-1987

Listen to folk

Whether it's fiddle-driven traditional forms or warped and weird nu-folk, there's all manner of folk to tickle your fancy.

Albert & Pearl
A shabbily chic ambience prevails in this dimly lit bar – home to the Softly Softly folk club. An acoustic 'celebration of all things folky', it's held on the first and third Wednesday of every month.
181 Upper Street, N1 1RQ (7704 1070, www.albertandpearl.com).

Apple Tree
Hosted by Alan Tyler, former linchpin of the Rockingbirds, Come Down and Meet the Folks happens here on the second and last Sunday of every month, between 4-9pm. It ranges across folk, roots, blues, country and Americana.
45 Mount Pleasant, WC1X 0AE (7837 2365, www.comedownandmeetthefolks.co.uk).

Betsey Trotwood
This Victorian corner pub is a great mix of bands and real ales. Monthly folk club Clerkenville West focuses on bluegrass, alt country and 'cosmic Americana'.
56 Farringdon Road, EC1R 3BL (7253 4285, www.thebetsey.com).

Bush Hall

Bush Hall
The music programme at this handsome hall is by no means limited to folk, but it does figure regularly, as do blues, country and Americana.
310 Uxbridge Road, W12 7LJ (8222 6955, www.bushhallmusic.co.uk).

Cabbage Patch
The home of Twickfolk, which has been running since 1983 and is one of London's most respected roots/folk music clubs. Held every Sunday, it presents established, highly regarded acts, both British and American.
67 London Road, TW1 3SZ (8892 3874, www.myspace.com/twickfolk).

Cecil Sharp House
The headquarters of the English Folk Dance and Song Society, this fine building has several halls which host dances, workshops, talks and multimedia events, as well as live music.
2 Regent's Park Road, NW1 7AY (7485 2206, www.efdss.org).

Dulwich Hamlet FC
One of two venues regularly hosting folk-particular club the Goose Is Out, which runs the gamut from unaccompanied traditional folk music to the twisted/wyrd variety, blues, roots and indigenous global sounds.
Edgar Kail Way, Dog Kennel Hill, SE22 8BD (7274 8707, www.thegooseisout.com).

Green Note
Pleasant vegetarian cafe/bar and venue featuring music five nights a week (and Sunday afternoons), with the emphasis on folk, roots and blues.
106 Parkway, NW1 7AN (7485 9899, www.greennote.co.uk).

Grosvenor
The Grosvenor's upstairs room hosts Acoustic Insurgency on the last Sunday of every month – dedicated to 'political folk, comedy and plotting the overthrow of absolutely everything.' On the first Friday, the No Frills Band host their night of 'folk music, drinking and shouting'.
17 Sidney Road, SW9 0TP (7738 4567, www.thegrosvenorsw9.co.uk).

Horseshoe
The band Rebetiko Odyssey hold a (free) jam session on the first Monday of every month, which is dedicated to the haunting sound of rebetika, or Greek 'blues'.
24 Clerkenwell Close, EC1R 0AG (7253 6068).

Green Note

Irish Cultural Centre

The music programme here embraces both adventurous contemporary music and more traditional forms.
Blacks Road, W6 9DT (8563 8232, www.irishculturalcentre.co.uk).

King & Queen

This is where the Musical Traditions Club – now in its 20th year – has its monthly, Friday night meets, presenting traditional singers and musicians from Britain and Ireland.
1 Foley Street, W1W 6DL (7636 5619).

King's Head

The downstairs room at this tiny Crouch End institution is home to the Kalamazoo Klub (www.kalamazooklub.co.uk), held every second Friday of the month. On the third Friday of each month, the King's Head also hosts the Local, a roving alternative folk/country-slanted club.
2 Crouch End Hill, N8 8AA (8340 1028, www.thekingsheadcrouchend.co.uk).

Kings Place

Vast, swanky new arts and media centre that boasts a large and comprehensive music programme; every Friday night brings Folk Union, featuring leading and upcoming exponents of folk music (both traditional and contemporary).
90 York Way, N1 9AG (7520 1490, www.kingsplace.co.uk).

Magnolia

A second home to the Goose Is Out, which takes place every Friday in the upstairs room. Here, the focus is on traditional folk (there's no PA).
211 Lordship Lane, SE22 8HA (8299 4116, www.thegooseisout.com).

North Star

The reliably excellent What's Cookin' club is at this community-minded, real-ale boozer, on the third Sunday of every month (out in the beer garden during summer). You'll hear blues, bluegrass and 'rockin' country-fried music'.
24 Browning Road, E11 3AR (01642 463920, www.whatscookin.co.uk).

Old Queen's Head

This groovily refurbished boozer is where you'll find the Magpie's Nest, a collective so dedicated to spreading the word about new and traditional folk and roots music that they've established two offshoot clubs, Two For Joy and Folklahoma!
44 Essex Road, N1 8LN (7354 9993, www.theoldqueenshead.com).

Passing Clouds

Occasional home to Magpie's Nest subsidiary events Folklahoma! and Two For Joy, this Dalston cultural centre runs the gamut from African drumming classes to klezmer orchestras.
1 Richmond Road, E8 4AA (7502 2789, www.passingclouds.org).

Selkirk

The upstairs room is home to the celebrated Wizz's Sitting Room, held every Thursday. Here, blues guitar legend Wizz Jones shows off his impressive chops, often accompanied by his sax-, flute- and harmonica-playing son, Simeon.
60 Selkirk Road, SW17 0ES (8672 6235, http://www.theselkirktooting.co.uk).

Slaughtered Lamb

The roving Pull Up the Roots (www.pulluptheroots.co.uk) night is a regular visitor at this music-focused pub.
34-35 Great Sutton Street, EC1V 0DX (7253 1516, www.theslaughteredlambpub.com).

Ye Olde Rose & Crown

The long-lived, warmly inclusive Walthamstow Folk Club is found here every Sunday evening, showcasing contemporary and traditional acoustic-folk guest acts.
53-55 Hoe St, E17 4SA (07740 612607 www.walthamstowfolk.co.uk).

A few of my favourite things

1988-1995

Simon Armitage,
poet & artist in residence,
Southbank Centre

If you become a member of the Southbank Centre (Belvedere Road, SE1 8XX, 7960 4200, www. southbankcentre. co.uk; £45 a year), you get access to the balcony bar that runs along the top, overlooking the Thames. It's a world away from some stuffy London club, where you'd sit in a leather seat next to some old boy having his afternoon nap. I love being there on my own, doing a bit of work and watching the river drift by. I'm trying to persuade them to offer free membership to every poet in Britain – we're a fairly fragmented lot, so it'd be nice to have a meeting place.
The British Library (96 Euston Road, NW1 2DB, 7412 7676, www.bl.uk) is next to my station home, King's Cross, so it's a good place to go if I'm early for a train. Even though it looks a bit like a post office depot, the exterior is very striking; inside, I love the huge glass vault of books that reaches all the way to the roof. It's like a battery of books, with all the charge of literature stored there. The further back you go in the building, the more complicated it gets in terms of access. I once had rather an excruciating moment when I marched in in a pair of wellies, having come down from Yorkshire, and asked to see the manuscript of Sir Gawain and the Green Knight. The lady on duty was probably looking for the panic button under the desk.
The Hunterian Museum (35-43 Lincoln's Inn Fields, WC2A 3PE, 7869 6560, www.rcseng. ac.uk) is inside the Royal College of Surgeons: unless you've heard of it, you'd never know it was there. It's like the inside of Damien Hirst's

mind, with lots of things bobbling around in formaldehyde. There's every part of the human body, some more diseased than others, along with various small animals. Some are at the foetal stage,and although that might sound gruesome, they're actually very beautiful. All in all, though, I think around 45 minutes in there is probably enough; no matter how good the seals are on those jars, there's always that vague whiff of embalming fluid. And I don't know what they've got in the gift shop...
I like the Lamb & Flag (33 Rose Street, WC2E 9EB, 7497 9504) – a tiny, stone-floored pub on an alleyway in Covent Garden. It always looks far too crowded, but it never really is; there's another room upstairs, and the crowd thins out as the night goes on. As long as you're prepared to breathe in for an hour and a half, it's fine. It's definitely a drinker's pub, and there's a good choice of beers; my mate belongs to CAMRA, so I'm happy to be guided along the pumps.
I used to stay at Hazlitt's (6 Frith Street, W1D 3JA, 7434 1771, www.hazlittshotel.com) in Soho, which was a lot of fun. All the floors were at different angles, and the rooms had four-poster beds and antiquated furniture. Rather than there being a breakfast room, they used to just knock on your door and leave a tray outside. It had a wonderfully secretive, no-questions-asked feel; *I* never asked any questions, anyway.
To me, Rough Trade had always been a record label; I didn't know they had shops. Penguin Books were based on Brick Lane for a while, though, which was when I discovered Rough Trade East (Dray Walk, Old Truman Brewery, 91 Brick Lane, E1 6QL, 7392 7788). It's a bit like a department store for indie music, and I really like going in there. I also go to a vinyl shop called Sister Ray (34-35 Berwick Street, W1F 8RP, 7734 3297, www.sisterray.co.uk). I don't always buy anything, but I love that feeling of walking your fingers across the top of the records.
Elena's L'Etoile (30 Charlotte Street, W1T 2NG, 7636 7189, www.elenasletoile.co.uk) is where I seem to end up after book launches and literary events. The main room is art deco, and covered in photographs of theatrical people, but there's also a series of private dining rooms going up the stairs. They become progressively smaller and smaller as you get to the top, like something out of *Alice in Wonderland*. I've generally had a few too many drinks by the time I get there, and it always seems quite magical.

1996

Appreciate a brand-new view

The year 2012 brings fresh perspectives to the city. By March, breathtaking views will be possible from the dramatic, looping ArcelorMittal Orbit Tower in the Olympic Park. Designed by Turner Prize-winning artist Anish Kapoor and engineer Cecil Belmond, it will stand 377ft tall. After the London 2012 Games, it'll open as a tourist attraction from spring 2013.

In summer 2012, meanwhile, a temporary floating boardwalk between Blackfriars and the Tower of London will create a different way of seeing Shakespeare's Globe and Tate Modern. At London Bridge, Europe's tallest building, the Shard (www.the-shard.com) will be finished in 2012, with a public viewing gallery and outdoor observation deck on the top (72nd) floor. And in 2013, the City of London's tallest building will be erected. Dubbed the Helter-Skelter, the Pinnacle (www.londonpinnacle.com) will offer incredible views from its restaurants and viewing deck.

1997

Look out for the little people

Slinkachu's 'Little People Project' (www.slinkachu.com) is both a series of street art installations and a photography project. Since 2006, the artist has been painting and remodelling model train set characters, which he then sets up as miniature scenes on London's streets. The idea is not only to surprise people as they come across them, but also to encourage us to be more aware of our surrounds. Being easily missed, however, means that the works have achieved more attention through the photographs of each project. These can often be viewed at the Andipa Gallery (162 Walton Street, SW3 2JL, 7589 2371, www.andipa.com), which represents the artist.

1998

Make some noise

During the summer holidays – which happily coincide with the Proms concert series at the Royal Albert Hall – the Royal College of Music turns its teaching skills towards the public, in the Sparks programme. Events are arranged for all ages, and are often linked to Proms happening later that day. Six- to 12-year-olds can make music and rhythm at creative workshops, with such themes as 'Musical Daydreaming', inspired by Debussy. Older children (to 18) can improvise their way to creating and performing a new piece. Adults can enjoy a Discovery Session, gaining an insight into the work of a composer, perhaps seeing hand-written manuscripts or the instruments they composed on. And everyone can join a family orchestra for the season. **Royal College of Music** *Prince Consort Road, SW7 2BS (7591 4300, www.rcm.ac.uk).*

1999-2010

Get all dressed up
(with someplace to go)

Bizarre Ball

Bizarre magazine (www.bizarremag.com) stages twice-yearly balls celebrating the zany, fetishistic and just plain weird. Wild bands entertain the swathes of crazily-dressed people, interspersed by burlesque and cabaret with a freakshow slant.

Blitz Party

Don 1940s thriftstore threads, period glam or home-front uniform to swing at these World War II-themed parties (www.theblitzparty.com). Expect big band tunes, performers and DJs.

Candlelight Club

A dazzling, clandestine cocktail bar with a 1920s speakeasy flavour, lit by flickering candles (www.thecandlelightclub.com). There's live music, period shellac spun by DJs, guest cabaret acts and monthly themes. Dress for the Jazz Age: think flappers, good grooming, LBDs and DJs.

Die Freche Muse

Promising decadent cabaret in the grand European tradition, host Baron Von Sanderson invites you to this soirée in a Dalston venue (www.diefrechemuse.co.uk). The dress code is 1920s to '40s, jeans and trainers strictly verboten.

Gangbusters

Tim's Jumpin' Jive hosts this great club at the Lexington on the first Sunday of the month (www.hellzapoppin.co.uk). There's a lindy hop dance class before DJs spin 1920s to 1950s swing, early jazz, jump blues and more.

Last Tuesday Society

'The future belongs to the dandy', say these party organisers par excellence, whose one-off soirées are masked, decadent and not a little kinky (www.thelasttuesdaysociety.org). Pay as much attention to your dress as they do to the artily sensual decor, food and entertainment.

Magic Theatre
Forget a theme: you can dress up any which way you want at Magic Theatre (www.magic-theatre.co.uk) – so long as you make an effort. The evening is based around a live band, with blues and retro dance DJs to follow. It's held at the Rivoli, London's only intact '50s ballroom.

Prohibition
It's back to the 1920s for these Prohibition era-themed parties (www.prohibition1920s.com), boasting jazz bands, tap and Charleston dancers, gambling tables and silent movie screenings. The dress code is stylish '20s (think flapper dresses, feathered headbands, tuxedos, top hats and spats), and the location secret.

Shore Leave
Sailor boys and girls wring the last drop of rum from their remaining hours on dry land at this itinerant evening (www.shoreleave.co.uk). There are bawdy bands and burlesque, DJs spinning sounds from far flung ports and a tattoo shack. Wear vintage nautical attire.

Volupté's Vintage Ball
Every third Saturday of the month at Volupté (www.volupte-lounge.com), 'The Most Decadent Little Supper Club in Town', the Black Cotton Club (www.myspace.com/blackcottonclub) hosts the Vintage Ball. Book a table for the early-evening burlesque-y dinner show, or arrive from 9pm for dancing until late. Dress for Prohibition.

White Blackbird
The country house party is alive and high-kicking at the White Blackbird (www.thewhite blackbird.com). It's held at Stoke Place, a 17th-century mansion-turned-hotel near Stoke Poges: stay overnight, or join the coach party from central London. Take your costume seriously, and dress to theme; previous soirées include a 'Tainted Love' Valentine's ball.

White Mischief
If White Mischief (www.whitemischief.info) is behind it, you can count on a cabaret extravaganza, with a Victorian/steampunk ethos infusing everything from poster design, decor and dress to theme: previous (irregular) events include New Year's Eve 1910 and Around the World in 80 Days.

2011 Own your own supermarket

The People's Supermarket (72-78 Lamb's Conduit Street, WC1N 3LP, 7430 1827, www.thepeoples supermarket.org) aims to provide an alternative to the big retailing guns. Inspired by New York's Park Slope Food Co-operative, the store is owned and run by its members. Pay the shop a visit or join the retail revolution by becoming a member, which entitles you to ten per cent off purchases. It costs £25 a year to join, and you'll need to contribute a minimum of four hours' work in the shop every four weeks.

2012 Let Time Out inspire you

Did you think this was the end? Think again; every day brings something new in this ever-evolving city. To hear about the latest events, openings and cultural highlights on our radar, download the free Time Out London app. And if 2012 Things weren't enough for you, tap the 'Inspire me' button to head off on another random and rewarding journey.

A-Z index

Note: number refers to page, not list entry.

Thematic index

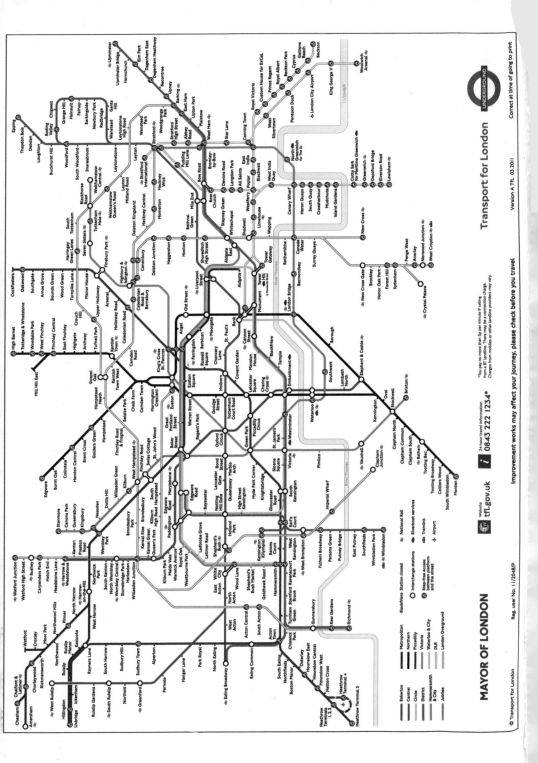